"Now that 'the political turn' in psychoanalysis and psych 'the relational turn,' it is nothing short of wonderful and lib collection of Lynne Layton's work. For those of us struggling field, Layton is the outstanding writer on how the social and ᴜᴇ ᴄᴌᴉᴜᴉᴄᴀᴵ interweave. We sit at her feet. She is also the go-to theorist on how psychoanalysis can still function as the best and most alert approach to critiques of the sorry political state of 'the West.' Layton's compassion, dedication, and knowledge of the relevant history are exemplary. Students and more seasoned practitioners, in both clinic and academy, will want to keep the book close at hand."

– **Andrew Samuels,** founder of Psychotherapists and
Counsellors for Social Responsibility, UK and author of
*The Political Psyche*

"In *Toward a Social Psychoanalysis*, Layton demonstrates her formidable scholarship, her incisive cultural critique, her clinical acumen, and her activist spirit. Over the last few decades, Layton has been devoted to integrating psychoanalysis with social justice. This book represents the pinnacle of that work. This is a profound query into, and rewriting of, the fundamentals of psychoanalysis, in search of cultural and political engagement. Highly readable and sophisticated, the book is interdisciplinary in scope and always immediate in its address to human suffering. In these dark times, this is essential reading. Layton inspires us to action and ameliorates our isolation and despair."

– **Sue Grand,** faculty in the NYU Postdoctoral Program in
Psychotherapy & Psychoanalysis and author of
*The Reproduction of Evil: A Clinical & Cultural Perspective*

"*Toward a Social Psychoanalysis* is an exciting and much needed contribution to the current awakening to the task of theorizing the social and political unconscious as embraced by the founders of psychoanalysis. Packed with wonderful insights, this masterful work offers an accessible and stimulating guide through the complex matrix of contemporary social theory and relational psychoanalysis, enabling a confrontation with the urgent problems of race, class, and gender as they affect patients in psychotherapy and society as a whole. Clinicians and academics alike will find this book indispensable."

– **Jessica Benjamin,** author of *Beyond Doer and Done To:*
*Recognition Theory, Intersubjectivity and the Third*

"Lynne Layton's brilliant essays hold the key to understanding how we have become the people we are in this society and to begin to imagine the people we might yet become in a more just and decent world. Challenging longstanding therapeutic models that divorce the psychic from the social, she connects the contours of our seemingly private and personal passions to the public process and practices of neoliberalism and racialized capitalism. I know of no single book that does as much to equip us with the tools we need to confront and correct the calculated cruelty and belligerent brutality of our time."

– **George Lipsitz,** author of *The Possessive*
*Investment in Whiteness*

"Lynne Layton has been among the most important and prolific psychoanalytic political writers of our time. She shows in understandable yet nuanced language the way psychoanalytic thinking can play a crucial role in understanding and healing our current personal and societal ills. Finding these marvelous papers collected in one place is a boon to students, practitioners, historians, and the general intellectual audience as we fight against the dark forces that presently threaten our society."

– **Philip Cushman,** psychology professor, psychotherapist,
and author of the recently published *Travels With the Self:*
*Interpreting Psychology as Cultural History*

k records the unique journey of a socially engaged psychoanalyst as she charts nkable consequences of power relations both in society and in the consulting /riting with passion, honesty and rigour, Lynne Layton undertakes a fascinating tion of the conflicts and struggles, both psychological and political, of neoliberal is in their encounters with racism, classism, sexism, and other social forces."

— **Professor Paul Hoggett**, Co-founder of the
Climate Psychology Alliance and the Centre for
Psycho-Social Studies, UWE, Bristol

Ne owe a great debt of gratitude to Lynne Layton for the work that she has done of many /ears to develop a social psychoanalysis that speaks across gender, sexuality, race, and class. This hugely important volume should be required reading not only for any therapist or analyst in training but for anyone interested in the complex relation of the social and psychoanalytic."

— **Valerie Walkerdine,** Distinguished Research Professor,
Cardiff University, UK

"Lynne Layton's newest book adroitly braids historical narrative, rigorous theory, and clinical vignettes into a necessary compendium for the psychoanalytic work we must do today, both in the privacy of the consulting room and in the public realms of social praxis. Layton's work shows how unconscious normative processes recreate structural inequities, locking psyche and society into fruitless repetition: psychoanalysis without social analysis can then only stumble clinically and remain ethically dubious. A probing critique and clinical companion, this book will help reshape how we think about psychoanalysis, making it an agent for the kind of change our discipline urgently needs."

— **Francisco J. González**, MD, Co-Chair,
Community Psychoanalysis Track,
Psychoanalytic Institute of Northern California

"Lynne Layton has written a brilliant and exciting set of interrelated essays that span her fascinating career, putting to rest any lingering doubts about whether the Freudian tradition can be at once individually and collectively liberating. With her notion of the normative social unconscious, Layton coherently links psychoanalysis with progressive critiques of class, race, and gender biases in sociology and anthropology; simultaneously, she solidifies the intellectual foundations of growing contemporary interest in psychosocial studies. Last but hardly least, she brings a self-reflexive lens to the therapeutic process itself as it enacts cultural as well as childhood influences."

— **Lynn S. Chancer**, Professor and Executive Officer, Ph.D.
Program in Sociology, The Graduate Center of the
City University of New York

"This book convincingly puts the case for a much-needed social psychoanalysis. It is a timely publication, highly relevant theoretically and clinically to our times. It should be read by all psychoanalysts, psychotherapists, counsellors, community, and social work professionals who are genuinely committed to putting the best interest of their clients and community first. Layton powerfully shows that social history and the social context into which we are born and develop are part of our unconscious and often not analysed in ourselves as practitioners and thus in our clients. She invites us to think about and grapple with the social embeddedness of ourselves and our clients, including our identifications in terms of class, race, gender, culture, and sexuality, among others, which can and are unhelpfully enacted consciously and unconsciously in our work with clients, trainees, supervisees, and colleagues."

— **Frank Lowe**, Psychoanalytic Psychotherapist and
Head of Social Work, Adults & Adolescents,
Tavistock Clinic, London, UK

# Toward a Social Psychoanalysis

Frantz Fanon, Erich Fromm, Pierre Bourdieu, and Marie Langer are among those activists, clinicians, and academics who have called for a social psychoanalysis. For over thirty years, Lynne Layton has heeded this call and produced a body of work that examines unconscious process as it operates both in the social world and in the clinic.

In this volume of Layton's most important papers, she expands on earlier theorists' ideas of social character by exploring how dominant ideologies and culturally mandated, hierarchical identity prescriptions are lived in individual and relational conflict. Through clinical and cultural examples, Layton describes how enactments of what she calls 'normative unconscious processes' reinforce cultural inequalities of race, sex, gender, and class both inside and outside the clinic, and at individual, interpersonal, and institutional levels.

Clinicians, academics, and activists alike will find here a deeper understanding of the power of unconscious process, and are called on to envision and enact a progressive future in which vulnerability and interdependency are honored and systemic inequalities dismantled.

**Lynne Layton,** Ph.D. is a psychoanalyst and part-time faculty in the Department of Psychiatry at Harvard Medical School. She supervises at the Massachusetts Institute for Psychoanalysis and teaches social psychoanalysis in the Department of Community, Liberation, Indigenous and Eco-Psychologies at Pacifica Graduate Institute. She is the author of *Who's That Girl? Who's That Boy? Clinical Practice Meets Postmodern Gender Theory*, and co-editor of *Narcissism and the Text: Studies in Literature and the Psychology of Self; Bringing the Plague. Toward a Postmodern Psychoanalysis*; and *Psychoanalysis, Class and Politics: Encounters in the Clinical Setting*. From 2004–2018, she was co-editor of the journal *Psychoanalysis, Culture & Society*. She is Past-President of Section IX of Division 39, Psychoanalysis for Social Responsibility, and founder of Reflective Spaces/Material Places-Boston, a group of psychodynamic therapists committed to community mental health and social justice.

**Marianna Leavy-Sperounis** received her Psy.D. from The George Washington University, Master in City Planning from the Massachusetts Institute of Technology, and B.A. from Oberlin College. She completed her predoctoral internship at Cambridge Health Alliance/Harvard Medical School and currently serves as a board member of Section IX (Psychoanalysis for Social Responsibility) of Division 39 (Society for Psychoanalysis and Psychoanalytic Psychology) of the American Psychological Association. Prior to clinical training, she worked as a community organizer in Lawrence, Massachusetts and on the 2008 Obama campaign in Colorado; she also served as a political appointee to the U.S. Department of Housing and Urban Development.

# Relational Perspectives Book Series

**Adrienne Harris,**
*Steven Kuchuck & Eyal Rozmarin*
Series Editors

**Stephen Mitchell**
*Founding Editor*

**Lewis Aron**
*Editor Emeritus*

The Relational Perspectives Book Series (RPBS) publishes books that grow out of or contribute to the relational tradition in contemporary psychoanalysis. The term *relational psychoanalysis* was first used by Greenberg and Mitchell[1] to bridge the traditions of interpersonal relations, as developed within interpersonal psychoanalysis and object relations, as developed within contemporary British theory. But, under the seminal work of the late Stephen A. Mitchell, the term *relational psychoanalysis* grew and began to accrue to itself many other influences and developments. Various tributaries – interpersonal psychoanalysis, object relations theory, self psychology, empirical infancy research, feminism, queer theory, sociocultural studies and elements of contemporary Freudian and Kleinian thought – flow into this tradition, which understands relational configurations between self and others, both real and fantasied, as the primary subject of psychoanalytic investigation.

We refer to the relational tradition, rather than to a relational school, to highlight that we are identifying a trend, a tendency within contemporary psychoanalysis, not a more formally organized or coherent school or system of beliefs. Our use of the term *relational* signifies a dimension of theory and practice that has become salient across the wide spectrum of contemporary psychoanalysis. Now under the editorial supervision of Adrienne Harris, Steven Kuchuck and Eyal Rozmarin, the Relational Perspectives Book Series originated in 1990 under the editorial eye of the late Stephen A. Mitchell. Mitchell was the most prolific and influential of the originators of the relational tradition. Committed to dialogue among psychoanalysts, he abhorred the authoritarianism that dictated adherence to a rigid set of beliefs or technical restrictions. He championed open discussion, comparative and integrative approaches, and promoted new voices across the generations. Mitchell was later joined by the late Lewis Aron, also a visionary and influential writer, teacher and leading thinker in relational psychoanalysis.

Included in the Relational Perspectives Book Series are authors and works that come from within the relational tradition, those that extend and develop that tradition, and works that critique relational approaches or compare and contrast them with alternative points of view. The series includes our most distinguished senior psychoanalysts, along with younger contributors who bring fresh vision. Our aim is to enable a deepening of relational thinking while reaching across disciplinary and social boundaries in order to foster an inclusive and international literature.

A full list of titles in this series is available at www.routledge.com/mentalhealth/series/LEARPBS.

## Note

1 Greenberg, J. and Mitchell, S. (1983) *Object Relations in Psychoanalytic Theory*. Cambridge, MA: Harvard University Press.

# Toward a Social Psychoanalysis

Culture, Character, and Normative Unconscious Processes

Lynne Layton
Edited by Marianna Leavy-Sperounis

Routledge
Taylor & Francis Group

LONDON AND NEW YORK

First published 2020
by Routledge
2 Park Square, Milton Park, Abingdon, Oxon OX14 4RN

and by Routledge
52 Vanderbilt Avenue, New York, NY 10017

*Routledge is an imprint of the Taylor & Francis Group, an informa business*

*British Library Cataloguing-in-Publication Data*
A catalogue record for this book is available from the British Library

*Library of Congress Cataloging-in-Publication Data*
Names: Layton, Lynne, 1950– author. | Leavy-Sperounis, Marianna, editor.
Title: Toward a social psychoanalysis : culture, character, and normative unconscious processes / Lynne Layton, Ph.D, Marianna Leavy-Sperounis, M.C.P., Psy.D.
Description: Abingdon, Oxon ; New York, NY : Routledge, 2020. | Series: Relational perspectives book series | Includes bibliographical references and index.
Identifiers: LCCN 2019049463 (print) | LCCN 2019049464 (ebook) | ISBN 9780367902056 (hardback) | ISBN 9780367902049 (paperback) | ISBN 9781003023098 (ebook)
Subjects: LCSH: Psychoanalysis—Social aspects.
Classification: LCC BF175.4.S65 L39 2020 (print) | LCC BF175.4.S65 (ebook) | DDC 150.19/5—dc23
LC record available at https://lccn.loc.gov/2019049463
LC ebook record available at https://lccn.loc.gov/2019049464

ISBN: 978-0-367-90205-6 (hbk)
ISBN: 978-0-367-90204-9 (pbk)
ISBN: 978-1-003-02309-8 (ebk)

Typeset in Times New Roman
by Apex CoVantage, LLC

We dedicate this book to our comrades in Psychoanalysis for Social Responsibility, Section IX of Division 39 (The Society for Psychoanalysis and Psychoanalytic Psychology), American Psychological Association and to Amalia Green Leavy-Mastman, born as this book came into being. To new life, new hope.

# Contents

# Acknowledgments

Social psychoanalysis is not exactly mainstream in the world of clinical psychoanalysis, and that makes it all the more important to acknowledge the work of all those who have been for me a community of people dedicated to transforming the field and fighting oppression. I hope you know who you are and know that this work rests on your outstanding contributions to the field of social psychoanalysis. I have space here only to acknowledge those who were directly involved in making this book a reality: Nancy Hollander, Sue Grand, Lara Sheehi, and, for unflagging support, superb organizational and editing skills, and great conversation, Marianna Leavy-Sperounis. I am extremely grateful to Donna Bassin, artist and psychoanalyst, for the beautiful photo that graces the cover of this book. Finally, I want to thank the past and present steering committee members of Reflective Spaces/Material Places-Boston, especially Dr. Natasha Holmes. I have learned so much from working with you all.

# Editor's introduction

## Social psychoanalysis: centering power dynamics and affirming our interdependence

### "That's the problem with your theory"

It was a spontaneous moment of self-disclosure at a talk I was somewhat nervous to give. I was an early career clinician at a local psychoanalytic conference, presenting a paper on intersectionality theory in psychodynamic clinical practice, which I contextualized with case material from a treatment that had taken place at the beginning of my training. I offered a literature review and then shared process notes from what I felt were several key moments in the treatment. In one particular vignette, the patient – a white, gay, working class, middle-aged, cisgender man – had reported a deep sense of loss as we explored an aspect of his class identity. In that moment with him, I chose to comment on and inquire about the sadness he had described. A member of the audience raised her hand. She said that she appreciated how I had stayed with the patient's affect. "It's interesting that you say that because I actually felt unsure of myself afterwards about that choice," I replied, unsure again in this moment how my disclosure would be perceived by the group. I proceeded nonetheless. I explained how I had questioned myself: Had I made a mistake by not choosing in that moment to further inquire about how class dynamics and their interactions with the patient's other identities had influenced his sense of self? I sensed that staying with his experience of sadness in that moment had been helpful to him and yet I wondered if I had still somehow erred in my choice, that I had let something potentially meaningful slip past. I shared this aspect of my internal experience with the group.

Someone else in the audience raised his hand. "That's the problem with your theory," he said and shared his sense that the doubt I described in that clinical moment was a byproduct of having incorporated direct attention to socio-political context and identities. In doing so, he said, I had set myself up either to neglect "the intrapsychic" or feel shamed for attending to it. It was an interesting critique, not unlike the refrain, "that's not psychoanalysis," delivered at times in more traditional analytic circles when political context is invoked, but I disagreed. At the time of the treatment I was discussing, I was a new trainee, beginning to read literature from classical theories of psychoanalysis and hoping to become a "good" psychodynamic psychotherapist. In retrospect, I can see the enormous split I experienced then: I sensed that in order to be a "good" psychodynamic clinician, I had to somehow preference what was understood to be intrapsychic over what was understood to be social, as though the two were not already inextricably linked. With this patient in that moment, I felt I had to choose affect over class identity, as though exploration of both could not co-exist in that moment or be interwoven throughout a treatment.

I had come to my training as a clinical psychologist from a career that had begun in community organizing, city planning, and federal urban policy. I knew from my work, my personal life, and my family history that there was in fact no separation between the intrapsychic and the social, that the politics of race, class, gender, and sexuality, of a place, and of a time in history all have profound impacts on our senses of self and others, the parts of ourselves that exist outside of our awareness, our identities, and our affect states. It seemed clear to me and yet somehow radical in this new field I was entering. Relatedly, my own socialization as an upper middle-class white woman likely had something to do, too, with my desire to be a "good" clinician at the expense of my own instincts. At the time of the treatment I was describing, I had highly supportive supervisors who thought similarly to me, but I had not yet encountered a body of theoretical work that both validated my nascent sense of a false dichotomy and offered a path forward.

It is safe to say that my subsequent exposure to Layton's work was a revelation. When a mentor wisely suggested I read her 2006 article, *Attacks on linking* (Chapter 3 of this volume), I felt that perhaps there was a home for me in the world of psychoanalytic thought and that I would not have to sacrifice the political lens through which I understand human experience. In *Attacks*, Layton speaks to the delinking of individuals from their social context as a product of the mid-nineteenth-century emergence of patriarchal capitalism in the U.S. She cites this delinking as similar to attacks on linking in the clinical space, as described by Bion (1984), in the way that psychoanalytic norms have historically called for a separation of the psychic from the political, an attack on linking that is then inevitably enacted in unconscious collusions between the patient and therapist. What I would come to understand is Layton's theory of social psychoanalysis names the bind I had felt, explains the origins of the psycho-social split within classical psychoanalysis, and liberates clinicians and patients alike to attend to facets of internal experience and context in equal measure.

Later, I would read in *Dreams of America/American dreams* (2004) Layton's succinct call for a more expansive understanding of psychody-namics and the unconscious: "I would like to see American psychoanalysis recognize that gender, race, class, and sexual orientation are not add-ons to psychodynamics; they constitute psychodynamics" (Chapter 1, p. 19). Her call for resistance to the separation of intersectional identities from the intrapsychic – a separation which, it is essential to note, appears unique to white, upper middle-class clinicians and theorists – is incisive and remains urgent. And from her body of work, I would better understand the way in which psychoanalysis has gifted us with a keen understanding of the dangerous, frightening, and traumatic conditions under which we restrict our own abilities and that of others to think, as well as the way in which it has succumbed to a neoliberal economic model – our current stage of capitalism and the focus of Section III of this book – that fosters these very conditions in the clinic and the culture. While some fields within mental health, such as social work and counseling psychology, have not histori-cally attended to unconscious process, they have arguably done a better job accounting for social context; clinical psychology and psychoanalysis have been slower to adapt in this way. Layton's theory of social psychoa-nalysis provides a crucial foundation for a necessary evolution.

Back at the conference, I responded to the audience member. "I don't think that's the problem with the theories I am drawing on. I think my uncertainty had more to do with the limits of the classical approaches to psychoanalysis that I was familiar with at that time." I explained how Lay-ton's thinking had helped me to understand this and the nodding in the group took on a new degree of intensity. Afterward, a steady stream of early career professionals in the audience approached me and asked that I send them her work.

While the hunger I sensed for Layton's writing is not new – and while what stands out to me in it is inevitably informed by my own identities as white, cisgender female, and upper middle class, my upbringing in a pro-gressive family, and a professional path that began in neighborhood-based, community organizing – I believe that the timing of this volume speaks to an urgent need. This need, particularly among a newer generation of clinicians, requires us to consider clinical work in a manner closer to an existing and robust tradition in liberation psychology, especially as has been written and researched by indigenous clinicians and practitioners. This need also requires a psychoanalytic approach more specifically, itself in the tradition of Frantz Fanon, in which exploration of intersectional identities, history, context, and power dynamics are understood as core to the therapeutic process, to our field's future relevance, and to our ability to address the collective, accumulating traumas in the U.S. since its geno-cidal origin. It is my hope then that readers of this impressive volume will heed Layton's call to action, which I believe directly supports the calls of clinicians and theorists of color, as she organizes our attention at a crucial nexus, one where the field of psychoanalysis recalls and centers its own subversive contributions and claims its potential to feed a movement of resistance.

## Resisting a memoryless present

Among the foundational contributions of Layton's body of work is her profound commitment to truth-telling as she frames the long-term, indi-vidual, and collective traumatic effects of a culture built on colonialism, genocide, slavery, patriarchal white supremacy, and capitalism. In doing so, she deftly illustrates how the history of a place infuses the psyches of its inhabitants and, in the case of the U.S., has led to a form of psychic collapse, a legacy of neglect of traumatic proportions. In her language of fighting "a memoryless present" (Chapter 1, p. 8), Layton demands the act of remembering as she lays bare the precariousness of a neoliberal ideology and economic model that invite the dangerous decontextual-izing of human experience, shut down a collective ability to think, and inhibit a collective capacity to mourn. This precarity – accelerating since the 1970s, as Layton writes, with the loss of secure manufacturing jobs, growth of low-wage service jobs without benefits, end of defined pen-sion benefits, hiring of temporary workers on short-term contracts, shift-ing of jobs overseas, and decline of union power to negotiate collective contracts (Chapter 13, p. 199) – has infused the white American psyche in particular, such that vulnerability is shamed, disavowed, and projected onto oppressed groups who are then attacked for their vulnerability, all

this is necessary?

the while eroding the capacity for social solidarity (Chapters 12 and 14). This, in turn, engenders a form of defensive autonomy predicated on the simultaneous denial of basic dependency needs and the promotion of a manic dependency on the approval of others. As Layton so poignantly states, defensive autonomy "is not a very autonomous kind of autonomy" (Chapter 8, p. 116). Put another way, this is no way to live, no way to heal, and no foundation for a healthy, well-functioning society.

As Layton describes, the realities of neoliberalism are baked into the American social fabric and psyche, infusing among many (particularly those who are extended racial and economic privileges) a passive collusion with social and economic policy decisions that leave Americans only more vulnerable, alone, and uncontained. As a specific expression of capitalism, the perniciousness of neoliberalism lies in the forced isolation it inflicts, undermining our public and private capacities for connectedness as it fetishizes a feigned independence (the seductiveness of which partly drives the collusion); in its inhibition of the capacity to engage in larger progressive and social political action as it both demands individual attention to meet basic needs and also offers countless outlets for individual self-preoccupation; and in its establishment of conditions of precarity through policies that shift risk from the collective to the individual, respond to social problems with market-based solutions, and promote the commodification of "self-care," as though individual, uncoordinated, profit-driven acts might remedy catastrophic violations to the social contract (Chapters 13 and 14). Indeed, in an economic system such as ours, true remedy is not part of the plan.

This, in turn, has generated a slow-building trauma response and a lying relation to reality (Chapters 13 and 14) that manifests in the dissociation of clinical work from political context and in the impossible expectation that clinicians treat social problems as individual problems with individual solutions, an expectation with which far too many white-identified clinicians and others in positions of power appear willing to collude. In resisting this state of a memoryless present, Layton identifies normative unconscious processes as the mechanism through which unequal power relations are reproduced in both the clinic and culture at large and invokes the historical traumas and disavowed realities that white Americans in particular must acknowledge and bear if they are to interrupt these processes and contribute to a relevant and vital psychoanalysis that, itself, wholeheartedly contributes to a more just and equitable society. Layton invites readers to consider that if a core tenet in the treatment of trauma is the eventual integration of the traumatic experience and traumatized parts of the self, no longer needing to be split off in the service of self-preservation and cohesion, then psychoanalysis must formulate new interventions to treat a population traumatized by the abandonment of a neoliberal economic order.

## Implications for clinical work

In effect, Layton calls for an invigorated approach to contemporary psychoanalysis – one that maintains its challenge of cultural hierarchies in the way that it honors vulnerability, dependency, and interdependence as essential qualities of the human experience – and opens discussion about the implications for clinical technique in a truly social psychoanalysis. In this approach, as she writes, "therapeutic action [. . .] lies in reconnecting patients with their histories and restoring the broken social link in a way that counters institutionalized individualization and neoliberal denials of embeddedness" (Chapter 5, p. 70). To facilitate this, she calls for enlarging the therapeutic frame to include "not only [. . .] the power differentials of race, class, gender, and sexuality, but also [. . .] the way that institutionalized individualization has become articulated with neoliberalism and marks conscious and unconscious versions of subjectivity" (Chapter 5, p. 72). Clinicians, she writes, must go beyond the traditional cultivation of empathy for self and other:

> I think that we are all skilled at helping our clients develop capacities for empathy and mutuality. This is a start. But it does not necessarily create subjects who have the capacity to connect themselves with broader social processes and inequities [. . .] Because clinical work has become so dissociated from its own political context, it is always at risk of creating subjects who do not question social inequities: not just the inequities that keep middle-class privilege unconscious, but even the inequities that keep us oppressed and powerless.
> (Chapter 2, p. 32)

Layton further questions our assumptions about empathy, first, as a state worth cultivating in patients if the concern fostered for others does not include acknowledgment of how one might be implicated in the suffering of others, and second, in the way that the clinician's capacity for it is often defined: "Many psychoanalytic schools' versions of empathy give the impression that the better we are at not getting stirred up by the patient's behavior, the more successful we are at sustaining an empathic stance – as though being stirred up indicates a failure of empathic capacity" (Chapter 12, p. 183). She posits the following conceptualization of the clinician's role relative to a patient: "If part of my job is to attend to his development as a citizen who recognizes his implication in the suffering of others, and I think it is, then I need to listen carefully for moments where the conflict [regarding mutual implication] emerges and might be further explored" (Chapter 12, p. 186). In sharing vignettes from her own clinical work, Layton also makes the case that essential to this work, particularly for clinicians whose identities are aligned with positions of power, is an ever-present awareness of one's own shame states that arise in this exploration, and the potential for unconscious enactments of unequal power relations, including the projection of that shame onto the patient.

## A bridge to organizing in the public sphere

Layton's concept of normative unconscious processes, alongside her reformulation of clinical technique, represents an essential contribution to how we understand and address abuses of power in the clinic and our professional institutions. And yet I believe that perhaps an even more impactful undercurrent in her work may be the blueprint she lays out for a bridge between social psychoanalysis and the fields of community organizing and progressive policymaking. In Chapter 8, she succinctly states, "Clinical work is by no means the equivalent of collective social action," (p. 120) but she is not satisfied by this reality. In the absence of a more progressive, robust public sphere and in a culture where participation in public life is challenged by the necessity for individuals and families to meet their own basic needs, we see, as Layton describes, that "collective action and political resistance, let alone participation in the public sphere, become severely hampered by a constant anxiety about just getting by day to day" (Chapter 14, p. 231). But what can a social psychoanalysis offer to counter the long-term psychic and collective effects of disinvestment in our interdependence? Or as Layton asks in Chapter 6, "Are there basic human needs that must be met for a democratic society to exist? If so, is there an important role for psychoanalysts to play in policy formation? Are psychoanalysts doomed simply to be lackeys of state and corporate power or might they offer a counter-discourse to contemporary social and political discourses?" (p. 80) In highlighting the gap between clinical work and collective action, Layton calls on and challenges the field of psychoanalysis, its theorists and practitioners, to question this gulf and to imagine a path to relevance and impact in the public sphere.

What I find particularly compelling here is that Layton's insights about the potential gifts of social psychoanalysis are the very same as the lessons I learned over several years as a community organizer on local and national campaigns, where long-term progressive change was not predicated on a single issue, a single victory, or a single organizer's ability to develop relationships with many people. Rather, what I learned over those years – and what leaders of successful, long-term organizing campaigns and social movements know all too well – is that in sustainable, progressive organizing, as in social psychoanalysis, unequal power relations must be constantly questioned, histories and struggles for power must be remembered and repeatedly named, our fundamental states of vulnerability must be honored and nurtured, a vast network of interdependent relationships (including strong links and weak links) must be cultivated to sustain the solidarity needed to withstand setbacks and attacks, and that all of this must be fortified by an active refusal to comply with social and economic policies that further erode our threadbare social contract, alongside the active advancement of a vision for a more just society and culture. In effect, where Layton identifies psychoanalysis' complicity with the carnage wrought by neoliberalism, she also lays the groundwork for a path forward for the field out of the false dichotomies of intrapsychic/ social, micro/macro, clinical/"real world" and toward a true means of psychoanalytic civic engagement and activism.

As Layton makes clear, the widespread erosion of a capacity for social solidarity must be met with the restoration of the internal and external links that have been attacked and disavowed. Clinicians do a grave injustice not only to their patients but to the collective good when their attention and inquiries are limited to purportedly de-politicized notions of the intrapsychic, when they fail to acknowledge the neoliberal hostage-taking of psychic life and of the field, and when they formulate and treat all distress as exclusively individual or located solely within the family. At its core, Layton's approach to social psychoanalysis centers power dynamics and affirms our interdependence. Her thinking is radical in its departure from more traditional approaches and elegant in its clarity. In this sense, the promise cannot be overstated of a social psychoanalysis that aligns with an ethic of organizing and progressive change, embraces an inclusive vision of social, racial, and economic justice as essential to health, and that is grounded in community, practiced across a range of spaces, and rooted in the power of interdependent relationships. Indeed, an interdisciplinary theory of mind and a practice of psychotherapy that legitimize vulnerability and interdependence at the same time that they invite and restore critical links between socio-political context and individual experience and situate intersectional identities in their historical and power-laden contexts – all the while defying hegemonic discourse – is something of a triple threat. It is worth noting that this volume comes at a time when Layton has immersed herself in political and racial justice organizing campaigns and publicly declared a commitment to the elevation of emerging voices that seek to decolonize the field of psychoanalysis (Leadership Award acceptance speech, 2019 Spring Meeting of Division 39, American Psychological Association). Thus, this volume represents not only a compilation of her most compelling writing over the last 20 years, but also a welcome and well-timed call to action for a newer generation of clinician-scholar-activists.

# Author's general introduction
## Toward a social psychoanalysis: culture, character, and normative unconscious processes

Before becoming a psychologist/psychoanalyst, I trained in comparative literature in the 1970s, a time when second wave feminist, British Cultural Studies under Stuart Hall, and Marxist frameworks were circulating in academia. Each of these left-wing theoretical paradigms had at least one strain that was inflected by psychoanalysis. As a graduate student, I was a member of the *Telos* collective at Washington University. Beginning in 1968, the journal *Telos* introduced an English speaking public to Frankfurt School critical theory. Founded in the 1920s, the Frankfurt School had made some of the first attempts to synthesize Marxist and psychoanalytic thinking. Alongside texts by Frankfurt School members Adorno, Horkheimer, Marcuse, and Fromm, my *Telos* collective study group, led by sociologist and *Telos* editor, Paul Piccone, read Nancy Chodorow's (1978) *Reproduction of Mothering*. These theoretical encounters, along with the various feminist and anti-capitalist activist groups in which I took part, became the basis for my commitment to a psychosocial and psychoanalytic way of understanding history, culture, and subjectivity.

Subjectivity, in my view, is "psychosocial" because from the outset it is shaped, though not determined, by the social structures and histories in which it is embedded. "Psychosocial," however, does not fully capture how I understand subjectivity and culture because not all who use that term would agree with me that unconscious processes are a major force in accounting for how we resist, reproduce, and transform those structures and histories. In fact, as some of the chapters in Section I of this book attest, even those who do take account of unconscious process often differ radically in how they define "the unconscious" and how they conceptualize the relation between the psychic and the social. For example, some theorists tend to idealize "the unconscious" as purely resistant to cultural demands (cf., Marcuse, 1955); at the opposite extreme are theorists who figure "the unconscious" as fully colonized by cultural demands. The challenge has historically been to resist either collapsing the psychic into the social or the social into the psychic. As Jacqueline Rose (1986, p. 12) might argue, the task is to "hover uncomfortably in between," that is, to account for the unconscious effects on identity of the pressure to internalize cultural norms and ideologies while also accounting for what such phenomena as dreams, slips of the tongue, and even repetition compulsions consistently reveal: the failure of cultural forces fully to colonize unconscious process, to exhaust subjectivity. Although many of the chapters collected in this volume emphasize the force of those unconscious processes that reproduce cultural inequalities in the clinic as well as in social institutions and socio-political life, I hope overall to stake a claim here for the resistant as well as the conformist nature of unconscious process.

In this introduction, I trace how I came to my own version of social psychoanalysis. The trajectory begins with my engagement in the white feminist activism and left-wing theorizing of the 1970s, travels through a dawning awareness of how my dominant white and upper-class positionings have made me complicit in unconscious enactments of racism and classism, and lands in the current antiracist, anti-capitalist activist and theoretical commitments that are deepening my understanding of what a social psychoanalysis needs to be.

As an academic in the 1970s and early 1980s, I was most drawn to 1970s work on social character, a term defined by Fromm (1941) as the typical character structure and typical defenses of a dominant socio-economic cultural formation. Societies, according to both Fromm and Reich (1933/1972), demand that people repress feelings and thoughts that come in conflict with existent power relations, and this demand produces particular character types and defenses. Reich's (1966) work focused on the deleterious effects of the demand to repress sexual desire. In Fromm's view, it is the fear of social isolation and loss of love that motivates people to conform to cultural mandates of what is proper to feel and think; the repression of all that people are not supposed to think or feel shapes what Fromm called the social unconscious. For most people, Fromm argued, identity is rooted in conformity with social clichés; to be aware of the truth is to risk loss of identity. In Fromm's view, however, the social unconscious does not exhaust unconscious process; a wider and ethical human unconscious exists and has the capacity to contest the dictates of the social unconscious. Fromm's work has very much influenced my own conceptions of what motivates conformity to social norms. My version of social psychoanalysis, however, puts more emphasis on the psychic conflict caused by cultural demands to split off part of our humanity, on struggles between resistant and conformist unconscious forces.

Psychosocial attempts to account for fascism in Germany led Fromm and other members of the Frankfurt School to investigate an authoritarian personality marked by a split between submissive behavior toward authority figures and tyrannical behavior toward intimate others (see, Fromm, 1984; Adorno et al., 1950). In the late 1970s and early 1980s, Lasch (1979) and Kovel (1980), following in this social character tradition, drew on Kohut (1971, 1977) and Kernberg (1975) to argue that consumer capitalism had spawned narcissistic characters and a culture of narcissism. Their description of narcissism bore a great resemblance to Adorno et al.'s description of the authoritarian personality and Fromm's (1947) description of the marketing orientation. My own reading of these texts contributed to my earliest social psychoanalytic writing on narcissism and literature (Layton, 1986; Layton and Schapiro, 1986).

My work took a different, but related, social psychoanalytic turn in the 1980s and 1990s, one informed both by my feminist activist and academic commitments and by my decision to train as a psychologist and, later, a psychoanalyst. From the 1950s to the 1990s and beyond, a variety of social movements emerged, each influenced by the other, to demand recognition for culturally devalued identities: civil rights, second wave feminism, black power, gay and lesbian liberation, Act Up, third wave feminism, queer and trans movements. Second-wave feminists, many of whom had wholly rejected psychoanalysis as irredeemably sexist, began to experience in their relational lives sexism's deeply unconscious psychic effects, effects that perpetuated the self-oppression of even the most socially-conscious feminists (see, for example, Dinnerstein, 1976; Chodorow, 1978; Benjamin, 1988; for the racist implications of internalized sexism, see davenport, 1983). Theorizing began to focus on the complexity and cultural shaping of identities. For me, as for others, these experiences led to an interest in clinical psychoanalysis, and I decided to train in the field and go into analysis myself.

During much of that period, I was also teaching in Women, Gender, and Sexuality Studies, and then in Social Studies at Harvard. There I continued to encounter left-wing academic theories, such as Queer Theory, third wave and intersectional feminist theories, Althusserian and Gramscian Marxism, critical race theory, and a variety of poststructuralist theories. I was especially influenced by the theories of Hall (1980, 1982) and Laclau and Mouffe (1985) because, in their anti-capitalist Gramsci-inspired work, they figured culture not as primarily marked by forces of conformity but rather by political struggles over meaning between hegemonic and resistant counter-hegemonic forces. Influenced itself by the political activity of various social movements and left-wing coalitions, this work captured the contingency and complexities of history and culture. Along with feminist writing on gender and sexual identities, Hall's antiracist work on the different ways alternately positioned subjects make meaning of the same cultural texts and events made me rethink the notion that one dominant character type could account for all that was going on in a given social formation.

When I began clinical psychology training in the early 1980s, I found the field to be decidedly individualist, focused primarily on defining and policing normalcy/abnormalcy and denying the effects on subjectivity of history, power differentials, and systemic/symbolic violence. This was, to say the least, disappointing if not, at times, mind-numbing. The only pieces of that training that interested me were the psychoanalytic courses and the psychodynamic clinical work because, for me, psychoanalysis was the missing link to the feminist psychosocial theory I was beginning to formulate. As it happens, Kohut's and Kernberg's theories were dominant during my 1980s clinical training and so I developed a more clinic-based and experiential understanding of the effects of narcissistic wounding on self structure. My clinical work and my own analysis suggested to me that narcissistic injury lay at the heart of most defenses and character structures. Further, it seemed to me that identity-forming narcissistic injury derived neither from innate drives nor innate conflict, but from the ways that the wounds caused by conscious and unconscious sexism, racism, and classism become lived as split binary structures. Indeed, I began to understand dominant white versions of femininity and masculinity as two subtypes of narcissism (Layton, 1988).

My early psychoanalytic feminist theorizing focused on gender because that was the place where I had experienced the most wounding in my life.

As a white, middle-class, heterosexual, cisgender woman born in 1950 and coming of age in the late 1960s, I sensed that my own unconscious conflicts, dreams, fantasies, relational struggles, ways of experiencing my body, dependency, shame, and assertion, were all marked by sexism. In 1985, I walked into my analyst's office scanning the bookshelves to try to figure out where she might stand in relation to psychoanalytic theory. I recall telling people that if she started to talk about penis envy I would be out of there. In my analysis, I discovered that the sexist norms of my 1950s upbringing had turned a young girl comfortable with being aggressive and sexual into an adolescent for whom assertion had become confused with unladylike aggression, and for whom an open enjoyment of sexuality could be deemed by others, and then actually felt to be, either slutty or dangerous. As a result, even though I came of age in the time of women's liberation and sexual freedom and was excitedly caught up in norm changes that challenged the norms of my earlier development, those earlier experiences had ongoing effects that greatly complicated my psychic life. In accord with 1950s gender norms, I had split assertion and connection and had unconsciously envied and raged against male assertion while consciously denigrating it as selfish, mean, and, most importantly, not-me (a social psychoanalytic reinterpretation, one might say, of penis envy). I made a virtue of passivity and of making myself small. I then bonded with other women who shared my conviction that making ourselves small was virtuous. I began to see how I had lived the wounds of sexism, the defenses and transferences that marked my experiences of love, work, agency, and dependency. At the same time, however, I rebelled, consciously and unconsciously, against the constrictions of those 1950s norms.

While my own analysis helped me connect social psychoanalytic culture theory to what I saw happening in myself and my clinical work, I did not find a psychoanalytic theory that felt "true" to me until I encountered relational psychoanalytic theory. One can find adherents of many psychoanalytic schools within a single country, but often a particular version of psychoanalysis becomes dominant in a particular place and at a particular point in time. The relational school was founded in the 1980s in the U.S. and its flagship journal, *Psychoanalytic Dialogues*, began publishing in 1991. Many of its founders came from the ranks of 1960s radicals, and true to the ethos of their era, they brought into the field of psychoanalysis a questioning of authority, of patriarchy, of the status of knowledge and certainty in clinical work. They rejected drive theory and highlighted instead the effects of relational experience on development and on unconscious conflict. The relational school of psychoanalysis became, for me, a home where I felt able to elaborate my version of social psychoanalysis (see Layton, 2008).

## My model of culture and identity

While in the 1970s and 1980s a rich body of feminist psychoanalytic work had emerged – often in film, literature, and cultural studies – by the end of the 1980s little if any feminist or other social psychoanalytic culture theory had yet been applied to what goes on in the clinic. In the third issue of the first volume of *Psychoanalytic Dialogues*, however, the journal made space for left-wing feminists (including Benjamin, Dimen, Goldner, and Harris) to author a special section on gender, and this kind of work, which I also had begun doing in the late 1980s, offered me a much needed community. Later in the 1990s, I joined this group of feminist psychoanalysts on the board of a journal called *Gender and Psychoanalysis* (which, in 2000, became *Studies in Gender and Sexuality*).

The articles collected in this volume were all written after the publication of my 1998 book, *Who's That Girl? Who's That Boy? Clinical Practice Meets Postmodern Gender Theory*. In that book, I tried to bring what I had learned from clinical psychodynamic practice into dialogue with poststructuralist, Marxist, and queer theories of gender and sexuality. It had sometimes seemed to me that while clinicians were largely unfamiliar with academic gender theories, academics were largely unfamiliar with the conflictual ways in which gender and sexuality were lived. Given my own experience in analysis and my work with patients, I had come to understand gender development as traumatic, subject not to the kind of traumas usually thought of as the "legitimate" realm of trauma – war, famine, poverty – but to the kind of traumas perpetrated by the prescriptions and proscriptions of rigidly binary sexist and heterosexist hierarchies. Academic celebrations of fragmented genders and decentered selves seemed to me often to deny the painful fragmentations of self caused by this kind of traumatic experience.

In the gender book, I argued that developing children encounter two kinds of gendered experience in their relations with their families and social surround. In one, their desires and agentic strivings are met with recognition and approval, regardless of whether those desires fall in line with gender

norms. In the other, their desires and agentic strivings are punished, usually by shaming; these experiences often enforce cultural norms and ideals
that prescribe which human capacities are feminine and which masculine,
and, in doing so, cause narcissistic injury. I proposed a model of identity
development in which these two modes of relational experience – recognition and narcissistic injury – are constantly being negotiated. Experiences
of recognition allow one to resist the binary gendering of capacities such
as assertion and vulnerability. As mentioned earlier, I argued that dominant cultural ideals of masculinity and femininity were themselves split
narcissistic structures, but I also maintained that other versions of gendered experience, some of which contest dominant norms, circulate in a
given culture and provide points of resistance. Against the academic writers, I suggested that identity categories of gender, race, class, and sexuality
can either facilitate or thwart individual growth and social change depending on how they become linked up with other social ideas and forces.
Women's experiences in sexist culture, for example, were crucial to the
development of different versions of feminism, but those linked to social-
ism were more progressive than those aligned with prevailing capitalist
norms.

Along with other relational psychoanalytic feminists in the late 1980s
and 1990s (Benjamin, 1988, 1991, 1995; Dimen, 1991; Goldner, 1991;
Harris, 1991; Layton, 1988, 1990), I began to write about how culturally constructed gender binaries enforce processes of splitting and projection in individual lives. My own contribution (Layton, 1998/2004) was
to focus on the psychological effects of having some human capacities
assigned to one side of the gendered split and others to the other side.
I wanted to understand what happens to the psyche and, later, to relationships when love and social approval are given only for certain ways of
being human and not others, when they permit certain identifications and
encourage disidentifications with what is socially considered undesirable.
I wanted to understand what it is like to LIVE the splits mandated by various binaries – to look at what becomes experienced as me and what not-
me and at how the not-me gets projected onto others.

In the 1998 book, for example, I spoke of a patient of mine whose father
had humiliated him by calling him female names, constantly suggesting
he was not the right kind of male. Trying to unravel his own history of
narcissistic wounding, the patient told a story one day about overhearing
his boss talking to his four-year-old son, who apparently was weeping

uncontrollably on the phone (reported in Layton, 1998, Ch. 7). After trying to cajole the boy to stop crying, my patient overheard the boss tell the boy to pull down his pants. He then asked, What do you see there? The boy must have said, "a penis." "That's right," the boss said, "so stop crying." How, we wondered, would this boy live the effects of coding vulnerability and emotionality as female/feminine; how would he live the demand to repudiate those states? How would it affect his relationships?

## Normative unconscious processes

Soon after writing the gender book, I became interested in exploring more about the way that split identity categories and internalized social norms not only impede growth but create narcissistic constellations that promote unconscious reproductions of racist, sexist, heterosexist, and classist social conditions. For this project, relational conceptions of enactment proved crucial. Many relational founders, including Stephen Mitchell, had been trained in the interpersonal tradition, some of whose members had argued that, in any analysis, there are two unconsciouses in the room. As early as 1972, Levenson pushed this premise further to assert that mutual enactments of traumatic experience that cannot yet be symbolized can be, and often are, at the heart of therapeutic action. Unconscious collusions within the dyad that re-enact (rather than analyze) earlier traumatic experience often lead to impasse, but working one's way out of such impasse can be key to promoting deep psychic change (for both participants). Clinical descriptions of enactments, especially mutual enactments, became central to my way of bringing into relation the psychic and the social, for, in my view, unconscious process in the clinical (or any other) setting is always inflected by cultural norms (the earliest example of my work in this domain is Layton and Bertone, 1998).

By the late 1990s, several clinicians, mostly within the relational and group psychoanalytic traditions, had begun writing about the ways that social inequalities are re-created in and sometimes sustained by unconscious enactments in the clinic (e.g., Layton and Bertone, 1998; Altman, 2000; Layton, 2002; Leary, 1997a, 1997b, 2000; Suchet, 2004; Hopper, 2003; Straker, 2006). These clinical descriptions of relational enactments of disavowed, split off, projected, and dissociated experience helped me formulate my own thoughts about how cultural inequalities become reproduced in both clinic and culture.

I first used the term "normative unconscious processes" in a paper that described enactments that seemed to me to reproduce a sexist and hetero-sexist status quo (Layton, 2002). Because the focus of that paper was on gender and sexuality, I referred there to a heterosexist unconscious. In one case, for example, I suspected that I had initiated a long enactment when I unconsciously shamed a lesbian patient whose desire for me had stirred my own anxiety about homoerotic desire. After I made my shaming comment, the patient stopped talking about desire and began instead to identify with my own version of femininity. This experience brought home to me in a visceral way Butler's (1995) argument that, in homophobic cultures, oedipalization and the incest taboo rest on a prior taboo against homo-erotic desire that splits sexual desire from identification, making them appear to be in binary and mutually exclusive relation. This socially con-structed, split binary "choice" is precisely the socially sanctioned outcome of oedipalization – in "normal" development, you are to identify with the same-sexed parent and desire the opposite-sexed parent. My own way of living the binary split between identification and desire had led me uncon-sciously to "heterosexualize" my patient. Elaborating on my concept of heterosexist unconscious, Stephen Hartman (2005) used the term class unconscious to describe both how class is intergenerationally transmitted to become part of one's identity and how internalized class struggles are enacted in the clinic.

Unfortunately, social psychoanalytic clinicians, mostly white, largely repeated in our publications the history of writings on identity by white academic feminists: even though some of our case descriptions were intersectional, we tended to take up one identity category of oppression at a time, beginning with gender, then sexuality, then race, and only infre-quently class. This category-by-category approach was not the one taken by feminists of color. The Combahee River Collective had already pub-lished their call for an intersectional analysis of identity and oppression by 1977; in 1981, Moraga and Anzaldua (1983) published the essays in *This Bridge Called My Back: Writings by Radical Women of Color*, and by the early 1990s, intersectionality (Crenshaw, 1989) was an established way of understanding the way identities are psychosocially shaped by power rela-tions and overlapping axes of oppression and privilege. Although I knew of this work long before I began writing about gender, it was not until I began to note the increasing number of clinical papers on unconscious enactments of unequal power relations, and had myself begun to write about intersectional aspects of class and racial enactments, that I more consistently used the umbrella term "normative unconscious processes" to describe enactments that reproduce traumatic experience related to subjects' overlapping and conflictual social and historical positionings, their location in multiple systems of oppression (Layton, 2006a).

In sum, normative unconscious processes are the lived effects on identity formation of unequal power arrangements and dominant ideologies that split and differentially value straight from gay, rich from poor, masculine from feminine, white from black and brown. Social hierarchies of sex(ism), class(ism), race(ism), heterosex(ism) mandate what one will have to split off to attain a "proper" identity. Indeed, norms and practices transmit historically specific and split prescriptions for what affects, attributes, behaviors, thoughts, and modes of attachment and agency are deemed "proper" to any given identity position, and all identities in a given social formation take up some relation – resistant, negotiated, conformist – to that society's dominant norms of class, race, sex, and gender. The binary identity structures that result from cultural inequalities and that keep those inequalities in place severely constrain human capacity. As Freud (1915a) once said, what has been repressed "proliferates in the dark . . . and takes on extreme forms of expression" (p. 149). This is true as well of what is split off and dissociated, and we should expect that dominant ideals of masculinity and femininity, for example, will be lived, at least in part, as defensive, symptomatic structures.

Culturally sanctioned "recognition," which takes the form of social approval, love, and conditions for social belonging, is a primary mechanism of the transmission of norms and practices, and this kind of "recognition" is generally granted, albeit often conflictually, to "proper" performances of identity. The risk of meeting with indifference, humiliation, and shame discourages "improper" performances and encourages subjects to split off as "not-me" disapproved of ways of being and relating, ways that provoke anxiety or shame in significant others. Thus, classed, raced, gendered, and sexed identities are often lived as painful, conflictual, binary (either/or) structures that include particular ways of living emotions such as shame, sorrow, and guilt, and particular ways of living such psychological states as dependency, love, vulnerability, and capacity for assertion. If social character is defined in terms of typical defenses and socially mandated norms of what is allowed to be thought and felt, then many social characters exist in a given culture, and each must be understood in the context of the different but related norms operating in specific social locations.

But social character is not all there is to subjectivity. Because what gets split off in normative unconscious processes are human needs, capacities, and longings, these do not disappear. Rather, they reappear in conflictual repetition compulsions: in symptoms and in relational struggles that often reinforce the splits even as they seek to undo them. And because identities form in relation to other identities circulating in a culture and subculture, relational enactments of normative unconscious processes often reveal that the ways in which we have been narcissistically wounded by heterosexism, racism, and classism stir up the wounds of those with whom we are engaged. The capacity to resist such repetitions, however, springs from multiple sources, especially relational experiences, inside and outside the clinic, that offer the kind of recognition that contests the binary structures of dominant culture. Section II of this book focuses most closely on how the struggle between normative unconscious processes and counternormative unconscious processes are enacted in the clinic.

Enactments of normative unconscious processes occur at individual, interpersonal, institutional, and societal levels – inside and outside the clinic – and the chapters in this volume explore each of these levels. By way of introduction, I offer a few examples here of how enactments of normative unconscious processes connect to the production and enforcement of different, but intertwined, versions of subjectivity and social character.

## Individual and interpersonal enactments of normative unconscious processes

If we pay close attention, we will find that everyday life provides some of the clearest examples of how normative unconscious processes operate. On a visit with friends, for example, I and other guests were told that the hosts' eight-year-old daughter Emily had been making movies with her nine-year-old male friend. We quickly discerned that the proud parents wanted us to watch the movies, and, although I was prepared to be bored, I found "Lovestruck I, II, and III" to be an astounding trilogy. In the short films, Emily and Joe had enacted a rather sophisticated presentation of class, race, sex, and gender conflicts. The theme of all three movies was the social barriers to the love between an upper-class white girl and a lower-class white boy. At first, the young lady, draped in an adult's fur boa, told her single dad, played by her father, that she was repelled by this "boy," whom they both call an "amateur" (which seemed to be their word for lower class). The boy earns her love by being good to his mom and the best student in the class; as they work on their projects together and she comes to see how very considerate and ambitious he is, the cold and distant emotional shield she had erected against whatever it is she considered to be associated with poverty begins to erode.

In all three films, money worries feature prominently. Lovestruck III concerns the financial difficulties they face in their married life. Attention is diverted from this problem when Emily is kidnapped by a lower-class black thief who shows all of the attributes of poverty against which Emily had erected her upper-class defenses in the first place – he's unkempt, loud, boorish, takes rather than earns money, and is a sexual predator. A happy ending resolves the tensions but also masks the fact that the film's social conflicts are unresolvable – and that they are psychic conflicts as well.

Emily, under the influence of whatever goes on and has gone on in her intergenerational family, in her largely white neighborhood, school, and peer group, is struggling her way into a gendered, sexed, classed, and raced position. Her fantasy suggests that this position is created and maintained by splitting off certain ways of expressing feeling, certain kinds of desire, disallowing certain kinds of activity, dehumanizing whole classes of people. Her conflict about her raced class position, which may involve such psychic phenomena as guilt over privilege or a longing to be able to enact some of the forbidden behaviors associated with the black lower-class male of her fantasy, or anger and confusion at her family's concern with money, is expressed in part in her desire for the poor boy. The conflict is managed in fantasy by the way she gives him the attributes that make him safe for marriage (i.e., the attributes that make him a good bourgeois, including his whiteness). The failure of her attempts at management surface in her alienated and disavowed envy of the black kidnapper, who grabs sex and money without guilt.

The intersectional social construction of identity apparent in Lovestruck also shows the way that the emotions and psychological structures that we work with every day in therapy – dependency, assertion, vulnerability, emotion – become gendered, raced, classed, and sexed in the process of identity formation – and how identities lived in conformity with various social inequalities play out in relation. One way we see them play out here is in Emily's seeking of distinction, which makes her complicit in the suffering of those less powerful. Emily and Joe's enactment of normative unconscious processes suggests that any conception of social character has to take into account how one's social location and different relations to power, privilege, and to other identity categories circulating in the same social milieu constitute psychic and social life. In other words, social character cannot be understood without looking at how each of us has been narcissistically wounded in particular ways by the group norms that operate in the intersecting inequalities of gender, race, class, and other forms of social oppression.

## Normative unconscious processes in clinical theory and practice

In a commentary on a 1974 paper by a well-known psychoanalyst, Lawrence Kubie (2011), I pointed to how normative unconscious processes operate in the clinic and in the theory that inevitably informs what happens in the clinic (Layton, 2011a). Kubie had proposed that some people, and many artists, have a neurotic drive to be both sexes; this drive, he felt, was crippling and highly resistant to analysis. He described several vignettes with patients suffering from this illness. In one example, he spoke of a male patient who, he said, was rather passive and not at all competitive. He then likened this man to an adolescent girl (p. 387), implying that adolescent girls are passive and not competitive, and that real men are supposed to be non-passive and competitive. Kubie's interpretations reflected his adherence to the strictly binary, white middle-class gender norms of the 1950s. These norms were articulated in many discourses, for example, in prominent sociologist Talcott Parsons' family theory (Parsons, 1949). Parsons lauded as natural and most desirable a social system that divided men and women along the axes of instrumental, bread-winner roles and expressive, caretaking roles. I earlier described the effect of such discourses on my own psychic life. Kubie's work suggests how clinical theory and practice can, in the guise of healing, further enforce oppressive norms.

In a lengthy vignette, Kubie described a female patient of his who, he writes:

> had a flair for writing, a fine dramatic gift, and great warmth in her attitudes toward children. In the course of her treatment she went through successive phases – working on the stage, writing, and teaching in

nursery schools . . . She did each extraordinarily well; yet each also carried its multiple and conflicting meanings.

(p. 421)

Kubie continued:

> For many months secret, lifelong fantasies of going on the stage had been completely absent from her material. Then as she approached the end of her analysis, she suddenly fulfilled a prophecy that I had made silently to myself by turning once again toward a stage career. This was buttressed by excellent rationalizations, including high praise from her dramatic coaches and her successes in certain competitions. *Her battle became . . . whether to have children or to have a stage career; or to put it another way, to be one sex or the other or both.*

(p. 421, my emphasis)

Kubie relates a dream from the end of this patient's analysis, in which the patient was auditioning for the role of Blanche Du Bois in *A Streetcar Named Desire*:

> In the dream, having auditioned successfully for the role of this unhappy psychotic prostitute, she wandered away. Then she stooped to pick up a half-dollar. But it was not a round half-dollar piece; it was one half of a round dollar, a half-moon. She picked this up, looked at it, and dissolved in tears.

(p. 422)

Kubie concluded, "In the course of time, with this warning in mind, I returned her to analysis with a woman, with whom she carried her therapy through to successful completion" (p. 422).

From the vantage point of having experienced the second wave feminist movement that was, at that very moment, in the process of deconstructing the gender norms Kubie was enforcing, I could recognize that this woman and the previously mentioned male patient were being asked by their analyst to be half a human. As I said, Kubie's diagnosis of these patients was that they suffered from the drive to be both sexes, a diagnosis that is not just descriptive, but prescriptive. For Kubie, a proper female should want to have children and give up any notion of a career. To want a career is to want to be male, evidence of the drive to become both sexes. As Butler (1990) has taught us, repeated utterances of the diagnosis, and the repeated interpretations dictated by the diagnosis are precisely what end up legitimizing the gender binary that makes half-people out of whole people. To put it psychoanalytically, the diagnosis and interpretations are not the neutral or universally true statements Kubie believes they are; rather, they unconsciously legitimize the splitting processes that one would have had to undergo at that time in order to occupy a social character culturally recognized as properly male or properly female. They enact, and thus enforce the particular classist, racist, sexist, and heterosexist social norms of the day.

It is easy to feel horror when listening to work like Kubie's, and all too easy to feel we are beyond enacting such egregious sexism in our clinical work. But I do not think it is fruitful to consider what Kubie did as a clinical "mistake." On the contrary, his theorizing and his work, undoubtedly characteristic of his era, caution us to think deeply about the way that mental health experts can consciously and unconsciously enforce and unwittingly legitimize only those performances of identity deemed proper by the culture and subcultures in which we live. In my experience, it is in fact not as uncommon as we might hope, even today, to hear case presentations in which human attributes like assertion and dependence are gendered.

## Institutional enactments of normative unconscious processes

Psychoanalytic conferences often provide multiple examples of the way that normative unconscious processes play out at the institutional level. I was once asked to discuss a case presentation by a young clinician on a panel set up explicitly to focus on intersectionality. The panel was titled: Intersectionality, The Trifecta: Gender, Race, and Sexuality. At first I barely noticed that class was missing as an intersectional category. As it happens, however, the case was shot through and through with class, and, in fact, the major unconscious enactment in the case was around class distinction. Interestingly, when the presenter sent me the case, she told me that she had to delete some material due to time constraints, but she had left in what she had crossed out so I could see it. Each instance of crossed out material was about class. This enactment of normative unconscious processes, like many such enactments, was overdetermined – for one thing, the panel's title and the task given to the presenter enabled her to know and not know, to hide in plain sight what she later revealed to be a vulnerable part of herself, particularly in this context of being a clinician in training presenting to more senior colleagues. But the omission in the panel's title and task is the product of a larger institutional enactment of classism – our conferences are quite costly and keep out those who can't afford to be there; they take place in upper-class venues; and institute power structures are generally oblivious to how the costs of training and analysis enact a classist and racist gate-keeping function. As Corpt (2013) has so eloquently written, many analysts of working-class origin silently bear the shame that this obliviousness inflicts.

At another psychoanalytic conference, I participated in a roundtable panel that featured the voices of Palestinian clinicians. I have been on many roundtable panels, but this was the first time I had ever found the room assigned for the panel literally to be outfitted with large round tables, an arrangement that severely limited the amount of seating. Audience members pitched in to move the tables to the side, and we brought in more chairs. Then we discovered that the table set up for the speakers had no microphones, also quite uncharacteristic. Nothing could be done about that. As the panel began, booming voices coming from the room next door penetrated our space, drowning out any possibility of hearing our "voices from Palestine." It felt like our "land" was occupied. This was not the first time that a panel on Palestine at a psychoanalytic conference had become the scene of unconscious institutional enactment.

## Neoliberalism, normative unconscious processes, and social character

While continuing to expand my conception of social character through writing about enactments of normative unconscious processes on these multiple levels, I found myself returning, around 2007, to some earlier social psychoanalytic ideas of social character. Even though I had written about class in the early 2000s (see Chapter 9), I had not fully recognized how changes in capitalism, specifically the vast income inequalities produced by neoliberalism, were shaping subject formation and relational interactions in all cultural groups. Capitalism as a central category of analysis had gone missing in the 1990s, not only in my work but in the work of many identity researchers (see Chapter 10). The chapters in Section III focus on the effects of neoliberal capitalism and its fostering of different types of social character, and they more explicitly bring together my earlier work on social character with work on normative unconscious processes. In Section III, I explore how normative unconscious processes function at the societal level, explore neoliberal versions of subjectivity, and describe how clinicians unconsciously normalize and, at times, resist normalizing neoliberal versions of subjectivity.

Although my conception of social psychoanalysis has deepened and changed over time, many of my early commitments have remained: to relational understandings of the causes of trauma and neurotic misery, to a conception of "unconscious" that does not define contents but rather recognizes how social positionings and power differentials shape continuous and ever-present unconscious processes in interactions between therapist and patient (see Fors, 2018), to a left wing anti-capitalist critique of culture and society. Finally, as I have evolved, I have made a deep commitment, most visible in the last chapter, to understand how the broader currents of history affect what happens in the clinic. Here I have been influenced by Davoine and Gaudillière (2004), who encourage us to understand present-day trauma as a consequence of earlier ruptures in what they call the social link – ruptures that affect the capacity to trust and that abandon subjects and whole collectives to a dyadic realm of kill or be killed. Davoine and Gaudillière (2004) have argued that the task of treatment is to unearth the truth that has not yet been able to be spoken and that has thus issued in symptoms. To restore trust, they argue, requires that therapists recognize our part in the BIG History. Although I had earlier recognized how those of us in positions of power become complicit in the psychic suffering of others, my last chapter reflects the – shamefully belated – beginnings of my engagement with historical narratives that run counter to the racist historical myths that formed my early subjective experience. This engagement has already clarified for me that, as a white woman, I need to go deeper in my thinking about the theory and practice of social psychoanalysis. As Fanon (1963, 1967) argued, a social psychoanalysis must not only account for the psychological damage wrought on oppressed (and dominant) populations but also work in whatever ways it can to dismantle the institutions that sustain that oppression.

As the final chapter in this book attests, I have been able to go deeper primarily because I have begun listening to the voices and writings of people of color and have become committed to doing antiracist activism.

This shift began when I read Michelle Alexander's (2010) *The New Jim Crow*. The way that book, and the many books authored by people of color that I subsequently read, trace the constantly morphing forms that racism has taken in U.S. history powerfully shook up my Obama-era white complacency. Black analysts have begun to speak out about their experiences in the field (Winograd, 2014), and I am listening. When the Movement for Black Lives formed, I wanted to figure out how I might be part of these new forms of radical antiracist activism. I co-authored an apology to Native populations for harm done by psychology, and I joined a black-led campaign for reparations that focuses on what we need to do to heal the soul disease that systemic racism has inflicted on both blacks and whites in the U.S.

These commitments are widening what I am able to be aware of in our field. For example, throughout my work, as you will see, I have criticized the field's separation of the psychic and the social, which I largely attributed to classist ideologies of individualism (Layton, 2006b, Chapter 3). But I only recently began to understand the racialized and racist core of that separation, and that realization only came about from working alongside colleagues of color in the Boston chapter of Reflective Spaces/Material Places. At one of our meetings, focused on the topic of social activism and clinical work, our cross-racial steering committee asked participants briefly to state how they connect their social activism to clinical work. Most of the white clinicians said they had not yet found a way to make that connection; this astounded the clinicians of color, for whom the connection was obvious. It came to me then that the separation of the psychic and the social is itself a normative unconscious enactment of the whiteness of the field – enabled by the multiple ways that the field has kept out or marginalized the voices of people of color.

I continuously have such decentering revelations, and, indeed, in going through my papers to prepare this book, I realized that a lot of what I have written assumes I am speaking to a white audience (which I largely was) about the psychology of white people. Nonetheless, I hope that the theories and methods I propose in this book offer ways to deconstruct whiteness and offer new insights into social unconscious processes. I am both thrilled and inspired by the entry into the field of more and more psychoanalytically-oriented clinicians of color. I have much to learn from them and others in our field who think psychosocially. In their company, I hope to continue to deepen my understanding of what it means to practice and theorize social psychoanalysis.

# Section I

# What is social psychoanalysis?

## Introduction to Section I

For the past few years, I have been teaching a course at Pacifica Graduate Institute that I call Social Psychoanalysis. I outlined in my introduction to the book an overview of what I mean by social psychoanalysis, central elements of which include the way identity categories are lived. I described one concept I developed to bridge the psychic and the social: normative unconscious processes. But because we draw from different psychoanalytic and sociological traditions, each of us who works at the intersection of the psychic and the social in fact has our own way of describing what is central to social psychoanalysis. The chapters in Section I of this book trace the development of my social psychoanalytic explorations from around 2000 to the present, and a few of the chapters were written precisely to differentiate my own view of social psychoanalysis from those of other psychoanalytic psychosocial thinkers. Although the sociology and psychoanalytic theorists I discuss here may disagree sharply about what constitutes a social psychoanalysis, we are all engaged in exploring the progressive and regressive ways psychoanalysis can be drawn on to understand subjectivity and its relation to the social and political world of a place and time.

In the late 1990s, Stephen Mitchell and Adrienne Harris invited me to participate in a special issue of *Psychoanalytic Dialogues* on "What's American about American Psychoanalysis?" Written in 2000, but not published until 2004, "Dreams of America/American dreams" (Chapter 1) reflects anecdotally on how European analysts, social critics, and some of my personal acquaintances experience Americans as superficial in relationships and "too nice" in the clinic. The chapter sketches out the strengths and limitations of what I perceived to be, in the U.S., a less tragic vision of humans and of psychoanalysis than the visions that predominate in other parts of the world.

Chapter 2, "Notes toward a non-conformist clinical practice," was written as a commentary on a paper by Philip Cushman, published in a 2005 issue of *Contemporary Psychoanalysis*. Disagreeing with what felt to me to be the hermeneutic tradition's somewhat homogenizing view of both culture and psyche, I laid out a perspective that put into a psychoanalytic frame the political and cultural theories of both Stuart Hall (1980, 1982) and Laclau and Mouffe (1985). In positing a constant dynamism and conflict between what Gramsci (1971) had described as hegemonic and counter-hegemonic forces, these theories helped me formulate what I hoped a social psychoanalysis might encompass: an understanding of the forces of capitalism and the forces of resistance to capitalism, a theory that could describe the unconscious processes operating in citizen subjects – understood to be complexly and contradictorily constructed, manipulable by media and other ideological formations, and both complicit in and resistant to hegemonic forces.

Chapter 3, "Attacks on linking," was published in 2006 in my co-edited book with Hollander and Gutwill, *Psychoanalysis, Class and Politics: Encounters in the Clinical Setting*. Here, I examine how difficult it was for me, as a clinician trained in paradigms that were never contextualized psychosocially, to resist the tendency to reduce psychosocial material that came up in the clinic to well-worn, decontextualized psychoanalytic interpretations of nuclear family relations. Re-working Bion's (1984) concept of attacks on linking, I began here to present a thesis that weaves its way through all my writings: that psychoanalytic theories and practices, in rupturing the links between the psychic and the social, unconsciously re-create the very kind of decontextualized individual that sustains a heterosexist, racist, classist dominant U.S. culture. The chapter suggests that the concept of normative unconscious processes, which describes interactions between patient and therapist that reproduce racism, sexism, and classism, can be applied as well at the institutional level: to the unconscious conservatism present in the theories and practices of psychoanalysis.

Chapter 4, "What divides the subject?," was published in 2008 for the inaugural issue of the journal, *Subjectivity*. This chapter again addresses the charge, made particularly by U.K. analysts, that the relational analytic theory that had become dominant in the U.S. is "superficial." The central critique was that relational psychoanalysis deals with "preconscious" rather than unconscious process. I argue here that what divides us against ourselves is neither innate drives nor the existential circumstances that befall all subjects. Rather, what divides the self are the historical, relationally inflicted traumas that each of us undergoes. I maintain that these kinds of intergenerationally transmitted traumas create the pain and conflict that most concern us in the clinic. I also assert that theories that claim that such traumas are secondary to existential universals, a trend found in many academic applications of psychoanalysis, function to deny the pain of such everyday abuses as heterosexist, racist, and classist macro- and micro-aggressions. Laying out the premises of a relational psychoanalysis and comparing them to premises of other psychoanalytic schools, I argue that the aggression against the self that is a marker of a divided subjectivity is not a drive but rather is a breakdown product of relational trauma – and therefore psychosocial.

The trajectory of all my thinking suggests that, to appreciate the singularity of individuals, a social psychoanalysis must contextualize, contextualize, and contextualize even more. Chapter 5, "Relational critique in socio-historical context" (2013, updated and revised in 2018), appeared in a book whose editors (Aron et al., 2018) had asked relational clinicians critically to appraise the now thirty-year-old relational theory and practice dominant in the U.S. In this chapter, I question why this theory became central to my work, what makes this theory feel "true" to me and to so many of us at this historical moment. Drawing on the work of U.K. sociologist Giddens (1991), and German sociologists Beck and Beck-Gernsheim (2002), I suggest that what the latter call "second modernity," marked by post-WWII processes of institutionalized individualization, created a fitting historical and sociopolitical ground in which a relational psychoanalysis could take root. At the same time that I question the ultimate "truth" of this theory and practice, I maintain the position that relational psychoanalysis is the school that best lends itself to a social psychoanalytic ethic and a progressive practice. The chapter ends with thoughts on how we might radicalize relational technique so that it can reach more deeply into the historical, psychosocial traumas that are lived out in the clinic.

Chapter 6, "Psychoanalysis and politics: historicizing subjectivity," originally published in 2013 in the journal *Mens Sana*, also draws on the work of Giddens and Beck and Beck-Gernsheim. This chapter begins by sketching an argument made by Young-Bruehl (2011) regarding what, to her mind, are the necessary constituents of a progressive psychoanalysis. I had raised this question more briefly and abstractly in 2005 (Chapter 2). Here, however, underscoring my deepening appreciation of historical contextualization, I contrast Young-Bruehl's interpretation of history and subjectivity, specifically psychoanalytic history, with the interpretations of theorists from two other theoretical paradigms: that of Giddens and Beck/ Beck-Gernsheim, described in Chapter 5, and that of Foucaultian social theorist, Rose (1989). For Young-Bruehl, Winnicott is a progressive hero. In Rose's historical account, Winnicott's papers and radio chats contribute to a discourse that normalizes a welfare state bent on administering not only public life but interior life. As he puts it, Winnicott's work normalizes the welfare state's project to fit subjects to a post-war status quo. Far from progressive, he sees such discourses as hegemonic, as contributing to the modern project of "governing the soul."

Rose's dark view of psychoanalytic thinkers and clinicians made me return to the question, "What then IS a social psychoanalysis?" What does one need to take into account to determine what a progressive psychoanalysis might be? The chapters in this section bring up many of the contested issues that go into answering that question. For me, the answer evolves and changes as I continually try to fight my own resistances, learn the lessons of history, and allow the circles of contextualization to widen.

# Chapter 1

# Dreams of America/American dreams[*]

My first acquaintance with psychoanalysis was as a theory, not a practice. In the 1970s, I was in graduate school studying comparative literature. In courses on the Frankfurt School, in an intellectual history course on Freud, and in feminist reading that included the work of Juliet Mitchell and Nancy Chodorow, I learned that psychoanalysis was both a product of a particular social world and a tool to understand that world and its inhabitants. Before I became a clinician, all of my psychoanalytic sources were left-wing academics, mostly European, who sought to understand the workings of bourgeois ideology: specifically, how people come to accept oppression and reproduce the very conditions that subordinate them.

My experience with psychoanalysis is thus quite different from that of most clinicians, and it is this background that shapes my thoughts on what's American about American psychoanalysis. The question pulls for reflections on differences in national character, and such reflections can quickly lead one to reify stereotypes and turn them into truths, to homogenize diversity and mistake the mainstream for the whole. While hoping to avoid such trivializations, I begin this chapter with three European views of America: the dream of a German friend, the reflections of a French critic, and the paradoxical views of Berlin Marxists in the 1970s. I do so because I would like to play with the idea that European stereotypes about America might tell us something useful about American psychoanalysis.

When I was in graduate school, a German exchange student (self-nicknamed Chanticleer) told me that he'd had the following dream: he was wandering through Disneyland holding the hands of his American friends, who appeared in the dream as children. His associations to the dream contained both positive and negative feelings about Americans. He felt that Americans had a sense of innocence, childlike-ness, and optimism to which Europeans (certainly Germans at any rate) could not lay claim. But he also felt superior to Americans and felt that there was something very superficial and childish about them. Indeed, many of my European friends would from time to time remark that Americans seemed very friendly on the surface but that the friendliness didn't go much deeper than "Hi, how are you?," with no real wish to have any answer other than "Fine." The Europeans' sense was that Americans are "nice," but perhaps only on the surface, that they are unwilling and unable to be adults: and that they deny, with a superficial cheerfulness signified so well by the ubiquitous Mr. Smiley Face, his logo "Have a nice day," and by Disneyland, the deep difficulties of life and loss. Had my European friends been acquainted with psychoanalytic theory, they might have understood the incredible violence of American everyday life as the dissociated cost of maintaining the smiley face. They might further have ventured the guess that there is something "borderline" about American culture. This borderline tendency is visible in things as profound as the media's inability to frame issues in any but a radically polarized form, with no shades of gray, and in things as mundane as the difficulty finding a greeting card that is neither overly sentimental and cloying nor downright hostile.

These many years later, I associate my German friend's dream with French theorist Baudrillard's (1983) notion that the reason such places as Disneyland exist in America and the reason that prisons proliferate is to divert attention from the fact that all of America is Disneyland and all of America is a prison. According to Baudrillard, Disneyland is not only a "digest of the American way of life, panegyric to American values" (p. 24), but also:

> It is meant to be an infantile world, in order to make us believe that the adults are elsewhere, in the "real" world, and to conceal the fact that real childishness is everywhere.
>
> (p. 25)

Baudrillard feels that Americans refuse to grapple with the horrors of capitalism, such as global exploitation of people and resources, radical

economic inequality, the unequal justice meted out to nonwhite populations, and the commodification of everyday life and relationships. Instead,
as Chanticleer's dream suggests, Americans take refuge in childish superficiality. Appearance and entertainment substitute for meaningful social
exchange, a false sense of being free masks a violent suppression of freedom. But what do we make of the fact that both the German dreamer
and the French theorist share an unmistakable attraction to Disneyland,
an attraction that surfaces despite their harsh critique of Americans and
American life?

When I lived in Berlin from 1978–79, I had the same sense that European Marxists were simultaneously rabidly critical and deeply envious of
American culture. In a strange twist reminiscent of Nazi anti-Semitism,
they saw the Marshall Plan as a violent American imposition of consumer
capitalism on a pure, essentially socialist German soul. Yet, there they
were in their American blue jeans, listening to American music, going to
American movies, and clearly participating in the pleasures of consumer
culture and of an American brand of freedom.

The similarity of the view of America in these anecdotes – and much of
what I can say on this topic is based on anecdote and personal reflections –
suggests there is a shared European fantasy about Americans against which
many Europeans define themselves (as superior). As is true of all stereotypes,
the ones in my examples reflect ambivalence: something about America and
Americans is simultaneously repudiated and desired. Insofar as the fantasy
is shared, I am imagining that, beyond the fulfillment of whatever psychic
needs the Europeans have for these fantasies, there may be something that
they are picking up on about America that is worth examining.

This chapter has two, somewhat loosely linked parts. In the first part,
I take up some of the elements of the European stereotype described in my
opening anecdotes, particularly cheerful optimism and superficial nice-
ness. I discuss them in the context of psychoanalytic anecdotes deriving
from European analysts' views of themselves and Americans. My purpose
throughout is to explore whatever approximation to truth the ambivalence
of the stereotype might reveal: what it is about America and American
psychoanalysis that might be worthy of envy, and what might be worthy
of disdain.

In both sections of the chapter, I look at that aspect of the stereotype that
condemns American superficiality. Whereas I contest the stereotype in the
first part, I later focus more narrowly on what might be its insight and what

role American psychoanalysis plays in keeping things superficial – which brings us back to Disneyland. The Disney Corporation, as you may know, is something of a false memory machine. It employs what it calls "imagineers," engineers who imagine and represent American history in just the way that the white corporate mainstream would like it to appear. This is a history that superficially celebrates American diversity while glossing over oppression and struggle and ignoring persistent class difference. The imagineers are charged with replacing sad thoughts with happy ones. Along with the news media and other American discourses that celebrate a memoryless present, Disney plays a prominent role in making it very hard for white Americans to have any sense of themselves as historical beings responsible for their world. These discourses further work to obfuscate the fact that we are not all equal, that we are placed within radically unequal power structures.

Psychoanalysis, American or otherwise, is seemingly unlike Disneyland in that it works against the denial of pain and the misery people cause one another. Nonetheless, it also participates in divorcing individuals from any social context and in ignoring the effect of cultural power inequalities on psychic life. This does lead to the kind of superficiality evident, for example, in the American tendency to reduce complex social problems to problems of individual psychopathology (for a counter to this tendency, see, among others, Benjamin, 1988; Altman, 1995; Cushman, 1995; Haaken, 1998; Fairfield et al., 2002).

My protagonist in both parts of the chapter is relational psychoanalysis, which I see as a distinctly American contribution. In the first part I take it as representative of what might be enviable about American institutions; in the second, I question its role in maintaining a separation between the psychic and the social.

## Reflections in a European eye, part I: American optimism

At a Massachusetts Institute for Psychoanalysis (MIP) symposium in 2000, on the 1942 British Controversial Discussions, Ron Britton, David Tuckett, and Peter Fonagy, each representing a school of British psychoanalysis, responded to an audience-provoked discussion about the cultural and philosophical differences between American and British psychoanalysis. While the ideas discussed regarding national character were admittedly anecdotal and rooted in fantasies about both self and other, and while the three participants themselves held differing views, there seemed to be a consensus that the two cultures' very ideas about human nature and the possibilities for personal transformation were quite different. In brief, British psychoanalysis seems to have a less optimistic view of human possibility than does American psychoanalysis.

British Kleinians have a darker vision of human nature than, for example, Kohutians (Kohut, of course, was Austrian – but it seems that those European theorists who found their way to America and became dominant voices, such as Hartmann, Kris, and Loewenstein, tended to be less pessimistic and to focus on adaptation to the environment rather than on the radical incompatibility between the individual and the requirements of civilization). Britton, a Kleinian, stated strongly his sense that one mind can never know another, that we are all, ultimately, alone and must come to terms with that existential fact. He expressed what I take to be a Kleinian assumption (also Freudian and Lacanian) that humans have an innate hostility to otherness. He said he felt that Americans had an "official optimism" and a belief, which he did not share, that words mend things. Fonagy, who did not agree with the belief in innate hostility, nonetheless spoke of the antisocial nature of British character.

Can we say that different visions of human nature lead to national differences in psychoanalytic theory and practice? I am hesitant to make such a statement, but I do think that theories that become dominant in a culture do so because they resonate at a particular historical moment with other things going on in the culture. There may be current ways of thinking about human nature and relationships in England, for example, which make certain Kleinian ideas appealing. The Kohutian tenet that aggression is a response to threat rather than an inborn destructive impulse or drive is held by many in American psychoanalytic circles today (see, for example, Mitchell, 1993). While this is consistent with a belief in innate human goodness that runs through much of American philosophy, literature, and psychological theory, there must also be other reasons why the idea has gained dominance in this historical period – perhaps because it resonates with the beliefs and experiences of those from the 1960s generation who are now some of our most prominent psychoanalytic theorists.

Britton's view of radical alone-ness and innate hostility is fundamentally incompatible with some of the basic tenets of relational psychoanalytic and other contemporary American psychoanalytic theories. Indeed, I would say that the vision of human nature and the relation to others expressed by all three of the panelists never could have eventuated in a theory such as interpersonal or relational psychoanalysis.[1] None was attuned to the way that analyst and patient co-create a reality. When audience members at the MIP symposium expressed a relational way of looking at what transpires in an analysis, particularly the way the analyst in the case presented had intruded upon the patient with her own reality, the "one-person" panelists seemed not to understand what they meant. Fonagy, who did think there might be something worth understanding about American relational psychoanalysis, nonetheless acknowledged that most of his British colleagues purposefully ignore this body of work or are disdainful of it. I believe that this British disdain has something to do with different views of human nature and human interaction, and with different relations to authority and certainty.[2]

A practitioner's view of the human condition must surely affect what she deems possible as the outcome of an analysis. The Kleinians seem much more circumspect about possibilities for character transformation; many do not feel that cure is what analysis is about at all. Similarly, I have heard Lacanians express a disdain for American "therapeutics." They suggest that psychoanalysis is something other than a means to alleviate suffering, for example, an ethics or a political defense of subjectivity and imagination against the onslaught of bourgeois society's demands for conformity. From a relational perspective, it seems to me that whatever the analyst believes the possibilities for outcome are will shape the possibilities for outcome. And here is where I see the clear advantage to patients of having a therapist who optimistically believes in the possibilities for radical personal transformation.

If this kind of optimism truly is "American," I think it is linked to American traditions of freedom and social mobility that are different from European traditions. In America, people tend not to "know their place" in the way they do in Europe. Most of our official ideologies, for example, deny class constraints and suggest, as the Army ads tell us, that we should be all we can be. Cultural pessimists such as Baudrillard believe that American capitalism has led the way in transforming citizens into consumers, in reducing political freedom to mere freedom to consume. While I agree with Baudrillard about the damage wrought by capitalism and consumerism, I also feel that there are American values that are incompatible with capitalism, values that are continuously drawn on by disenfranchised

groups that demand that America live up to its promise of liberty and justice for all. Americans feel entitled to a kind of personal freedom that is
unique, the kind my Marxist German friends seemed to envy. It is this
stance towards life, in part, that makes America a "therapeutic society" in
which so many seek either treatment, or, more frequently, self-help books.
There are clearly at least two sides to this aspect of America. On the negative side, Americans tend to reduce political and collective problems to
individual psychological ones (more on that later). On the positive side, a
therapeutic society is one in which individuals refuse to accept misery as
their lot, and rather express the right to be free, to speak up, to be treated
equally, to treat others as one would like to be treated, and to have a measure of inner peace.

## Reflections in a European eye, part II: I wonder why Americans are so nice

The Europeans in my opening anecdotes connect American optimism,
which they see as naïve, with American nice-ness, which they see as, at
best, superficial, and at worst, masking aggression. In a group supervision session I attended led by British Kleinian Elizabeth Bott Spillius, she
chastised us American analysts for worrying too much about being nice.
Her point seemed well taken in that many of us shy from confrontation
with our patients' aggression.[3] But when she gave her clinical thoughts
about case material, I was struck by the way that she interpreted much of
what patients did as hostile and envious (frequently the case with Kleinians). I sense that this way of selecting out what is important is linked to a
particular view of human nature.

The patients' strengths were consistently ignored and vulnerabilities
were not treated gingerly, indeed were often interpreted as attacks on the
analyst. A group supervision session with James Grotstein, on the other
hand, suggested to me what an American re-working of Klein might look
like (inflected by Bion, but also by Kohut). Grotstein listened for and
interpreted the patient's anxiety, not the patient's hostility. He argued that
hostility and aggression are always secondary and that it is not empathic
to focus attention there. Empathy is a value that is salient in American
psychoanalysis but not so very salient in European Lacanian and Kleinian
schools, for a variety of theoretical reasons. Grotstein's is a kinder, gentler,
more American Kleinian practice.

Bott Spillius also criticized the Americans for phrasing things tentatively. Why do Americans say "I wonder" when in fact they know what they think?, she asked. At first this intrigued me because I believe that I often say "I wonder" when I feel fairly certain. But "fairly" is the operative word here. I admired Bott Spillius's certainty and felt that there is indeed a dishonesty and covert coerciveness in some uses of "I wonder." Nonetheless, I think what she saw as the American tendency to hypothesize might also be seen as a well-founded suspicion about authority and certainty that dates back at least to Watergate and anti-authoritarian social movements, if not to the very beginnings of the country's history. Are contemporary American analysts afraid of speaking as authorities or are they simply more comfortable about revealing uncertainty – or both? Balint (1968), foreshadowing the relational analytic idea that the analyst co-creates the trajectory of the analysis, hypothesized that his Kleinian colleagues' authoritative certainty was probably the very thing that produced hostile patients (p. 107).

When I spoke later to some of my female colleagues attending Bott Spillius's supervision, they had similar questions about her certainty and her disdain for being nice. But why hadn't we spoken up about our misgivings – too nice to criticize such a charming and authoritative guest? "I wonder" if the American stake in empathy and nice-ness that has developed since Kohut has to do with the increasing number of middle-class white women in the field, women trained to be nice and deferential to authority?

We need here to distinguish between what are likely two different forms of nice-ness, each with its own relation to authority and each perhaps characteristic of American psychoanalysis. On the one hand, there is a nice-ness associated with white bourgeois norms of politeness and self-control that arise from a repudiation of aggression (which then gets projected onto other classes and races). This operates in an extreme form in bourgeois norms of femininity. In this latter case, conformity to bourgeois norms entails a submission to authority and a difficulty being authoritative oneself (or an oscillation between submissive and authoritarian). As I said previously, I imagine that the contemporary American psychoanalytic dominance of such ideas as empathy, mutuality, and relatedness has something, if not a lot to do with the increasing numerical dominance of non-M.D. women in the mental health field (Philipson, 1993, has made a similar argument).

But this form of nice-ness is not limited to women in the field. In my experience, it shows up as well in the way criticisms are handled in psychoanalytic circles. In academic settings, the critique of other people's work is accepted as a way to expand knowledge. Granted, an academic meeting can get aggressive, but this may arise from a conviction that what is at stake is the importance of ideas, not the state of the thinker's ego. When I first began attending psychoanalytic conferences, I noticed that papers are greeted with very little critique. Discussants try to be nice; their critiques are often exercises in doing and undoing what seem to me to be assertive claims but what must seem to them to be aggressive ones. I'm not sure I yet understand this phenomenon in American psychoanalysis; perhaps it hearkens back to how careful one had to be in criticizing Freud, the way power in psychoanalytic circles depends more on being anointed by charismatic leaders than on expertise (Kirsner, 2000). Perhaps it has to do with how narcissistically vulnerable we all are when we do and share the results of our clinical work. Or perhaps it is more broadly American and connected to what I earlier referred to as the American borderline split between violence and sugary nice-ness, revealed in the scarcity of instances in popular culture, media, and everyday life in which ambiguity, ambivalence, and shades of gray are acknowledged. In order to tolerate ambivalence, one needs to be able to tolerate both one's own and another's aggression. Whatever the reasons, I have found that there is a low tolerance for criticism in the field and a definite sense of "you're either with us or against us" that I think stifles innovation.

There is a second form of nice-ness, however, that does not entail the repudiation of aggression and is found in many of the egalitarian tenets of relational analytic theory, particularly in Benjamin's (1988) notions of recognition and the regulatory ideal of subject-subject relations, as well as in Mitchell's (1988) relational-conflict model. This form of nice-ness – care for the self and the other – involves the capacity to tolerate ambivalence and aggression, and to engage in a serious critique of the uses and forms of authority. Indeed, I see a clear relation between this form of nice-ness, the capacity to question authority, and the capacity to see patients as simultaneously aggressive and loving, hostile and longing for love. This form of nice-ness entails as well a capacity to invest in neither a tragic nor a naively optimistic view of human nature and human possibility.

Before getting too carried away with praise for American antiauthoritarianism, however, I must admit that the history of American psychoanalysis from the 1920s to the 1970s does not reveal much questioning of authority. Kirsner (2000), who discusses moments in the history of four American institutes, finds unquestioned conformity to dogma, elitist holds on power rarely based on merit, and the establishment of hierarchies, such as restriction of practice to MDs, that went beyond anything Freud and his circle had dreamed up. When feminists began questioning male authority in the 1970s, many targeted the way that psychoanalysis and psychiatry kept women in their place via interpretations of penis envy and prescriptions for tranquilizers. It was precisely such questioning, which grew out of the social movements of the disenfranchised, that led to the awareness that authority claims to speak for all but in fact speaks for its own power interests.

It is ironic that the decline of the cultural significance of psychoanalysis has occurred simultaneously with an unprecedented creative blossoming of American theoretical and practical psychoanalytic innovation. It may be the very lack of psychoanalysis's cultural authority that has permitted it to focus on ideas rather than on enforcement of dogma. But the ideas inherent to relational analytic theories have also surely been influenced by the undermining of authority that is the legacy of the social movements of the 1960s. Indeed, the undermining of analytic authority opened the field to non-MDs, which meant that a lot of women gained entry (and which also may explain why the field has lost cachet – most fields lose cachet when women begin to dominate). At this particular historical moment, American relational psychoanalysis is refreshingly non-dogmatic and egalitarian, especially when compared with European variants such as Kleinian and Lacanian theory. But as I will argue in the next section, while relational psychoanalysis makes more space for integrating the psychic and the social than perhaps any other version of contemporary psychoanalysis (see, among others for example, the work of Altman, 1995; Benjamin, 1988; Corbett, 2001b; Dimen, 1991; Goldner, 1991; Harris, 1991; Domenici and Lesser, 1995; Schwartz, 1995; Leary, 1997a), much of it yet participates in the same depoliticizing and decontextualizing tendencies that pervade most dominant American discourses. This, too, is American.

## American dream syndrome

In 1981, John Demos wrote a fascinating piece in which he investigated what it was about 1850–1900 American culture that made it receptive to

Freud's ideas. Among other things, he cited the increasing disjunction between men's and women's roles resulting from the migration from rural to urban areas; the increasingly clear demarcation between generations as parents began to have fewer children and to regulate reproduction such that all of their children were close in age; and the rise of experts who advised parents how to raise children. Having studied advice books, Demos found certain assumptions compatible with Freud's, for example, that children's characters are set at a young age. Ideal children were to be both independent and to exercise self-control in accord with their parents' wishes; to develop a conscience; and, as the parent-child bond became more and more intense, to understand that their wrong doing hurt not only themselves but their parents. Demos noted that this guilt-based model indicated a shift from earlier shame-based models of child-rearing. He suggested that this shift had to do with perhaps the most significant nineteenth-century social development: the increasing separation between public and private spheres, with men becoming associated with the former and women with the latter, and with the home taking on sentimentalized connotations of refuge from competitive capitalism. In this context, first the family, then individuals, became understood as separate from their social and political circumstances. Arguing that these conditions made the American family ripe for Oedipal dynamics, Demos suggested that the American fantasy of the self-made man was enhanced in this period when competition grew between sons and their ever more absent fathers.

Demos's thoughts about the American psyche actually describe not all Americans but rather its white, middle-class heterosexual citizens. Cultural critics have amply documented the fact that these ideals perpetuate themselves by omitting from their self-understanding, even splitting off from themselves, the different values and family systems of those who are not white, middle-class, and heterosexual (see, for example, Gilroy, 1993; Walkerdine, 1997). The story of America becomes quite different when others' struggles and contributions are taken into account. The fact that they are generally not taken into account, however, reflects the power held by majority patriarchal ideals and norms, which I refer to as dominant culture. Dominant culture has shaped psychoanalytic theories from the beginning. In many ways, as Demos's article suggests, psychoanalysis provided a fitting theory to account for the conflicts, fantasies, and anxieties of those who were aspiring to be part of dominant culture. With the collapse of communist and socialist alternatives, more and more people aspire to be

part of dominant culture, and, as Philip Cushman (1995) has well documented, dominant culture has been increasingly marked by consumerism.
There are many manifestations of this, some economic and some psychological. A number of dominant discourses, especially television (Lipsitz,
1990), promoted and taught consumerism in the post-WWII period (see
Cushman, 1995, who describes the post-war empty self that consumerism
creates and psychoanalytic theories legitimate). The contemporary obsession with consuming may be a symptom of a collective inability to mourn
such losses as the Vietnam War and the idealism of the 1960s, to face
the global exploitation of people and resources that marks contemporary
capitalism. Consumerism, and the media that promote it, have become the
communal glue that binds Americans together, and it is their message that
success is measured by how many toys you have, which in part accounts
for the superficiality of our Disney-produced culture.

I want to take up some of the psychic consequences of the way the
American social world is structured. The first derives from the observa-
tion that most of my white middle-class clients spend a good deal of their
waking moments beating up on themselves. They do not feel successful
enough and have a great deal of difficulty regulating self-esteem (which
undoubtedly contributed to the popularity of Kohut's views in America, as
well as to the popularity of greeting cards that directly proclaim, "You're
special."). In America, the longings of an older generation are all too often
formulated in the impoverished terms of material and career success.
Unfulfilled longings are projected onto the next generation, which comes
to feel that it can win love and recognition only by achieving the success
that eluded its parents.

Whether they are artists struggling to survive financially and spiritu-
ally in a materialist culture (and a disproportionate number of my clients
are artists or people who would love to do art full time if their "practical"
selves, shaped in part by their culture, would let them), or successful professionals who never feel quite successful enough and measure themselves
constantly against the success of real and imagined others, or women who
don't feel thin or pretty enough and who measure success by marriage and
male attention – even when they have achieved career success – all seem
beaten down by a diagnosis I would like to see in DSM: American Dream
Syndrome.[4] This is a pernicious illness that builds on what Demos saw
taking root with the rise of industrial capitalism in the U.S.: the ideology
of the self-made man who pulls himself up by his bootstraps, goes from

rags to riches, etc. Deep-rooted individualist ideologies and contemporary consumerist ideology, which defines the good as that which makes the most money, combine to form a deadly mix.

Demos connected the ideology of American individualism with the second issue relevant to understanding what's American about American psychoanalysis: the ever-increasing literal and figurative separation of individuals from their social context. The separation is figured in just about every form of dominant discourse, from the Declaration of Independence to self-help books to psychoanalytic theory (for example, developmental theories that hail separateness as the most mature form of being). Discourses do not just describe; they have formative effects. And so individuals in American society are shaped in such a way that they are able to remove themselves from their social contexts when necessary, e.g., all the middle-class seventeen-year-olds who go away to college, the executives or army personnel who move when the corporation needs them to move, uprooting self and family and cutting off whatever connections have been made. There is certainly a kind of freedom inherent in this form of individualism. It seems to fulfill one aspect of the Enlightenment project: self-determination. At the same time, however, it destroys community and impoverishes individuality by creating individuals who defensively deny their connections to other people and to the environment. Until recently, when many in the psychoanalytic profession began to accept criticisms of the developmental model of ego psychology (see, for example, Stern, 1985 and Benjamin's use of Stern, 1988), psychoanalytic developmental and clinical theory had been one of the many discourses that normalized this kind of monadic development. What is American about American psychoanalysis, then, is not only what distinguishes it from European analysis, but also the way it legitimizes and colludes with other American discourses that separate the psychic from the social.

Americans never feel successful enough. And they generally believe that their fortunes rise and fall by dint of their own effort and motivation. And so they blame themselves not only for failures beyond their control but also for their inability to achieve extraordinary successes. Those who feel that Americans are too optimistic might prefer the tragic view of human nature to explain the way people beat up on themselves – human beings are innately cruel or innately hostile to others and the otherness within themselves. Alternately, from the social psychoanalytic perspective I favor, we could try to understand why so many parents need their children to fulfill their unmet needs, and we could incorporate our findings into our theories. Further, we could ponder what it is about American contemporary culture that breeds a narcissistic misuse of both self and others (cf, Lasch, 1979; Sloan, 1996).

The fact that individuals are not understood in social context is a deeply political phenomenon – in a capitalist economy, material wealth is the major criterion of success, and it serves a capitalist status quo to have people think that it is their fault if they do not have material wealth. They're just not trying hard enough. Before the economy went into its recent downturn, *The Boston Globe* (July 6, 2000) reported that 57 percent of New York City residents were living at or below the poverty line. That's a lot of people not trying hard enough. What the article omitted is that America redistributes less of its wealth to those in need than just about any other Western capitalist nation, and the statistic was and remains a shameful counter to the celebratory rhetoric of the 1990s that endlessly glorified the free market system. No one says it, but statistics such as this reveal that there is no way that everyone can enjoy the fruits of capitalism, no matter how hard they try, and that most of those who succeed have cultural and/or economic capital to begin with. It is remarkable to me that, given the gross inequities in social and economic capital, and despite high crime rates and more violence than in all other industrialized countries, there is not more protest, more crime, and more revolutionary activity in America. I suppose that this is because American ideologies work so well and in such concert to convince people that their misfortunes are their fault and not due to structural inequalities. They go to therapy rather than form social alliances and rebel.

American psychoanalysis works to mitigate the power of the harsh, punitive superegos our patients bring to us. And indeed, much of the theory of the past 30 years is concerned with self-hatred and difficulties regulating self-esteem. At the same time, American psychoanalysis does little to question the socio-economic system that makes so many people self-punishing; on the contrary, its theory also removes the individual from any social context beyond pathological family dynamics and so contributes to the ideology of the American Dream's brand of individualism – or is an apology for it.[5] Those who try to bring the social and political context in are often labeled non-psychoanalytic. But as Altman (1995), Cushman (1995), and Samuels (1993) make clear, there is no logical barrier that keeps psychoanalysis from integrating the social and the political into its domain. The barrier is ideological.

As I said earlier, I believe that relational analytic theory is the least dog-matic and most egalitarian theory we currently have and the theory most capa-ble of recognizing diversity of experience. Nonetheless, much of relational theory does not take cultural contexts into account. When cultural context is considered, it often appears as an add-on to traditional psychodynamic constructs such as dependence-independence, enmeshment-separateness, or the capacity for love. I would like to see American psychoanalysis recog-nize that gender, race, class, and sexual orientation are not add-ons to psy-chodynamics: they constitute psychodynamics. They entail and put limits on the very way we Americans define our sense of agency, our feelings of dependency, our way of loving. Benjamin (1988) and Chodorow (1978), among others, have well described the way that gender norms shape the agency and attachment patterns of middle-class white heterosexuals, but few have truly taken this work into account in their theory-building.

Like many other dominant discourses, psychoanalytic theory often sug-gests that things that are actually specific to a cultural formation and a historical moment are instead universal. To conclude this chapter, I'd like to give one or two more examples of psychoanalysis's contribution to the American cultural pull towards depoliticization and decontextualization. To do so, I return to the European view of America and quote Eva Hoff-man, a Polish immigrant who moved to Canada at age 12 and then to the U.S. for college. In her autobiography (1989), Hoffman writes about two staples of current American life: obsession with mothers and obsession with achievement – neither of which ever seem good enough. Hoffman is disarmed when her Polish friends ask, "What's this thing Americans have about their mothers? Why do they talk about their mothers all the time?" (p. 265). She says of the Americans:

> The oppressive mother, or the distant mother, or the overloving mother, is an accepted conversational trope, like the weather or the stock mar-ket or the latest Mideast crisis. My American friends pay their moth-ers the indirect tribute of incessant and highly subtle scrutiny. They measure the exact weight the mother exercises upon their psyche and they practice careful equilibriating acts between letting the mother too much in and keeping her too much out.
>
> (p. 265)

Polish daughters, she claims, do not have such emotionally fraught rela-tions with their mothers. She hypothesizes that this is because Polish daughters remain in close physical proximity to their mothers whereas American middle-class daughters must be psychologically prepared to live far from theirs by about age seventeen. Polish daughters maintain an ongoing adult relation to their mothers, one in which fears and angers and joys are negotiated and shared on a day-to-day basis. Because American daughters do not have the mother's "concrete presence to wrangle with or get angry at" (p. 267), commonplace dramas become psychological ones. This is indeed part of a larger difference Hoffman points to: the fact that, as emphasized earlier, American discourses construct and explain problems in almost exclusively psychological terms. In part, this is what makes Americans seem superficial to their European contemporaries.

Hoffman's Polish friends do not psychologize; they find the root of their problems in social and political circumstances. Censorship, not mothers, is what they blame for their woes. Her American friends root their problems in weaknesses of self. Bad or good mothering becomes the guarantor of the well-being of the children, not the social, political, or economic system. When I criticize American psychoanalysis for not taking the social system into account, I mean that psychoanalytic discourse contributes to the successful reproduction of an unfair socioeconomic system by encouraging white, middle-class subjects to blame themselves and their parents for their unhappiness rather than to examine their social circumstances (and this dominant frame for understanding the world affects non-dominant groups as well). Motherhood is a social institution, lived differently depending on class, race, gender, sexuality, and nationality. Psychoanalysis ignores that fact as it theorizes the universals of maternal experience and describes/prescribes proper maternal behavior (Layton, 2000).

Hoffman also ponders the peculiarities of American ambition:

> The French, in the eighteenth century, classified ambition – a new phenomenon in the topography of behavior and emotion – as an illness . . . Ambition, achievement, and self-confidence are the pieties I've picked up from the environment, and if I don't always work hard, I compensate by a sort of anxiety, an inner simulation of running hard. My friends and I tell each other heroic stories of how much we've accomplished, how we manage to get to the health club between high-powered conferences, how much energy we have, and how effectively we expend it. Like everyone I know, I'm in a hurry all the time.

Her Polish parents cannot understand what the purpose is of all this running. Hoffman says:

> Clearly the purpose is not only accomplishment, for even after I gather a modicum of it, the need to keep in seemingly forward motion doesn't become assuaged.
>
> (pp. 270–271)

This is the American Dream Syndrome (with nightmare features). So many of my patients have it. Does American psychoanalysis confront it? Or do we rather build egos better equipped to handle it? I must say that theories promoting flexible, multiple selves capable of dealing with high levels of fragmentation sometimes read to me as liberating but other times read as the psychological theory that creates and legitimizes the kind of subject who will function best in a global capitalist economy.

To conclude, my concern is that American psychoanalysis has always been too likely to take bourgeois norms as guideposts of healthy functioning. Lacan's (1977) critique of ego psychology was precisely that Freud's idea of the insuperable divided-ness of the subject was replaced by a theory that promoted a unified self (the ego) and that encouraged adaptation to bourgeois norms. Perhaps the European tendency to avoid speaking of cure has something to do with the wish to avoid endorsing this or that way of life as superior. Certainly there is a tendency towards the judgmental in such theoretical notions as good-enough mothering (again, an idea not of American origin but one that is embraced with fervor in American psychoanalysis). Whatever the case, I have been arguing here that any psychoanalytic theory that divorces individual dynamics from social inequality and historical reality in some sense shores up the status quo. In so doing, it supports Europeans' assertions of American superficiality and immaturity (I say this knowing full well that European analytic theory is also guilty of separating the social from the psychic, although Freud and many early analysts, for example, Fenichel and Reich, saw the two realms as inextricable).

Contemporary American psychoanalysis is not easy to characterize. Besides the fact that there are many schools that vie for dominance, each with its own view of human and relational possibility, there are also many different versions of America that vie for dominance. American subcultures live America in quite different ways. I have looked here at some

European views of Americans and have used these as a way to understand a few of the contradictions of contemporary American social reality and their relation to psychoanalysis. I believe that relational analytic theories, especially their feminist and socially-informed variants, belong to one of America's most honorable traditions: the ongoing struggle to recognize and respect the diversity of Americans, which is perhaps what is best about America, and the struggle to complete the never completed project of securing equality and justice for all. I would like to see relational theory incorporate further into its clinical practice a way to contest the American tendency to divorce individuals from their social and historical context. Psychoanalysis already contests one level of historical amnesia, and in doing so, it breaks with both the narcissistic American fantasy of an individualism without constraints and with the borderline enactments characteristic of many American discourses. I think it can challenge a deeper level of historical amnesia if it reconnects with its European Marxist and socialist forebears and breaks with mainstream thinking devoted to preserving existent power relations.

## Notes

* Used with permission. Layton, L. (2004) Dreams of America/American dreams. *Psychoanalytic Dialogues* 14(2): 233–254.
1 This is so despite the fact that theorists such as Winnicott have had such a profound influence on American theory or that theorists such as Fairbairn and Balint (a Hungarian émigré to England, and a student of Ferenczi) held ideas that clearly were forerunners of both self psychology and relational theory. Balint (1968), in fact, made it clear that he and those like him who thought about the analyst's role in provoking regression, were, as he put it, on the fringe: "We are known, perhaps even read, but certainly not quoted" (p. 155).
2 I do not mean to say that pessimistic views of human nature cannot be found in America, only that they are not consonant with mainstream American self-understandings – as evidenced by the enormous popularity, at one extreme, of positive psychology.
3 Again, it seems to me that Kohut's theory dovetails remarkably well with American nice-ness and the shying away from confrontation. My guess is that Kleinian ideas are taking root in America currently in part as backlash against some of the difficulties dealing with aggression inherent in self psychological practice.

4  Tartakoff (1966) identified a similar syndrome that she called the Nobel Prize Complex. She saw in American culture an institutionally supported fantasy that activity and achievement will guarantee success. She likened the syndrome to an addiction and included denial of dependence among its features. Patients with such a syndrome, she argued, enter treatment with the fantasy that if they are good patients, therapy will bring them the success that has evaded them – a fantasy that can prove to be a difficult resistance to treatment. See also Lesser, 2002.

5  There have of course been exceptions in the history of American psychoanalysis, for example, Fromm (1970). More recently, I would cite Kovel (1988) and Altman (1995).

# Chapter 2

# Notes toward a nonconformist clinical practice

## Response to Philip Cushman's "Between Arrogance and a Dead-End: Gadamer and the Heidegger/ Foucault Dilemma"*

Phil Cushman sounds a cautionary note for those who subscribe to the relational analytic paradigm or to any other paradigm influenced by what he calls the interpretive turn. He wants us to take heed of the flaws in our philosophical mentors' lives and philosophies, and he spells out those flaws with care and balance. He also offers a way out of them: to redress Heidegger's arrogant monologism and monoculturalism, he prescribes Gadamer's correction to and extension of Heidegger's theory of authenticity, particularly Gadamer's emphasis on dialogue. Dialogue, he argues, counters Heidegger's disrespect for the interpersonal and social realm. To address Foucault's flaw, i.e., a missing moral perspective that might offer a counter to the abuses of power, he prescribes both Gramsci's theory of hegemony and Gadamer's theory of dialogue. For Gadamer, dialogue is work, and it involves knowing our own history and the source of our convictions, and then continually putting our convictions into question so that we can have a meaningful encounter with difference. We must draw on what we have learned from the encounter with difference if we are to engage in building something new. Cushman argues that while Foucault's practice of genealogy opens us up to the recognition of difference, only dialogue enables us to do anything constructive with that recognition and to avoid nihilism.

I imagine that the occasion of Cushman's scrutiny of these theorists is that he sees something of those flaws operating within our own analytic theories and practices. Nonetheless, Cushman concludes that the therapeutic encounter is a privileged site of dialogue and, sadly, one of the few places left in our world where there is the good will for dialogue and the capacity to take on another point of view.

It is with regard to this sad state of affairs that I formulate my response, hoping not so much to critique what Cushman has to say but rather to draw out some of the implications of his essay for clinical practice. Specifically, I want to think here about what a nonconformist psychoanalytic practice might look like. To do so, however, requires an examination in some detail of difficult philosophical and social theory that may be unfamiliar to many clinicians. I hope readers will bear with me as I work my way from social theory to clinical practice.

My response has two interconnected threads: (1) in order to have the kind of therapeutic practice Cushman wants (and here I refer largely to Cushman, 1995), I think we have to face a very serious problem: the good will for dialogue and the capacity to take on another point of view are developmental capacities, and these capacities have been and continue to be severely compromised by the effects of capitalism, bureaucracy, sexism, racism, and heterosexism. This is why there are so few sites of dialogue, and why, as I will argue, even the clinical encounter can rarely begin with dialogue. To elaborate this point, I look to those who have written about the relation between narcissism and capitalism, particularly members and heirs of the Frankfurt School (Adorno et al., 1950; Fromm, 1941; Habermas, 1971; Kovel, 1980; Lasch, 1979; Layton, 1986; Livesay, 1985; Marcuse, 1955; Sloan, 1996; and, with regard to clinical issues, Altman, 1995; Benjamin, 1988; Kovel, 1988; Layton, 1998, 2002, 2004a). These authors have argued that capitalism brings about particular kinds of relationships, instrumental ones, and these are in fact inimical to dialogue (indeed, they are precisely what bring people into therapy); (2) I am particularly delighted that Cushman brought Gramsci into our dialogue. I agree with him that Gramsci's theory of hegemony is crucial to articulating critical, non-conformist views, and I want to extend Cushman's discussion by proposing what I consider a most important revaluation of Gramsci in Laclau and Mouffe's (1985) *Hegemony and Socialist Strategy*. I think that if we can figure out a way to bring Laclau and Mouffe's theory into dialogue with clinical theory, we will be a step closer to recapturing the revolutionary vitality of psychoanalysis.

Cushman's argument here suggests that relational analytic theory is by its dialogic nature anti-conformist and critical of the status quo. But I think that this is only partly true, and I would draw on his own work (1995) to prove my point: there, Cushman argued that we must add to our two-person theories a notion of thirdness, which he defined as the historico-socio-cultural realm (see also Altman, 1995; Samuels, 1993). This call implies that relational analytic theory, like all theories, alters its meaning depending on the context in which it is articulated. It can be artic-ulated into a variety of ideological formations, some that are politically radical and some that are not. I agree with Cushman that relational theo-ry's dialogic nature contests the authoritarian form of dominant discourse, but I do not think that it prepares subjects to be as radically questioning of their culture as it might. Because the questioning usually stops short of the social and political realm, it does not in fact contest political conformity.

Laclau and Mouffe's re-articulation of Gramsci's theory of hegemony explains why the radicality of theories can only be judged by their *use* at any given historical moment (see also Hall, 1982); Laclau and Mouffe's theory of ideology can also explain some of Cushman's other findings. But their theory contradicts Cushman's argument in one respect: this view of hegemony suggests that therapists falter not so much because they don't understand the flaws in the models of those who instantiated the interpre-tive turn. Rather, they "falter" (if indeed they do) because, in their theo-ries and practices, they consciously and unconsciously articulate (a word Laclau and Mouffe use to mean "link" as well as "express") elements of conformist ideologies together with elements of hermeneutic or postmod-ern theories. In this way, a potentially radical theory can be rendered quite mainstream.

## Capitalism and narcissism

The Frankfurt School was one of the earliest groups of philosophers and sociologists to explore the link between Marx and Freud, and much of their critique centered on what Marcuse (1964) called the one-dimensionalization of contemporary life, the utter conformity that marked both liberal democracies and fascist states. Even earlier, Erich Fromm (1941), another Frankfurt School theorist as well as an analyst, described the way that relations between people become instrumentalized under cap-italism. For the Frankfurt School, the version of reason practiced within capitalism and modern bureaucracies perverts the Enlightenment defini-tion of reason, which centered on the capacity for subjects to assess criti-cally the given. The perversion of reason arises from the rational quest to predict, control, and calculate. As this quest began to take on a life of its own and dominate modern life, it bred institutions in which facts were split from such Enlightenment values as equality, autonomy, and the capacity for critique (a situation that Horkheimer and Adorno (1944) referred to as the "dialectic of Enlightenment"). Reason degenerated into an instrumental rationality, separate from morality, that threatens the ego, the natural world, and the world of human relations. This is the kind of reason proper to a world in which relations between humans take on the character of relations between things (reification), a result of capitalist commodity fetishism and bureaucratic administration of everyday life.

In 1950, Adorno, one of the early members of the Frankfurt School, participated in a study of the authoritarian personality, the description of which did not greatly differ from what Kernberg (1975) and Kohut (1971) many years later called narcissistic personality. In 1979, Lasch made use of Kernberg's work to write about the ways that capitalism, particularly in its consumerist post-WWII version, brought about and sustained narcissistic personality disorder. His focus was on the continual sapping of the kind of ego strength necessary to self-reflect and to evaluate or criticize authority. He, like so many other critics of Western culture, wrote about the anomaly of a culture that insists we bring ourselves up by our bootstraps, depend on nothing and no-one, and at the same time encourages self-doubt and a reliance on experts (who tell you that you ought to be able to bring yourselves up by your bootstraps!). Cushman's groundbreaking critiques of self psychology and of Daniel Stern's theories (1990, 1991) are squarely in this tradition – there, he cautioned that therapy patches up and sends back into the world the empty selves brought into being by consumer capitalism. Cushman warns that therapy can function not so much as a critical practice but as a salve, analogous to the consumer goods that fill up empty selves.

Kovel (1980, 1988), Livesay (1985), Sloan (1996) and others wrote eloquently about the damaging psychic effects of capitalism, but the links they made between capitalism and narcissism are at risk of falling too soon into the dustbin of history (see Chapter 15). We cannot afford to lose Kovel's and Livesay's penetrating analyses of how narcissism functions in the middle-class white family, how the unachieved aspirations of parents get transmitted to children in such a way that the children come to feel simultaneously special and gifted but also smolderingly resentful that they are used as instruments to fulfill their parents' unfulfilled needs.

In the years since the earliest of these critiques appeared, much of the anti-conformist and politically resistant literature that has attracted clinicians has come from feminists, queer theorists, and antiracists. Few have connected that work to class and capitalism (exceptions include Altman, 1995 and Cushman, 1995), and I think that our best hope for a nonconformist, politically resistant clinical theory and practice is to begin to make those connections. I do not think this will be terribly difficult, for much of the work on gender, for example, deals precisely with the way unequal gender arrangements and gender socialization create narcissistic difficulties (Benjamin, 1988; Chodorow, 1978; Dimen, 1991; Goldner, 1991; Kaftal, 1991; Layton, 1998, 2002, 2004a). But connections have to be made between class, gender, race, sexuality, and other subject positions.

## Gramsci, Laclau, Mouffe, and hegemony

Work on capitalism and narcissism can illuminate what Fromm (1941) called the "social character" of our era and can help clinicians place in social context the kinds of problems they see daily. But we also need to connect that work to more contemporary, poststructuralist theories of ideology. Gramsci (1971) has been central to poststructuralist radical theorists, for he was one of the first to explain that ideologies are lived in material practices and that *all* ways of understanding the self in relation to culture are ideological (not just dominant versions).

For Gramsci (1971), the notion of hegemony was a way out of the impasse of the socialist theory and reality of his time. Marxist theory was weak in at least two areas: (1) the assumption that, by virtue of its place in the system of production, the working class would automatically come to class consciousness and overthrow capitalism to establish a communist democracy. As it turned out in practice, the working class had several distinct fractions within it, many of which were finding ways to accommodate to capitalism. And people of other classes, intellectuals, for example, were vying for the role of "revolutionary subject" (which led to such unfortunate structures as Lenin's vanguard party); (2) Marxism did not provide a complex theory of ideology and subjectivity.

While not giving up on the idea that the working class was the revolutionary subject, Gramsci nonetheless recognized that ideologies were not just ideas but were lived in material practices and discourses. To translate this insight into clinical terms, one might say that ideology is lived as character, evident in the most mundane of acts and emotional attachments. Further, he argued that at any given historical "conjuncture," antagonistic ideological discourses undermine the hegemony of the discourses that the powerful hope will keep the subordinate in their place. To win consensus, Gramsci argued, dominant ideologies have to incorporate at least some elements of subordinate discourses, meeting some of the needs of those who do not hold power. In his view, then, ideologies are articulated (put together and expressed) by historical agents; ideologies can be hegemonic, counter-hegemonic, or a mix of the two. If a new consensus comes into being, new, more radical hegemonies can displace older, conservative ones. Dominant ideologies serve the powerful, but those in power can never become complacent, for, as Stuart Hall has said (1982), no matter how many stray dogs the dogcatchers capture each night, new stray dogs will roam the streets by daybreak. Because language is polysemous, the powerful can never control the process of meaning-making, much as their agents in politics and the media might try to do so.

For Gramsci, then, there is indeed dialogue: dialogue between those in power and those not in power. But the suggestion is that those in power only make concessions in order better to consolidate their power. There is also dialogue among the subordinate as they join their separate struggles together to form a "historical bloc" (Gramsci's term). But perhaps more central to Gramsci's theory than dialogue is "antagonism," a concept Laclau and Mouffe develop. Laclau and Mouffe try to elaborate a socialist theory of politics and ideology that fits the post-war era. In this period, a variety of radical social movements arose whose revolutionary subjects were NOT the working class, but rather antiracists, gays, feminists, anticolonialists, students, etc.

How do these new subjects and new movements relate to earlier struggles? In their view, democratic revolution began with the French Revolution and its elaboration of an "egalitarian imaginary," expressed in such documents as the Declaration of the Rights of Man. Henceforth, relations between those in power and those outside of power were experienced as "not fixed," as neither ordained by God nor by a king who represents God. The concept of hegemonic formations can only emerge in such a political reality, not in one in which people accept their place in a hierarchy. The "egalitarian imaginary" is an ideal that continuously gets "yoked" to a variety of Western political struggles for hegemony, most of which gained steam in the late nineteenth and early twentieth century. The movements arose to fight new, monopoly forms of capitalism that had instituted dehumanizing "inventions" such as the assembly line. While assembly lines standardized work life, increasing the alienation of large parts of the workforce, new mass media arose to standardize leisure time. Capacities for mass manufacturing and mass distribution led to a shift in capitalist focus from production to consumption, especially after WWII. To ensure continuous consumption, coordinated apparatuses (including advertising, mass media) worked to create new needs and convince citizens that the greatest good was to consume, discard, and consume. At the same time, bureaucracies increasingly invaded private lives and individuals were increasingly cut off from participation in public life. All of this contributed to the commodification of selfhood, of the relations between people, and the relation between humans and the environment; indeed, these are some of the social developments critical to what Kohut and others identified as a rise in the occurrence of narcissistic personality disorders.

Drawing on poststructuralist work (especially Foucault, Lacan, and Derrida), Laclau and Mouffe describe their view of subjectivity: decentered, constituted in relation to other identities, constituted in relation to dominant power structures, and made up of a multitude of subject positions (race, class, sex, etc.), some lived in a complementary fashion and others in contradiction. The unfixed nature of subjectivity and subject positions, their multiple meanings (polysemy), creates the conditions for plural and radical democratic demands that can never be associated with one fixed subject position, e.g., a particular class. Subjects' different demands, each of whose referents is an "egalitarian imaginary," will ideally be yoked together in a hegemonic formation that counters dominant formations. Hegemonic formations, then, are socially constructed (Laclau and Mouffe's word for this is "discursive") and constitute themselves in opposition to other formations, in antagonism. Antagonism sets the limit frontier both to what is inside and what is outside the formation but also to the possibility of constituting a fixed identity. In other words, identities can be partially or temporarily fixed such that they can constitute a "historical bloc" and take political action, but it is the nature of subjectivity that identities can never be fully fixed. What a hermeneuticist might call a "horizon," Laclau and Mouffe conceptualize as a battleground of antagonistic hegemonic formations.

In this view, there can be no one revolutionary subject and certainly no guarantee in advance that this or that subject will be revolutionary, because subjectivity is multiple and contradictory AND because antagonistic formations, such as feminism for example, are also available for multiple articulations. This is a most important point, and one that I think explains in different terms what Cushman argues about Heidegger. Because subjectivity and discursive formations have no fixed center, feminist ideas can be articulated to liberal ideologies, to socialist ideologies, even at times to neoconservative ideologies (issuing in liberal feminism, socialist feminism, difference feminism, ecofeminism, etc.). Feminism itself isn't radical; it depends on how it gets articulated, what other discourses are yoked to it. Cushman illustrates such a perspective when he argues that we need not throw out Heidegger's theory altogether, even though it is flawed. When yoked to Gadamer's theory of dialogue, the concept of authenticity is disarticulated from the monocultural and monological context and rearticulated in a more radical context.

Laclau and Mouffe would also agree with one of Cushman's main points: a hegemonic formation as a strategy of opposition cannot just be AGAINST the given or it will be reduced to marginality; it also has to offer a strategy for the construction of a new social order. Nonetheless, nothing guarantees that radical democracy will be the outcome of historical struggle.

Here we have a relational, open systems theory that includes a theory of the relational way that power operates. It posits moments of partial unification, partial fixity, which guarantee the possibility of political action and provide a safeguard against nihilism. The tensions between concurrent articulations and between new and old articulations, the antagonisms, always militate against the possibility of total unifications, of fixity. This is a postmodernism without nihilism. Indeed, the proper term for Laclau and Mouffe's articulation is poststructuralist, the radical egalitarian version of postmodernism that we also find in the work of Derrida (1976, 1978), Butler (1990), Irigaray (1985), Bhabha (1994), and others who speak from clear ethical standpoints.

But what does any of this offer clinicians? I think it offers a lot if we can figure out a way to translate it into the work that we do. Cushman gives us a good starting point that reveals precisely what is missing in Laclau and Mouffe: a psychology. When Cushman speaks of Heidegger's inability to empathize or to value the interpersonal realms, he adds to this theory of antagonisms and hegemonic formations a focus on the emotional and developmental capacities that underlie the very *possibility* of articulating a progressive ideology. Articulations are not just the cognitive events that Laclau and Mouffe's theory suggests they are; they are deeply emotional and personal ones. To be able to engage in dialogue, one needs, at a minimum, the capacity for empathy, the capacity to respect and be curious about the other. Most clinical treatments do not begin as dialogue in this sense of the term; rather, their goal is dialogue.

We have to find a way to connect the psychological damage wrought by capitalist relations (in which, for example, relational and agentic capacities are often split and gendered – see Layton, 1998 and this volume, Chapter 8) to our ideas about fighting conformity and inequality. I think that we are all skilled at helping our clients develop capacities for empathy and mutuality. This is a start. But it does not necessarily create subjects who have the capacity to connect themselves with broader social processes and inequities (for example, that we in the U.S., 4% of the world's population, consume 25% of the world's energy). Because clinical work has become so dissociated from its own political context, it is always at risk of creating subjects who do not question social inequities: not just the inequities that keep middle-class privilege unconscious, but even the inequities that keep us oppressed and powerless. Indeed, I would argue that the way the socio-historical thirdness that Cushman has elaborated enters the clinical dyad is often via enactments. These conscious and unconscious collusions between therapist and patient, motivated by what I have called normative unconscious processes, often do not in the least contest social inequalities but rather actually shore them up, either by performing them in the treatment, failing to contest them, or missing chances to articulate them.

The notion of normative unconscious processes is one of many possible concepts that we could use to account for the way dominant ideologies express themselves materially in social character and its unconscious and conscious defenses, object relations, repetition compulsions, and enactments. Only by articulating such concepts, I think, can we work toward a kind of clinical dialogue that truly resists conformity and that creates subjects who are able to link their experience to their social world and enact mutuality not just in the private but in the public sphere. Only then might we have a kind of dialogue that connects us ethically not just to ourselves and our intimates, but to our common bond with humanity and nature – the kind of dialogue, in other words, that enables us to become something more than healthier narcissists.

## Note

\* Used with permission. Layton, L. (2005) Notes toward a non-conformist clinical practice: Response to Philip Cushman's "Between arrogance and a dead-end." *Contemporary Psychoanalysis* 41(3): 419–429.

# Chapter 3

# Attacks on linking

## The unconscious pull to dissociate individuals from their social context[*]

Cultural norms erect barriers to what can be thought, felt, and articulated in speech. Because in certain ways they share the same dominant middle-class culture, therapists and their clients often adhere, consciously and unconsciously, to some of the same cultural norms. These norms not only condition thought, feeling, and behavior, but create dynamic unconscious conflicts as well. Such unconscious conflict, in turn, can generate particular kinds of clinical enactments, ones in which therapist and patient unconsciously collude in upholding the very norms that might in fact contribute to ongoing psychic pain. In this chapter, I want to focus on a particularly dominant norm in U.S. culture: the unlinking of individuals from their social contexts. This unlinking derives from many historical and social sources. Its origins lie in the rise of capitalism in mid-nineteenth-century America, in response to the increasingly sharp separation of the public from the private sphere that was mandated for the middle and upper classes both by urbanization and industrialization's division of labor. White middle-class patriarchal norms split and gendered the two spheres, and the disparate functions of these separate white male public and white female private spheres created the psychic split between agentic capacities and relational capacities that for so long have defined dominant gender positions (even though white women played key roles that melded the private and the public in such historical movements as the fight to prohibit prostitution and alcohol, the right to divorce, own property, work in healthy conditions, and the right to vote). Emotional attachments were only culturally valued in the private sphere, not in the dog eat dog world of capitalism (Lasch, 1977). Indeed, despite today's public rhetoric in favor of family values, now, as always, if a corporation or the military want to send you and your family to a different part of the country or world every few years, you go – regardless of what clinicians and others know about how significant a prognosticator for psychological difficulties frequent moves can be.

The liberal ideology that legitimizes the public/private split has traditionally idealized an autonomous white male whose subjectivity resides in reason and will. The ideology of the "free individual" is, particularly in the U.S. context, closely connected with self-reliance and an extreme individualism that denies connections of all kinds. As Barthes (1957) and others have written, two of the main tropes by which bourgeois ideology operates are dehistoricization, which involves naturalizing and universalizing what is actually specific to a given historic moment and a given constellation of relations, and what Barthes calls ex-nomination, by which the class that has the most economic and symbolic power refers to itself as "man" or "human," anything but white or upper-middle-class or owners of the means of production. As Barthes (1957) writes:

> practised on a national scale, bourgeois norms are experienced as the evident laws of a natural order – the further the bourgeois class propagates its representations, the more naturalized they become.
>
> (p. 140)

Both dehistoricization and ex-nomination are ideological forms of decontextualization, the unlinking of things that, if experience is to make sense, need to be linked. Indeed, what primarily sustains the ideology of the "free individual" is an active and continuously constructed process of decontextualization, most obvious in the media but clear as well in every one of President Bush's speeches, in most discussions of corporate wrongdoing, in the medicalization of psychological problems, in discussions of what is wrong with our schools and in most discussions of social policy. Dominant ideology works very diligently on a number of fronts to hide the systemic nature of inequalities of all kinds, to make sure that an individual's problems seem just that, individual.

As political theorist Wendy Brown (2004) claims, liberal ideology has always been deeply suspicious of groups and their public display of passions such as anger and love. Ardent attachments are deemed dangerous and must remain private and individualized. Many key documents of liberal ideology view groups as sites where perfectly rational individuals become regressed, primitive, and de-individuated beings. Liberal ideology then draws on such "expert evidence" to relegate group aspects of identity, such as culture and religion, to background status, to a place that is not deemed constitutive of subjectivity.

As entrepreneurial capitalism gave way to consumer capitalism, liberal individualist ideology became ever more entrenched. The autonomous individual, once figured in liberal discourse as public citizen, is now largely figured in the media and elsewhere as private consumer. The continuous subordination of sensuous human existence and morality to the "facts" of the marketplace and technical rationality severs, instrumentalizes, and commodifies connections between individuals and between individuals and their environments. All of these processes unlink individuals from each other, from themselves, and from their social and natural world.

Even to speak of the individual and the social as separate is a distortion, except insofar as that separation is the truth of this society's dominant culture, and, as such, appears to most of us as "common sense" (see Adorno, 1967, 1968). As Althusser (1971) argued, all the apparatuses of capitalist culture – the family, the education system, the media, religion – function to shore up the notion of a free individual separate from social context. Free individuals, free to succeed or fail on their own, generally have no idea that their freedom is conditioned by the lack of freedom inherent in the wage-labor system (Žižek, 1994). Yet, despite the mystifications of ideology and the way ideologies are enacted consciously and unconsciously, it is clear that social context is woven into one's psychic fabric in myriad ways, from the ways bodily processes are experienced and tastes developed (see Bourdieu's 1984 discussion of class, habitus, and taste, discussed in Chapter 9), to the ways one experiences and enacts the most taken for granted psychoanalytic staples, such as dependency and agency. The way the power structure of a culture defines what counts as dependency and what counts as agency, the way it mandates which social classes or strata will be "dependent," which "independent," plays a large role in determining the kinds of psychic conflicts inherent to that culture.

Certainly, there are subordinate cultures in the U.S. whose members are painfully aware of the connections between social systems and their own individual struggles. Nonwhite populations, for example, are far less likely to buy into the unlinking norm than are whites of all classes. Nonetheless, all subcultures have to wrangle psychically with dominant ideology; it is hard to imagine that even the most impoverished black man doesn't on some level feel personally responsible for his failure to be successful. And because dominant ideology is so tied into the one system NO ONE is allowed to question, capitalism, we find that as minority subcultures rise in social status their prominent members sometimes become the most rabid defenders of the unlinking norm: think of the Ward Connerly's and Clarence Thomas's of the world who, once achieving individual privilege, seem to want to close the privilege gate behind them.

By limiting to the family the context in which it views patients' conflicts, psychoanalytic therapy is one of the many practices that enforce the norm that unlinks the psychic from the social. Following Cushman (1995), Altman (1995) and others, I argue that, in so doing, we establish a norm for what counts as mental health that aims far lower than it might. As a consequence, we contribute to constricting the possibilities of our patients, even as we are enhancing them in many other ways. Indeed, if we believe that the individual ought to be a social individual and that his or her happiness should have something to do with connections beyond the self and beyond intimate relations, we should perhaps be troubled by the fact that, too often, our work produces only healthier and happier versions of narcissism.

Although many psychoanalytic theorists have spoken about the relation between the psychic and the social (my notion of normative unconscious processes owes a debt, for example, to Fromm's notion of social character 1941, 1962), Samuels (1993) was perhaps the first to insist that the political development of the person is a proper and necessary topic for inquiry in the clinical setting. In the clinical vignette that I describe next, we can see that the patient's political conflicts are also psychic conflicts. What I want to add to Samuels' observations is (1) an analysis of the way that norms that separate individuals from their "political psyche" generate unconscious conflict and (2) the way this shared conflict plays out in unconscious collusions between therapist and patient.

## Clinical vignette: work and love and the passion for civic life

In the spring of 2003, just after the U.S. went to war in Iraq, a patient reported a dream in which she wondered whether or not to tell her state senator her views on what is currently going on politically in American life. In exploring the dream with her, I found myself struggling throughout the session against the urge to close off this inquiry with an interpretation that would reduce what she was saying to the kind of psychological insight that separates the psychic from the social. Granted, we are living in difficult political times, times in which historical events such as 9/11 force their way into the consulting room. But this experience revealed to me my own resistance to linking the psychic and the social, a resistance of which I had been largely unaware. Fighting my urge to interpret enabled the two of us to discover that there are realms beyond those of work and love that are clinically relevant.

Before reporting the dreams, I want to say something about other ways that the separation of the individual from the social affects this patient's psyche. The patient owns a small business, and like many small businesses these days, hers has not been doing well. But she never understands her failure in that context. She, after all, is part of the Smith family, and Smiths are winners, not losers. She suffers in a special way, one that doesn't seek affinity with other forms of suffering and makes it seem as though to suffer or not depends on her capacity to get it wrong or get it right. She is failing, she thinks, because she isn't organized enough, isn't getting enough done during the day. In the childhood scenes to which she associated one day as we discussed this, she was a very special person by virtue of being a Smith, but there was always a particular way to be a Smith if you wanted love, and that way included wearing your hair and your shirt collars a certain way, not reading when you're supposed to be out playing with friends, in short, figuring out what it entailed to be the right kind of person. The psychic cost of living the ideology of the free individual is precisely in living this paradox: self-reliant, what common sense calls independent, but always unsure of oneself and therefore utterly dependent on the outside for clues as to how to be (a dependency consumerism is only too happy to manipulate).

On the particular day in which the enactment I report on next took place, she entered saying that she was feeling very good about certain things at work; for the first time in memory, she said, she feels that she is instituting changes that are making her small business function more the way *she* wants it to. She also reported that as she has become more hands-on in her workplace, she feels more connected to her staff. A primary focus of treatment has been analyzing her desire to feel connected to people and her equally strong defenses against that desire. Then she reported two dreams that she had written out in a dream journal:

*Dream #1:*  She is in the backseat of a car with someone else. John Kerry is outside the car and he's in a wheelchair. She lets him into the car and wonders if she should use the opportunity to tell him what she thinks about what's going on politically.

*Dream #2:*  She's with a group of people and they have to flee. She's supposed to make a fire by rubbing things together and it works. She's very surprised that it worked and feels good about herself. But the fire is going to burn everything up and she's anxious that it will all burn before she and the others figure out what they need to take with them to start over.

I asked for her associations to the first dream and asked her what she would want to tell the senator, who had recently declared his interest in running for President. She began to talk about her political opinions, that she doesn't like what's going on and that she's been annoyed with Kerry because he wasn't sufficiently critical of the Iraq war. Her wondering about whether or not she should say something to him made me associate to what we'd recently been talking about: that it is difficult for her to make herself accountable for things. A psychic dilemma we've long looked at involves her tendency either to give everything over to another, to make that other all powerful, or to take it all on herself and be unable to ask for help. Often she feels that she's not accountable for things such as the upkeep of her house or her business; she puts herself in a child position, hoping the adults will get the job done. I said something about this dilemma, but I also thought to myself that I'd like to hear more about what she wants to tell Kerry, and when I allowed for that she began to go more deeply into what she feels about the state of the country, evincing a level of passion and a state of conviction that I rarely have glimpsed in her.

Passionlessness, an unlived life, has been her chief complaint. As she began to get more passionate, she pulled her legs up on the couch and sat cross-legged. She looked at me and hesitantly asked: can I really talk about this? I asked her why not. She wasn't sure if it was a proper therapy topic. I assured her that it is certainly a legitimate topic. I told her that I want to know what she's passionate about, and I could see that she feels deeply about this. As I said that, I realized I should just let her talk without jumping in with psychological interpretations, that jumping in and interrupting her experience of passion would in fact repeat her original wounds. For, in childhood, her spontaneous passions of all kinds were often found wanting and even mocked. But also, I realized that I in fact was struggling with the same question she asked: is this a therapy topic? At the moment, I didn't think that we could have explored her question further, which might have enabled us to understand more about her doubt. At that moment, I was wondering more about my own doubt. I know her politics are left of center, as are mine, and it is perhaps knowing this that made me mistakenly feel that what she was going to say was known territory, that I was just indulging my own wish to hear her bash the Bush regime and the Iraq War. She broke into my reverie when she asked if it was alright to have her feet up on the couch like that – she said she was thinking about that on the way over: is there a couch etiquette? I wasn't sure what to make of this sudden concern, but in retrospect I wonder about the meaning of the associative sequence. Does speaking about one's political convictions in therapy carry the same kind of taboo of impurity or of being uncivilized as does putting one's feet on the furniture? Was there a connection between her child-like attitude toward political responsibility and her child-like feelings about putting her feet on mommy's couch? Was she simply doing all in her power to interrupt her *own* experience of passion?

She went on to say that she would tell Kerry that she feels that everything she grew up believing about America was being taken away from her, all the values she learned, like doing unto others. She began to cry and I asked what was upsetting her. Crying more intensely, she wailed that she feels betrayed. This is a woman who rarely is able to cry in another's presence, who, in fact, has spoken many times about her longing to be able to express feelings while with me in the room.

She then brought in the second dream, associating to what she called a Jewish theme, "maybe like there was a pogrom." Her association to the fire burning was that something very bad was happening and it will be too late by the time we realize what it is. Again, I thought about what was happening to her business, which was falling apart, and felt pulled to interject something about that; but I had the sense that while her passion about what is happening politically may have had multiple psychic sources and motivations, it would be a mistake to understand what she was saying as mere displacement. In part, I did not interpret in this other frame because

I share her feelings that what the country stands for is being rapidly dismantled; her passionate feelings of betrayal are clearly valid in their own right. I also just wanted to see where she would go next.

Still crying, she repeated, with more intensity, that everything she feels America stands for is being betrayed and she feels helpless to do anything about it. I asked her to say more about her feelings of helplessness. She said that she supposes she could write letters but she doesn't. I asked her why not. She answered: last night she got home and her partner wanted to watch the Red Sox game and she didn't. She wanted to sit outside and read the newspaper (the day before she told me she had stopped reading the newspaper because it was too depressing). And then she talked about her partner, who is very left-wing and very voluble about it. Apparently *she's* been writing letters. At this point, a link between the psychic and the social became clearer – in the face of her partner's very big passion, my patient's passion drains away and she detaches, letting the partner carry the political feelings and political activity. My patient doesn't feel quite the same as her partner on these issues, but her feeling of helplessness seems to come from a sense that the partner owns this realm because her passion and anger are so much bigger. I thought about Bush's 70 percent approval rating (in that period) and wondered if she might be allowing the other side to own civic life because the other side is louder and so deaf to dissent. Again, a part of me was thinking that, like all other roads, this political road led us back to a particular psychic conflict, the one that gets in the way of her feeling like an autonomous and passionate being. Her parents were also louder, and also deaf to dissent. My first association, the one about accountability, fits into this larger repetition scenario, for she long ago had made a conscious and unconscious pact with her parents that went something like this: "I'll do as you say but then you're in charge: I refuse to take any responsibility myself for my life." And yet, again, I felt that we were both discovering something new that day, which I stated at the end: that her passion for a certain kind of America is not a lesser passion than the ones we had been exploring, the passion to work well and to love well. Indeed, the parental interference with her autonomy and passion had led to a kind of isolationist machoism, which coexisted with a smolderingly resentful feeling of helpless passivity. All too frequently the resentment issued in acts of passive aggression. Her character style well illustrates one typical way that American ideology's unlinking of the individual and the social is psychically enacted.

The session ended with what I consider to be an enactment worth think-ing about, one I'm a bit embarrassed to admit to: I told her about some political letter-writing activities on the Internet that I was aware of. She smiled and left. I think that through the session she was consistently invit-ing me to be larger and louder, as when she asked me about whether it was okay to talk about this, okay to put her feet up on the couch. Each time I resisted making an interpretation, I think I was resisting that pull to be larger – although I *did* give permission rather than ask why she sought it. And then at the end, in suggesting something she might do, I went large, and I am not sure why.

The next day she told me how good the day before had felt to her. She was quite surprised and a little embarrassed that her political feelings had made her cry – she doesn't think that most people take these political things so personally. She'd have to describe herself as in some way an innocent, she said, and that is embarrassing. And when I asked what about the session had made her feel so good, she told me that it was because she allowed herself to follow my questions without resistance, that there was something about my encouraging her to keep speaking about it that had put her in touch with her feelings and enabled her to go on expressing them without shame. My sense is that what enabled the passion to emerge, enabled her resistance to recede, was precisely my capacity to put a muz-zle on my interpretive impulse. Here was the anti-enactment: shutting up made me less large which enabled her to come forward.

Again, what was striking to me about this hour was how hard I had to struggle to stay out of her way and simply let her feelings develop. I do not generally find myself having irresistible urges to cut in and interpret in my sessions with her. My guess is that this urgency reflected at least two things: (1) my anxiety that because I did not explore what Samuels (1993) calls the symbolic/intrapsychic/transferential aspects of my patient's speech, I wasn't being a proper analyst. Had I expressed the doubts I had at the point when the patient asked if it was a proper therapy topic, we might both have unconsciously colluded with the social norm that keeps the psychic and the social separate; and (2) the sense of urgency about jumping in may well have come from an unconscious pull (hers? mine? ours?) to re-enact this patient's repetition compulsion – to quash her spon-taneous gestures by finding them not quite right, to play the larger one and make her small. This illustrates a paradox of the American version of autonomy – we are encouraged to pull ourselves up by our bootstraps – by experts who tell us how to do it (Lasch, 1979). How many of our patients come in wanting the therapist to provide the "Ten Easy Steps to Thinking For Yourself"?

In more recent work, this patient has confronted on a deeper level her tendency to see the world and its rules as adversaries that endanger her individual autonomy. She has become aware of how she passive aggressively breaks rules, simple ones such as not paying bills on time or trying to send a package 5 minutes after the post office closes. When the other refuses to "cut her slack," she self-righteously positions herself as a victim. She has also confronted the way that her sense of being an individual has been based on a refusal to be part of ANY group, again because she experiences others as intruders on her autonomy. As she has become more able to feel that she can remain a self while engaged with others, as she has had less fear that she will be taken over by others, she has tentatively begun to sustain connections to others. And, most interestingly, some months after the reported vignette, this patient, who is gay, became terrifically excited by politics and made the first political gesture of her life: she sent out an email to friends and acquaintances with a copy of an article a straight woman had written about gay marriage. The writer, who was about to be married, had a gay brother, and the article revolved around her conflicted feelings about her own right to marry and the state's attempts to limit the rights of her brother. My patient noted that in the past she might have sent the article around with an introduction such as, "Here's an article you might find interesting." But this time she wrote a preamble in which she urged people to call their representatives and senators or just to intervene when they hear homophobic conversations. She spoke in that session of feeling alive, and ended the session with the statement, "I'm pumped."

Several things strike me about both this vignette and another enactment I experienced with a patient, one concerning talk about class privilege. Most striking is that at the end of each session this patient shamefully admitted, "I'm not politically active." Hollander and Gutwill (2006), from an object relations perspective, and Althusser (1971) and Žižek (for example, 1989), from a Lacanian perspective, see psychoanalysis as uniquely suited to shed light on how and why people attach to the very social forms that oppress them. In this patient's history, and in the histories of so many of my patients, a choice was made to constrict spontaneity in the face of parents who were certain they were right. This was the only way to pre-serve some autonomy, even if it was a form of autonomy that doomed the patients to a sense of ineptitude and helplessness. These phenomena open up two areas for further investigation concerning the relation between the psychic and the social: (1) how that sense of helplessness is transferred from the familial to the relational and then to the political realm; and (2) what it is about the society that makes so many parents absolutely certain about how things ought to be done, that makes them frightened of the otherness of their children. This is more than just a question of genera-tional difference; I am questioning a particular way that generational dif-ference is lived. In this form, children are mere extensions of their parents, props the parents need to accomplish psychically and socially whatever it is they feel they have failed to accomplish (Kovel, 1988). The child's response of submission, on the other hand, brings about a form of "auton-omy," if we can call it that, that results in attacks on the self and a convic-tion that failure is individual and not systemic. The continuous enactment of this unlinking norm produces narcissistic personalities, defined both by the difficulty regulating self-esteem that Kohut (1971, 1977) theorized, and by the difficulty establishing relations of mutuality that Benjamin (1988) theorized. In splitting the individual from the social, bourgeois ide-ology brings about an impoverishment of individuality in which depend-ence is repudiated and difference not tolerated. This dynamic leaves so many of us vulnerable to manipulation by media, government, advertising, and public relations – even as we desperately try to assert our individual-ity and autonomy. Rather than enable people to live happier lives as "free individuals," I feel strongly that clinical theory and practice have to figure out how to re-establish the links between the psychic and the social that dominant ideologies work tirelessly to unlink. Somehow we have to find a way to allow the passion for civic life to take its rightful place beside work and love in the clinic.

## Note

* Used with permission. Layton, L. (2006) Attacks on linking: The unconscious pull to dissociate individuals from their social context. In: Layton, L., Hollander, N.C. and Gutwill, S. (eds.) *Psychoanalysis, Class and Politics: Encounters in the Clinical Setting*. New York, NY: Routledge, pp. 107–117.

# Chapter 4

# What divides the subject?

## Psychoanalytic reflections on subjectivity, subjection, and resistance[*]

The object of psychoanalysis *is* the subject, subjectivity. But what do we mean by subjectivity and how does subjectivity come into being? Feminists and others, both within the field of psychoanalysis and outside, have deconstructed the traditionally male version of subjectivity, the bounded, rational, autonomous subject, and many other versions of subjectivity have been proffered in its stead. In this sense of the term, subjectivity is situated, socially constructed, historically mediated, gendered, raced, classed, etc. – subjected to social norms, to be sure, but not necessarily riven by unconscious conflict. While few psychoanalysts feel that the social and historical situatedness of the subject has much to do with psychoanalytic subjectivity, psychoanalysts of all camps agree that the subject is divided, and, more particularly, divided against itself. And, yet, there is controversy here, too, for the many schools of psychoanalysis that currently co-exist define the causes, mechanisms, and stakes of this division quite differently. Is it birth that divides the subject internally? Separation? Annihilation anxiety? Innate aggression and omnipotence? A result of an originary and prolonged state of helpless dependence? Castration and the Oedipus complex? Unconscious narcissistic identifications? Acute trauma? Ongoing interpersonal strife? The answer given to this question differentiates one psychoanalytic school from another.

Assuming, then, that the conceptualization of subjectivity is itself a "site of struggle" – even within psychoanalysis – I will begin by highlighting certain debates among Anglo-American psychoanalysts, debates that shed light on the relation between subjectivation, that is, the process of becoming a subject, and subjection. I will then take up what has most vexed those of us engaged in theorizing psychosocial subjectivity: on the one hand, the need to address psychoanalysis' collusion with ideologies that separate subjectivity from its situatedness in the social, and, on the other hand, how to address the subject's emergence within particular power structures without reducing subjectivity to social determinism.

## Two psychoanalytic debates on the nature of subjectivity

How one answers the question of "what divides the subject?" depends in large measure on how one conceptualizes the relation between self and other, for, in most psychoanalytic theories, it is the encounter with otherness that divides. And in most analytic theories, this encounter is figured as antagonistic. Thus, the tension between subjectivation and subjection is at the heart of psychoanalytic theory, even if social structures besides the family are rarely considered as sources of subjection. A recent psychoanalytic controversy has led to new ways of thinking about subjectivity and about the relation between self and other. The controversy centered on whether we are born fused with the other, in a symbiotic tie (Mahler et al., 1975), or whether we are born with an at least incipient form of subjective agency. Daniel Stern's (1985), Lou Sander's (1983), and Beatrice Beebe's (1985) groundbreaking studies of infant development challenged Mahler's view that babies begin in symbiotic fusion with the mother by claiming to demonstrate empirically that infants show signs of a separate subjectivity from the outset, including an innate capacity and need to intuit the intentions of others with whom they engage. In many psychoanalytic theories, the mother is figured as narcissistically enmeshed with her baby and therefore a third figure is needed, usually conceptualized as the father, to rescue the baby from maternal engulfment (and thus begin the process of subjectivation). The infant researchers contested the notion that the first tie is a narcissistic one and contested the idea that subjectivity begins only with separation from the mother. This opened new psychoanalytic possibilities for feminist theorizing about the mother's and the baby's subjectivity, and about the co-construction of subjectivity within relationship.

In feminist psychoanalytic theory, Chodorow (1978), working within the object relations and separation-individuation analytic tradition, had already elaborated the differing effects of 1950s white middle-class sexist norms on male and female subjectivity. These norms denied mothers any agency beyond caretaking and tending the home; yet, as primary caretakers, mothers were the main figures with whom the child had to negotiate separation and differentiation. Building on Chodorow's work, Benjamin (1988) argued that in conditions in which mothers are denied subjective agency and fathers do not allow their daughters to identify with their agency, a boy's subjectivity is likely to be based in omnipotent denial of need for the other, while a girl's is likely to be based in submissive attachment to the other.[1] But equally important was Benjamin's counter-model of subjectivity. Influenced by Beebe, Sander, and Stern's observations of mother-infant play and mother-infant co-creation of patterns of mutual regulation and mutual affective attunement, Benjamin contested traditional (and individualistic) psychoanalytic views that the primary task of individual development is a progressive process of becoming separate from and independent of others, particularly the mother. Alongside the Oedipal law of "renounce, renounce," she elaborated a law based in the pleasures of attunement and the pleasures of being recognized as a subject by another subject. This revision of psychoanalytic theory proposes a kind of tie to the other that is neither a tie of identification nor a tie of subjection. Although subjectivity here is inextricably intertwined with (but not pathologically fused with) the subjectivity of the other, the other is not figured as necessarily oppressive or intrusive (nor is the baby figured as destructive and torn by love and hate). We can certainly find in Freud some instances in which the development of subjectivity is grounded in loving relationships with others (for example, in *Group Psychology and the Analysis of the Ego*, 1922), but these instances are few, and what dominates instead in Freud's work is a vision in which subjectivity begins and develops in antagonism toward the other. This view, of course, is one that tends to pathologize dependence and vulnerability, or, perhaps more accurately, it is a view that is unconscious of its anxiety about dependence and vulnerability and rids itself of these dread states through a particular version of developmental theory and Oedipal law (see Irigaray, 1985).

Within psychoanalysis, there continues to be a tension between those who see the endpoint of healthy development as the achievement of separateness from the other, and those whose theories convey less anxiety about dependence and connection. At one end of the spectrum are theories in which the subjection of the subject to the desires and needs of the other is paramount, and the other is figured as narcissistic. Other developmental theories, for example, Kohut's (1971, 1977), posit an original merger in which functions first performed by the parent (e.g., soothing) become internalized by the child, who eventually performs them him/herself. Although Kohut's theory recognizes the ongoing need for what he calls "selfobjects," these are objects used in the service of stabilizing the self, and are not subjects in their own right. At the other end of the psychoanalytic spectrum are theories that assert that subjects develop within relational matrices and negotiate differentiation and connection throughout life. Some of these theories (for example, see Lyons-Ruth, 1991) argue that an ongoing sense of secure attachment is the necessary ground of the development of capacities for autonomy. In a similar vein, Fairbairn's (1954) model for health emphasized what he termed "mutual interdependence," a capacity simultaneously to be both connected and separate, dependent and independent. And in Benjamin's (1988) model, a hallmark of both health and ethical subjectivity is the capacity to sustain what she calls the assertion-recognition dialectic: a form of subject-subject relating in which each subject is both able to assert its own subjectivity and recognize the subjectivity of the other.

A second and related contemporary debate that bears on both the nature of subjectivity and on the question of what divides the subject centers on how one understands the origins of aggression. And this depends on one's view of human nature: are we born with and primarily motivated by destructive wishes and omnipotent strivings? Are we primarily motivated by relational strivings, longings for love, or, as Hirsch has put it (describing the view of early interpersonalists such as Harry Stack Sullivan), the "striving for safety and security of self and for loved others" (1998, p. 518)? Are we born with both aggressive and erotic drives and is the primary developmental task to temper one with the other (for example, in Kleinian theory, where reparation arises from guilt about destructive wishes and acts against the mother)? Most psychoanalytic theorists suggest that we all contend with an originary omnipotence, a wish to impose our agenda on the other. Benjamin (1988), for example, draws on Winnicott's (1971) essay on object usage and object relating to support her view that intersubjectivity, the capacity for mutual recognition, is a developmental achievement that arises from a process of "destroying" the other and experiencing the other's survival of our destruction. Only then do we have the capacity to conceptualize the other as external to the self. Crucial to healthy development is the experience that interpersonal ruptures can be repaired. While I agree with the latter assertion, my sense is that Benjamin's view of originary omnipotence is not compatible with her views on mutual accommodation and the pleasures of attunement.

My own thoughts on subjectivity and aggression are more indebted to Kohut (1971, 1977), who contested the twin psychoanalytic beliefs in originary destructive omnipotence and aggressive drives. For Kohut, founder of the psychoanalytic school of self-psychology, omnipotence and aggression are break-down products of narcissistic injury, that is, they arise to defend against further wounding, shaming, trauma. Stephen Mitchell (1988), a founder of relational psychoanalysis, also argued that aggression arises as a product of relational breakdown. In these paradigms, the subject is seen to be divided against itself as a result of either acute trauma or ongoing relational injury. Thus, these theories assert that it is not the mere encounter with a desiring other that inaugurates a subjectivity divided against itself, but rather the nature of that encounter.

## Relational trauma and the divided subject

The re-introduction into psychoanalysis of the effects on subjectivity of actual trauma thus provides different answers to the question of what divides the subject, and, in particular, what divides the subject against itself. While my own thinking is largely indebted to the interpersonal/relational schools, which means that I believe that subjectivity is constructed from ongoing relational engagement with both internal and external "objects," I yet have learned what I know about subjectivity from a wide variety of psychoanalytic and non-psychoanalytic sources. From Freud, I take the idea that all subjects are riven by unconscious conflict, but my work with patients draws me to Kohut's, Winnicott's, Fairbairn's, and Ferenczi's beliefs that what causes neurotic misery is not originary helplessness, castration, or Oedipal struggle, but rather the unconscious conflicts produced by relational trauma – including shaming, humiliation, gross relational unpredictability, and empathic ruptures that are consistently met with retaliation and withdrawal rather than with attempts at repair [Benjamin's (1988, 2004) term, doer-done to, well captures this kind of relating, in which one is treated as an object rather than as a subject]. I find Klein's (1946) work on splitting and projective identification most useful for understanding the sometimes rapid-fire relational breakdowns that take place between patient and analyst in the consulting room. Seligman's (1999) work on the way parental projections and infant introjections fly back and forth from the earliest moments of life and become sedimented into repeated patterns suggests to me that the most painful forms of alienation from self, and the repetition compulsions that are the source of most people's suffering, have their roots not in the human condition but in early and ongoing relational struggle. Ordinary human unhappiness is a result of what we all have to do to make sense of loss, mortality, generational difference, the birth of siblings, the indifference of the universe, constraints on getting what we think we want. But our cognitive, affective, and behavioral reactions to the way our significant others love and nurture (or withhold love and nurture) are, to my mind, the source of neurotic misery. The other's consistent or intermittent abuse of our vulnerability, mild or major, the other's consistent or intermittent misrecognition – these are the events that fragment the subject and divide the subject tragically against itself (thus, I have always found the postmodern impulse to celebrate a fragmented subject to be the absolutely wrong response to the bourgeois celebration of a unified rational subject, see Layton, 1998, Ch. 5).

At the same time that I maintain that relationally-induced trauma and responses to it are at the heart of the neurotic misery of the divided subject, I also believe that subjectivity is more than what is captured by theories that reduce subjectivity to subjection. For I believe that we weave our subjectivity – in complex and non-linear ways, to be sure – from our conscious and unconscious responses to the *two* kinds of relational experience that most of us have: one in which we are treated as objects by the significant figures in our lives and one in which we are treated as subjects. One could state something similar in other psychoanalytic terms: for example, Kleinians might say that subjectivity alternates between paranoid-schizoid and depressive positions. But the difference between this view and mine would be that, for Klein, these states arise from the infant's responses to his/her innate destructiveness, and Klein and her followers place far less emphasis than I on what the parents or other significant figures have actually done. In other words, while I do think that mutuality, or subject-subject relating, is a developmental achievement, I believe that it is a capacity that grows from good-enough parenting, the earlier mentioned "pleasures of attunement," and from having been recognized as a subject by others from the outset (see Benjamin, 1990, on the developmental line of mutuality).

*[margin handwritten notes: "nothing about the social here...? this is a development perspective"]*

## Models of psychosocial subjectivity

From the earliest days of psychoanalysis, there have been attempts to account for the relation between the psychic and the social as well as attempts to understand the results of subjection to oppressive cultural norms. One early model conceptualized society as the primary cause of neurotic conflicts, social defenses, and particular character structures. Freud (1908/1959), for example, wrote about the ways that a sexually repressive society could cause neurotic anxieties, and Fenichel (1953) wrote about anal neuroses caused by capitalist culture. Many early analysts and social theorists (for example, Reich, Fromm, and other members of the Frankfurt School) understood character structure to be a precipitate of socio-economic structures and contradictions. Christopher Lasch's (1979) *The Culture of Narcissism* and Tod Sloan's (1996) *Damaged Life* are more recent works in this tradition.

Another early model posited the very opposite: that neurotic conflicts are primary in defining the form of a society. In *Totem and Taboo* (1913/1955), *Moses and Monotheism* (1939), and *Group Psychology and the Analysis of the Ego* (1922/1959), Freud argued that the origins of the social lie in conflicts within the primal horde. Here, the sons' rage at the primal father's freedom to exercise his sexual and aggressive instincts without restraint leads them to murder the father. The ensuing sense of guilt ushers in a more egalitarian, but at the same time a far more repressed version of society, in which no one is allowed to enact the primal father's instinctual freedom.

What are some of the implications for a social psychoanalytic theory of the relational views of subjectivity that I have highlighted here? Elaborating a relational view of the development of subjectivity, one in which we are always internally and externally imbricated with others, Butler has pointedly challenged psychoanalytic views that stop short of engaging with social constraints on subjectivity:

> The "I" who cannot come into being without a "you" is also fundamentally dependent on a set of norms of recognition that originated neither with the "I" nor with the "you" . . . The task is . . . to think through [humans'] primary impressionability and vulnerability with a theory of power and recognition.
>
> (Butler, 2004, p. 45)

One of the main difficulties for those of us who do recognize the effects of the social is how to account for the effects of the social without succumbing to the reductionism of social determinism, and how to account for the idiosyncrasies of human subjectivity without removing subjectivity from its social and historical context (as most dominant discourses are wont to do). How can we capture the way that subjectivity tends to resist subjection to oppressive social norms and simultaneously becomes complicit in sustaining them, the way we simultaneously strive for mutuality and yet tend to replicate doer-done to relations?

As I said earlier, my own way of conceiving the relation between the psychic and the social suggests that subjectivity emerges from an ongoing conflict between relational experiences in which we are treated as objects and relational experiences in which we are treated as subjects. Each of us, if we are lucky, grows up with some predictable experiences of mutuality in relating. But each of us as well is vulnerable to the shaming assaults that arise from being treated as objects. One major source of these shaming assaults is cultural hierarchies of classism, racism, sexism, and heterosexism – the power structures that establish norms of recognition. Such hierarchies tend not only to idealize certain subject positions and devalue others, but tend to do so by splitting human capacities and attributes and giving them class or race or sex or gender assignments. The culturally desirable attributes go to the dominant group; the ones the culture least rewards go to the subordinate. Thus, social processes such as gendering, racing, classing, and sexing are at the very heart of subjectivity and subjective trauma, not accidental add-ons (as they are conceived to be in most psychoanalytic theories). We may all be born dependent and helpless, for example, but the way dependency is lived subjectively is very much marked by the ideals of proper masculinity and femininity that circulate within and between classes and races. And these ideals are bound up with a culture's norms concerning whether or not it is shameful to be dependent. Psychoanalysis is well suited to explain how cultural demands to split off capacities such as vulnerability, assertion, connection, and dependence are lived both intrapsychically and interpersonally.

Because cultural hierarchies split and categorize *human* attributes and capacities, subjectivity is marked by unceasing conflict between those unconscious processes that seek to maintain the splits and those that refuse them. I call the ones that seek to maintain the splits "normative unconscious processes," that is, processes that pull for us to repeat those affect/

behavior/cognition patterns that uphold the very social norms that cause psychic distress in the first place. Repetition compulsions (Freud, 1914) are the place where the struggle between coercive normative unconscious processes and counter-normative unconscious processes are enacted, where we will find the conflict between those parts of self that are shaped by relational trauma (and that divide the subject against itself) and those parts of self that have known and are able to seek out relationships based in mutual recognition of self and other as separate but interdependent subjects. These repetitions tend to be stirred up and played out in relation, particularly at moments of heightened vulnerability. Because the result of splitting is to keep what has been split off near, because we project what we repudiate onto others, the ways in which WE have been wounded will inevitably stir up the wounds of those with whom we seek intimate contact. Thus, the defensive aspects of our identity investments implicate us in each other's suffering. *we create the suffering* *\* by projecting (not-me)*

## Conclusion

Unconscious conflict, to be sure, is not produced solely by oppression. The subject is divided by experiences of loss, by confusing experiences that the organism might be too immature to comprehend, by desires that are blocked by various kinds of limits. But I have argued that it is relationally inflicted wounding, not ordinary human unhappiness, that is most inimical to the development of the kind of subjectivity that a psychoanalysis mindful of the workings of power and mindful of the cultural constituents of subjectivity would hope to nurture: a subjectivity with space for reflection, for imagination, for dreaming, for the capacity to be both self-critical and critical of authority, for engagement with the wider world, a subjectivity that can acknowledge both destructiveness and vulnerability, a subjectivity that fosters versions of agency and connection that acknowledge mutual interdependence and accountability to intimate and non-intimate others. *\* includes at dyad and social level.*

My sense is that the kind of subjectivity psychoanalysts want to foster cannot emerge from a psychoanalysis that splits the psychic from the social, one that does not take cultural power differentials and oppressive social norms into account (Layton, 2006b, and Chapter 3, this volume). Indeed, a psychoanalysis that separates the psychic from the social is likely to collude with contemporary individualist trends and to produce healthier versions of narcissism, thereby failing to produce subjects who can see themselves in others outside the intimate circle of family and friends. Clinicians who know what trauma does to subjectivity, clinicians mindful of the way that social norms and social policies affect processes of subjectivation, subjection, and resistance, can at the very least challenge splitting processes and thus challenge the ways that difference becomes vulnerability-denying distinction. To do so requires, among other things, coming to terms with how our own identity investments sustain both our suffering and the suffering of those with whom we relate. To that end, we need to understand that the very way our psychic structures become intertwined with split gender, race, sexual, class, and other identity investments not only divides subjects against each other, but divides the subject against itself.

## Note

* Used with permission. Layton, L. (2008) What divides the subject? Psychoanalytic reflections on subjectivity, subjection, and resistance. *Subjectivity* 22: 60–72.

# Chapter 5

# Relational theory in socio-historical context: implications for technique*

Those of us who read widely in contemporary theory will surely be struck by the fact that just about every discipline, theoretical or practical, and certainly most forms of critique, have committed themselves to a relational ontology in the past 25 years or so. Indeed, I've begun to notice that not just within relational psychoanalysis, but in various other high theory fields, relational ontologies are just beginning to be critiqued – often for not putting enough emphasis on the singularity of the individual. Here, I take a step back from critique in order first to focus on some of the features of contemporary social life that may account for the popularity of relational ontologies in general, and relational psychoanalysis in particular. I then explore the implications of this approach for expanding the boundaries of relational technique.

From the time I began to train in clinical psychology, in the early 1980s, through my time teaching feminist psychoanalytic theory and then finally training as an analyst in the 1990s, I have been attracted to relational theories because they feel "true" to me. Because of my own family and cultural history, Freud has never spoken to me in quite the same way as Ferenczi, Kohut, the British Independents, and U.S. relational theory. I have shunned theories that divorce the individual from social context, that commit to an ontology of innate forces that will manifest no matter what the environmental situation might be, that do not question authority or take into account the analyst's influence, both pernicious and benevolent, on treatment. But, even more than that, what I mean when I say that I am committed to a relational ontology is that I favor a poststructuralist and Bourdieusian sense that individual psyches are embedded in and forged in the context of history and in social relations that themselves exist in fields permeated by power differentials. I believe that identities are in some important psychic senses collective – not just defensively so but facilitatingly so. For example, I have argued (see Layton, 1998/2004), against poststructuralist conceptions of identity categories as solely oppressive, that identifications with social categories can facilitate change, as seen very clearly in social movements such as feminism. In turn, I also believe that individual and group psychic phenomena, including fantasy and other forms of unconscious and conscious process, participate in the forging of new historical contexts, new social relations, new collective identities, and new fields.

My commitment to a relational ontology means that I understand individual and group identity formation as occurring always in relation to other culturally available identity positions. I believe that cultural ideals of what it means, for example, to be a "proper" white middle-class female, emerge in relation to and confrontation with cultural ideals not only for white middle-class males, but for nonwhite middle-class females and both white and nonwhite working-class females. Psychologically, these identity-forming relational fields require identifying and disidentifying with certain ways of being and loving. The splitting, projections, and dissociations that go into both identifications and disidentifications create symptoms, defenses, and character structures that permeate what happens in the clinic. What relational theory has enabled me to do, particularly relational theories that center on the analyst's conscious and unconscious contribution to what transpires, is to develop a theory of the ways in which cultural inequalities of race, class, sex, and gender enter into what happens in the clinic. My focus has been on the ways that cultural inequalities are at times unconsciously and performatively reproduced. Thus, I am a relationalist in what I would call a broad sense, that is, I try always to think not only about the individual and family context of patients and therapists, but also about how cultural forces and power differentials shape those contexts. And yet, like all psychoanalysts, my clinical focus is on the singularity of the patient. For example, if a patient is a white working-class female, I want to know how this particular person has lived and is living both the facilitating and constricting aspects of class, sexuality, gender, and race. I think about these categories as existing intersectionally; for example, the way that gender is lived is always marked not only by gender relations but also by class, sexual, and racial relations.

What relational theory has not enabled me to do is to conceptualize what the consequences of thinking this way about identity might be for re-working or adding to relational ideas about technique. While many relational thinkers have proposed theories about how the psyche is shaped by culture, I can think of few who have extended that thinking into the realm of technique (as an exception, see Samuels, 1993, 2001). Attempting both  a historical and a forward-looking approach to evaluating the impact of relational theory, I want first to place relational theory into its historical and social context. I ask what has happened culturally, politically, and historically that might help us understand why so many of us have found relational theories compelling (I focus here on the U.S. context) and why they feel so "true" to us. Second, I want to begin to think about what technical innovations might be necessary to enable us more fully to elaborate a relational ontology that includes relations beyond the family.

## Relational theory in socio-historic perspective

In *The Lonely Crowd*, David Riesman (1950), a sociologist influenced by the "culture and personality" anthropological school prominent in the mid-twentieth century, argued that every culture produces a dominant character type that insures the efficient functioning and reproduction of that culture. The close connection between psychoanalysis and sociology in that period/school is attested to by the fact that Riesman was analyzed by, and remained a close colleague of Erich Fromm, who himself was one of the founders of the Frankfurt School critical theory sociology tradition, as well as an analyst working in the interpersonal tradition. Fromm's ideas about social character focused on individual and collective "escapes from freedom" (1941), and, later, on what he called the "marketing personality" (1947); Riesman's concern was with what he saw as a shift in the dominant form of social character in the post-WWII U.S.: from "inner" to "outer-directed" (note that Fromm's marketing personality exemplifies the epitome of an outer-directed character). The "inner-directed" character arose in the late nineteenth century, spanning the period in which entrepreneurial capitalism was oriented toward production. The "outer-directed" character, consonant with a consumer society, is primarily oriented toward the various relational matrices in which it finds itself. Unlike the "inner-directed," this character needs social approval for its achievements, seeks recognition, and becomes adept at understanding the emotional nuances of what goes on in the relational worlds of work and home. For the outer-directed character type, the autonomy precious to the inner-directed type is mediated by a greater value on, and anxiety around, what others think of you. Riesman was one of the first sociologists to describe a social reality in which meaning-making and the internal experience of the self are rooted in our multiple and contradictory relational matrices. It is in such conditions that a relational theory staple such as the need for "recognition," for example, becomes key to psychological health. As we look further at the social context within which the popularity of relational analytic theories emerges, we might keep the implications of Riesman's work in mind: psychological theories both reflect and shape broader cultural changes that affect the ways that people experience life and what is meaningful (see Cushman, 1995, 2019, for more recent reflections on the connection between social change, changes in self construction, and psychological theories).

Once the culture and personality school fell out of favor, few academic works sought to combine sociology and psychology; in fact, mainstream sociology became rather hostile to psychology. In the past 25 years, however, several prominent sociologists have argued that, in what they refer to as "late modernity" (post-WWII), sociology and psychology are "bound up in a direct way" (Giddens, 1991, p. 33). Among these sociologists, a relatively recent consensus has emerged that one cannot grasp the objective social circumstances of late modernity without a deeper and more nuanced understanding of subjectivity and intersubjectivity. As Giddens (1991, pp. 140–142) writes, for these sociologists "the real meaning of modernity is the construction of the self," beginning to say *I*. At the same time, Giddens (U.K.), Beck and Beck-Gernsheim (Germany), Touraine (2009) (France), and others describe dilemmas of contemporary subjectivity that relational theory and practice are perhaps particularly well suited to address.

## Individualization, reflexivity, and risk society

A patient spent most of a session talking about how a visit from her sister-in-law had "unnerved" her. The sister-in-law seemed so happy with her life, so content with her choices. While noting that something about her seemed "not real," my patient was nonetheless very self-critical about her own dissatisfactions with her relatively privileged life. Toward the end of the session I asked her if it was common for her to go through this kind of comparison.

I think I was perhaps pathologizing what seemed like shaky self-esteem. She replied, "Doesn't everybody?" And then, "I do have the tendency to second guess myself." And then, "Well, I'm aware there are a lot of different ways to do things, and I think that's positive. And that can be unsettling." Indeed, the patient's plight is captured in several relational tenets, well summed up in many of Hoffman's principles of dialectical constructivism (1998): for example, the assertion of the ambiguity and indeterminacy of much of reality; the "principle of uncertainty" that requires respect for the differing convictions put forth by patient and analyst; the multiplicity of possible "good" options for living the good life; the ambiguities of truth that demand continuous reflection on previous choices; the urgent feeling about choices we make as we search for what for us will be the good life; the changing truths that the process of reflection upon choices itself brings to the fore; the questions that the patient's plight raises for the "expert" analyst. My patient exemplifies what the sociologists refer to as a "reflexive" subjectivity that exists within a socio-historically particular "architecture of choice" (Illouz, 2012). She presents a major dilemma of life in our times: at least among the privileged, never before has there been so much opportunity for the uniqueness of the individual to emerge and to discover what, for him or her, the good life might be. At the same time, rarely before have there been so few traditions or such little cultural consensus to appeal to for guidance – nor so much conflicting expert advice telling us what's best for us to do.

Sociologists concerned with subjectivity refer to the post-war period in which this patient and her analyst dwell variously as "late modernity" (Giddens, 1991) and "second modernity" (Beck and Beck-Gernsheim, 2002). For Beck and Beck-Gernsheim, late or "second" modernity is marked by "institutionalized individualization," a result of the disembedding of individuals from any of the traditional frameworks that once provided an anchor for knowing how to live: nation-state, class, ethnic group, kinship ties, community, religion, or any other authority. While this loss can dispose us to "radical doubt" (Giddens, 1991, p. 181), it is also true that institutionalized individualization produces the possibility for many of living "a life of one's own" for the first time, the opportunity (and demand) to create a "do-it-yourself biography" (which is not to be confused with the ideology of individualism). This condition is the very one that relational theory describes as normative, and from which many of its theoretical and technical innovations have emanated.

Individualization processes have been at work since the urbanization and industrialization of the late eighteenth and nineteenth centuries in the West, but they have rapidly accelerated since the end of WWII. These processes include not only the disembedding from tradition but also the construction of legal frameworks that aim more at insuring individual freedom than at protecting collective life. Social movements such as feminism and civil rights have also played a role in individualization, widening the opportunity in the middle classes – beyond the world of privileged white men – to live for oneself rather than solely for others. "What is historically new," as Beck and Beck-Gernsheim assert, "is that something that was earlier expected of a few – to lead a life of their own – is now being demanded of more and more people and, in the limiting case, of all" (2002, p. 8). "In modern life," they write,

> the individual is confronted on many levels with the following challenge: You may and you must lead your own independent life, outside the old bonds of family, tribe, religion, origin and class; and you must do this within the new guidelines and rules which the state, the job market, the bureaucracy etc. lay down. The new element is, first, the democratization of individualization processes and, second (and closely connected), the fact that basic conditions in society favour or enforce individualization (the job market, the need for mobility and training, labour and social legislation, pension provisions, etc.).
>
> (p. 11)

The new ethic becomes enshrined as a duty to oneself; Beck-Gernsheim (in Beck and Beck-Gernsheim, 2002, Ch. 5, n. 94, p. 80) cites as a prime example Fritz Perls's popular 1960s motto: "I do my thing and you do your thing . . . I am not in this world to live up to your expectations, and you are not in this world to live up to mine. You are you and I am I; if by chance we find each other, it's beautiful. If not, it can't be helped."

Perls's words suggest that the individualized self is highly stable and confident. But individualization processes themselves are dialectical: the very forces that open the self to opportunity simultaneously create what the sociologists refer to as a "precariousness" of the self. As an example of these forces, we can look at changes in the organization of work. "Flexibility" is the watchword of what Sennett (2006) calls the "new" capitalism (loosely equal to free market or neoliberal capitalism). "Flexibility," which includes short-term contracts, willingness to move from job to job, and so on, emerges largely to guarantee short-term profit for corporate shareholders. It has heralded a major change for a workforce that in the recent past often stayed in the same job for entire careers. For a mobile elite, "flexibility" seems to work well and seems to offer freedom of choice, particularly in good economic times. But for the non-elite, and for everyone in times of downsizing, outsourcing, and the imposition of other demands of global capital, flexibility can create enormous insecurity and anxious feelings of disposability (see Section III of this volume; Stein, 2000). Indeed, part of what Beck and Beck-Gernsheim mean by "institutionalized individualization" is a historical, political, and legal situation in which institutional structures are conceptualized around individual rights and duties and not around the interests of collectivities. The decline of unions as a source of collective support is a symptom of institutionalized individualism as it intersects with neoliberalism.

An important aspect of second modernity that simultaneously has existential, psychological, and social ramifications is what Beck (1999) refers to as "risk society." In his model, first modernity, the period of industrialization, was marked by the sense that society could calculate and insure against risks by socializing and collectivizing them – for example, workmen's compensation and social security. Second modernity, on the other hand, is marked by the unforeseen risks and "manufactured uncertainties" produced by first modernity, for example, nuclear threat, genetic engineering, and ecological destruction. These dangers cannot be insured against and many of them threaten not just local populations but the whole world. To live in "risk society" we have to be able to keep in the background of consciousness our awareness of the potential disasters that could occur; yet we must also be able to face and deal with those dangers that, if denied or only selectively attended to, could destroy all life as we know it.

Risk society encompasses both the manufactured uncertainties produced by first modernity and the precarious corporate work world described by Sennett. Risk society and institutionalized individualization have been intensified by the dominance of neoliberal economic and political principles, which devalue dependency and deny the ways in which we are interdependent (see chapters in Section III; Hollander, 2017; Layton, 2014a). Neoliberalism requires individuals to be enterprising selves in competition with other enterprising selves (du Gay, 2004; Rose, 1989). Neoliberalism's offloading of formerly public responsibilities onto individuals,

which began with the Reagan "revolution" against "big government," contributes to an institutionalized individualization that is primarily individualistic – and thus contributes to the creation of precarious selves (Peltz, 2005; Rustin, 2014).

## The psychological requirements of institutionalized individualization

The loss of traditional anchors and the conditions of a "multi-option" society produce "reflexive" subjects, like my patient, who draw on constantly changing and contradictory expert knowledge that they, in turn, shape as they create their individual life narratives (Giddens, 1991, pp. 14–15). In late modernity, Giddens asserts, the question "how shall I live?" has to be answered daily (p. 14). He argues that if the hysterics of Freud's day experienced symptoms of a sexually repressive society, the self-hating, self-punishing patient of today expresses symptoms of a society in which the coherence of the self and trust in abstract systems are absolutely necessary to function – because you are on your own in both positive and negative ways. The sociologists of late modernity well describe the fine line we all walk between successful individuation and complete breakdown. As Beck and Beck-Gernsheim assert, "Depending on the economic situation, educational qualifications, stage of life, family situation, colleagues – [the do-it-yourself biography] can easily turn into a 'breakdown biography'" (2002, p. 7). If individuals are to thrive in the conditions prevalent in second modernity or risk society, that is, if individuals are to avoid breakdown, they need to rely more on inner psychological resources than on the social surround.

Echoing Erikson (1959) and British Independents, Giddens (1991) suggests that to avoid "breakdown," one must establish "basic trust," which, in turn, depends on good-enough early attachments that promote "ontological security." The resulting "protective cocoon" enables one later to have enough trust in abstract systems to function without tremendous anxiety (which also requires bracketing much of what we know, e.g., the threat of "an ending to everything," Giddens, p. 183). But it seems to me Giddens' own work suggests that the constructs "basic trust" and "secure attachment," not to mention other contemporary psychoanalytic mainstays such as "multiple selves," have themselves arisen from a need to make sense of the social realities of second modernity – they are not timeless universal

truths describing subjectivity. Rather, they describe what becomes necessary psychologically to navigate modern life. To develop basic trust, for
example, attachment and other dependency needs must be attended to,
precisely the domains of post-war psychoanalytic "discovery" that have
so influenced the development of relational theory (Young-Bruehl, 2011).
The literatures on risk and on institutionalized individualization suggest
to me that it is no accident that many post-war analytic theorists have
found the need for safety and security to be a more compelling explanation of what motivates human behavior than sex and aggression. Nor is
it any wonder that, at the very moment in which our collective containers began to abandon us (Hollander and Gutwill, 2006; Peltz, 2005; see
Chapter 12), that is, the moment when neoliberal economics and ideology,
with their relentless attack on the caretaking functions of big government,
became more pervasive (the late 1970s to the present), analytic theories
foregrounding attachment, dependency, and vulnerability, holding and
containment began to feel so existentially relevant and "true."

## Reflexivity, risk, and the pure relationship

In a world of risk, detraditionalization, and contradictory expert knowledge
claims, the capacity to depend on intimate relations crucially replaces the
capacity reliably to depend on social holding environments. Indeed, one
of the few anchors against existential anxiety available in contemporary
life lies in what Giddens calls "the pure relationship" (1991, pp. 88–98).
By pure he means that nothing extrinsic keeps such relationships in place
(as did, for example, arranged marriages or religious beliefs). For the most
part, in the contemporary West, friendships and love relationships are held
together largely by psychological gratifications, the "fulfillment of inner
needs" (Beck and Beck-Gernsheim, p. 71). Thus, the pure relationship,
like the reality that makes it feel so necessary, is itself precarious: since little anchors it but the emotional and psychological satisfactions it brings to
the partners, it is constantly subject to question and to possible dissolution:
is this right for me? Am I happy? Such questions simply were not asked
in earlier eras – even as recently as the 1950s – and are still not asked in
many cultures. The way we answer those questions in the West is highly
influenced by what experts of all kinds write and say (Layton, 2013c;
Rose, 1989). But the increasing need to have a certain kind of relationship ground us itself creates new definitions of intimacy, new demands,

and new problems. Some of the principles of relational theory are in fact consonant with what Giddens claims is required for pure relationships to function well, for example, the openness to the truth of each other's perspective and the vulnerability necessary to establish trust. Indeed, the precariousness of the pure relationship and the pressures of individualization are alleviated by the stability and consistency of the (paid for) therapeutic relationship (see Hoffman, 1998, on the dark side of the analytic frame).

Thus, the conditions of late modernity create particular ways of being human, particular kinds of attachments and attachment needs, particular human struggles, and particular responses to them. Among these responses is the relational analytic practice that has been elaborated in the past 25 years. Relational psychoanalytic theory, influenced by attachment theories, interpersonal theories, the British independent tradition (with its influences from Ferenczi), and self psychology, all of which are concerned with deficits in environmental care, has, I am arguing, developed in tandem with the development of the particular kind of subject demanded by the social forces of institutionalized individualization and risk society. Our work enhances capacities for reflexivity, for determining what for each individual the good life might be. We work to keep the do-it-yourself biography from becoming a breakdown biography. In many ways, too, relational theory and practice counter institutionalized individualization's and neoliberalism's devaluation and denial of dependency and mutual interdependence. At the same time, however, like most analytic theories, relational theory and technique, while making a space in its journals for political critique, tends to collude with institutionalized individualization's demand to neglect the collective components of subjectivity. One of the features that Stern (2013) recently pointed to as distinguishing interpersonal/relational field theories from Bionian field theories was the former's belief that "it isn't possible to be uninvolved in the meanings and ideologies of the world at large, even while you are inside the psychoanalytic session," and its belief "that it is possible to have an impact on the reality of the world and not just on the inner world" (pp. 679–680). Yet, much relational theory and practice does not take into account the impact of the meanings and ideologies of the world at large. Thus, while recognizing that most psychoanalytic theories separate the psychic from the social, I address my critique specifically to relational theory – precisely because its own assumptions challenge that separation. I now turn, then, to consider how enlarging the frame to take into account unconscious and

Counter argument is that absence → have to continually
a flesh leaves 'natural attitude'... revise / search cultural
argue is in communities! assumptions in self and
Relational theory in context 65 theory...

[to whom, not in project]

conscious collective identifications and power differentials can lead to an
expansion of relational technique, one that I feel is necessary to contest the
psychological damage wrought by cultural hierarchies, neoliberal versions
of individualism, and institutionalized individualization.

⊛ not challenging the frame, but filling out the frame

## Notes toward a socio-cultural expansion of relational technique

Relational clinicians have contributed greatly to re-thinking questions of
technique and drawing out the technical implications of our theories. Our
roots in interpersonal ideas about analyst-patient interaction, Ferenczi's
(1949) thoughts about professional hypocrisy, Winnicottian ideas on holding (e.g., 1965) have led to respect for, as Mitchell (1988, 1997) put it,
the varieties of interaction and their effect on treatment. Relational theorists have deconstructed the authority of the analyst, our particular form
of expertise, emphasizing its ironic and dark sides (Hoffman, 1998, 2005);
we have explored mutuality and asymmetry (Aron, 1996; Mitchell, 1988)
and we have offered profound work on how the analyst's vulnerability and
fallibility implicate us in enactments (Altman, 2000; Cooper, 2000; Grand,
2007, 2013; Hirsch, 2008; Layton, 2006a, 2006b, 2009; Levenson, 1972,
1983; Maroda, 1999; Slochower, 2003; Suchet, 2004, 2010, and others
too numerous to mention). We have elaborated numerous ways of thinking about enactments, along with some technical ideas for recognizing
them and disengaging from them (Benjamin, 2004, 2009; Davies, 2004;
Stern, 1997, 2010); in this work, the emphasis on dissociation has been
crucial (Bromberg, 2001; Davies and Frawley, 1994; Stern, 1997, 2010).
We have questioned analytic dogma around neutrality and recognized the
therapist's role in what has traditionally been understood as the patient's
resistance (Gerson, 1996; Stein, 2005). Hoffman (2009) has perhaps most
persuasively examined and re-valued the role of suggestion, arguing that
we ought to take an active role in battling our patients' bad introjects.

Those of us committed to thinking about cultural power differentials
and their effects on treatment have been tremendously influenced by all
of these theoretical and technical developments. To instances of enactment, we have added the interactional effects of a socially constructed
and relational unconscious (Altman, 2000; Bodnar, 2004; Bonovitz, 2005;
Botticelli, 2012; Dimen, 2003; the authors in Dimen, 2011; Grand, 2007,
2013; Gump, 2010; Guralnik and Simeon, 2010; Harris, 2005, 2011, 2012;

Hartman, 2005; Layton et al., 2006; Layton, 1998, 2002, 2004c, 2006a; Leary, 1997a, 1997b, 2000, 2012; Straker, 2006; Suchet, 2004, 2010). Andrew Samuels (1993, 2001) has proposed techniques for unearthing what he understands to be an important aspect of development, urging us to take account of our patients' political development. Crucial to the ethic I hope to elaborate is Benjamin's (2004, 2009, 2017) idea of the acknowledgment of harm done, an ethical form of self-disclosure. I consider this to be one of the most important innovations in technique in the relational canon.

In 2014, I began teaching a course in comparative technique. I inherited a syllabus from the previous teachers, and, only at the end of the course did I realize that, as is usual in courses that aren't specifically devoted to culture or gender or sexuality or race, there was not one paper on the syllabus that reflected anything cultural. Determined to add papers to the syllabus that take culture into account, I was struck by a short paper by Rozmarin (2014) written at the height of the Israel-Gaza summer, 2014 war. Here, Rozmarin makes the absolutely correct claim that most analysts have neglected to attend to the collective dimensions of subjectivity. It is in this way perhaps that we most clearly collude with institutionalized individualization and the culture of neoliberalism, particularly when we frame socially-generated pathologies (e.g., racism) in terms of intrapsychic pathology (see Eng and Han, 2002).

Rozmarin writes that his Israeli expatriate patients, when speaking about a war in which they feel deeply and intimately implicated, "are not only enacting personal dramas, although they invariably do. They are also wondering, sometimes desperately, how one ought to live in this world as one of many, as a social, ethical being with collective identities" (p. 1). One thing that struck me deeply in reading this was a conviction that, in fact, all patients, at all times, wonder how to live in the world as one of many, as social and ethical beings with collective identities. At times of war, as Rozmarin says, the wondering is explicit. But what about at other times? Are collective identities, our implication in our own and others' suffering, our quest to be ethical beings, not operating all the time? Might it be the case that an absence of such wondering would reflect not the state of nature but rather something about the way our culture radically separates the individual from the social?

Rozmarin goes on to say that when his patients talk about the war, they are also "talking about belonging and alienation, about conforming and resisting, about our place in a collective that has its own history and conflicts, and anxieties and madness" (p. 2). As he says, "We should be able to address this register of human experience in our work." But how? Rozmarin goes on to talk about the effects of ideology on collective identities and how to make those effects conscious, and I think that here he begins to adumbrate the kind of technical innovation that I have in mind.

Rozmarin notes that, in his experience, because of an "inherent need of and therefore surrender to collectively, politically and ideologically generated narratives," "questioning collective identifications is often harder, more troubling, than doing so in the context of one's relations with one's family" (p. 2) (see, also, Rozmarin, 2009, which emphasizes the damaging effects of collective identities and argues that our job is to resist colluding with them when they are damaging). I agree, although I do not see the two, collective and individual, as mutually exclusive. They may well *appear* to be mutually exclusive, but that appearance itself is an effect of ideology. For one thing, those of us in the U.S. who were born into an era of institutionalized individualization are not even aware of our collective identifications until there is some threat to them (see Volkan, 2004, on conditions in which large-group identity becomes salient, and Aviram, 2009, on prejudice and the large-group mind). This works in the service of neoliberalism's denial of the ways we are mutually implicated in each other's lives and histories. Rozmarin suggests that it may be questionable to challenge people on unconscious ways in which their identity has been organized, noting (ironically), "After all, it is not my role to unsettle what makes my patients feel secure" (p. 3). Actually, that is precisely our role, isn't it? Why do we hesitate to recognize that it is just as much our role to unsettle unconscious facilitating and/or defensive collective identities as it is to unsettle individual identity commitments that might be blinding us to the psychologically damaging ideological cultural work that they are doing?

Within the relational canon (broad tent relational), there has been some important theorizing about collective identities and how they impact treatment. For instance, work on the intergenerational transmission of trauma often addresses collective identity. Davoine and Gaudillière (2004) argue that ruptures in what they call the social link (following Lacan), war, for example, produce quests for restoration of trust that require analysts to give something of themselves, the missing piece of "terra cotta" that will restore trust in a moral social order. Technical suggestions include a deep engagement with both one's own and the patient's social history, for they suggest that there will inevitably be a way in which the two histories intertwine and that the therapist will somehow need to make that known to the patient. To that end, Gaudillière (2012) writes that if he dreams about a patient, he will tell the patient the dream. He insists that the dream is a co-construction of their unconscious process and belongs as much to the patient as to himself. For Davoine and Gaudillière, the small histories revealed in their patients' fragmented narratives and symptoms are inextricably intertwined with the BIG History in which they and their ancestors lived their lives. Thus, intergenerational transmission of traumas cannot be understood or treated without comprehending (and resonating with affectively) the particular ruptures in the social link, in history, that have produced them.

Relational theorists (small tent) who write about intergenerational transmission of trauma have offered gripping narratives of the ways that the conflicting collective identities of patient and analyst often come to the fore in clinical enactments. Like Davoine and Gaudillière, Altman (2000); Bodnar (2004); Gentile (2013, 2017); Grand (2000, 2007, 2013, 2014); Hartman (2005); Leary (1997a, 1997b, 2000); Suchet (2004, 2010), and others, make it clear that analysts need to immerse themselves in learn-ing about the intergenerational cultural history of their patients and themselves in order to understand and find their way out of enactments. Grand, all of whose work integrates the social being that lies at the core of psychic exploration, focuses often on the body clues emerging in the analyst, clues that can lead to a more conscious appreciation of her own unconscious collective identifications. A striking example is her account of the case in which she came to recognize that her patient was living a collective identity with collective commitments that stood in stark contrast to the individualized ethos of psychoanalytic treatment (Grand, 2013). The patient was asking Grand precisely the question that I am addressing here: does psychoanalysis have any way of speaking to the collective self? As Grand notes (private communication), patients are often the ones who pose the very questions that psychoanalytic theory and technique must next address.

Guralnik and Simeon (2010) persuasively argue that the symptoms many of us treat (in their case, depersonalization) are disorders produced by the disparity between our longings for recognition and our interpellation by the discourses of a social order that recognizes only what conforms to its norms. They theorize that we are humiliated by our dependence on recognition from a social order that requires us to yield on our own sense of reality (see my case vignette in Chapter 3). Further, they recognize that psychoanalysts are, and are perceived by their patients as being, agents of interpellation; thus, analysts are always present as potential sources of shame. Technically, Guralnik and Simeon identify moments of counter-transferential confusions and ruptures, particularly ones involving shame, as moments that signal "the presence of mixed and seductive transmissions from the *great big hegemony*" (p. 410), that which dislocates the patient from his/her reality and to which patients unconsciously and repeatedly succumb. They interpret in a frame that enables their patients to under-stand how their symptoms derive from their social context, how socially allowable discourses are calling into question the patient's counterhegem-onic personhood.

Gentile (2017) recognizes that taking account of, and making ourselves accountable for, our cultural positions and positions of power in relation to those of our patients, affects even such a common technical choice as how, in any given moment, we offer our empathic attunement. Describing work with a Latina patient who was lovingly attached to a father who had sexu-ally abused her, Gentile, aware of the father's own complicated history of racial and gender oppression as well as of her own privileged position of whiteness, writes, "Integral to this [holding space for multiple identifica-tions] was sustaining a vigilant awareness of how, when, where I deployed empathy, the power based roots of it, and to what ends" (p. 179). What strikes me as crucially important in such theorizing is the idea that the more aware we become of our own and our patients' cultural embedded-ness and collective histories of privilege and oppression, the less likely we are to pathologize our patients' intimate others in the rather concrete and uncomplicated ways we often do. Gentile argues that the way that she responds to her patient must take into account the fact that the patient's father's psyche, too, was formed within a history of racial and gender oppression; Gentile's own white privilege had to be spoken as well.

Such self-disclosures have played an important role in the technical tool-kit of those relational theorists engaged in investigating the ways that the ideological underpinnings of collective identifications are enacted in the clinic. One of Bodnar's (2004) vignettes with an African American patient culminates in Bodnar disclosing her envy of her patient's beauty – which opens up the treatment to the unconscious racial assumptions of both patient and analyst. The patient could not imagine a white person being envious of a black person, and yet, it became clear that she had been unconsciously engaged in trying to prove that her analyst was racist (that is, that she could not possibly envy the patient's beauty) by often attending to beauty rituals that caused her to be late for her therapy appointments. Here, collective identifications transmitted intergenerationally, bonds wrought from unconscious racism, were lived as questions of who can be beautiful.

In this case, as well, we learn that the source of an intergenerational transmission of seemingly inexplicable outbursts of anger lies in an emotionally abusive ancestor whose rageful strictness toward his children emerged in good measure from his need to protect his children from the greater abuses likely to befall them at the hands of Jim Crow southern whites. The process of making this history conscious not only makes conscious a source of the patient's outbursts of rage, the symptom, but also locates the symptom in a depathologized collective narrative (or, rather, it relocates the pathology from the black grandfather to the white culture in which he had to make his way). I would argue that the therapeutic action here lies in re-connecting patients with their histories and restoring the broken social link in a way that counters institutionalized individualization and neoliberal denials of embeddedness. As I argued in earlier work (Layton, 2005), colluding with the separation of the individual from the cultural too often leads to producing a subjectivity that we might think of merely as a healthier version of narcissism than the version with which the patient entered treatment.

Bodnar's case suggests to me as well that we not only have to understand the historical dimension of collective identifications but also need to understand the relational field in which current identifications take place. To do this, we have to take note of the intersectionality of identifications. The beauty issue that comes up in Bodnar's case is about gender every bit as much as race, about raced ways of living gender. Intersectionality is a complex concept, but it is rendered even more complex if we think about the psychic costs entailed in inhabiting various collective identifications. My concept of normative unconscious processes rests on a belief that those versions of collective identity that garner social approval often require that we split off and project various ways of being human, ways of loving, ways of being in our bodies. Cultural binaries such as male/female, black/white, straight/gay exist in hierarchical relations conditioned by cultural power differentials, and each side of the binary comes with an array of psychological attributes considered proper to it. The technical implications of being aware of how ideologically-produced binaries operate, how they require psychological splitting, entail challenging normative ideologies and revealing what options for being have been cut off by one's attachment to binary either/ors (see Aron and Starr, 2013). The challenge probably occurs most frequently when played out between patient and analyst, since the effects of projecting the unwanted, not-me ways of being are generally enacted in sadomasochistic relational scenarios (see Benjamin, 1988; Goldner, 1991).

Where commitments to binary forms of collective identities have been made, analysts can hold fluidity as a challenge to the splitting and projection that keep sadomasochistic relations to self and others in place. Thus, I would suggest that doing analytic work requires understanding the effects on subjectivity of normative and counter-normative ideologies. We need to be mindful of how our identifications and disidentifications are intertwined with hierarchies of class, race, gender, sexuality, and nation – and how these are experienced psychologically in ways of being and loving that are differentially valued and are often lived via splitting and projection. As Gentile (2017) argues, making power relations and cultural hierarchies of oppression explicit in our work produces new possibilities for relating that contest the damaging structures of institutionalized individualization and neoliberal forms of individualism.

In a vignette first reported in Layton, 2014b, I described a clinical situation that highlights how technical choices can either contest or reproduce a neoliberal individualism. A middle-class white female patient of mine had become ashamed of what she felt family members condemned as too much desire for attention. When I began seeing her, she was in fact quite constricted. Sometime during our work together I moved into a home office, which I had decorated in higher style than the office I had been renting. In our first meeting in the new office, the theme of entitlement and selfishness arose. The patient spoke about having just read Barbara Ehrenreich's (2001) book, *Nickel and Dimed*, and said she felt guilty and indulgent about having hired a maid for the first time. I said, "It's hard to acknowledge that you're privileged." She agreed and held out her hands to show me her nails. She said, "I get my nails done, I have a therapist in Brookline in a place like this." My own privilege having been invoked, I think I felt anxious and vulnerable and did not know what to do with the deserved shame evoked by the harm done by privilege: hers, mine, and ours. I remember having tried to normalize the privilege, saying something like, "You don't have to feel guilty for having nice things." I think this comment closed down something the patient was trying to say, something that went against the neoliberal grain because it attempted to connect her fortune to the misfortune of others. My first comment had kept the question of privilege open; the second one closed it down. There was  something significant to explore here about our mutual discomfort about our privilege and its connection to the lack of privilege all around us, and I would suggest that normalizing privilege is perhaps a neoliberalizing practice that keeps class inequality in place. This example suggests that technical choices that focus on the individual as separate from the social are quite different from those that focus on the individual as psychosocial.

In conclusion, I would argue that relational work needs to take account not only of the power differentials of race, class, gender, and sexuality, but also of the way that institutionalized individualization has become articulated with neoliberalism and marks conscious and unconscious versions of subjectivity. I believe that changing the frame of treatment in a way that addresses conscious and unconscious social and collective aspects of identity/identifications demands a re-thinking of relational technique, and I hope here to have begun to adumbrate some possible directions this re-thinking might take.

## Note

* Used with permission. Layton, L. (2013b) Dialectical constructivism in historical context: Expertise and the subject of late modernity. *Psychoanalytic Dialogues* 23(3): 271–286, and Layton, L. (2018) Relational theory in socio-historical context: Implications for technique. In Aron, L., Grand, S. and Slochower, J. (eds.) *De-Idealizing Relational Theory*. New York, NY: Routledge, pp. 209–234.

# Chapter 6

# Psychoanalysis and politics

Historicizing subjectivity[*]

In a recent article, Elisabeth Young-Bruehl (2011) writes about various attempts that have been made to synthesize psychoanalysis and political progressivism since Freud. The story Young-Bruehl tells is one version of how to understand the relation between subjectivity and modernization in the Western world, a view that focuses squarely on a universal vision of what humans need in order to thrive and on countering all forms of social exclusion. In this chapter, I shall place Young-Bruehl's historiography in juxtaposition to two other very different stories about the history of subjectivity and modernity. These versions of history do not talk about what humans need. Instead, they tell a story about how social changes and social agendas produce individuals whose needs and character emerge from what it takes to thrive in the particular social and political conditions of Western modernity (conditions they do not necessarily equate with "democracy"). The first such version is proffered by theorists of "risk society" and "institutionalized individualization" (see Chapter 5; Beck, 1999; Beck and Beck-Gernsheim, 2002), who argue that post-war modernity is primarily characterized by the continual disembedding of subjects from any kind of "tradition" to which they might have recourse when trying to ground their decisions about how they ought to live. The second derives from the work of Foucault and focuses on the role psychological sciences have played in what Rose (1989) has called "governing the soul," an increased interference by experts in the conduct of the daily private lives of families and individuals (with particular focus on subjectivities produced by welfare states). More recently, theorists in this same Foucaultian tradition have pointed to a historical shift away from the kind of welfare state subjective practices Rose discussed. These authors, trying to understand neoliberal versions of subjectivity, have highlighted cultural and political demands on subjects to adopt practices that will enable them to become the "enterprising" selves necessary for functioning well in neoliberal social and economic conditions (see, for example, du Gay, 2004; Binkley, 2009). These latter writings are not psychoanalytic, but I draw on them to elaborate my own psychoanalytic understanding of relations among social character, historical conditions in the contemporary West, and what humans might need to thrive. I juxtapose these different perspectives on our current situation in the West in order to raise questions about what humans need, about what psychoanalysis might contribute to the making of a more politically progressive world, and about the ways in which contemporary psychoanalytic discourse itself is and is not progressive.

## Young-Bruehl

In her article, "Psychoanalysis and Social Democracy," Elisabeth Young-Bruehl (2011) constructs a narrative about the historical relations between psychoanalysis and post-WWII social democracy (with particular focus on the U.K.). Shaping this narrative is her view of the two most important post-war developments in left-wing psychoanalytic theory. The first is a realm of instinct theory that, she argues, Freud left undertheorized once having committed himself to the dual instinct theory of life and death: the ego-instincts, which include dependency needs, attachment needs, needs for love, care, and security. Post-war U.K. attachment theorists and British independents are the heroes of Young-Bruehl's narrative, for they not only brought to the fore the importance of such needs, they also influenced social democratic policy. In so doing, these analysts contributed to what Young-Bruehl calls the general principle psychoanalysis and political progressives both came to champion: "human beings cannot live well or happily in their families or communities or political arrangements unless these do not thwart their ego instincts" (p. 192).

The second psychoanalytic realm of theory to which Young-Bruehl draws attention is characterology, a field to which Freud contributed but which found its deepest elaborations in the work of left-wing analysts and theorists such as Reich, the Frankfurt School, and others concerned with problems of social inclusion and exclusion (problems that Young-Bruehl places under the umbrella term of "prejudice"). The neglect of the ego instincts again enters the narrative in her claim that Freudian characterologists were limited by a sole focus on sexual instincts. The post-war characterologists, on the other hand,

> convinced postwar pragmatic socialists that they needed to focus their attention not just on class conflict and class struggle, but on all forms of social and political exclusion as well as production of inequality – on all forms of prejudice considered as a social disease. Social democracy came to mean, in this sense, maximally inclusionary democracy, and the European social democrats designed programs for bringing excluded peoples into citizenship and into the welfare states.
>
> (Young-Bruehl, 2011, p. 193)

Young-Bruehl goes on to discuss theorists who focus on dominant types of character within a society (for example, Adorno et al., 1950, and the authoritarian personality), as well as on the intergenerational transmission of dominant character types. Her narrative ends with the suggestion that the two realms, ego-instincts and characterology, need to be thought together. As she puts it, ego instinct theory tells you what humans need and characterology focuses politics on "equality and maximal inclusion of once-excluded groups, on human rights, and on political structures moving beyond nation-states and exclusionary sovereignty" (p. 194). Young-Bruehl's own life work was in fact dedicated to the elucidation of different kinds of prejudices and the character types most closely associated with each kind. Her final work (2012) took up a prejudice she felt she had overlooked in her earlier work (Young-Bruehl, 1996), one closely connected to the thwarting of ego-instincts: the prejudice against children.

## Alternate histories of modernity and subjectivity

### (a) Institutionalized individualization

What strikes me about Young-Bruehl's historiography is how different it is from two other stories about subjectivity and the politics of modernity that I had drawn on in a paper in which I had sought to understand why relational analytic theory has become a dominant psychoanalytic force in the U.S. In this paper (Chapter 5), I looked at the socio-historic changes in subjectivity and intersubjectivity to which, I argued, relational analytic theory has been a response.

Many contemporary sociologists, for example, Beck (1999), Beck and Beck-Gernsheim (2002), and Giddens (1991), have, with slightly different emphases, focused their historiography of modernity and subjectivity in the West on the increasing disembedding from tradition of post-war subjects and the role played by experts in supporting the demand that subjects create themselves in the absence of socially sanctioned and agreed-upon traditions on which they might depend. Beck (1999) characterized the post-WWII West as "second modernity," a condition prominently characterized by the kinds of "risk" against which populations cannot insure themselves. Beck describes many of these risks as the "manufactured uncertainties" produced by first modernity (e.g., the threat of nuclear holocaust, environmental destruction). As I noted in the previous chapter, Beck and Beck-Gernsheim (2002) use the term "institutionalized individualization" to describe a historical, political, and legal situation in which institutional structures are conceptualized around individual rights and duties and not around the interests of collectivities. Without recourse to tradition, and subject to a range of contradictory and ever-changing expert opinion, increasingly more people, they argue, are in the position of daily having to question how best to live their lives. The more enfranchised the segment of the population, the more options are available; but given the shift away from public responsibility for the welfare of populations that has taken place in many Western countries in the past 30 years, nearly everyone has found themselves left on their own to find their way. The condition of institutionalized individualization in risk society means, on the subjective level, that more and more people can – and must – create what these theorists call "do-it-yourself biographies" that constantly teeter on the edge of becoming biographies of nervous and other forms of breakdown.

Theorists of institutionalized individualization suggest that, in a world without traditional anchors, the only thing that anchors many of us is our intimate relationships. Giddens (1991) speaks of the "pure relationship," by which he means one not held together by any moral, religious, or social tradition but rather by whether or not the relationship meets the psychological needs of its participants. Individualization means, then, for privileged individuals, an ability and a demand constantly to reflect upon whether or not a career or a relationship is making them happy, bringing personal fulfillment, and if not, whether or not they should stay in it. Beck-Gernsheim (in Beck and Beck-Gernsheim, 2002, Ch. 5, n. 94, p. 80) cites as a prime example of this ethos the Fritz Perls motto that became so popular in the 1960s:

> I do my thing and you do your thing . . . I am not in this world to live up to your expectations, and you are not in this world to live up to mine. You are you and I am I; if by chance we find each other, it's beautiful. If not, it can't be helped.

The individualization and risk society literature suggests different historical reasons from those on which Young-Bruehl relies to explain a shift in psychoanalytic theory regarding what lies at the heart of human motivation. Rather than positing, as she does, that psychoanalysts were crucial in recognizing what humans need, these theories would likely suggest that the shift in psychoanalytic theory away from seeing sex and aggression as primary motivators of human desire toward, instead, seeing needs for safety and security as primary, is a function of living in an increasingly insecure world in which individuals have little to rely on besides their own psychic fortitude and, perhaps, intimate relations. This literature suggests that the ego instincts central to Young-Bruehl's account might have become more important to tend to in the post-war period because, even in the welfare state, institutionalized individualization proceeded apace – and because, as Giddens (1991) suggests, late modernity is characterized by abstract systems that require of individuals a solid capacity for basic trust. Thus, if individuals are to thrive in these conditions, that is, avoid breakdown, they need to rely more on inner psychological resources than on the social surround. To develop basic trust, for example, attachment and other dependency needs must be attended to. In a world of risk, detraditionalization, and contradictory expert knowledge claims, the capacity to depend on intimate relations crucially replaces the capacity reliably to depend on social holding environments. Thus, post-war social conditions that foster individualization are progressive in some ways and in some ways not. One implication is that attending to attachment and dependency needs might not be the *sine qua non* of a progressive politics or a progressive psychoanalysis. Young-Bruehl's stance in favor of attending to ego instincts is perhaps only progressive in welfare state conditions. Even that argument is challenged by the following historicization of subjectivity.

## (b) Governmentality

The governmentality literature is influenced by the work of Foucault on genealogies of subject positions and techniques of governance and normalization (see, for example, Foucault, 1978, 1980). As elaborated by Rose (1989), one clear line in the history of Western institutions from the nineteenth century on is an increasing demand for self-surveillance and self-control. Contrary to the individualization theorists, Rose and others argue that normalization techniques arose concurrently with industrialization and urbanization in order to maximize opportunity for the middle class and minimize the threat to the middle class of the poor and working-class masses congregating in cities. Individualization, according to Rose, means the production not just of individuals, but of knowable individuals.

In the Foucaultian paradigm, "the disciplines 'make' individuals by means of some rather simple technical procedures" (Rose, 1989, p. 135). Central to this paradigm are "regimes of visibility": where people gather *en masse*, they can be observed (e.g., in the school or the workplace, with the model being Jeremy Bentham's eighteenth-century design for penal institutions, the Panopticon). Regimes of visibility allow for institutions to operate according to a regulation of detail; a grid of codeability of personal attributes emerges:

> They act as norms, enabling the previously aleatory and unpredictable complexities of human conduct to be charted and judged in terms of conformity and deviation, to be coded and compared, ranked and measured.
>
> (pp. 135–136)

The phenomenal world becomes normalized, "that is to say, thought in terms of its coincidences and differences from values deemed normal" (Rose, 1989, p. 136).

Given this theoretical backdrop, Rose (1989) finds, in the British welfare state, an increased social regulation of subjects. He argues that this was in no small measure accomplished by the intrusion of psychological and other experts into the private sphere practices of family life and the socialization of children. Winnicott's radio chats and childcare manuals come in for special censure, because, according to Rose, Winnicott's discourse masterfully masked experts' techniques of normalization beneath a language about what is "natural" for a mother to feel and do. For example, Winnicott tells mothers that feeding is a natural act of love at the same time that he gives them advice about how to perform this natural act. Rose writes,

> on the one hand, in the attachment discourse, the family tie appears as 'natural'; on the other parents can only carry out their task effectively when educated, supplemented, and in the last instance supplemented by psychologically trained professionals.
>
> (Rose, 1989, p. 177)

For Rose, a mother's desire for a hygienic home and healthy children, and parents' conviction that love is essential to raising a normal child, are not natural convictions and desires but rather are socially produced in order to fit subjective desire with institutional requirements.

## Comparing historiographies

In Rose's argument that "love" became thought of as the element that would produce normal children in the two decades after WWII we find a historiography that is diametrically opposed to the ones offered by both the individualization theorists and by Young-Bruehl. Where Beck, Beck-Gernsheim, and Giddens suggest that an increasing "disembedding from tradition" promotes individual autonomy and particular kinds of intimate relationships, Foucaultian theorists argue that experts and their expertise have *become* the new tradition. In this view, post-war subjects feel free and yet are increasingly regulated by regimes of what is considered to be "normal":

> The representations of motherhood, fatherhood, family life, and parental conduct generated by expertise were to infuse and shape the personal investments of individuals, the ways in which they formed, regulated and evaluated their lives, their actions, and their goals.
>
> (Rose, 1989, p. 132)

In Young-Bruehl's account, Winnicott and others in the independent psychoanalytic tradition developed their theory, practice, and public policy in response to the trauma, devastation, and abandonments of WWI and II.

Rose, on the contrary, places Winnicott's work in the context of a long history of expertise, the primary effect of which is to abet and normalize a self-regulation designed to bring the individual into harmony with the culture's institutions – an effect Rose describes as "governing the soul."

In suggesting that an important element in the history of Western modernity has been the kind of normalization that supports prejudices, the governmentality literature challenges both Young-Bruehl's thesis as well as her historiography. This literature raises several important questions: are the positions and practices that define the good and the healthy precisely those that work in the service of regulating the poor or unruly, those that normalize and optimize middle-class opportunity? Are they practices that fit subjects for a certain kind of society, one in which alternative practices are pathologized? As Cushman (2019) argues, the discipline of psychology has tended to address and treat the problems society creates in a way that normalizes and reproduces them (for example, a culture that produces the conditions for prejudice to thrive also spawns psychological theories and practices that treat prejudice as a pathology and not as an effect of social and political arrangements).

Such questions and arguments perhaps challenge Young-Bruehl's assertions that humans need a certain kind of care to thrive and to be more resistant to prejudices. But Rose skirts the question central to Young-Bruehl's project: are there basic human needs that must be met for a democratic society to exist? If so, is there an important role for psychoanalysts to play in policy formation? Are psychoanalysts doomed simply to be lackeys of state and corporate power or might they offer a counter-discourse to contemporary social and political discourses?

## Staking a claim

I write and think in a relational analytic tradition that is very much influenced by both the Budapest psychoanalytic school of Ferenczi and Balint and the British Independent tradition on which Young-Bruehl bases her analysis. Yet, at the same time, my work differs from Young-Bruehl's, particularly in our understandings of social character. In this domain, I have been more influenced by the Frankfurt School and its heirs than by Freudian notions of character. From the 1980s on, I have written, for example, about the relation between capitalism and narcissistic personality. Much of my work is related directly to the clinic and focuses on how the normalizing practices of both the psychoanalytic field and of class, race, sex, and gender identity production are replicated in unconscious collusions between patient and therapist. But, like Young-Bruehl, I also assume in my work that humans need reliable caretaking to thrive and to be able to negotiate among their dependency needs, needs for self-assertion, and needs for recognition. In different ways, both the individualization literature and the governmentality literature suggest that such negotiations are not basic to being human but are rather a product of a particular historical formation. For example, as the Foucaultian tradition moves into researching post-welfare state subjectivities, we find arguments about how subjects now have to wrestle with the demands of neoliberalism. Binkley (2009) argues that in order to produce the "enterprising" selves necessary to function in a world in which responsibilities for the population's welfare have shifted from the public sphere onto the individual, people have to disidentify with the practices that had made them comfortable with dependency on the state (and dependency in general) and identify instead with practices that enable them to thrive in neoliberal free market and sociopolitical conditions. Looking at self-help books, the field of coaching, and positive psychology, Binkley (2011a, 2011b) persuasively identifies some of the practices that experts encourage people to adopt – and most of them work in the service of demonizing dependency and interdependence. While I find this work quite valuable, I think about these same phenomena somewhat differently. In my view, agentic strivings and strivings for connection are likely universal and basic to being human, but I believe such strivings are negotiated quite differently depending on prevailing norms for what a "proper" human in a particular time and place needs to do to get love, social recognition, and a sense of belonging.

From my 1990's papers on gender to recent papers on neoliberal subjectivities (see Section III), central to my work has been the effects of the cultural repudiation of what Young-Bruehl includes under ego instincts (most of which have been historically associated with femininity). I concur with Young-Bruehl that the classical psychoanalytic literature and the ego-psychological literature that was dominant in the U.S. until recently generally valued most highly an autonomy based in separation from the other and denial of or overcoming of dependence.

This way of conceptualizing an autonomy that splits off attachment needs connects quite directly with characterology, and so, like Young-Bruehl, I believe that the thwarting of "ego instincts" does indeed produce certain kinds of character. But, unlike Young-Bruehl's version of characterology, which is rooted in Freudian character types and the defenses particular to each type, I focus on the way character is formed by economic and socio-historical conditions of inequality and the intergenerational transmission of the effects of inequality. More particularly, character, in my view, emerges in part from the social possibilities for negotiating autonomy and dependence that are available and/or denied to particular social groups, and with the way that inequalities of race, gender, class, and sexuality inform practices that inflict humiliations and other psychological damage. In any culture or subculture, some ways of being and acting are recognized as "proper" by the social groups and families to which one wants to belong and be loved by, and some "improper." What is unrecognized or felt to be improper is often split off. Disavowed "not-me" states have to be repeatedly defended against in identity performances and relational enactments that affirm the norm that caused psychic pain in the first place. Various kinds of character – or versions of subjectivity – or versions of living dependency and autonomy – are produced and sustained by these unconscious repetitions that I refer to as normative unconscious processes.

An example: in my early work on gender (Layton, 1998/2004), I argued that the dominant ideals and ideologies of masculinity and femininity in the post-war U.S. bred two subtypes of narcissism, each marked by cultural demands to split off some part of what it is to be human. Heterosexual masculinity, I argued (along with many other feminists), was marked by a self-centred version of autonomy produced by a denial of attachment needs and other ego instincts discussed previously. The ideal of femininity was marked by a repudiation of autonomous strivings, which often led, in practice, to hostile versions of dependency and severe conflicts over self-assertion. Different groups are subject to different forms of narcissistic wounding, but what gets split off and either dissociated or, as a Freudian might see it, repressed, are human needs and capacities, and character issues emerge when, for example, a man comes to feel that he cannot be both masculine and dependent. In my version of characterology, the narcissistic wounds suffered, for example, in conforming to socially and historically specific ideals of masculinity produce particular defences and ways of relating (transferences and counter-transferences) that become normative. Each social group's ways of defending against its wounds tend to inflict wounds on both dominant and marginalized groups – and these processes of mutual wounding need to be studied always with reference to the particular power arrangements within which they unfold.

In more recent work (see Chapters 13 and 14), I, too, have tried to historicize what seems to me to be, since the Reagan and Thatcher era, an increasing general revulsion toward dependence and vulnerability. Before being conscious of "neoliberalism" as a form of governmentality, I wrote, for example, about the way that television shows of the 1990s were normalizing for middle-class women the same counter-dependent norms for subject formation that had until then prevailed for middle-class men (Layton, 2004b) – again producing a particular kind of social character with particular psychosocial defences. When dependence and interdependence are repudiated and made shameful, as they have been in the neoliberal U.S. – where the attack on the poor and vulnerable continues unabated, where social policies tear away at the containment and care offered by the welfare state, and where income inequality is at or close to historic highs – you find characteristic narcissistic defences against trauma: retaliation and withdrawal, oscillations between grandiosity and self-deprecation, devaluation and idealization, denials of difference, and the rigid drawing of boundaries between who is "in" and who is "out."

## Psychoanalysis and progressive politics

In "normalizing" dependency and interdependence as part of what it means to be human, and in critiquing versions of autonomy that deny an embeddedness in relation, contemporary psychoanalytic theory (particularly relational analytic theory and all those theories indebted to the Hungarian and British Independent traditions lauded by Young-Bruehl) offers something of a counter-discourse to hegemonic neoliberal discourses. All of the psychoanalytic theories of which I am aware certainly counter what Binkley describes as the versions of subjectivity promoted in neoliberal discourses, that is, theories and practices that have no use for looking within for understanding suffering, for thinking about an individual's problems in the context of relationships, or for any notion of unconscious process that divides the self against the self. Where psychoanalysis certainly falls short, however, is in its continued separation of the psychic from the social, its general refusal to understand what people suffer from as having something to do with societal conditions. So I do believe in the importance of Young-Bruehl's project to question and think historically about what psychoanalytic theories promote as the good. I do not think that the practices promoted by psychoanalysis are inherently democratic, precisely because of the way the social is dissociated from conceptualizations of subjectivity.

One effect of the way psychoanalysis separates the psychic and the social is that psychoanalysts today, in the U.S. at least, have little impact on public policy. But the marginalization of psychoanalysis is not the fault of psychoanalytic theory alone: it is also in no small measure due to the dominance of neoliberal discourses. Perhaps precisely because psychoanalysis has lost its hegemony and become a minority discourse, we find current trends in psychoanalysis that do connect with progressive politics, trends that likely also grew out of the progressive politics of the 1960s, a time in which many of our current theorists came of age. Among these trends I would include the radical questioning and re-thinking of the authority of the analyst and the awareness of the effect of the analyst's unconscious on treatments (e.g., Mitchell, 1997; Hoffman, 1998); re-formulations of theory that acknowledge the power inequities inherent in many social norms and that thus work to challenge power and depathologize non-normative ways of being; and a commitment, in some quarters at least, to think about the ways that politics enter the clinic (Samuels, 2001; Layton et al., 2006).

To summarize, on the one hand, in my work I draw on many psychoanalytic theorists who talk about tending to what Young-Bruehl calls "ego-instincts": Bion on containment, Winnicott on holding. And on the other, I focus on defenses like splitting and projection that arise from failures in containment and holding. As Young-Bruehl might suggest, this is where a kind of characterology comes in. But unlike the version of characterology she favors, I look at character formation more relationally. I ask if there are particular patterns of defenses, particular kinds of repetition compulsions, transferences, and counter-transferences that arise in relation to particular power arrangements, policies, cultural trends, and discourses. More broadly, I try to understand denials of the ways in which in-groups and out-groups are related, and the sado-masochistic forms of power struggle that often result from such denials (see also Scanlon and Adlam, 2008). Psychoanalysis is thus, for me, necessary to understand what might be essential to achieving a progressive democratic politics in which humans might thrive.

At the same time, drawing on the governmentality and individualization literatures, I also think about ways that therapists might unconsciously collude in sustaining neoliberal practices that favor performance and achievement over comfort with dependence, or that favor a kind of care of the self that disregards care for the collective good. Here, I see psychoanalysis as at times contributing to anti-democratic and anti-human practices. Thus, I understand psychoanalysis to be a culturally embedded discourse and practice that cannot be characterized as either uniformly democratic or anti-democratic. Rather, to be able to assess what is progressive, we have to understand each version of psychoanalytic theory in its particular historical context, and interrogate both a theory's assumptions as well as the socio-cultural uses to which it is put.

## Note

* Used with permission. Layton, L. (2013) Psychoanalysis and politics: Historicising subjectivity. *Mens Sana Monographs* 11(1): 68–81.

# Normative unconscious processes

## Reproducing cultural hierarchies of class, race, gender, and sexuality in the clinic

### Introduction to Section II: normative unconscious processes – reproducing cultural hierarchies of class, race, gender, and sexuality in the clinic

As I mentioned in my introduction to the book, until the early 1990s, with an emerging body of feminist psychoanalytic work, few social psychoanalytic thinkers had applied their post-1960s political and cultural critiques to what goes on between patient and therapist in the clinic. But, as I also mentioned, those of us who applied academic feminist, social constructivist, and poststructuralist theories to the clinic tended to apply one category at a time, and you can see this reflected in the chronology and themes of the chapters in this section. Because I taught in academia through the 1980s, 1990s, and into the 2000s, I did indeed know about and had even taught intersectional theories of identity and oppression; yet, and I think this is because I was a white middle-class clinician largely treating white middle-class patients, I only gradually began writing and thinking about race and class dynamics in the clinic when I began to think of myself as white and upper class. I was also better able to understand how different social positionings and different matrices of power operate in the clinic after other clinicians had begun to write about race and class enactments in clinical encounters (e.g., Leary, 1997a, 1997b, 2000; Altman, 2000). It was an even more gradual process to start to think about how racism operates in white-white dyads.

Chapter 7, "The psychopolitics of bisexuality," published in 2000, marks a conceptual bridge between Section I's emphasis on psychoanalytic theory and Section II's emphasis on normative unconscious processes as they unfold in the clinic. The chapter was written at a time when some prominent feminist gender theorists were conceptualizing bisexuality, a sexual position, as a gender position. I felt that, consciously or unconsciously, their work was neutralizing Freud's radical psychoanalytic view that all humans begin as bisexual, thereby turning bisexuality into a less threatening construct that proposes that each of us is both masculine and feminine. Further, much of the theory accepted as "normal" the dominant and highly questionable position that certain attributes are masculine and others feminine. At this point, I had not yet formulated the concept of normative unconscious processes. Yet, I had been aware since the mid-1990s of clinical instances in which hierarchical, binary conceptions of gender and sexuality, shared by patient and therapist, had functioned to reproduce heterosexism (Layton and Bertone, 1998). This chapter shows how theory and practice, even seemingly radical theory, can enact normative unconscious processes.

In the contemporary world, people have found multiple ways of living and theorizing non-binary configurations of gender and sexuality, which may make this chapter feel a bit dated. Nonetheless, I decided to include it because, for one thing, it introduces a particular way of doing cultural analysis, one that looks at what cultural work a theory is doing. How are terms and categories deployed at a particular historical moment, and in whose interest are they deployed? How does the way the terms are used in psychoanalytic discourse relate to the use made in other cultural discourses? I include the chapter as well because, in general, psychoanalytic gender and sexuality theory still very much needs to be interrogated. Rapoport's (2019) recent work on bisexuality, for example suggests that the psychoanalytic reduction I discuss here may still be operating in theory: once it is operating in theory, one can be sure that it is operating in the clinic. Indeed, as mentioned in my introduction to the book, I still hear clinicians apply gendered assignations to characteristics like aggression and passivity in case reports.

As I relate in Chapter 8, "Relational no more: defensive autonomy in white middle-class women," published in 2004, sometimes a confluence of events in one's life and work begin to bring new cultural patterns into bold relief. I had found theories that described the psychic life of women as grounded in and motivated by relationship "true" to my own experience growing up in the 1950s, so I was rather startled to find that these theories did not feel "true" to the experience of my college students in the 1990s. Nor did they accurately account for the psychological experience of my younger female patients. When several television shows in the 1990s began to feature female protagonists who were anything but "relational" (Layton, 2004b), I began to sense that a construct often used to describe the psychic experience of men, defensive autonomy, in fact had fairly accurately begun to describe the experience of these middle-class women. At that point, I did not understand this in the context of the broader socio-economic currents of neoliberalism, but I was aware, for example, that the television shows were doing some "cultural work" to normalize a kind of autonomy for women that denigrates relational capacities, just as television had earlier done "cultural work" to normalize the "relational female."

Chapter 9, "That place gives me the heebie jeebies," published in 2004, also began with a personal experience that made an intensive engagement with the social class theory of sociologist Pierre Bourdieu come emotionally alive for me. Bourdieu studied the intricacies of class by looking at the tastes of different class fractions. After a friend of mine became emotionally overwhelmed during a visit to a low-end store and said the store gave her the "heebie jeebies," I decided to survey some colleagues and friends to see how emotions subtend shopping experiences and do the cultural work of keeping class relations in place. This chapter was first published in a special issue on psychosocial research methods, edited by Wendy Hollway, in the *International Journal of Critical Psychology*. Hollway was a member of the collective that had written a ground-breaking 1984 book that was very important to my thinking, *Changing the Subject: Psychology, Social Regulation and Subjectivity* (Hollway et al., 1984). A founding document of critical psychology, this book brought Foucault into relation with psychoanalysis. Hollway later was a founding member of the U.K. Psycho-Social Network, and her interest in my work brought me into relation with a whole new world of international colleagues engaged in critical theory, critical psychology, and psychoanalytic culture critique.

Although the cases in Chapter 10, "Class in the clinic: enacting distinction," were first discussed in a paper published in *Psychoanalytic Inquiry* titled "Grandiosity, neoliberalism, and neoconservatism" (Layton, 2014a), the chapter is an unpublished reckoning, written in 2015, with the long marginalization of class in both academic sociology and psychoanalysis. By the time this paper was written, I had been immersed for a while in writings about neoliberalism and subject formation, and here I tried to offer an intersectional analysis of some different ways my patients were living class inequality, and how conflicts around class emerged in our clinical work.

Chapter 11, "Racial identities, racial enactments and normative unconscious processes," was first published in *Psychoanalytic Quarterly* in 2006. It was in that paper that I most fully laid out my theory of normative unconscious processes, a description which, for the sake of avoiding repetition, I have mostly removed from this chapter and placed in my introduction to the book. The theory I formulated for this 2006 paper was drawn from my reading of earlier papers in the relational canon that had described racialized enactments (e.g., Altman, 2000; Leary, 1997a, 1997b, 2000; Suchet, 2004) and the previous work I had done on class and gender. The chapter describes my work with Michael, a gay Asian American man, and focuses on how my psychosocial positioning as a white heterosexual female of a certain age came into contact and conflict with the way that he lived his own singular psychosocial positioning. The paper was later updated for a book edited by Grand and Salberg (2017). For this version, the authors asked me to think more deeply about my own history and how it affected the treatment. In the original paper, I had written that at that particular historical moment, and for most of my life, I had been considered white, and I spoke there of "passing" as white. I described it that way because I am Jewish, and because there have been times historically when Jews were not considered to be white. But I had not really included my Jewish positioning in my earlier analysis of what had happened between Michael and me. When I thought more deeply about my own racialization history, I realized that this particular intersection of whiteness and Jewishness in my history did indeed have relational significance for the encounter. Social psychoanalysis, and attention to normative unconscious processes in the clinic, demands historicization, a conception of how different identities are positioned in relation to each other, an awareness of the operation of power relations, and recognition of the effects of intersectionality.

# Chapter 7

# The psychopolitics
# of bisexuality[*]

In the past few years, I have been to a number of conferences and symposia sponsored by groups calling themselves "lesbigay," or "gay, lesbian, transgendered, and bisexual." But bisexuality has rarely if ever been on the agenda, although it is clear that a bisexual community exists. Curious about the discrepancy between the visibility of the category on the conference circuit and the absence of actual talks about it, I began to research bisexuality both in psychoanalytic literature and outside the field of psychoanalysis. Outside of psychoanalysis, I found a large number of recent books and articles on bisexuality, most of which are written by bisexuals who define bisexuality in terms of fluid object choice (see Weise, 1992; George, 1993; Klein, 1993; Weinberg et al., 1994; Garber, 1995; Rust, 1995; Tucker, 1995; Hall and Pramaggiore, 1996; Michel, 1996; Rose et al., 1996; Eadie, 1997). Many of these writings focus precisely on the invisibility of bisexuality in a variety of discourses (see, for example, Klein, 1993, several essays in Rose et al., 1996). The authors point out that homosexual discourse of the 1970s and 1980s, heterosexual discourse, medical discourse, and all other discourses predicated on the assumption that one is either straight or gay (monosexuality) argue that there is no such thing as a bisexual: people who claim to be bisexual are homosexuals trying to pass as heterosexuals, or heterosexuals wanting a taste of the forbidden; they are going through a phase, they are confused.

The insistence in these discourses that bisexuals do not exist has played no small role in the emergence of bisexual movements and writings on bisexual identity. The writings tend to be historically specific, focusing either on some of the reasons for the emergence of contemporary bisexual identities or on what it is like to be bisexual in this historical moment. Many of the texts place bisexuals in their historically shifting relations to lesbians and gays, discussing, for example, the way gays and lesbians marginalized bisexuals in the pre-queer 1970s and 1980s. They talk about the ways that bisexuals were scapegoated during the AIDS epidemic as carriers of AIDS to the heterosexual community. Both of these historical marginalizations contributed in important ways to the emergence of specifically bisexual communities. Another much discussed topic in this literature is the way that, in the current historical moment, bisexuality functions to challenge the dominant view that sexual identity is not a choice.

Many of the works cited previously on bisexuality are either anthologies or empirical investigations of the way that those who call themselves bisexual live their lives. The effect of these formal choices is to emphasize the multiple ways that one can be bisexual. Some bisexuals are monogamous and others critique the constrictions of coupling; some bisexuals are anti-marriage and others are happily married. Some call themselves gay-identified bisexuals, and others call themselves heterosexual-identified bisexuals. Yet others decry the way that monosexual discourses force descriptions of bisexual practice into a heterosexual and/or homosexual frame; many bisexuals feel, for example, that the relationships they forge with opposite-sex partners are not heterosexual relationships but rather bisexual relationships. Bisexuality has a specificity that cannot be reduced to homosexual and heterosexual desire. Curiously, however, not much has been written on the specificity of bisexual sexuality (an exception is Wark, 1996).

There is a tension in this literature between the tendency just described to allow for diversity and to be historically specific and a tendency to want to define a bisexual identity and make it stand for a transgressive radicalism. Claims for radicalism occur both within writings by bisexuals and within psychoanalytic writings. Du Plessis (1996), who dislikes this trend, catalogues the uses to which bisexuality has been put in various discourses, many of which are psychoanalytic. He cites Juliet Mitchell, who used the term bisexuality to signify the uncertainty of identity, and French feminists, who, using it to signify a female resistance to phallocentric culture, argue that the two-in-one defies the univocal sameness characteristic of patriarchal culture and that bisexuality signifies a different way of treating the other. Queer theorists, du Plessis argues, use bisexuality to do the work of exemplifying border crossing, deconstructing, contesting binaries (one should note that in the not too distant past, the constructs "woman" (see, for example, Rabine, 1988), "lesbian" (for a critique, see Martin, 1996; Layton, 1998), and "mestiza" (see Anzaldúa, 1990) have also been called on sequentially to do this work). Du Plessis, like many others, notes that all these uses have *no* use for *actual* bisexuals; many of them, in fact, keep bisexuality firmly rooted in fantasy, not reality.

Bisexual writers such as Jo Eadie (1996, 1997) are troubled by those who want to make bisexuality a new radical identity, particularly because the latter tend to create new hierarchies in which bisexuality is superior to monosexuality and in which nonmonogamy is superior to monogamy. Sometimes these new hierarchies are ironically created in the very act of declaring that bisexuality's essence is to contest gender, sexual, racial, and all kinds of other culturally dictated binaries. Bisexuals' responses to this work range from a clear joy at finding themselves placed in an avant garde position to annoyance at being homogenized and used abstractly to further a postmodern cause. Those most critical of these uses are those researchers who want to focus on the way bisexuals are living their lives in this historical moment.

In contemporary psychoanalytic literature, bisexuality is a contested term as well, influenced by a curious mix of Freud and feminism. A currently popular and prevalent use of the term draws on the work of Fast (1984, 1993) and defines bisexuality in terms of early cross-sex and cross-gender identifications. This use echoes one of the ways that Freud understood bisexuality: as a mix, in all of us, of masculine and feminine strivings, of masculine and feminine physical matter.[1] But theorists who currently use bisexuality in this way are by and large feminists. As is true of some of the bisexual writers mentioned, one of the analytic theorists' primary assumptions is that bisexuality is our best defense against gender binaries (Bassin, 1996; Benjamin, 1996). Cross-sex and cross-gender identifications, they argue, function to ground the possibility of contesting rigid gender polarities. Bisexuality is used, then, as a way to mediate between polarized cultural gender norms and a more complex or even resistant psyche. In general, however, the psychoanalytic literature neither discusses bisexuality as an identity nor legitimizes, except in fantasy and transference, fluid object choice. And so contemporary psychoanalysis is one of the discourses that renders the practice of bisexual sexuality invisible.

In this chapter, I look more closely at the cultural and political work that the term bisexuality is doing in current psychoanalytic theory. To do so, I focus on a few essays on bisexuality that appeared in the 1990s in mainstream psychoanalytic journals, particularly Donna Bassin's (1996) "Beyond the He and the She: Toward the Reconciliation of Femininity and Masculinity in the Postoedipal Female Mind," Barbara Stimmel's (1996), "From 'Nothing' to 'Something' to 'Everything': Bisexuality and Metaphors of the Mind," and Dianne Elise's (1997) "Primary Femininity, Bisexuality, and the Female Ego Ideal: A Re-Examination of Female Developmental Theory." When I speak of "cultural and political work," I mean to suggest that the way that the term bisexuality is currently defined and deployed has political consequences. In particular, I argue that the dominant use of bisexuality in contemporary psychoanalytic theory 1) erases bisexuality as a sexuality; 2) heterosexualizes identity; and 3) assumes that preoedipal identifications are somehow free of the splitting that is inherent to the very definitions of masculinity and femininity (see Magee and Miller, 1996, for a broader critique of the gender polarizations that pervade analytic developmental theory).

Bassin (1996), like many theorists who want to ground the deconstruction of gender polarities in the preoedipal period, has recourse to Fast's theory of early gender "overinclusiveness" (a term which itself suggests pathology). Fast (1993) makes it pretty clear that so called "appropriate" gender activities and attributes are socially imposed by caregivers – it is caregivers who determine what is sex- and gender-congruent. She posits, however, that in the undifferentiated period children do not differentiate "the sex and gender aspects attributable to themselves and those that belong exclusively to other-sex persons. Therefore, they include in their inchoate selves representations of both male and female aspects of the persons in their lives" (p. 180). While this statement includes both sex and gender attributes, all of Fast's examples of bisexuality tend to center on anatomical differences and the capacity to bear children. Again, she makes it clear that, while these are biologically based, the meanings that children give to them and the attributes that get associated with these differences are cultural. But the differences between anatomical and cultural representations become quite blurred.

When Bassin cites Fast's discussion of overinclusiveness, she describes things that, as she says, really have nothing to do with gender at all, or, I would emphasize, with identification: for example, Bassin cites Fast's discussion of "modes of relating or going at objects based on early body experiences, e.g., grasping, receiving, penetrating, and inserting" (p. 158). But here is where the blurring and gender trouble begin. These four actions are not arbitrarily selected from the arsenal of what bodies – which include hands, feet, and mouths, as well as genitals – can do. Rather, they evoke connections with genitals, connections that many gender theorists go on to make explicit. For instance, Bassin associates the girl's desire to penetrate not with sticking her finger or foot in her mouth, but with her fantasy of having a penis.

After discussing Fast, Bassin cites Erikson, who said that "the infantile genital stage is dominated in both sexes by combinations of intrusive and inclusive modes and modalities that become differentiated only during puberty" (cited on p. 158). She wants to know what happens to these countermodalities after puberty. Her thesis, the thesis of her article, is that cross-sex identifications do not disappear. Having symbolized them in the overinclusive phase, men and women can call them up in postoedipal life and so contest gender polarity. Further, she argues that the girl's fantasy of having a penis ultimately is her means of making an empathic connection with the Other, by which she means the Other Sex. Bassin thus derives psychic phenomena, physical capacities, and even heterosexual harmony from preoedipal cross-sex identifications.

These theories, like Freud's own, unwittingly tend to legitimize normative associations between penis and activity, vagina and passivity, rather than contest them. The theorists use the term bisexuality to make it possible for women to be aggressive, competitive, assertive, but in so doing they implicitly code these attributes masculine or male. As soon as particular body parts become either metaphorically or literally associated with particular kinds of activities and not with others, as soon as genitals, and not fingers and toes and tongues and mouths, become the primary bearers of intrusion and inclusion, gender inequality is legitimized. When bisexuality is defined as a mixture of feminine and masculine strivings or a fantasy of having male and female genitals, bisexuality functions to sustain rather than contest gender polarities.

Bassin's patient, Ms. A, presents with "anxieties about penetration during intercourse and an intense fear of driving a car" (p. 161). In further elaborations, it appears that Ms. A is afraid of being intrusive and aggressive; she seems to feel that her lover's wish to penetrate her is intrusive. She comes to experience her analyst's interpretations and the frame of the analysis as intrusive. Further, she finds that she has a lot of curiosity about her analyst but that she does and does not want to know the answer to her questions. These questions center on the analyst's sexual life, feelings about men, sexual fantasies. She is afraid that if the analyst answers her questions she herself will be found to be intrusive.

Bassin suggests an origin to this conflict about intrusion. Ms. A used to like to "sneak" into her mother's closet:

> The closet was filled with beautiful women's things, such as silky nightgowns and lounge wear. The garments were soft and pliable and were saturated with her mother's perfume. She remembered many such visits to her mother's closets, touching the wonderful fabrics, and stopping herself from trying on the garments. She had been frightened that she would be caught doing something or looking at something she was not supposed to.
>
> (p. 163)

Bassin suggests that a memory that arises in connection with these incidents is a key to understanding Ms. A's conflict: Ms. A remembers being slammed or slapped by her mother for going into the closet, which Ms. A interprets as a punishment for her curiosity and for her intrusion. Later in the vignette, Ms. A makes it clear that both parents demanded that she be a good girl, which she enacted by becoming passive, disembodied, floating, by splitting off the offending curiosity. Given this demand, Ms. A associated her curiosity and assertiveness, which had already been punished as intrusive, with the masculine. The masculine, in her conception, is the equivalent of what a good girl is not.

How does Bassin interpret this vignette? Her theoretical moves mirror the earlier moves in the article. Bassin equates the patient's wish to know about the inside of her mother's closet with a wish to know about the inside of her mother's body and to get inside. Thus the theorist begins to create a temporal hierarchy. Primary is not a fear of intrusion based on signals from her mother about what she is allowed to know and do; primary is a wish to penetrate. Like many contemporary gender theorists, Bassin assumes, with Freud, that sexuality and anatomy are primary motivating forces in behavior as well as the origin of psychic attributes.

I do not believe that sexuality is a privileged motivating force or that any number of psychic correlates – curiosity, assertion, competitiveness – are outgrowths of sexuality (at least not in the narrow sense connected to genitalia; all the attributes certainly do evidence desire and libido). Rather, I see these as human capacities that take meaningful form only within particular modes of attachment and agency. But even if we grant that sexuality is a primary force, must we go along with the way that Bassin reduces the sensuousness of touching and smelling her mother's clothes to a desire to penetrate? Once sexuality is reduced to penetration, we are but a hair's breadth away from the familiar anatomical associations to penises and vaginas. A complex relational event regarding how mother and daughter negotiate privacy and knowledge of each other, how much the daughter is allowed to be like and desire mother, is reduced to the universal wish to get inside the mother's body. And then further reduced to having or not having the right genital equipment.

This reduction reflects, I think, an unreconciled contradiction between a feminist position that wants to contest gender polarities, and a classical analytic position that reinstates them: activity and passivity have nothing to do inherently with masculinity and femininity, the feminist Bassin says (p. 179). But, for the analyst Bassin, intrusion and inclusion are respectively male and female, a position that is both sexist and heterosexist. The only way the theorist Bassin can make intrusion and inclusion possible for the female is to invoke bisexuality. Having refused to associate intrusiveness and inclusiveness with gender, Bassin yet associates them with sex and hopes that a sexual polarity will deconstruct a gender polarity. My sense is that, on the contrary, the symbolic equation of male=masculinity =penis=penetration=activity is the very thing that keeps gender polarities in place. When theorists root a female's desire to penetrate in male genitalia, they perpetuate the very gendering of attributes that they had hoped to escape.

How do I view this vignette? Ms. A calls her act of going into the closet "sneaking"; she seems to know, if only in retrospect, that it was an act that was likely to be punished if discovered. That she seems to know her act will be punished suggests to me that in this family guidelines exist that strictly define what is intrusive, what is forbidden. I would guess that Ms. A's visits to the closet were not intrusions until they were punished – or that previous messages about intrusion made her worry that her visits to the closet would be seen as intrusive – or that messages about intrusion created a desire to know that could only be accomplished in "sneaky" ways.

The trauma that turns curiosity and desire into intrusion is connected for her with another trauma: that of gender socialization, and Ms. A begins to associate intrusion not only with all forms of curiosity and assertion but with masculinity. These are things that good girls don't do but men do. Her fear of penetration by the penis, then, is one among many manifestations of a conflict about intrusion, not the primary manifestation from which all others derive. If anything is primary, it is probably the fear of being slammed if she is too curious or aggressive, the fear of losing love.

To be loved, Ms. A splits off curiosity and assertiveness. And she becomes passive, disembodied, floating. What we call her femininity, then, is something produced in the act of trying not to be what she considers masculine and taboo. But as a product of splitting, the "feminine" passivity, disembodiment, floating will contain some form of "masculine" aggression and resentment as well. So Ms. A is undoubtedly inhabited by both sides of the gender polarity, and this kind of mix of masculinity and femininity is crippling. When used to describe masculine and feminine strivings, bisexuality can only describe the very process of splitting it is meant to contest because masculinity and femininity are cultural constructs defined psychically in relation to each other; they do not exist apart.

The cure that Bassin proposes is the restoration of Ms. A's capacity to use a fantasy of having a penis with which to penetrate without fear of retaliation. Ms. A's curiosity and entries into the closet, however, have nothing to do with maleness, masculinity, having a penis versus having a vagina; these are simply things that her body and mind can do. Even if we say that the entry into the closet was symbolic of a wish to enter her mother, we still have no need to invoke the penis. So it does not seem useful to me for psychoanalytic theory to call on bisexuality to legitimize the problematic cultural connection that has been made between penetration and masculinity or curiosity and masculinity. Bisexuality is used here in two suspicious ways. First, by Bassin's saying that the patient expresses her desire for her mother by a wish to penetrate her, she calls on bisexuality to place the patient's mode of desire for her mother in a heterosexual frame. Second, the rooting of curiosity and assertion in a bisexuality that is defined by the couplet penetration/being penetrated colludes with rather than deconstructs Ms. A's association of activity and curiosity with masculinity.

Bassin's clinical work focuses on restoring to the patient what the patient has split off – curiosity and assertion; the problem for me emerges in the theorizing, the thesis that what heals the split is the patient's early cross-sex identifications. Bassin writes:

> Entrance into the female genital stage requires integration, acceptance, and symbolic elaboration of the body ego genitals of both sexes within the psyche. To the extent that a woman cannot call upon her early overinclusive body ego experiences and use them in playful symbolic representations, she will be dominated by a vaginal world, her inner generative space, or an empty hole. Finding herself surrounded only by this vaginal world, she forecloses a true object relation with a man.
>
> (p. 187)

In this concluding formulation, Bassin undoes the possibilities opened by her clinical work. This explanation heterosexualizes a complicated case in which the patient gets "slammed" for expressing her desire for her mother. It also suggests that the primary means of contesting gender inequality is found in a woman's early fantasy of having a penis rather than in the work of uncoupling conventional associations that have been made between attributes like curiosity and genitals and gender. Where the clinical work made it clear that the patient could not really come to empathize with or love another until she had dealt with what she had split off from herself, the theory suggests that a woman's Other is always male, and that heterosexuality works because women can imagine what it is like to have a penis. Rather than heterosexualize her, the clinical work might in fact have revealed to Ms. A the fluidity of her sexual desire. It might have made desire for both sexes – my preferred connotation of the term bisexuality – available to her. In fact, one could argue that Ms. A's heterosexuality might in part have been produced from traumatic interactions with her mother, interactions that punished her expression of same-sex desire at the same time that they punished her curiosity (Elise, 2000, discusses in greater detail the heterosexual mother's role in discouraging her daughter's desire for her).

Like Bassin's work, most recent analytic literature on bisexuality is clearly marked by contemporary changes in analytic ways of understanding women. But I keep picking up an uneasy tension between the writing analysts' attachment to gender equality and their attachment to classical analytic theory. They are committed to proving that women are not lacking, that penis envy is not primarily about wanting to have a penis but about wanting to be able to display intelligence, or be assertive; yet they want to find a way to make these findings compatible with analytic theory. Bisexuality does the work of reconciling writers' feminist strivings with contradictory classical analytic strivings.

Stimmel (1996), for example, begins her essay by noting that we are in an exciting period when "Partial and mistaken ideas from the past are being completed and corrected, particularly having to do with making more accurate sense of the sexual and psychological lives of women" (p. 191). Here, as elsewhere, psychoanalysis, rather than the feminist movement that spurred analysts to question old truths in the first place, is credited as the source of these truths. Indeed, Stimmel goes on to say that we should not allow the revisions we are making in understanding female sexuality to blind us to the universal truths that classic psychoanalysis has uncovered. One of these truths, in her opinion, is our bisexual core, by which she means the mental representation of both sets of genitals that we all need to have accomplished in order to have available to us such things as a healthy capacity for creativity. She, like other analysts, draws on bisexuality to do the work of legitimizing so-called "masculine strivings" in women: wishes to display one's intelligence; wishes to be active, assertive, or aggressive; to be competitive.

Rather than look at the way that culture and psyche intersect, as, for example, in the cultural gendering of attributes that makes splitting inevitable in the construction of a gender identity (Benjamin, 1988; Dimen, 1991; Goldner, 1991; Harris, 1991), writers such as Stimmel divert attention from these processes by rooting psychic characteristics in genital characteristics. For these writers, the language we use to talk about our psychic selves derives from what our genitals do. Stimmel talks about a woman describing herself as spacey and suggests that the analyst look to the genitals and other body parts for the origin of that assessment. A culturally informed analyst would see this in quite the opposite way: the origin both of the way one thinks about the genitals and the way one thinks about the mind is the language and behavior available in culture. In our case, the language of most cultural discourses, and the structure of most institutions, including the family, are informed by or built on gender inequality. A language whose use is shaped by gender inequality, and available behavioral models also shaped by gender inequality permeate the way we come to think about our bodies, what we think our bodies can do, and what we think our minds can do.

The analytic underpinnings of Stimmel's notion of bisexuality prove this point. She, like Bassin, argues that genitals are the primary body part in the determination of psychic life. Where, for Bassin, what genitals do is penetrate and be penetrated, intrude and include, for Stimmel they primarily want to impregnate and be impregnated. Here, bisexuality is called on to reduce sexuality to its reproductive functions. In the bisexual identity literature, we find bisexuality serving the opposite function – to promote an opening to all kinds of desire (see. e.g., Eadie, 1996, 1997; Hall and Pramaggiore, 1996; Rose et al., 1996). In the analytic literature, desire is subtly kept in a heterosexual frame. This constraint is accomplished first and foremost by reducing sexuality to reproduction. It is no wonder that Stimmel's case material involves a woman who, before analysis, had decided not to have a baby, but during analysis had one.

Stimmel's female patient began analysis because she found herself unable to present her intellectual ideas in public, particularly to a male audience. The patient, Stimmel reports, was happily married, had a good sex life, and had decided she wanted no children. Stimmel's work links the patient's fertile, creative mind to her fertile, creative genitals; she helps the patient to see that what blocks her ability to thrust her ideas forth is that she has disavowed an identification with male genitalia. During the analysis, the patient becomes pregnant and has a baby. Stimmel assumes that everyone wants both to impregnate and be impregnated; this is our bisexual core, which, if denied, leads to neurosis. If accepted, it seems to lead to having a baby. We will never know but can only guess what role the analyst's implicit conviction that not to want to have a baby is pathological played in her patient's change of mind. Nor will we know if the baby she had is the one she wanted to have with her husband or her analyst or both.

Which brings us to the question of what happens to the idea of bisexual object choice, an idea Stimmel finds in Freud and wants to preserve. In Stimmel's theory, little girls and little boys both want to impregnate mother and be impregnated by father. Little girls and boys, then, are bisexual; indeed, female analysands want to impregnate and be impregnated by their female analysts and so are also bisexual. But outside of the analytic hour, in "reality," *mothers* are impregnated and *fathers* impregnate. Analysands' yearnings for their same-sex analyst never lead to the possibility of a bisexual sexuality in any but the metaphoric sense. Indeed, bisexuality is called on precisely to keep bisexual desire in the metaphoric realm.

And so the bisexual core also ironically serves as a support for hetero-sexual object choice. As Stimmel concludes:

> Finally, in the back-and-forth between self and object, the oedipal child successfully traverses this phase by identifying not only with both parents' superegos, but by incorporating their genital anatomy as well . . . They would have to in order to satisfactorily bring closure, such as it is, to the oedipal phase with its positive and negative object-related lures.
>
> (p. 211)

You need a penis to desire mother and a vagina to desire father. Stimmel's use of bisexuality does the cultural work of keeping bisexual object choice in the mind and out of enactment.

Bassin's and Stimmel's recourse to bisexuality makes them confront the way that many analysts dismiss bisexuality: by equating it with the narcissistic wish to have everything. Analysts who dismiss bisexuality in this way feel that a key developmental task is to confront the limit of being either male or female and relinquish narcissistic longings to be both. Now Stimmel does not differ from these analysts in her sense that the division into male and female is universal and natural. But her view is that the representation of both sets of genitals is one of the ways that we cope with limits, and, as I said earlier, she, like other writers on sexuality, sees this version of bisexuality as necessary for creativity. Recall that Bassin dealt with the charge of narcissism in a slightly different way. She argued that bisexual identification, far from narcissistic, is the very route to empathy for the other gender.

The charge that psychic bisexuality is a symptom of narcissism functions largely to keep women out of the male preserve. The cultural demand for sexual division goes hand in hand with the privileges of the phallus (Butler, 1990). So the need to meet the charge of narcissism head on, I would argue, stems from Bassin's and Stimmel's commitment to gender equality. Bisexuality is called on to do the work, within psychoanalytic theory, of legitimizing gender equality. I am in sympathy with the wish to legitimize gender equality. But my feeling is that bisexuality is the wrong concept to do that work: once you have divided the world into male and female, masculine and feminine strivings, you have placed yourself in a sphere of gender polarity. Defined by anatomical difference or gendered

attributes, bisexuality as a concept diverts attention from the task of looking at culturally-induced splitting, the heart of gender inequality.

Stimmel says:

> The wish for everything (for bisexual completeness) is not in itself a
> problem; rather it is the disruption of bisexual symbolization, in men
> and women, which follows the guilty disavowal of such a wish. This
> disruption is at least one possible determinant of the neurotic inhibi-
> tions of intellect, creativity, and ambition in women – and men.
>
> (p. 193)

I am not arguing that bisexual symbolization does not exist. It simply is
not primary, and its disruption does not originate in intrapsychic dynamics. Rather, I would locate the disruption of bisexual symbolization in the
same source in which I would locate inhibitions of intellect, creativity, and
ambition in women: in culturally supported sexism, which can be conveyed by either parent, and which promotes each gender's disavowal of
those attributes that have been exclusively associated with the other gender. With regard to the charge of narcissism, what is longed for here is not
limitlessness, the wish to have everything; what is longed for is the wish
to be allowed to do what you in fact know you can do, what you enjoy
doing – without being punished for it. To confuse a girl's desire to be able
to express her intellect freely, a boy's desire to weep in public, with a narcissistic longing for completeness is pure sexism.

Elise (1997) has also recently contributed to the psychoanalytic literature on bisexuality. Elise questions the way that primary femininity, as
addressed in the work of such theorists as Phyllis Tyson and Elizabeth
Lloyd Mayer, confuses core gender identity, the cultural assignment to
male or female, with masculinity and femininity, categories that are purely
cultural and whose definitions are shot through with gender inequality. In
the work Elise critiques, there is the same quick leap from body characteristics to psychological characteristics that I have found in the work of
Bassin and Stimmel. Primary femininity in Mayer's work, for example,
arises from the girl's early awareness of her body, and in this first phase of
body awareness the body image is not of something lacking. Elise agrees
with this conclusion, but she does not go on to assert that the awareness of
a vagina is necessarily associated with wishes to be penetrated by a penis
(the innate heterosexual imperative) or with wishes to be passive (cultural

femininity). In Stoller's work, Elise argues, core gender identity is not primarily about the body at all: "although core gender identity may be fixed and unalterable and although it is an idea *about the body*, it does not necessarily stem from the body or even correspond with actual chromosomal or anatomical structure" (p. 497). So Elise's work differs from that of Bassin and Stimmel in that Elise does not conflate characteristics, such as intrusive, with the wish to penetrate; nor does she seem to label as a masculine striving the wish to let the contents of one's intellect come forth.

In the section of her essay on bisexuality (1997), Elise criticizes the way Tyson and other mainstream psychoanalytic writers on gender have used primary femininity as a way to get rid of the concept of bisexuality. Tyson argues that, if primary femininity is bedrock, then bisexuality is not. And it is a small step from there to normalizing heterosexuality. Elise sees no reason why a primary sense of femaleness, which, in her view, is a girl's earliest sense of self and derives from the mental representation of her female body, might not coexist with psychic bisexuality, which she partially defines as same and opposite gender self-representations. Following Fast, Elise argues that the original matrix holds the unconscious fantasy of *potential unlimited by gender* – unlimited, and, in the girl, also not male. She cites Fast, who says that cross-sex bodily and psychosocial characteristics are not easily given up. Indeed, Elise, citing Fast, notes that, in the phase in which children become aware of difference, "both sexes 'vigorously assert those sex and gender aspects they believe they must renounce'" (p. 502). Elise, like Benjamin (1996), Aron (1995), and others, argues that such fantasies are never wholly given up, and she wants the concept of bisexuality to "illuminate the wish to *be* both sexes (self-representation) and to *have* both sexes (object choice and representation)" (p. 505).

I am generally sympathetic to that formulation. But I have an easier time understanding what it means to desire both sexes than I do understanding what it means to be both sexes. Fast writes about the phase in which children must renounce bisexuality: I find it easy to understand what it means that a girl becomes aware that she does not have a penis, but I do not understand what it means that she has to renounce "inappropriate" cross-gender identifications. What can it mean to have an inappropriate psychosocial gender characteristic? This notion is comprehensible only if "inappropriate" refers to a social order and its gender norms, norms which in no way necessarily connect to what girls and boys can feel or do.

Nor do I exactly know what cross-gender identifications are, although many theorists seem to agree nowadays that they are the great hope for overturning rigid gender polarities. I certainly understand that since, in this culture, the dominant options for identification are men and women, children will probably have associated some of their attributes and desires and behaviors with men and others with women. But I would never want to conclude, for instance, that if a girl identifies with her father's intelligence and her mother's sexiness (identifications that I would refer to as paternal and maternal rather than masculine and feminine), intelligence is a male identification and sexiness a female one. In this girl's life they may be, but these very cross-gender identifications will complicate her life if, at the same time, intelligence is not associated with women and sexiness is not associated with men.

If we are aware that gender inequality dictates what culturally is associated with men and what with women – and that, in large measure, culture, not biology, dictates how men and women talk to, play with, separate from, and touch boys and girls – then we are led to acknowledge that preoedipal cross-gender identifications must also be tangled up in gender polarities. When a girl, even a preoedipal one, identifies with her father's autonomy, she is identifying with a particular version of autonomy, one that is very much a cultural construct formed by the splitting of masculinity and femininity. Indeed, if cultural femininity is defined by what masculinity is not, and if splitting is characterized by the co-presence of what is performed and what is split off, then statistically "normal" feminine gender identity probably can be characterized as the uneasy coexistence of avowed femininity and disavowed masculinity.

The problem here seems to be that even Elise, who is highly cognizant of gender inequality and the problem it poses for a girl who is supposed to valorize positively a sense of femininity, understands the categories femininity and masculinity as separate entities rather than as inextricably related entities that emerge from a process of splitting. Because of this, she ends up obscuring the distinction between gender difference and gender inequality.

The differences between Elise's and my position may seem to be those only of semantics, but I think that, in the end, the differences have political and clinical consequences. I will try to illustrate this by looking at one of Elise's more recent papers on bisexuality, "Gender Repertoire: Body, Mind and Bisexuality" (1998). In this paper, Elise does an excellent job of uncoupling associations between penetration and masculinity; she makes points similar to mine regarding girls' capacity for penetration. She roots this capacity, as I have, in the girl's experiences with non-genital body parts (sticking fingers in mouths), but she goes beyond my assertions when she roots it as well in the capacity psychically to take both roles in the nursing couple – an idea most promising for feminist gender theory. But when Elise wants to refer to all of this as bisexuality, it seems to me that she reinstates the very gender binary she so eloquently critiques. What piece of the nursing process is masculine, what piece feminine? Faulting those who naturalize associations between masculinity and penetration, Elise wants to equate bisexuality with gender equality. Citing Aron approvingly (1995), she criticizes those who pathologize the wish for bisexuality (and the usual means of pathologizing, as I stated in my discussion of narcissism previously, is to charge that the wish for bisexual completeness indicates a delusion of omnipotence). Elise writes: "Bisexuality . . . is the recuperation of the lost aspect deemed gender inappropriate or possibly even annihilating of gender" (p. 360). To call this recuperation bisexuality is to agree that some attributes are masculine and some feminine, even if you simultaneously argue that men and women ought to be able to have both sets of attributes. To speak of the wish to be both sexes as an omnipotent fantasy (Aron, 1995), whether a healthy one or a pathological one, is to obscure gender inequality – because the cultural problem is not that humans wish to have it all but rather that culture enacts traumatic proscriptions on what humans would be perfectly capable of being and doing if they were left to their own devices.

What fosters and enables creativity, then, is not bisexuality but, rather, social equality. What inhibits creativity is the gender (and race and class) splitting deemed normal by dominant culture. Fast's (1984, 1993) dictum about how children of both sexes vigorously assert those sex and gender aspects they believe they must renounce sounds rather to me like the child's last stand before giving in to the culturally required splitting that *produces* dominant femininity and masculinity. Because they use the terms femininity and masculinity without regard for their culturally dominant meanings, those theorists whose concept of bisexuality centers on cross-gender identifications do not escape the problem of cultural splitting.

## Conclusion

What are the implications of using bisexuality to mean a mix of masculine and feminine strivings? I have argued throughout that the theory that cross-sex or cross-gender identifications, the bisexual core, undermine gender polarities is not convincing. I question several parts of this theory: are identifications themselves primary in establishing a gender identity? Are a girl's identifications with father male identifications, with mother female identifications? Does this use of bisexuality get entangled in the very notions of splitting, of gender polarity that it wants to contest? Is this use of bisexuality ultimately homophobic?

I have argued that dominant versions of masculinity and femininity do not exist separately, that both sides of the polarity are internalized in some fashion. A little boy is humiliated for crying in public, and, adopting a stoic attitude to painful situations, he never cries again. The stoicism is now a part of what defines his masculinity, and that definition involves a differentiation from girls, who are allowed to cry in public. The stoicism itself is conditioned by the need to guard against desires and impulses that will bring humiliation upon him: masculinity is characterized by the co-presence of what is performed and what is split off (Butler, 1995). Has the boy given up a cross-gender identification to establish this aspect of his masculinity? I don't think so. More likely, he, like his sister, cried as a baby, and everyone found that fine until he did it in a group of boys and was shamed. Another example: a little boy identifies with his mother's way of walking and begins to walk like she does. In what sense is this a cross-gender identification? Only in the sense that his mother may walk in a way defined culturally as feminine. But all cultural definitions are rooted in splitting: feminine is what is not masculine and vice versa. Masculinity and femininity, male and female, are each largely defined by what the other is not – and cultural value is placed on male and masculine. In a homophobic culture, same-sex desire is supposed to be split off and is denigrated; homosexuality and heterosexuality have meaning only in relation to that split. So it is politically very problematic to talk about bisexuality as a mix of masculine and feminine strivings. For the same reason, it is problematic to talk about bisexuality as a mix of heterosexuality and homosexuality.

To return to the example of the boy who stops crying in public: much of what theorists call cross-gender identifications are in fact capacities that have nothing to do with gender and are gendered only retrospectively. Because of this we don't need to posit a primary bisexuality in order to legitimize gender equality. If anything can be said to be primary, it is perhaps what the body can do. And the body can do a lot more than it is given credit for in theories that give primacy to a sexuality grounded in genital penetration and heterosexuality. Both male and female bodies can push and shove, cry and laugh, yell and whisper, bite and kiss, punch and snuggle, run and sit quietly. These activities are retroactively endowed with such meanings as "aggressive," "competitive," "passive," and it is gender inequality, not gender difference, that says "penetration" is masculine (for elaboration, see Elise, 1998) and that makes penetration absorb a range of attributes such as "curious" or "assertive." What might contest gender polarity, then, is the early connection a child might make between being a female and the bodily pleasure she derives from yelling loud or jumping high (Layton, 1998).

Primary, too, are the relationships in which bodies take shape. I would say that along with identification, along with wishes to be like and sexually to have, are wishes to be loved. Gender theory has made much of identification, but it has not made nearly enough of the role that permission and humiliation play in the creation of gender identity and sexuality. Goldner (1991) has alerted us to the way that gender takes shape within conflictual relational matrices in which children make their identifications and disidentifications according to how they understand what they need to do to be loved. Humiliation and the wish to be loved play a primary role in the splitting off of attributes not considered gender-appropriate. Some of those attributes have been attained through complex identifications; many of them, however, are gender-neutral inborn capacities for agency and attachment that develop in relationships that are culturally gendered, with men and women who are culturally gendered. To use bisexual as a term meaning the combination of masculine and feminine is to collude with the way those capacities have been gendered and split.

If it is not early cross-sex or cross-gender identifications that heal the split, what might? Here is where politics unavoidably enters into psychoanalysis in one form or the other. Bassin's and Stimmel's clinical achievement does not restore an originary bisexuality; their achievement derives from their awareness of the damage wrought by gender socialization and gender inequality. It derives from their feminism, not from their allegiance to psychoanalytic theory. In both Stimmel's and Bassin's cases, what helped the patient was not the patient's early bisexuality but probably the patient's relationship with and identification with a woman who had not disavowed intellect, creativity, ambition, and so was able to recognize and question that disavowal in her female patients. When the theorists try to reconcile their feminism with their allegiance to classical theories of bisexuality, a different kind of politics emerges: heterosexist assumptions about desire and sexist assumptions about what is masculine and what is feminine. There may be intrapsychic resistances to gender inequality, but there is no intrapsychic solution to this cultural problem.

To conclude, I would define bisexuality the way bisexual theorists do: exclusively in relation to object choice, which I do think has psychic origins in erotic ties to male and female caregivers. But I would also listen to those bisexual writers who insist that an adult bisexual identity has, at best, highly mediated ties to an infantile disposition. Much as I wish that bisexuality, in this or any sense, would contest gender or sexual binaries, I do not think that this is possible. In a world in which hetero- and homosexuality, like femininity and masculinity, are mutually defined by processes of splitting, within relations of domination and submission, I would argue that only a mode of relating based in mutuality and aware of culturally-mandated splitting might produce a transgressive subjectivity.

I want to end where I began, with the literature on bisexuality, because I think it offers clinicians a lot to think about. Therapists need to be aware of what Simon (1996) has referred to as the function that building an identity and joining a community serves in an atomized world; I would want to understand all sexual identities in connection to sexual communities. I appreciate the awareness in the literature on bisexuality of how many ways there are to incorporate a sexuality into a life. I would not want to let preconceptions about the health of coupling close off the possibility, for any patient, of alternate forms of loving and living, for example, triangles. I would listen for what makes bisexual sexuality, whether acted on or not, irreducible to either hetero- or homosexuality. I would continue to interrogate whether or not the origins of some heterosexualities lie in the cultural prohibition on homosexuality enacted by parents. Finally, some bisexual theorists have noted that unlike a coming out story, which has a clear telos, and unlike a lifelong unquestioned heterosexuality, a bisexual narrative is an ongoing construction (Michel, 1996). I find this most useful as a way of thinking about how to listen to any patient talk about his or her sexuality; it is a therapist's job not to foreclose on the form or object choice a patient's or our own sexuality might take.

## Notes

* Used with permission. Layton, L. (2000) The psychopolitics of bisexuality. *Studies in Gender and Sexuality* 1(1): 41–60.
1 Despite this early reference to psychological bisexuality, Freud (1933) warns that it is an error to think that masculinity and femininity have any fixed referents in the psychological realm. He notes that whenever we use these terms to refer to psychological attributes rather than biological ones, we commit the "error of superimposition" (p. 115).

# Chapter 8

# Relational no more

## Defensive autonomy in
## middle-class women[*]

This chapter focuses on what I perceive to be a change in the psychic structure of many middle-class white heterosexual women. Nearly every Western theorist writing on the relation between the psychic and the social is struck by the fact that Western culture holds as an ideal the autonomous individual while it simultaneously creates people who are insecure, status-craving, and dependency denying, yet deeply dependent on the approval of others. While those who follow Althusser (1971) argue that every capitalist institutional apparatus centers on creating individuals who fantasize themselves as free agents, and that it is this fantasy that keeps them reproducing the very conditions that require their subordination, I believe, following arguments made by Frankfurt School theorists (Adorno, Horkheimer, Marcuse, Fromm) that the ideal of an autonomous individual can also play a role in generating resistance to domination. In my model of the relation between the psychic and the social, reification and instrumental rationality, central to the Frankfurt School's theory of the effect of capitalism on individuals and their relations to one another, do not pervade all aspects of character and are not just characteristic of masculinity. Nonetheless, the effects of the character structures and relational possibilities fostered by capitalism are pervasive enough that all people find it difficult if not impossible to sustain both mutual relating and autonomous striving, or, as Benjamin (1988) has called it, the assertion-recognition dialectic. Different social positions produce somewhat different forms of breakdown of the dialectic, which is not to say that every person in a particular social position will have the same experience. I do not believe that it is possible fully to sustain this dialectic in conditions of stark inequality such as exist in the U.S. But I do believe that even the most damaged among us hold some capacity for mutuality and longing for the kind of recognition Benjamin describes. This is what we count on in clinical work to get us through the long, painful struggle of a treatment. What is less clear to me is whether or not our treatments remain partial, more adjustment-based than what one might call "critical," if they do not in some way open to an awareness of those stark inequalities.

As a transition to the clinical vignette I would like to use to illustrate my model, let me say a bit more about why I have tied Benjamin's work on gender difference and domination to narcissistic character structure. In 1990, I published an article that stemmed from my dissertation research, which challenged Kohut's notion of two separate lines of development, the line of object love and the line of narcissism (Layton, 1988). My conclusion was that Kohut had mistakenly attributed to human nature something that is in fact an effect of patriarchal capitalism. I argued that the appearance that autonomy is distinct from relational capacities is an effect of a social system in which autonomy is marked by instrumental reason and defined by splitting off relational needs and any sense of social context; and in which relational capacities are defined by splitting off the capacity for separateness and for setting one's own agenda. Further, the two sets of capacities, I argued, had been gendered male and female respectively (cf, what Benjamin refers to as gender polarity, 1988). As a clinician, I am always struck by the way that normative unconscious processes cause clients to make the same assumptions Kohut did. Indeed, many of my clients have been so narcissistically wounded by sexist projections that they experience autonomy and relatedness as two separate lines of development. One way then that clinicians can contest the psychic structure on which patriarchal capitalism depends is to work to deconstruct such culturally enforced dichotomies.

The vignette that follows, which investigates defensive autonomy in middle-class white women, addresses one particular clinical phenomenon that I think shows the way gender, race, class, and sexuality are linked to each other and to our specific historical moment. Up until the late 1960s, the proper way to live a white, female, middle-class heterosexual identity was to be educated but plan to marry a man who would support you financially. The children of the middle-class were expected to go to college, and this meant that parents and children alike had to prepare themselves for separation when the child was around age seventeen. This is still true, and I think that many of the psychic issues clinicians treat are consequences of the strong cultural pull for children of all classes to be independent at younger and younger ages and to leave home by 17 (see Hoffman, 1989; Erikson, 1950). The increased pull to be independent of nurture comes in part from the demands on children of the two working parent family as well, a structure that has few social supports that might compensate for the loss of family nurture. And it also comes in part from the feminist movement, which, by the 1970s had begun to change the proper way to live a white, middle-class female heterosexual identity. The liberated woman was supposed to be relational and nurturant as always, but now she was also expected to have a career – not a job, a career. Alas, the version of feminism that prevailed was not the one that demanded alterations in the structure of work, childcare, and consumer capitalism but the one that "stalled" (Hochschild and Machung, 1989) by focusing too narrowly on career equality for women. Since few family or workplace conditions were changed, the pressure for change was placed instead on the psychic structure of middle-class women. To fit into a man's world, to attain status and economic privilege, she had to be able to inhabit the male version of autonomy, the psychic requirements of which conflict dramatically with those of the so-called "relational female."

I first became aware that the relational female might be giving way to a female psyche marked by defensive autonomy when I taught my Harvard women's studies seminar on gender and psychoanalysis in 1998. I had been teaching this seminar since the late 1980s, and in 1998 I taught the course as I usually did: I began with Freud's theories, Horney's challenges, then turned to Klein, and then to the work of feminist object relations and relational theorists, for example, Nancy Chodorow (1978) and Jessica Benjamin (1988). Chodorow's work focused on psychic differences between white middle-class heterosexual men and women, differences that had emerged from particular changes in family and parenting structures in the 1950s. Chodorow argued that women's self-worth derived from their on-going identification and connection with their mothers and, thus, from a value on maintaining connection, nurturance, and emotional availability. Men's self-worth, she argued, derived from disidentifying with their mothers and with all things deemed by the culture to be feminine. Thus, men attained a sense of self that was based in a disavowal of being embedded in relationship, an intolerance of dependence, and a repudiation of vulnerability. After teaching this material, I introduced a group of papers by the men (e.g., Pollack, 1995; Kaftal, 1991) who had taken up the psychological problems that this version of defensive autonomy, considered culturally normal, caused for men. For several years, the women in the class had identified with the "relational" female described by the feminist analysts. But in the 1998 iteration of the class, a woman raised her hand and said that these papers on male defensive autonomy were the first course papers with which she could identify. A chorus of women echoed her sentiment, and students began to talk about how their mothers, many of whom were divorced, had cautioned them to get good jobs so they would not be dependent on a man. My students were largely upper middle-class white women and women of color who are the highest of high achievers, the women who will garner the advantages brought about by women's liberation. They had not found Chodorow's and Benjamin's submissive, non-autonomous, relational woman familiar. If they are to be believed, it is possible that one psychic result of women's liberation is the kind of female psyche best suited to a male work environment, the kind based in defensive autonomy.

Martha is a 35-year-old white female patient who exemplifies this recent trend (NB: she was born in the late 1960s). Martha is fairly successful in her law career but has had great difficulty establishing love relationships – while she craves love, she is quick to experience the other's demand for love and caretaking as intrusive, clingy, and as slowing down her career progress. Her romantic fantasy is to meet a man who is in an advanced stage of her same career and who could thus facilitate her career aspirations. And what perhaps best reveals that she painfully experiences love and achievement as two separate lines of development is her fantasy of giving up her law practice to run a bed and breakfast. Only in a career like this, she asserts, might she have a chance of integrating her conscious needs for achievement with the split off relational longings that are just becoming conscious in treatment.

For a variety of reasons, Martha has gendered her autonomous strivings as male, and her gender identity is another source of torment for her, as are her class and race identities. Raised as solidly middle-class but in a family that she experienced as emotionally impoverished, she is drawn to men of other classes and races. While these men are capable of nurture, they "drag her down" by their lack of ambition and wishes that she not work so much. She is also drawn to those lesbian women whom she fantasizes are both capable of nurture and successful in careers. But this is complicated because it is often when she experiences herself as not feminine and not successful with men that she wonders if she is a lesbian – which exemplifies the way normative unconscious processes function to align femininity with heterosexuality. While struggling to make a place in her life for the man she was dating, a man of a lower social class, she ended a session one day by saying to me: "Nice shoes." Since I'd been wearing the same femmy shoes all summer, I took it to be significant that she had just noticed them. Knowing her conflicts and aware of some fantasies she was beginning to articulate about what my life is like, I speculated that she was positioning herself in relation to me with regard to femininity and to class. A few days later, she asked if I was married. When I explored her fantasies, she said she thought I was a lesbian with a partner and a child. At this point, she acknowledged that she had gotten involved with the boyfriend just as she was making tentative steps to explore her lesbian desire. Martha seems to want me to be a feminine lesbian female who is both successful in her career and nurturant, although her skepticism about the possibility of reconciling achievement and nurture often emerges in fantasies that I experience my patients as burdensome. At different moments of the transference, I am asked to hold each of her split off projections or am drawn into the normative unconscious's wish to maintain the splits. Part of our work involves disentangling the straight-gay, masculine-feminine, white-nonwhite, upper-class and working-class binaries that are bound up with what she feels able and unable to do in her life, whom she is able and not able to love, and what kind of love she is able to experience.

What relational and socio-historical matrix produced these splits and Martha's conflicts? Martha's mother, a tennis pro before marriage, had five children by the time feminism burst on the scene in the late 1960s and early 1970s. In accord with the white, middle-class heterosexual norms of the time, her mother had become a full-time housewife and caretaker of the children while her father, a domineering and rather needy man, pursued a professional career. Her mother had tremendous difficulty handling the demands of motherhood while keeping her identity as a professional alive. Martha remembers her mother's group of feminist friends – mostly women with professional aspirations, now housewives married to professional men – sitting around the den criticizing men and male dominance.

It seems that during Martha's early childhood in the 1970s, her mother was depressed and, according to siblings, not very good at nurture. The nurture Martha remembers getting from her mother came after fights Martha had with her father, usually about his controlling behavior. Interestingly, this mother, who in some contexts was strongly feminist, never confronted her husband herself, submitting passively to his domination and letting Martha take his rage. Her father would often turn pale and seem to wither during his angry fights with Martha, and this left her feeling ugly, unfeminine, and that her assertiveness was damaging. Her mother comforted Martha after the fights and told her that she was in the right.

Martha felt both parents discouraged the children from forming heterosexual love relationships. Her mother mixed her feminism with her anger at her husband in frequent admonitions that she take care not to let herself become dependent on any man, that is, "don't be like me," a rarely successful injunction. Her father, whose family had cut off contact with him after an argument about money, needed his new nuclear family to stay close; he discouraged his children from forming bonds outside the family and overtly criticized most of his children's friends and lovers. Her mother and father showed little interest in their children's weddings and have been generally critical of their choices to have children; they worried about relationships interfering with career advancement. Indeed, her mother was not very interested in things maternal and domestic, often saying that such things make one boring. She tended to equate autonomy with professional development. Thus, although her mother was hostile to male sexism, she nevertheless had her own way of disparaging nurture and other capacities traditionally thought of as women's work.

The history thus far suggests reasons why Martha has equated career and autonomy with freedom from relationships. But there is more to Martha's story: in my experience, and certainly true of my work with Martha, the cultural dichotomization of relatedness and autonomy leaves neither pole functioning very well. What most accounts of defensive autonomy perhaps slight is not only the way in which this kind of autonomy is carried out at the expense of relationships, but also the way in which it is not a very autonomous kind of autonomy, certainly not the kind called for by the Frankfurt School. Martha is as conflicted about autonomy as she is about nurture; it may be that this is more characteristic of a female form of defensive autonomy than a male form, or it may be that the split itself makes confusion in both arenas inevitable. In Martha's case, there is a strong gender component to this conflict. One of the many double binds in which she finds herself results from the fact that her father, while encouraging career aspirations, nonetheless also seems to have disparaging feelings towards independent career women; to be loved by her father, Martha felt she had to gender her autonomy male.

How does her autonomy disturbance manifest? For one thing, even though she worries that the time she puts into therapy and her boyfriend slows her down, she often pulls for me and the boyfriend to organize her: he should help her get up on time; I should tell her what to do. Second, her difficulties nurturing create some of the very constraints on her freedom she dreads: she will, for example, forget to tell her boyfriend she has a late meeting or forget to call me to cancel an appointment. If we come after her with a worried or desperate "Where were you?," she feels put upon, slowed down. Indeed, a major piece of the treatment is dealing with her lateness and missed sessions, most of which allegedly have to do with conflicting work demands. She expects me to be critical and therefore not supportive of her autonomous strivings; she wants permission to devote all her energy to her work (tempting me to be like her parents). What is unconscious is her terror of being dependent on me and the way she deprives herself of my nurture.

Here is a typical example of the complex way that her conflicts about nurture and autonomy operate: we have a session that centers on the very painful topic of the unpredictability of caretakers. She will inevitably miss the next session, but in the most interesting of ways – she may be on her way to the appointment but spill coffee on something she had drawn up for a meeting right after. Then she has to miss the appointment to re-do the document. Or she may intend to get up at 5:30 am to do her work, not hear the alarm, get up at 7:30, then cancel the 8 am appointment because she has to be prepared for her 9:30 meeting. Career priorities are a defense that masks her difficulty sustaining closeness to me. The irony is that what slows her down is not, as she thinks, the time she spends in treatment but rather the psychic energy that goes into the defense against being there – which makes her both unpredictable as a partner in our undertaking and also unpredictable with her clients, for whom she is often late or unpredictable as well. So while she experiences her autonomy and relational life as dichotomized enemies of one another, the truth is that her autonomous activities are fully conditioned and disrupted by her relational conflicts.

Her problems with autonomy also manifest themselves in cognitive confusion – she is easily convinced that her take on things is completely wrong. A fight with her father exemplifies what happens: she tells her father that her boyfriend's anger at how much time she spends at work sometimes feels intrusive and threatening to her sense of independence. Her father, setting Martha straight, replies that it is she who is the angry person. At first Martha is upset and hopes her mother, who is in the living room with them, will defend her. But, just as in childhood, her mother says nothing. Then Martha forgets it until she arrives home and finds herself mildly angry. In her next session, she talks about it and becomes furious. She seems to seek permission from me and her friends to be angry, but no response that I or others give seems to soothe her. She phones a brother who tells her he thinks their father has always been threatened by career women. This information is impossible to process: she has sacrificed her relational life to devote herself to her career, which is what she always thought her parents wanted. The emotional turmoil is so great that she soon wonders if her father is right – who, in this fight, and who, in her relationship with her boyfriend, is the victim and who the perpetrator? Does her independence damage others? As she got more and more upset, she became more cognitively confused and less able to work.

What seemed most insidious about this event, and what it repeated from childhood, was her father's questioning of her own capacity to understand herself and her relationships better than he. Independent thinking was a sign of disloyalty to him. On top of that, this particular piece of independent thinking had come of her work with me, an outsider to the family. To be obedient to her father requires that, in certain instances, she has to kill her capacity for independent thinking AND for forging outside relationships. If not, she kills him and is destructive and unlovable. To be a good daughter to her mother is to be an independent woman who stands up to her sexist father, unlike she. But it also entails repudiating tasks her mother associated with a powerless womanhood, such as nurturance.

In *The Bonds of Love* (1988), Benjamin argued that so long as only men are accorded the position of agency in our culture, daughters need to be able to identify with their fathers to become subjects, rather than objects, of desire. Analyzing gender as a polarized, split, complementary structure that derives from a sexist culture, Benjamin foresaw that, as is true of all complementarities, the male and female positions can be reversed; for example, given women's entry into the public sphere, it was conceivable that women might take on the male position of defensive autonomy (p. 83). Martha is one of many examples I could cite in which I see white, middle and upper middle-class heterosexual women taking on that psychic structure. As Martha's case suggests, the developmental prerequisites for this change seem to entail identification with a father's defensive autonomy and a denigration of whatever has been regarded as feminine.

I do not mean to argue that sexism is the only root of Martha's troubles, but I think her situation shows well the way that the family mediates sexist and other cultural hierarchies that split, gender, and give class attributes to such human needs as dependence and independence. Defensive autonomy has been her idiosyncratic solution to the conflicts passed on to her, but I am arguing that there is something about those conflicts, their origin, and her solution that are not solely individual but collective. Indeed, a plethora of new and popular TV shows – *Crossing Jordan, Alias, CSI: Crime Scene Investigation, Karen Sisco* – feature women who work all the time and cannot seem to commit to relationships; most of these women, too, identify with their father's defensive autonomy, have outside intimate relationships only with their fathers (whose careers they largely share), and have repudiated nurture and dependency. The cultural work these television shows do is to normalize this particular psychic structure for middle-class women (see Layton, 2004b). By the time they got to my Harvard class, my female students had perhaps experienced familial dynamics that were somewhat akin to those Martha had experienced, and they had also been swimming in cultural waters that were normalizing the kind of psychic structure that worked best for the contemporary expansion of consumer capitalism.

In conclusion, I offer some further thoughts on the psychic and the social indebted to Erikson's (1950) attempt to think about the same. In his analysis of "momism," Erikson was struck by all the expert opinion stating that mothers were the biggest threats to children's health – professional and popular literature denigrated the overprotective mother, the rejecting and cold mother, the schizophrenogenic double-binding mother. The tack Erikson took was that of the clinician: regard the noxious behavior as a defense against some deep vulnerability, and try to understand what these mothers faced that might have made them rejecting, cold, or overprotective. Hypothesizing that the American psyche was marked by strict polarities, foremost among which was the split between a frontier mentality and a sedentary one, Erikson looked at the impossible and contradictory tasks that the American woman faced as both wife and mother – for example, to prepare her child to be adventurous and live far away from her while providing the closeness experts claimed important for healthy development.

Erikson's model suggests we look at some of what capitalism and other social inequities require of a population to understand its psychic results. What must parents do to raise children who will be able to meet demands for a mobile workforce? Who will be able to meet the demands of a fiercely competitive work environment? Who will be able to meet the demands that stem from the fact that the jobs that have status are the ones that pay the best and that few caretaking, service positions or positions in the arts pay well? Who must not nourish deep connections that might make it too psychically uncomfortable to compete? Who must not be so connected to the species and the environment as to worry about what happens to the peoples and resources of the so-called "Third World" and to the planet? Who must consume, and therefore must have the latest and finest objects to feel adequate and to fit in? Who must be able to multi-task? Who, if they are women, must be attractive? Who, if both parents have to work, must be able to take care of themselves at a very young age? Is it any wonder that we have so many instances of separation disorders among the upwardly mobile? Eating disorders? Attention deficit disorders marking those who can't multi-task, or, among children, those who perhaps react against not having enough attention? How many people do clinicians see who are conflicted because they really wanted to be artists but have internalized their parents' anxiety about the vow of poverty artists are forced to take? How many people do clinicians see who beat up on themselves because they are not successful? How many people do clinicians see who feel so inadequate that the only way they can keep their minds from anxiously reproaching them all day long is to make sure they own the best car or best clothes or whatever it takes to feel they are above any possible reproach from the outside? And how many people do we see who dread abandonment and yet simultaneously feel that they can only be ok if they are separate from others, people for whom independence entails a dreadful, numbing isolation but for whom connection undermines the capacity to think and act?

Clinical work is by no means the equivalent of collective social action. But my sense is that clinical work does challenge cultural hierarchies in the following ways: first, even if the hierarchies are not named in treatment, the patient comes to understand the splits that they have created, what attributes have become associated with each end of the split, and how each set of attributes has been valued by loved ones and by the culture at large.

Second, it helps the patient identify what has been repudiated and how what has been repudiated haunts and conditions what has not. Third, it is one of the only cultural discourses that does not denigrate or deny dependency; indeed, I would argue that the cultural contempt for dependency is perhaps the central symptom of both male and female forms of narcissistic personality disorder. Finally, it helps the patient empathize with, then own or otherwise rework what has been split off, dissociated, projected.

Martha is an upper class white woman who feels poor and is drawn to poor men of color; a woman who often feels like a man and whose mode of autonomy is defensive, a mode which doesn't work as well as it is supposed to, either for her work life or her love life; a heterosexual who is terrified by her desire for women. These splits reveal the way that social inequities get played out in the psyche. The ensuing narcissistic character structure and narcissistic modes of relating impoverish possibilities for agency and mutuality that would challenge the status quo. I have looked here at one contemporary way that social conditions disturb what ideally would be experienced as a dialectical relationship between agency and mutuality, but which all too often become experienced as two separate and conflicting lines of development.

In conclusion, I suggest that there are different ways that narcissistic disturbances are inflicted and lived depending on one's social location and that it would be a fruitful endeavor for psychoanalytic social critics to examine these specificities. Psychoanalysis and psychotherapy in part work by contextualizing what has been decontextualized or too narrowly contextualized, or erroneously contextualized – our work can only be enriched by enlarging our definition of context to include the psychic effects of the social inequities that permeate all aspects of our identities and relationships.

## Note

* Used with permission. Layton, L. (2004) Relational no more: Defensive autonomy in middle-class women. In Winer, J.A., Anderson, J.W. and Kieffer, C.C. (eds.) *The Annual of Psychoanalysis 32, Psychoanalysis and Women.* Hillsdale, NJ: The Analytic Press, pp. 29–42.

# Chapter 9

# That place gives me the heebie jeebies[*]

I needed a garden hose and took a friend shopping with me to a store called Ocean State Job Lot. As we left the store, my white, upper middle-class friend looked utterly disgusted and said, "That place gives me the heebie jeebies." I tried to find out what she meant, what emotion "heebie jeebies" describes for her, but as I asked and it became clear that the emotion had to do with a disdain not only for the lower class goods in the store but for the lower class shoppers, shame set in and she refused to keep talking. The incident brought to mind Pierre Bourdieu's (1984) work on class, taste, and distinction, and it suggested to me that emotions such as "the heebie jeebies" play an important role in sustaining the tastes that keep class hierarchies in place. I personally had felt completely comfortable in the store, which undoubtedly has to do with my own class origins. I hail from what Bourdieu would identify as the rising petite bourgeoisie, marked by a mild asceticism combined with the search for a good bargain that, in my case, is articulated with the Jewish immigrant experience. I have crossed over, via education, into what he would call the new petite bourgeoisie. As I discussed the connections between shopping and emotions with my friend, I recalled my own feelings of discomfort and shame in upper class stores such as Neiman Marcus. Having found some hints in Bourdieu that emotions secure the tastes that differentiate one class fraction from another, I wanted to explore further the unexplored psychoanalytic dimension of his work. After a discussion of the clues Bourdieu provides, I turn to a very informal survey I made of my friends' and colleagues' emotional experiences when shopping in high end vs. low end stores. While this method does not have the advantage of providing a random sample from which one might generalize, it did, because I know the people and the complexities of their class identifications, enable me to read between the lines of self report. The results point to some of the issues that sustain class conflict, particularly connections between emotions and unconscious process, conflictual internalizations of class relations that sustain well-defended identities.

In his book *Distinction*, Bourdieu (1984) largely discusses the tastes of the different class fractions as they appear to the conscious mind of his survey subjects. His empirical methods rely on self-report, and he defines each class fraction by its relative volume and mixture of social, educational, and economic capital as well as its members' personal historical trajectory (i.e., from one class fraction to another). The focus is on how each fraction distinguishes itself from the others and how all but the lowest fractions struggle to distance themselves from the necessity that marks the lives of those at the bottom. Although Bourdieu's work is not psychoanalytic, and in some respects might be seen as rather anti-psychoanalytic (see Ch. 6 of *Distinction*, where he critiques the profession), he nonetheless opens his investigation with the following sentence: "Sociology is rarely more akin to social psychoanalysis than when it confronts an object like taste, one of the most vital stakes in the struggles fought in the field of the dominant class and the field of cultural production" (p. 11). What might he mean by a "social psychoanalysis"? *Distinction*'s significance for psychoanalysis lies in the fact that the core sociological concepts Bourdieu identifies operate largely on an unconscious level. For example, his notion of habitus – the schemes and dispositions that class fractions draw upon to make ethical and taste judgments that distinguish them from other fractions – is something that performatively takes shape from repeated relational and other early tactile and visual experiences that remain unconscious:

> The schemes of the habitus, the primary forms of classification, owe their specific efficacy to the fact that they function below the level of consciousness and language, beyond the reach of introspective scrutiny or control by the will. Orienting practices practically, they embed what some would mistakenly call *values* in the most automatic gestures or the apparently most insignificant techniques of the body – ways of walking or blowing one's nose, ways of eating or talking – and engage the most fundamental principles of construction and evaluation of the

social world, those which most directly express the division of labour (between the classes, the age groups and the sexes) or the division of the work of domination, in divisions between bodies and between relations to the body which borrow more features than one, as if to give them the appearances of naturalness, from the sexual division of labour and the division of sexual labour.

(p. 466)

This version of the unconscious might be thought of as something akin to Stern's (1997) concept of "unformulated experience," which describes a not necessarily conflictual realm of what forms one's horizon of meaning-making possibilities. But other passages, such as the following, suggest that the habitus is grounded in a dynamic unconscious and that tastes derive from relational conflicts highly charged with emotion. Bourdieu writes:

If a group's whole life-style can be read off from the style it adopts in furnishing or clothing, this is not only because these properties are the objectification of the economic and cultural necessity which deter-mined their selection, but also because the social relations objecti-fied in familiar objects, in their luxury or poverty, their 'distinction' or 'vulgarity', their 'beauty' or 'ugliness', impress themselves through bodily experiences which may be as profoundly unconscious as the quiet caress of beige carpets or the thin clamminess of tattered, gar-ish linoleum, the harsh smell of bleach or perfumes as impercepti-ble as a negative scent. Every interior expresses, in its own language, the present and even the past state of its occupants, bespeaking the elegant self-assurance of inherited wealth, the flashy arrogance of the nouveaux riches, the discreet shabbiness of the poor and the gilded shabbiness of 'poor relations' striving to live beyond their means; one thinks of the child in D.H. Lawrence's story 'The Rocking-Horse Winner' who hears throughout the house and even in his bedroom, full of expensive toys, an incessant whispering: 'There must be more money.' Experiences of this sort would be the material of a social psy-choanalysis which set out to grasp the logic whereby the social rela-tions objectified in things and also, of course in people are insensibly internalized, taking their place in a lasting relation to the world and to others, which manifests itself, for example, in thresholds of tolerance of the natural and social world, of noise, overcrowding, physical or verbal violence – and of which the mode of appropriation of cultural goods is one dimension.

(p. 77)

As Bourdieu's citation of the D.H. Lawrence story suggests, the child's relational world is the ground of a *conflictual* internalization of class antagonisms, an internalization that causes neurotic misery. It is this kind of dynamic conflict that I have tried to capture with the concept of normative unconscious processes, that is, those processes that are produced by social hierarchies of various kinds and that, in turn, work to reproduce and secure a hierarchical status quo. If one casts Bourdieu's description of distinction into the terminology of a dynamic unconscious, one could say that class identities are formed via a defensive splitting off of parts of self too closely associated with anything felt to characterize other, especially lower but also upper class fractions. One distances oneself from the lower class's closeness to necessity, but that very splitting creates a haunting anxiety about necessity that is ever-present and must be vigilantly guarded against. In different ways, we distance ourselves as well from those who have what we can never hope to have. These processes make class, like gender, a melancholic structure (Butler, 1995).

The anxiety born of distinguishing oneself both from those below and those above is precisely what Bourdieu discovers to be the motor of social reproduction, but the emotions are not his primary focus and in fact get a bit lost in the welter of empirical data. Bourdieu does occasionally speak about emotions, particularly the anxiety, disdain, and resentment people in one class fraction may feel when they find themselves in the institutions, sites, or among objects that are considered the legitimate domain of another class fraction. Any particular habitus, in other words, is shot through with the emotions that hold its series of dispositions and strategies in place, that mark them as morally good, nay superior to other sets of dispositions. The habitus, he writes, "is a virtue made of necessity" (p. 372), and the most common words, such as "practical," "sober," "odd," "clean" are used to defend or condemn a given habitus, used in ways that mark one fraction off from another (pp. 193–194). An example lies in the way the new petite bourgeoisie distinguishes itself from the rising petite bourgeoisie by rejecting its ethic of asceticism for one of pleasure. Each fraction describes the other's choices in negative terms, e.g., what the ascetic rising petite bourgeoisie calls ethical in terms of body discipline, necessary purchases, etc., the new petite bourgeoisie pathologizes in terms such as masochistic and self-denying.

So even though Bourdieu does not explore emotions, it is clear that emotions are central to his investigation of what reproduces the social status quo, perhaps even more central than taste: indeed, it is precisely the kind of shame or anxiety I feel in the upper-class Neiman Marcus store that keeps the likes of me OUT of Neiman Marcus, no matter how much I may like their goods. On the rare occasions that I go there, I try to make myself small and inconspicuous, anxious that at any moment I will be too loud, take up too much space, or make some other social gaffe that will give me away as not belonging. More comfortable in my own element, my unconscious anxiety is denied by the conscious thought that what I like is the best, but the anxiety that makes me stick close to my own stores simultaneously legitimizes the upper class's right to have more, to have better, and to dominate. I may make fun of what will appear to me to be their extravagance, or, more likely, morally disdain it, both strategies of the less powerful, but I will deploy my own set of values and lifestyle choices, my habitus, to justify turning my back on their domain, all the while possibly envying if not their goods, then certainly their place at the top of the hierarchy. As one respondent to my survey admitted:

> Sometimes when I am in a store like SAKS [an upper-class store: note that she prints it in large letters] and can't afford things, I feel better by telling myself that the clothes, etc. are really not worth even close to what they are asking and I feel that I am empowered by NOT buying them (whether I'd like to or not). It's my personal form of protest.

What is conscious is the shame or anxiety she and I experience in the store; what is structuring the unconscious is the taboo on having a proprietary relation to culture and knowledge. As Bourdieu writes: "Objective limits become a sense of limits, a practical anticipation of objective limits acquired by experience of objective limits, a 'sense of one's place' which leads one to exclude oneself from the goods, persons, places and so forth from which one is excluded" (p. 471).

To get more of a sense of how emotions sustain class identifications and differentiations, what gets split off and how what is split off haunts, I undertook an informal survey of friends and colleagues, most of whom are also part of the new petite bourgeoisie, a class fraction of cultural intermediaries that tends to repudiate both the other fractions of the petite bourgeoisie as well as the dominant class fractions. This fraction, Bourdieu writes, in fact often sees itself as allied with the dominated classes and the dispossessed, understands itself as marginal, déclassé. I suspected, then, that there might be some conflict between the liberal or left values held by this class fraction and reactions, such as the "heebie jeebies," to the habitus of their lower class allies. To begin to explore the emotions structuring the habitus of the new petite bourgeoisie, I sent around an email that said the following:

> I'm working on a research question that I need my friends to help out with. I'm writing about shopping and emotion and social class. I'm finding that some people can't bear to be in stores like the Christmas Tree Shop [a store that buys odd lots of varying quality goods and sells at a discount] – as one person put it, these stores give me the heebie jeebies. I want to know what the heebie jeebies means, what emotion does it describe and what does it have to do with class relations. I myself experience shame when I'm in places like Neiman Marcus, like I'm going to make some terrible social faux pas and I'll be discovered not to belong. These are examples of what I'm interested in – what emotions sustain antagonisms between classes, or, put another way, what emotions sustain class identity? In what shopping situations does one get anxious, shame-filled, repelled, and why? What do those emotions have to do with class? Do you have any anecdotes you'd be willing to share? Thanks in advance.

The responses to this question produced a few broad themes that I analyze next: responses that show how taste is underwritten by the fear of falling back into the class from which one has come and/or falling for the first time into the state of necessity of which the poor are constant reminders; responses that show that those whose origin is upper class have attained and maintain that position by disdaining whatever is associated with the lower classes; responses that reflect something that Bourdieu mentions but does not consider in any detail in *Distinction*: the way that gender and other aspects of identity intersect with class to mediate the emotions behind taste; and, finally, responses that reflect a kind of pity or sadness for the lower classes and the quality of goods with which they are "forced" to make due.

One set of responses came from the wives of men whose social trajectory had taken them from white working class to highly paid professional. The wives reported that their husbands NEVER go into stores like Ocean State Job Lot, which also seems to be true of those born into the upper middle class. But there are interesting emotional differences behind the similar behavior of these two groups. In the store, both groups might feel the heebie jeebies, but it seems that the emotional reactions of those who rose from lower class origins center on the fact that it all feels painfully familiar, while those from upper class origins find such stores simply alien. For both groups, entering the stores might reactivate all that they have split off to attain what they have, and both groups' emotional responses suggest a fear of contagion by contact with the lower classes. But whereas the heebie jeebies among those born into the upper class seems to be something akin to revulsion, for the group whose class status has risen these stores also evoke shame, even humiliation. Responses suggest that low-end stores recall painful experiences of having less than other kids, the wrong kind of clothes, of seeing family members working there at low pay all their lives. One respondent who has moved, via education, from a lower to a higher class fraction, said:

> When I was a kid, my mother used to shop at a place called King's, which I think was an early Walmart . . . I felt humiliated that we were buying stuff there and embarrassed that my clothes came from these discount-y places (or were homemade) when my friends were all buying stuff at Ann Taylor [at the time, upper class women's clothing] . . . I found the people at King's and Caldor's scary and the colors ugly and the smells horrible. I still do.

The humiliation felt in relation to the upper class seems to produce the heebie jeebies reaction toward the lower class.

In thinking about the reactions of both groups, made up largely of liberals, I was reminded of Patricia Williams' (1997) analysis of why the white lower classes don't trust liberals. Williams writes that while liberals may politically fight for the poor, they make it clear in many other ways that they don't want to be anywhere near the poor. They have nothing but disdain for the poor habitus, and the poor know it. Yet it is significant for a social psychoanalysis to recognize that the disdain has different emotional underpinnings for the two class fractions.

Respondents who have moved up in class – especially men – characteristically expressed a wish for "only the best" goods. They expressed it in terms of "better quality," but my guess is that in some cases this hides a fear of being "revealed" as not truly upper class if you *don't* have the best. In my clinical work, I had a client whose obsession with getting "only the best" consumer goods hid an ever-present anxiety about being judged inadequate. This client, who was born into the working poor but who became a successful entrepreneur in his 20s, once said that the only way he can know for sure that no one is putting him down (as he was put down constantly in childhood) is if he exclusively buys those things that legitimate culture considers the best. Bourdieu recognizes the psychic cost that these fractions, who come from poverty, pay:

> The nature against which culture is here constituted is nothing other than what is 'popular', 'low', 'vulgar', 'common'. This means that anyone who wants to 'succeed in life' must pay for his succession to everything which defines truly humane humans by a change of nature, a 'social promotion' experienced as an ontological promotion . . . a leap from nature to culture, from the animal to the human; but having internalized the class struggle, which is at the very heart of culture, he is condemned to shame, horror, even hatred of the old Adam, his language, his body and his tastes, and of everything he was bound to, his roots, his family, his peers, sometimes even his mother tongue, from which he is now separate by a frontier more absolute than any taboo.
>
> (p. 251)

The emotional implication is that a kind of melancholia or dysthymia is the price of that separation from one's former self and earliest attachments (Eng and Han, 2002).

Alternately, the attainment of the higher class status might provide a manic defense against what has been lost. One respondent who moved, via education, from middle to upper middle class said:

> I used to hate getting a bargain . . . But that was 20 years ago when I was moving up class ranks. Now I'm pleased not to overpay and willing to go almost anywhere . . . although I still think of myself as belonging in the Nordstroms, Neiman Marcuses, Williams Sonomas and Bread and Circuses of the world [all high-end upper-class stores].

> Guess it's sort of like dressing a certain way most of the time – but enjoying dressing in drag – because you're pushing the boundaries and somehow "getting away" with something.

This respondent, whose mother aspired to upper class status, was one of the few Jews in his town growing up, and I wonder if he also perceived that Jewishness, often associated with getting a bargain, stood in the way of rising in class status. He did not repudiate Judaism, just getting a bargain; his comment reveals the interesting difference between how one passes while moving up in rank—by disdaining association with those who need a bargain—and how one passes once having achieved the desired status: he can now take pleasure in frequenting the bargain store because he no longer feels an emotional kinship with those who have to do so. Here we see that distinction is marked, at its core, by relational rupture.

The next set of responses suggests that gender inflects the habitus in particular ways; for example, within a class fraction such as the new petite bourgeoisie, men and women may have different emotional ways of internalizing class difference, ways that have to do in part with their relation to their bodies, to knowledge, and to their right to dominate. A 52-year-old female geriatric social worker, whose parents are Holocaust survivors who did factory work when they first came to the U.S., spoke of her discomfort looking at clothes in Bloomingdale's [upper-class department store] in an upscale suburban mall:

> First of all, all the saleswomen were young and thin. It's not true of other large department stores like Filene's [a middle-class department store] . . . It made me feel different. The women that shopped there were all well manicured, and looked like they spent time on themselves. I felt schleppy in comparison. The clothes they were selling also left me feeling left out. There were only a few items in each size and they seemed to say "not for you." . . . On the other hand I had been to Chicos in the Burlington Mall [a more middle-class mall] a few weeks before. I felt more comfortable there. Perhaps because their clothes were geared toward someone like me (older and rounder). Also the saleswomen were friendly and there is a sense of camaraderie amongst the customers.

Conscious of systemic age discrimination, she also wrote that she's aware that it is the unspoken policy of some stores not to hire older women.

Like myself, this respondent did not feel that she has the right body for these high-end stores. A male respondent to my email asked if I felt similarly uncomfortable in high-end restaurants and hotels. I do not, which made me think all the more that the shopping issue is about having the wrong body. My large educational capital, consonant with my Jewish identity, makes me see myself as someone with excellent and sophisticated taste that entitles me to frequent the finest restaurants and hotels with no sense of shame. Another Jewish female psychologist respondent seemed to feel similarly:

> I often have conversations with myself when I find myself having feel-ings of superiority about such things as taste in clothes, music, books (or should I say literature), accents, plays (or should I say theatre), etc. I tell myself that taste is subjective, but part of me persists in feelings of superiority, which feels good, sad to say, since like you, Lynne, I have feelings of inferiority in stores like Neiman Marcus, etc.

So it is not just class that keeps this class fraction out of high end stores, but the intersection of class and gender.

Worried far less about his body, a male, gay, Jewish psychologist wrote:

> I don't often feel (aware of anyway) discomfort related to shame or class when shopping. However, on the rare occasions I have been in an extremely upscale store or boutique, I am more aware of "how I pass or read" than usual. In those situations, I can feel imperiled of feeling (or seeming) "less than" – so I might want to convey an air of "I know what I'm looking for" or "I know Armani," or maybe even "I am a person who could/does wear this clothing, or owns home furnishings like this."

He further wrote that he does not usually feel as though he doesn't belong in high end stores; he has a sense of entitlement that enables him to go there. But what does cause him discomfort is to be perceived as a "neo-phyte, or a pretender." He wondered if there is a gender component to this, that men don't like to "not know," to be perceived as an "unknowledgable consumer." I imagine that another aspect of the gender component is that, as a male, he feels a right to have what the upper class has in a way that the females of this class fraction might not. Although my sample was quite small (with an N of 20), I would say that most of the males claimed this right to have the best, and most of the females felt as though they did not belong in upper class stores.

I conclude with the responses of a few avowedly left-wing members of my sample, who said that they feel sad in stores such as Ocean State Job Lot; one said she feels the stores are an assault on poor people:

> When I am in a store like a Christmas Tree shop, or a place with scented candles and knickknacks for instance, I get a sick feeling that I would describe as existential agony. I feel that everything in the world is worthless junk and that there is no point in striving or in trying to do anything of substance. I often feel this way at malls. I rarely go to them because of it. . . . If I go to shop, I soon become "world weary" and just want to go home immediately. Some of the stores have sickening smells in them which I think is a combination of poor air circulation and evil gases coming from the products. It's got to be unhealthy, but beyond that it's just awful to smell. Yet, no one seems to notice it. I want to shout to everyone to wake up and see what a horrid environment they're in, but I of course know that would be "crazy."

Another respondent wrote:

> I find those low-end places horribly depressing. They make me angry for AND at the people shopping there. And maybe horrified at/scared of the idea of living that kind of life? I don't like the high end Neiman Marcus stores, either. In fact, I really loathe shopping – except in bookstores and hardware stores, for books and hammers and paint. Those are okay. Classless, perhaps? . . . Even when I was a kid I minded (resented) the ugly brownish colors and sleazy fabrics and horrible mirrors in the dressing rooms and the way you often don't have private dressing rooms in stores like that. Maybe I was picking up my mother's resentment that she had to shop there, that my father didn't make enough money to live the way they'd been brought up to live? I find it all a kind of assault on poor people and yet, I suppose, don't like being WITH those people. Any more than I like being with

the people at Saks or Neiman's or just about any place that isn't a small store . . .

All of this is what makes catalogues such a great way to shop. You can do it at 11:00 at night if you want and you don't have to undress with those ugly fat ladies yelling at their kids AND you don't have to deal with snooty salespeople in expensive stores.

As with the upper class respondents, heebie jeebies for these respondents had to do with the quality of the goods, the way they're thrown all over the place, the dirty floors, the noise, the overstimulation, the crowdedness – mixed in with some condescension towards the people who shop there. But the sadness also reflected empathy for those who HAVE to shop there.

Bourdieu suggests that this sadness, too, might be merely a guise of the way distinction operates. He argues that the dominant classes generally impose their own view of what is desirable (in terms of noise, clothing quality, cleanliness) on the working classes, not recognizing that their own taste marks nothing objective, nothing superior, but only their internalization of class struggle. He writes:

> So the search for distinction has no need to see itself for what it is, and all the intolerances – of noise, crowds, etc. – inculcated by a bourgeois upbringing are generally sufficient to provoke the changes of terrain or object which, in work as in leisure, lead towards the objects, places or activities rarest at a given moment.
>
> (p. 249)

Bourdieu's theory has been accused of being overly deterministic/ structuralist and pessimistic, and here is one place where I think we see evidence of that. For he suggests that there is no stance from which to make an objective judgment; there are only subjective rationalizations that legitimize one's own place in the hierarchy. Clearly, he has a point, and we can see it in the respondents' distaste for noise, for dressing in open rooms, for the "ugly, fat people." Yet, perhaps Bourdieu is not attentive enough to emotion and misses the possibilities for a class alliance that exist in this class fraction's empathy for the poor. If there are indeed gases coming out of the goods and the people who have to buy those goods can't, in any of several ways, afford to notice, it seems a good thing that some do notice that bad goods and unhealthy food are being dumped on the poor.

Bourdieu's logic suggests that the poor develop their habitus out of necessity. While at times he seems almost to glorify tastes that are closer to everyday needs and experiences, critiquing the aesthetic distance central to the taste of dominant fractions, would he want to argue that values that rationalize the constraints of necessity are emancipatory? Isn't part of the goal of social equality to make it so no one has to live dangerously close to the edge of not having basic necessities? Bourdieu's system presupposes a narcissistic subject and so holds little place for getting outside oneself and caring about what happens to those not of your class; he assumes that negative value judgments on the habitus of a lower class are rationalizations meant to maintain your class status at a safe distance from that class. My results suggest that this class fraction's emotions are complex, operating simultaneously to secure distance from necessity and to make one decry and fight actively against social injustice. Still, speaking as someone who himself is from the working class, Bourdieu does have a point: the ambivalence that this class fraction has toward the poor inevitably makes allyship problematic.

## Conclusion

Psychoanalytic social theorists know that social change does not come about by suggesting that people "just say no;" they know that fantasy and the emotions that drive fantasy largely pull to keeps things as they are, or, alternatively, to motivate change. What drives Bourdieu's work is the psychoanalytic view that the internalization of class relations, manifest in taste and people's fantasies about what tastes represent about them, is responsible for the social reproduction of things as they are. His work inspires a deeper investigation of the unconscious processes of internalization and the role emotions play in social reproduction. I suggest that to elaborate a social psychoanalysis, we must investigate the workings of a dynamic normative unconscious, that aspect of the unconscious born of having to suppress and/or split off whatever feelings, desires, and attributes that those who offer us love insist, consciously and unconsciously, are not part of a proper way of being human. "The Rocking-Horse Winner" exemplifies the way in which parental anxiety about money becomes a child's anxiety. Another example: a friend whose early life was dominated by a father who wanted him to go to medical school was repeatedly asked, whenever he did something that did not show enough scholarly promise,

in a particular individual, for example, could account for a reading of consumerism in opposition to that of most Americans. One left-wing female respondent, a Jewish immigrant who came to America as a child, wrote that her family was "not steeped in consumerism as a means of selfhood or sense of emotional security. In fact, my parents thought Americans foolish in their spending habits."

It seems important to think about the fact that even those in my sample who were aware of systemic discrimination did not seem aware of what might underlie their fear of contagion by the poor, be it a fear of humiliation or the separation from an earlier self of which Bourdieu speaks. Recall that the friend I spoke of in my opening anecdote stopped talking as soon as she realized that her heebie jeebies was not only about the goods but about the people. I conclude by suggesting we look at the shame about need and dependency that is part of this class fraction's identity, for it is likely to be the very thing that blocks a closer political alliance between the left-liberal new petite bourgeoisie and lower class fractions.

## Note

* Used with permission. Layton, L. (2004/2006) That place gives me the heebie jeebies. *International Journal of Critical Psychology* 10: 36–50. Reprinted in Layton, L., Hollander, N.C. and Gutwill, S. (eds.) *Psychoanalysis, Class and Politics: Encounters in the Clinical Setting.* New York, NY: Routledge, pp. 51–64.

# Chapter 10

# Class in the clinic
Enacting distinction[*]

In her introduction to the 2005 special issue of *Sociology* on Class, Culture and Identity, Lawler (2005a) briefly reviews the history of sociological work on class. In the 1980s and early 1990s, Lawler notes, research on class and research on other identity categories, for example, race, tended to develop separately. However, the title of the 1991 volume *Bringing Class Back In* (McNall et al.) suggests that even outside of sociological work on identity, class had fallen off most sociologists' research agenda after the late 1960s and early 1970s. In part due to its antipathy to sociology, psychology has largely ignored class altogether, with the very important exception of those critical psychologists, e.g., Walkerdine, 1986, 1992; Walkerdine and Lucey, 1989, for whom class was never off the agenda.

Lawler is nonetheless correct to highlight the general disappearance of class as a category of identity research. Outside of work focused directly on identity, what became prominent in sociology in the post-Marxist and increasingly neoliberalizing academic milieu of the 1980s and 1990s was work on de-traditionalization and individualization (Giddens, 1991; Beck, 1999; Beck and Beck-Gernsheim, 2002). Intentionally or unintentionally, this work contributed to the mainstream consensus that class affiliations (like religion and other traditional collective identity categories) no longer effectively or affectively bind people together. As those who write about neoliberalism and class suggest (e.g., Walkerdine, 2003), this sociological literature "disappeared" class by focusing on the contemporary Western demand for self-invention, do-it-yourself biography, "self-fashioning" (although, to be fair, individualization theorists did emphasize that the absence of collective support systems, and the increasing shift of risk from the public sector onto the individual, created a tendency for "do-it-yourself" biographies to issue all too frequently in "breakdown" biographies (Beck and Beck-Gernsheim, 2002, p. 7)).

The publication in English of Bourdieu's work (particularly *Distinction*, 1984) proved crucial in expanding the concept of class beyond definitions centered on job category or income. Bourdieu's relational definition of class, which understands class position to be a complex amalgam of economic, social, and cultural capital, lived as differentiated and embodied versions of habitus, enabled researchers to articulate class with such psychosocial variables as taste, affects, and competition for educational and social networking advantage (see, for example, Bennett et al., 2009; Reay et al., 2011). Drawing on Bourdieu, Skeggs (2005) and others have persuasively argued that class has hardly disappeared: rather, it is expressed as differences in taste, differences that are used to pathologize the working class as subjects with bad taste who make bad moral choices. As Lawler (2005a) writes, by the end of the 1990s (probably due to the noticeable effects of new levels of income inequality), class had once again become central to several theorists, many of whom were themselves working-class in origin. By the time the 2005 special issue appeared, there was a consensus among feminist (and other) theorists that (1) class is a category that can only be understood relationally; (2) subjectivities are not only raced, sexed and gendered, but also classed, i.e., class is integral to the construction of subjectivity; (3) class is a dynamic process, a "site for political struggle, rather than . . . a set of static and empty positions waiting to be filled by indicators such as employment and housing" (Lawler, 2005b, p. 430).

By 2005, a powerful means of researching class had emerged from psychosocial interview work aimed at understanding how class is lived. Class researchers have increasingly turned their attention to the particularities of class cultural practices and how they are forged in relation to the practices of other class fractions. Given the increasing interest in investigating class as lived relational experience, it has been surprising to me how few psychosocial theorists of class have taken into account the power of unconscious process, unconscious affects, and unconscious intergenerational transmission. As noted in the last chapter, Bourdieu (1984) himself had called for a "social psychoanalysis" in *Distinction* (p. 11), and there, as well as in *The Weight of the World* (1999), he pointed to various effects of

*a feeling small / not fitting in / seen as key intelligent, etc.*

unconscious process on the way class is lived: for example, he described unconscious effects of disavowed histories of class struggle, embedded in the very concept of habitus; he also elaborated the internal conflicts and self-repudiations inherent to moving up in class. Although Bourdieu linked "distinction" specifically to the habitus of the bourgeoisie, he also described the way each class makes a moral virtue of its own way of being, shaming and repudiating the ways of other classes both higher and lower (Skeggs, 1997; Lamont, 2000; Sayer, 2005; Reay, 2015; Aarseth et al., 2016).

Among psychoanalysts who write about class, few, until very recently, have grappled with how class relations play out in the clinic (exceptions in contemporary psychoanalysis include Samuels, 1993, 2007; Altman, 1995; Whitson, 1996; Bodnar, 2004; Hartman, 2005; Layton et al., 2006; Ryan, 2006, 2017; Botticelli, 2007; Corpt, 2013). Danto (2005) has usefully traced the history of the psychoanalytic establishment's relation to class, highlighting Freud's endorsement of the early twentieth-century free psychoanalytic clinics in Berlin and Vienna. Altman (1995) wrote of the many class and race issues that emerged in his work in a clinic in a poor area of New York City. Hartman (2005), elaborating on my concept of a heterosexist unconscious (Layton, 2002), wrote about his own conflictual class formation and how it affected his clinical work. Ryan (2009, 2017) chronicled the elision and disavowal of class in psychoanalysis, while she herself (2006) significantly advanced work on class and the clinic in her study of middle-class and working-class clinicians who described the kinds of transferences and countertransferences they experienced when working with patients from classes different from their own. Among Ryan's fascinating results was the finding that middle-class patients often were contemptuous toward their working-class therapists, who then had to work very hard not to retaliate (2006, p. 132). In what follows, I look at classed clinical enactments of normative unconscious processes, focusing specifically on how class identities are subjectively created and relationally lived in our particular historical moment.

## Class struggles in neoliberal times: enacting the demand for upward mobility

Two vignettes drawn from my own clinical work illustrate some of the effects, as Walkerdine (2003) has put it, of the neoliberal intensification of the demand for upward mobility. Set against a backdrop of a decline in working-class collective institutions; the fraying, if not rupture, of a social safety net and the accompanying "responsibilization" of the individual; a growing consensus that competition is at the heart of an intensely individualistic conception of human nature; the conviction that a successful human is a rich human; and the high value put on self-fashioning (or, as some have put it, e.g., du Gay, 2004, on being an entrepreneurial self), the following vignettes demonstrate how the demand for upward mobility in a culture of increasing class inequality promotes sadomasochistic patterns of relating that are part and parcel of class formation and class struggle.

The two patients I shall describe came of age in the post-1970s U.S. atmosphere of neoliberalism and neoconservatism (the vignettes were first reported in Layton, 2014a). Both of their families, conflictually to be sure, demanded that they show their worth by rising in class status. Sandy was born in the late 1970s, the first child of a white mother who grew up in poverty and a white father who rose from blue collar to bureaucratic white collar. Father never let mother forget where she had come from, and much of Sandy's specialness to father was wrapped up in his often-stated aspirations that she rise in class and status. Because she was so special, he asserted, she could do and have whatever she wanted. Intuiting this source of father's love, Sandy worked much harder academically than any of her peers, and she did indeed rise to become a professional in a high-income field. She thus secured her place as her father's favorite – which involved joining together in denigrating mother. What Sandy always knew, but couldn't really know until therapy, is that her father's capacities for love were rather damaged, and a largely unconscious part of her greatly resented what felt like a love contingent on performance. Her fragile sense of specialness was bolstered by her utter disdain for peers who didn't work as hard as she: "someday they'll be cleaning my toilets," she thought when she saw them out having fun while she studied.

Sandy fell in love with a working-class man who himself had risen to be bureaucratic white collar. As her therapist, I listened over and over again to her mocking denigration of his working-class ways. I surmise that Sandy thought she was bonding with me and my, in her view, exalted class position when she was denigrating the classlessness of her boyfriend. But, of course, it was her own anxiety about not being classy enough that she feared would be revealed – and dreams did at times reveal it. At the point where I could no longer bear her contempt and could find a way to confront it calmly, I pointed out to her that she seemed to need to mock her boyfriend, and we ought perhaps to look at why. The first time I brought this up, she practically had an anxiety attack on the couch. She had an instant moment of recognition that, in fact, much of her sense of who she was rested on this defensive kind of class mockery, and she suddenly felt herself unraveling at the prospect of being shorn of this defense. It took much work to understand where her class distinction had come from, how it related to class disidentifications with mother and identifications with father's disdain for what, in mother, reminded him too much of his disowned class insecurities. More importantly, she came to understand how the class grandiosity was a defense against recognizing that father's love was contingent on her achievements – her mockery was aimed as much at hated parts of self that she had come to associate with classlessness as at her boyfriend.

Class wounds run deep. When it feels like love is contingent on performance, love itself gets tangled up in sadomasochistic enactments. Indeed, until she met this boyfriend, Sandy was entirely cynical about love. For years, she had been cheating on her previous upper middle-class boyfriend with a lower-class man she'd dated in high school – another way of externalizing and interpersonalizing her class struggle. But Sandy's denigration of love was abetted by a fairly new subject position offered to professionalizing women, one formed at the intersection of neoliberalism and a middle-class version of feminism. Here, dependency is denied and caretaking capacities devalued in favor of a single-minded focus on career goals – and, indeed, before analysis Sandy occupied this position without seeming conflict (see Chapter 8). Love was for fools, she would often say. In her determination to rise in class, Sandy had become the kind of non-relational maximizer of self-opportunity described as exemplary in neoliberal literature. She had come to hate her own vulnerability and to project it onto her boyfriend and lower classes in general. But we might guess that she fell in love with this boyfriend not only to have an object from whom she could distinguish herself and whom she could denigrate, but also because he was comfortable with his class, with all she had come to call not-me, other. She would try repeatedly to get me to laugh with her at him for wearing a gold chain or showing some other sign of belonging to the white working class, but she was head over heels in love with him and she had never been in love before.

Sandy's case illustrates that disgust and distinction can operate not only between classes but within class – and that here, too, the "disgusting" other has to be kept close. Sandy was not only defending against her fear of falling back into the lower class, represented by her mother; she was also disavowing her love for her lower-class mother and retaliating against that mother's difficulty giving love and nurture. Sandy became a "disgusted" subject (Lawler, 2005b) and expected to find in me someone who would share her disgust for the lower class. When I did not play that part, her defenses and the form of classed subjectivity she performed began to crumble.

Another patient, Paul, was born in the early 1970s and was the second child of a working-class mother from several generations of working-class and unskilled laborers. His father was a white-collar small business owner, but he had left when Paul was three, plunging the family into poverty. His mother's grandparents had been proud working-class union people, but his maternal grandparents and his mother, the people who raised him, aspired, unsuccessfully, to rise in class (a generational shift perhaps due, in part, to the declining political and collective power of unions – see Lamont, 2000). Although he was only occasionally present in Paul's life, from time to time bestowing a bit of money and heavy doses of advice, his father stood as a family example of someone who had "made it" – but also as someone who was felt to be immoral, irresponsible, and an object of family derision. Paul, who did very well in school, seems to have been the target recipient in the family of the (conflicted) parental wish to advance in class. Like Sandy, Paul, too, had a vague feeling that the love of both parents was contingent on rising in class, on bringing the family a more legitimate social status.

The arena in which Paul chose to rise, academic science, was one that truly was dear and meaningful to him, but the rage at the almost desperate demand put on him to rise kept getting in the way of achieving what he hoped to achieve. The question "who am I doing this work for?" plagued him constantly, and because he perceived his parents as tyrannical and unloving, achievement always had the flavor not of self-fulfillment but rather of submitting to a rejecting, judgmental authority. An important basis of his sense of self involved a constant courageous fight against parental and other unjust authorities. But what we began to recognize was that part of the repeated transference scenario entailed a need to turn any authority perceived as "higher" than he into a potential immoral tyrant; more than once Paul was fired from jobs after getting explosively angry at a superior.

For Paul, the very structure of analysis frequently and painfully evoked the feeling of unjustness, for while the caring attention of analysis promised love, each of its many limits were felt as unduly punishing and rejecting – although he rarely acknowledged that he felt hurt by these constraints. Rather, from time to time, we became engaged in a struggle in which he defended the underdog world of patients against the injustices of arrogant analytic authority. Notable in Paul's case was a need to see me as powerful and punishing both so that he could have a perch from which to feel justified waging battle against the perceived (and real) injustices of the analytic situation AND so he could keep me at a distance so he would not be at risk of being overtaken by me, swallowed up, and destroyed. At the same time, his exquisite sensitivity to abuses of authority forced me repeatedly to examine the defensively grandiose aspects of my analytic stance. More than once, I wounded Paul when my own class-blindness was enacted unconsciously as class arrogance, for example, by pathologizing some of his protests against injustice.

Sandy and Paul's ways of living class illustrate how split states of grandiosity/pride and, on the other side of the split, self-hatred/shame can ensue when children perceive that parental love is contingent on rising in class and economic status. The parents in these cases carried the intergenerationally transmitted wounds of being lower class and treated by multiple authorities in degrading and condescending ways. Their way of loving their children produced different kinds of wounds that issued in split relations both to authority and to those lower in class. Such are the narcissistic wounds that create class character. But, as Ball et al., 2004, and Vincent and Ball, 2007, have suggested, even within the same class fraction class can be lived quite differently, depending not only on variables such as gender, age, geography, history, and politics, but also on what Levine-Rasky, 2011, pp. 247–248 (citing Anthias), describes as a distinction between social position (differences in resources) and social positioning (how one deals with those differences). In other words, even within the same class fraction, differences in libidinal loyalties and investments affect whether and how one challenges, conforms to, or otherwise negotiates class inequalities. Sandy identified with professional class authority and generally denigrated those lower. Paul's relation to authority alternated between deference, rage, and panic. What crippled Paul was precisely an intergenerationally transmitted split relation to authority.

As is so often the case, both Sandy and Paul had made a virtue out of the very place in which they had been wounded: Sandy, encouraged by a neoliberal culture that can only envision winners and losers, felt those who achieved middle-class status were better humans than those who had not, and yet, as in all cases of splitting, she had to keep the degraded other close so as to continue to feel special and perhaps, as I suggested, also to stay close to some part of her that, in her class rise, she had lost and not grieved. Indeed, along with therapy, it was her love for him that offered an opportunity to heal her classed psychic splits.

Unlike Sandy, Paul had made a virtue of refusing to comply with authority, of rebelling against rules, of NOT seeking accolades. The cost, however, was high: he could neither shake a pervasive sense of being unlovable nor a conviction that culturally-sanctioned middle-class ways of doing things were the "right" way and the only way deserving of reward. Thus, he would repeatedly use his academic credentials to enter an upper-class world, and then he would fight with the boss about all the injustices he saw, thereby risking, and often incurring, either demotion or expulsion. For Paul, entering the middle-class world meant a loss of integrity. For both Sandy and Paul, the splits and projections resulting from the way class wounds were lived played out interpersonally in sadomasochistic relations, central to which were enactments externalizing internalized "distinction" between inferior and superior. Sandy's were performed in the relation with her boyfriend rather than with me. Paul's were performed with me. Indeed, as sadomasochistic forms of relating began more clearly to define my relationship with Paul, I was able to see that one thing that continually got in the way of his ability to work on his projects was inextricably tied to class inequality: feelings of illegitimacy and the simultaneous impotent reverence for and hatred of power WERE and ARE his maternal family's way of living class.

As I've said, Sandy and Paul came of age in an era in which U.S. parents of all classes are anxious about whether or not their children will "make it." Their stories illustrate some of the psychic fallout that can arise from the demand to rise in class, and they clearly reveal how class gets connected to particular ways of being, knowing, and loving – and how the demand to rise can cause one to hate those parts of self that are connected to the practices of the "inferior class." Neoliberal regimes publicly sanction the repudiation of vulnerable and dependent psychological states, and thus render such states shameful (for an example, see Jimenez and Walkerdine, 2012). Indeed, Chase and Walker, 2012, p. 740, describe poverty as a "meta-arena for the emergence of shame, especially in contemporary British society where success is largely measured according to the attainment of economic goals." In such conditions, certainly true as well in the U.S., ordinary human self-states like dependence, exacerbated by the inequalities of neoliberalism, are likely to become "not-me," other, dissociated and then associated with those others who are lower on the social scale.

In conclusion, I hope not only to have demonstrated the significance of unconscious process in the creation of conflicted class identities and class distinctions, but also to have suggested some new avenues for thinking about how class struggles are historically specific and both driven and perpetuated by vicious circles of sadomasochistic relating. In Section III, I explore further the sadomasochistic individual and large-group effects of neoliberalism.

## Note

* Used with permission. Adapted from Layton, L. (2014) Grandiosity, neoliberalism, and neoconservatism. *Psychoanalytic Inquiry* 34(5): 463–474.

# Chapter 11

# Racial identities, racial enactments, and normative unconscious processes*

## On racial/ethnic identity

What do we mean when we speak of racial or ethnic identities? Do we refer to categories that are coherent, socially constructed, and inherently oppressive, as many theorists assert? Dalal (2002), for example, argues that racism precedes the concept of race, and Rustin (1991) asserts that "'Race' is both an empty category and one of the most destructive and powerful forms of social categorization" (p. 57). Lacanian cultural critics often argue that coherent identities are oppressive fictions, and Morgan (2002) cites DNA evidence that "the term 'race' is a constructed idea with no objective basis in biology" (p. 567). Or, as those who see "identity" as less problematic argue (e.g., Volkan, 2004), is it human nature to need a large-group identity and to form that identity by creating an us-them divide?

Or, as liberal multiculturalists might claim, are racial and ethnic identities simply based in cultural and/or biological differences not necessarily built on repudiation of otherness, differences that ought to be celebrated rather than denigrated? Do we understand racial and ethnic differences as discrete (the liberal as well as conservative model) or as related to each other and interimplicated (the poststructuralist model)? More particularly, do we think that nonwhite, non-Protestant identities are built in reference to dominant whiteness and Protestantism? And do those in subordinate positions then create hierarchical relations among and between themselves, all marked in some way by white dominance (Friedman, 1995; Gooding-Williams, 1993; Layton, 1998)?

If we believe the latter, how do we understand such relations psychologically? In terms of perpetrators and victims? Do we then focus politically on redressing long histories of systemic prejudice and discrimination? Or, as "colorblind" adherents claim, do racial and ethnic identities rest on cultural and/or biological differences that ought to be ignored, ought not to be taken into account, when, for example, hiring or admitting to college? Finally, does it even make sense to speak of racial identities without simultaneously speaking of the way they intersect with class, gender, and other identity categories (R.M. Williams, 1997)? Can we assume, in other words, that a racial identity is homogeneous, that blacks and whites of all classes and both genders experience race in the same way?

Obviously, thinking about racial and ethnic identities requires us first to do some thinking about identity tout court. Currently, there are any number of theories that contest the definition of identity, and the struggle to define both identity and race is definitely a political matter, the outcome of which has important social consequences (which is obvious when we think of the differences in policy that derive from liberal ideology, e.g., affirmative action, versus colorblind ideology). In this chapter, I draw on the poststructural, feminist, and relational negotiation model of identity that I described in my introduction to the book, and I describe the operation of normative unconscious processes as they operate in racism, racialized identities, and racialized enactments in clinical work.

With the term normative unconscious processes, I refer to the psychological consequences of living in a culture in which many norms serve the dominant ideological purpose of maintaining a power status quo. My assumption is that class, race, gender, and sex hierarchies, which confer power and exist for the benefit of those with power, tend not only to idealize certain subject positions and devalue others, but tend to do so by splitting human capacities and attributes and giving them class or race or gender assignations. Such assignations cause narcissistic wounds that organize the desire to belong to one group rather than another. These wounds become lived as class, race, gender, and sexual identities. As Bourdieu (1984) and other social theorists have made clear, no social location exists without reference to all the others, and all people create their own identities by taking up some cognitive and affective position toward dominant cultural ideals. Power hierarchies create and sustain differences that mark out what is high and low, good and bad, pure and impure, and there is certainly a general tendency for those not in power to internalize the denigrating attributions that come at them (see Dalal, 2002; Clarke, 2003; Moss, 2003; White, 2002). Nonetheless, as my model of identity suggests, it would be a mistake to think that norms are internalized without conflict (Layton, 1998, 2002, 2004d). Because the hierarchies split and categorize human attributes and capacities, we find in the clinic and in our lives unceasing conflict between those unconscious processes that seek to maintain those splits and those that refuse them.

Normative unconscious processes, then, are one of the psychic forces that push to consolidate the "right" kind of identity and to obfuscate the workings of unequal power hierarchies. They protect the psychic splits that cultural norms mandate, and they do so because the risk of contesting them is loss of love and social approval. But let us not forget that the result of splitting is to keep what has been split off near. Repetition compulsions are the very place where the struggle between coercive normative unconscious processes and counternormative unconscious processes are enacted. And since all identities are relational and not individual possessions (in Dalal's words, "who I am" really boils down to "where I belong" [2002, p. 187]), these repetitions are stirred up and played out in relationships.

## Race and ethnicity: psychoanalytic views

Psychoanalytic views of race differ depending on the way a school (or theorist) formulates its theory of aggression and its theory of what constitutes the self-other relation.[1] Dalal (2001) surveyed the psychoanalytic clinical literature on race and discovered that, in all cases, it was assumed that the differences between races are essential rather than constituted historically. None of the authors in his survey wondered, he notes, how "whites" come to be white. He found that there were two types of assumptions in the psychoanalytic literature: either that, deep down, we are all alike and culture is just an overlay; or that, deep down, we are all unique, and the social contaminates or swamps our uniqueness. In either case, culture is considered external to internal psychic functions.

Further, Dalal found that the actual fact of cultural racism was just about never taken into account as a cause of problems in the clinical psychoanalytic encounter. The patient is frequently assumed to be acting out infantile fantasies; at best, race becomes intertwined with those fantasies, but it is never determinant. Racism is conceptualized as an effect of individual prejudice, never as a cause of it. Dalal (2001) hypothesizes that external reality is kept out of psychoanalytic explanations of racial prejudice because of white guilt.

More recent clinical discussions of race do take external racism into account, and these often lead inexorably to discussions of the effects of trauma, particularly traumas that are unspoken but passed on intergenerationally (Apprey, 1993; George, 2001; Layton, 2002; Volkan, 2004; Walls, 2006).[2] The hatred involved in racist policies and racist projections tends to issue forth in all the well-known sequelae of trauma: intense shame and self-hatred, splitting, dissociation, suicidal or homicidal wishes (Walls, 2006; White, 2002). Herman (1992) writes that the psychic consequences of trauma often result in a three-part internal structure that includes the positions of victim, perpetrator, and rescuer. As the clinical vignette I will present suggests, it is important always to keep all three positions in mind as we work – as well as the ways in which all three will be stirred in us.

Clinicians influenced by poststructuralist antiracism walk the fine line between skepticism toward the category of "race" and respect for the fact that the "fiction" of racial difference is nonetheless a traumatic, lived reality, because of the forces of racism and the many possible responses to them. Leary (1995, 1997a) and Altman (2000) have both argued compellingly that, whether or not it is spoken about, race is always in the room when the dyad is interracial, and the analyst who does not bring it up risks avoiding difficult but likely present material. The trauma of racism affects both "victims" and "perpetrators" alike. It affects each differently, but as Altman's (2000) clinical example demonstrates, victim and perpetrator are psychically connected, and the two roles are easily reversed.

In my own clinical experience, I have at times found it useful to bring up race, or at least race privilege, even when patient and analyst are both white (see Chapter 3). On the other hand, Dalal (2002) asserts (with reference to voluminous data on the historicity of the processes of racialization) that racism historically preceded the concept of race, and, in his view, any reference to race assumes a basis for differentiation of races that is spurious (see also Kovel, 1970, 1988).[3] If we take this to be true, then bringing up race in therapy is as complicated as pretending that it is not there, for what exactly is racial difference? While physical distinctions might anchor our notions of racial difference, what it actually is, in its oppressive mode, has to do with the power to split asunder human capacities and to call some white and others nonwhite. It has to do with an ideological means of maintaining power differentials, of assigning, as Bourdieu (1984) might say, distinction to one group of people and a lack of distinction – or, at best, second classness – to others.

As Dalal (2002) notes, citing Elias (1991), words and categories carry embedded emotions, and the positive or negative valence of words and categories derives from power relations: "Emotions are evoked and utilized to fulfill functions of differentiation. The emotions are a *technique* that is exploited in the task of differentiation, and not the 'cause' of differentiation that they are mistakenly taken to be" (Dalal, 2002, p. 131, italics in original). When we look more closely at the content of racialized splitting (as I shall in the vignette discussed later in this chapter), we find all sorts of effects of these splitting processes: among others, cognitive effects, effects in the way attachment and agency are defined and valued, and effects in emotional states, expression, and range.

On the other hand, drawing again on the negotiation model of identity, racial difference also has to do with whatever the people labeled as racially other – i.e., nonwhite – collectively and individually have fashioned historically from being so labeled. Where my views differ from many determinist views on identity is in my sense that racial identities and the relation between dominant and subordinate identities are not closed systems; subordinate groups' identities are never fully determined by the power of dominant groups. As Hall (1982) and Laclau and Mouffe (1985) assert, elaborating on Gramsci's (1971) concept of hegemony, social and political life in modernity involves a ceaseless struggle between subordinate and dominant groups over the power to define precisely such constructs as race.

Thus, aspects of the identities that nonwhite groups fashion for themselves are healthy, at times psychologically healthier than the psychic states of those who identify with the split cultural ideals of whiteness. Leary (1995, 1997a) and Altman (2000) persuasively argue that, because of racism and the different living conditions it entails, blacks and whites in U.S. culture see the same phenomena quite differently, another argument for the need to address racial difference in the clinical setting. Dalal's theory of race, which implies that calling attention to race is itself racist, suggests that we cannot avoid racist enactments in the clinic, no matter what we do: we enact racializing processes when we bring racial difference into the consulting room, as well as when we deny the significance of such differences.

In the next vignette, I explore this problem via a series of enactments with an Asian American patient, one with whom normative unconscious processes pulled me, all too comfortably, into a position of whiteness. After examining the clinical significance of the ambivalence of stereotypes, I will go on to discuss the increasing discomfort I felt with this patient as I explored what I considered to be his tendency to self-abnegation. And, finally, I look at the patient's struggle to know what love is, a struggle that showed the ways that love – as well as many other constructs that analysts rarely think of in cultural terms – is itself racialized. The interactions I have selected reveal as well the way that race intersects with gender, class, and sexuality.

## Clinical vignette

Michael was a gay, Asian American male in his mid-30s who entered therapy because he could not get his former boyfriend, who was white and middle-class, out of his mind. The patient was worried that this would get in the way of his new relationship, and hoped that therapy, which he had never done before, might help him extirpate disturbing thoughts of the ex-boyfriend, particularly the compulsion to compare himself unfavorably to the ex and to feel socially inept in relation to him. Michael had long felt socially inept, and at least part of the origin of this feeling was that his mother, who strongly valued family and education, did not let him have much of a social life outside the family. He was expected to focus single-mindedly on schoolwork.

His mother and father had emigrated from Asia to a suburb of a big city while in their early 20s, and Michael considered many of his thoughts and feelings to be products of his non-Western culture – and he valued them as such. Nonetheless, he felt that he had problems with self-esteem and hoped that therapy might help with that. At the same time, he was clearly conflicted about being in therapy from the outset. It seems that one of the ways his parents had differentiated themselves from "Westerners" was by feeling superior about their capacity to be private people; Westerners, the parents felt, talk too loudly, too publicly, and too long about their private business. They also make far too much of their emotions. Michael often thought so, too.

Michael's lived experience illustrates the splitting, and, in this case, racializing and nationalizing, of human capacities: in the family, emotion and rationality were split off and labeled Western and non-Western, respectively. This is not the way capacities are usually split by dominant Western groups, to be sure, but if the parents saw their best shot at success in being rational and scientific, then it served them psychologically to distinguish themselves from the other in terms of superior rationality. Yet, how much more complex these things are than they first appear. It turned out that Michael's mother could herself become highly "irrational" at times – yelling, screaming, and imposing rules that to Michael made no sense. Ironically, this only heightened Michael's identification with rationality and against emotion.[4]

In high school, Michael was aware of longings to be part of the white in-crowd, but he also joined his Asian friends in denigrating the popular kids' practices – for example, derisively noting that whites seemed to keep switching romantic partners, but only took partners of the same racial group. Michael figured that he was the only one of the Asian kids who longed to be part of the white crowd; as he told me, it would not be logical for the Asian kids to denigrate something that they really desired to join. (Here I gently noted that this was precisely what he was doing, and perhaps logic is not always all that it is cracked up to be.) Because of his longings, Michael must have felt a certain degree of alienation from his friends as well, which exacerbated his feeling of being socially inept. What was striking about his ambivalent place between Asians and whites, East and West, was that it left him quite uncertain – both about what he felt, and about the value of what he felt, for it pulled him into denigrating the very things he longed for.

From my first sessions with Michael, I saw two grids begin to form, one that associated certain attributes with white Westerners and others with superior Asians, and another that denigrated Asians and idealized white Westerners. These stereotypes were not just racial and ethnic; they were nodal points that stitched together race, ethnicity, gender, and sexuality. Michael and I were both aware of the grids, and, at one point, he laughed and said, "I rely on stereotypes a lot, don't I?"

I invoke Michael's story because his way of splitting and racializing attributes, sometimes with whiteness in the superior position, sometimes in the inferior, stirred a lot of thought and feeling in me and a lot of questions about how best to work with him. It also kept me conscious of my own ways of categorizing and judging, and made me wary of some of the certainties with which I found myself operating. The therapy raised a number of issues about the way intersecting identity categories are lived and the way power differentials create differences: differences in emotional range and expression, in the relation between emotion and cognition, in modes of separation and attachment, in one's very experience of love.

I do not take Michael to be representative of Asian Americans in general;[5] rather, I draw on our work together to explore in more depth the way ideologies of race, ethnicity, gender, and sexuality intersect and are lived and enacted in treatment.

As I mentioned earlier, Michael both idealized and denigrated whites, which put me now in a superior, now in an inferior, position. Although he was conscious of his tendency to stereotype, what was unconscious for Michael was the splitting upon which this rested, and the trauma that caused the splitting in the first place. Splitting and projection may be universal mechanisms of defense, but racism creates the wounds that marshal such defenses, and it is within a racist field that people enact the repetitions that simultaneously keep the wounds fresh and seek to heal them (Dalal, 2002; Layton, 2002).

Michael's ex-boyfriend (who was in fact a mid-level corporate employee and not a higher executive, as the patient's admiration had implied) incarnated in Michael's fantasy everything that Michael was not: he was handsome, dashing, well dressed, athletic, a corporate success, and, most important, socially suave and popular. Michael's attraction was clearly a mix of sexual desire and the desire to have what he thought the ex-boyfriend had. To be the right kind of male in Michael's economy, one had to be white. The fantasied ideal of whiteness that organized his desire was upper class, worldly, popular, and – as the ex-boyfriend was not fully comfortable self-identifying as gay – at least semi-straight and homophobic.

Michael denigrated what he thought of as Asian masculinity, and did not think he could be attracted to an Asian male. He felt that neither white men, the ones worth having, nor Asian men were attracted to Asian men. At the same time, he and his Asian friends had disdain for what was seen as his ex-boyfriend's culture of self-serving, false sincerity. As Bourdieu (1984) noted, one of the central mechanisms of the aspect of identity formation built on a repudiation of otherness is to claim virtue for whatever social group one finds oneself in (thus, the title of Bourdieu's book, *Distinction*).

Michael's Asian friends served the function of asking, "Who wants to be white, anyway?" Whites are selfish. Indeed, the patient's ex and his friends pretended to be concerned for others, Michael said, but, really, they were always manipulating social scenes to get what they wanted. Michael even complained that his current, loving boyfriend had that white Western way of thinking of himself first. For example, in restaurants, Michael observed, his white friends would pour water or tea for themselves when they wanted it, whereas he and other Asians he knew would always pour for everyone else first, and for themselves last. So here was yet another stereotype: that white Westerners are self-absorbed and Asians more polite and considerate of others.

## The ambivalence of the stereotype

While the content of Michael's beliefs and observations is important and tells us the way that he and his family split and racialized human capacities, I want first to look at the form the stereotyping took: the oscillating idealization and denigration. Michael's conflicts and the way stereotypes functioned for him as pseudosolutions resonate with, and even extend, theorizing about the ambivalence of the stereotype.

Writing in a Lacanian frame about colonial discourse, Bhabha (1994) argues that stereotypes function as fetishes: they attempt to fix a signifier to a signified, to a particular meaning (e.g., blacks are animals, Jews are cheap), and so deny the fact that signifiers are always open to multiple signifieds, and that identities can never be fixed. Subjectivity ceaselessly disrupts identity categories because it is, by nature, split by the existence of the unconscious and the unsymbolizable. (That split between meaning and being is what Lacan [1998] refers to as castration.) The fetish-stereotype operates in the narcissistic economy of the Lacanian Imaginary, the register in which the ego itself comes into being.

In this Lacanian economy, the child of eighteen months of age or so sees an image of itself that appears as a coherent whole (Lacan, 1977). Yet, the child experiences the self as a fragmentary and chaotic jumble. The child identifies with this coherent version of self, the ideal ego. For Lacan, then, the ego is founded on the misrecognition that we are not castrated. We know that we are castrated beings, and yet we disavow it by trying to fix ourselves in seamless identities. If we have the power to do so, we use whatever is at our disposal – scientific knowledge, gender dominance, consumer goods – to deny the fact that subjectivity is essentially split, that the ego is not in control. Whatever reminds us of our fragmentary nature stirs aggression and narcissistic rage.

Stereotypes issue from the mind of the colonizer, who, for psychic reassurance, renders the other the same, all the time knowing that the other is different, and attempts to eradicate otherness in the self. To sustain the disavowal, the colonizer must not give the other a chance to speak. For when the other speaks, the fixity of signification that the colonizer seeks to impose (in, for example, colonialist ideologies of what blacks are like) is revealed to be fictional. The oscillation between knowing and not knowing is thus central to colonial discourse, which fantasizes the other as knowable and same, and yet is aware that the other is different, thus posing a challenge to attempts to fix him/her within the stereotyped grids of dominant discourse. The other's difference, and acknowledging differences within the self, are both threats to the colonizer's fantasy of wholeness and sameness.

Bhabha (1994) exemplifies the way that colonizer and colonized become co-implicated in colonial discourse via a well-known "scene" in *Black Skin, White Masks* (Fanon, 1967, pp. 109–114). In this account, told in the first person, a child on a train sees Fanon and says to his mother, "Look, a nigger" (p. 109). At first amused, Fanon then becomes increasingly disturbed as he feels his humanness evaporate, his multiplicity as a man reduced to only a "black body" (what he calls a racialized epidermal schema). He shivers from cold. The boy, unconscious of his own aggression, now interprets the shiver as a shiver of rage, and, suddenly, he is frightened of the black man, scared that the "nigger" is going to eat him up. For Bhabha (following Lacan), the shaky ground upon which the bourgeois ego forms ensures that the attempt to deny or dominate difference will unleash continued aggression against both self and other.

Writing in a Kleinian frame about the relation between African Americans and whites, Balbus (2004) argues that the dominant version of whiteness in the U.S. requires that whites split off emotion from reason, body from mind, nature from culture. Blackness becomes the container of what is split off from whiteness. Balbus maintains that white stereotypes of blacks yield significant evidence that whites both love and hate blacks, and that whites have tremendous guilt about what they have historically done to blacks in this country. The guilt, however, is not expressed in making reparation; rather, structural racism causes depressive anxiety at every phase of development – oral, anal, genital – to issue in the regressive splitting and projection characteristic of paranoid-schizoid relating. The stereotypes that whites develop about blacks at each developmental level reflect the split between unintegrated love and hate.

Balbus (2004) catalogues some of the contradictory evaluations in white stereotypes of blacks, including white perceptions that blacks are "lazy and shiftless," but "laid back and cool"; that they are denigrated as "animals," while being simultaneously idealized as "natural athletes." Balbus argues that reparations, monetary ones, would be symbolic of an emotional reparation in which, rather than continue to split, whites would acknowledge the harm they have done to blacks and deal with the anxiety and guilt produced by this knowledge. His argument is that the taking back of white projections is crucial to the well-being not just of blacks, but also of whites themselves.

In essence, I come to the same conclusion as these writers, that the nature of the stereotype is ambivalent, but I come to it from a different psychoanalytic frame, for I locate ambivalence as deriving neither from an originary destructive instinct, nor from an originary split in our feelings about the breast/parent, nor from an originary refusal to acknowledge limits and loss. Rather, I think it derives from racism (Boulanger, 2007): from the fact that dominant identity categories are defined by dividing up into binary pairs the human capacities and attributes that can only develop and thrive in tandem, such as dependence and independence, connection and agency, emotion and reason. Such dividing determines the ways in which we love, hate, and create. And the reason why such divides exist has little to do with human nature. Rather, they exist so that those in power, those with the power to define the proper identity, stay in power.

The oscillation between denigration and idealization that marks my patient Michael's stereotyping is characteristic of narcissism, and it is part of my argument that racism and other cultural inequalities produce not just narcissistic injury, but narcissistic character and defenses as well. Michael frequently got caught in his web of projections, now disdaining what he in fact longed for, now disdaining what he felt he was. Is the fantasy behind the stereotyping process one of a "lost" wholeness that no one ever can or did attain (Bhabha, 1994)? Is the love-hate relationship with whiteness rooted in originary destructive and libidinal drives, torn asunder by racism (Balbus, 2004)?

I suggest that fantasies of lost wholeness and racist-driven splitting and projection arise from the ashes of racist-driven narcissistic wounding, which leads us to seek a place, a fantasy space, where we might no longer be vulnerable to hurt, humiliation, and isolation. Michael's ex-boyfriend, who incarnated whiteness and whose rejection of Michael only made him more desirable, represented such a fantasy space for Michael. In this fantasy space, which Michael resisted relinquishing with all his might, he would either be loved by the ex or would himself be more like the ex – and he would never again feel the pain of inferiority.

## Whiteness

For Bhabha (1994) and others (e.g., George, 2001), the colonial ideal ego is white, and whatever threatens one's claim to whiteness is apt to unleash anxiety and aggression. A major stake of discourses that reinforce racial difference is to define who can lay claim to whiteness/wholeness and who cannot (Lipsitz, 1998). In their article on racial melancholia, Eng and Han (2002) argue that different stereotypes haunt Asian Americans from those that haunt African Americans. These authors focus specifically on the psychic effects of the model-minority stereotype. In their view, many middle-class or upwardly mobile Asians become melancholic because to be successful in white America often requires a rejection of part of who they are. Further, Eng and Han assert that, while Asian Americans can become wealthy and successful in their fields, they can never become white; if the inclusion that comes with whiteness is what they covet, the psychic mission is doomed to failure.

My patient Michael felt that he had the wrong attributes, including body type, to be the right kind of man. The love that Michael felt for his ex-boyfriend reminded me of the psychic positions Benjamin identified in *The Bonds of Love* (1988), which I understand to be versions of narcissism. For, in that relationship, Michael had taken up the self-denying, submissive position typical of dominant white femininity in its relation to dominant white masculinity. His wish seemed to echo the Kohutian formula, "You are perfect and I am part of you" (Kohut, 1971).

All this felt fairly obvious to me, and I believed that, in the course of therapy, Michael would probably come to see that he did not so much want the ex-boyfriend as he wanted what this man represented that he himself lacked. What was less obvious to me until later was that, in the many interchanges about his desire, Michael had put me in – and I had unconsciously assumed – the position of the white one. While it is certainly true that in our particular historical moment, I am called and call myself white (as opposed to historical moments when Jews were considered nonwhite), and while it is true that I have many of the privileges of whiteness, it is also true, as Lacan (1977, 1998) might have said, that whiteness embodies a fantasy of wholeness to which no one can lay claim.

My pretense to incarnating whiteness is precisely the kind of normative unconscious process that sustains racial inequality. Only much later (Layton, 2017) did I realize that, for me, this pretense enacts an intergenerationally transmitted imperative, held by all four of my grand-parents, to escape, via assimilation, the traumas of Eastern European pogroms, Western European associations of Eastern Jews with dirt and darkness, and American anti-semitism (see P. Williams, 1997). My "wish" to occupy the position of "invulnerability," an unconscious collusion with Michael's wish, demonstrates that racism and class inequality do not only split the psyche of the subordinate; they also bolster the split, fantasmatic position of the dominant – and both parties want to hold to the fantasy that – again, as Lacan might say – someone has the phallus and is invulnerable to pain and loss. The collusion acts as a mutual resistance to experiencing psychic pain, what Ruth Stein (2005) called a perverse pact. By claiming the whiteness my ancestors, as immigrants, so longed for, I, in fantasy, secure my attachment to those ancestral ghosts, keep them alive, remain loyal to them. To be recognized as white was, and to a large extent still is, to be recognized as American, to be safe and loved.

It seems to me important to think about how, technically, we might reckon, in our work, with the splitting inherent to racial categories without fostering a fantasy of wholeness/invulnerability. It was while listening to a talk by Leary (2003) one evening that I suddenly realized I had that very day adopted the position of whiteness vis-à-vis my patient. Michael and I had been talking about the psychic function that his ex-boyfriend had served for him, the connection to whiteness that that relationship brought him, and I recall saying something like, "And you can never be white." Thinking of the Eng and Han (2002) article, I recall adding to myself something like: "Poor guy. He'll never be white and he shall have to mourn that." So long as I was putting myself in the place of whiteness, I must have been acting somewhat superior, which probably enabled me to tolerate his envy and idealization, and to empathize with his feelings of inferiority. But I did not realize that I was in some ways re-enacting the very scene of humiliation by sustaining a superior stance. Indeed, while I well know intellectually that "whiteness" is a fiction, a cultural ideal created by repudiating undesirable attributes labeled nonwhite, I unconsciously held onto the privileged position because it enabled me to keep a certain distance both from my own ethnic vulnerabilities and from the pain caused this man by racism, not to mention homophobia. In doing so, however, I was enacting the humiliation of racism and the projection of vulnerability that underlies it.

Once aware of my collusion with the norm that splits white and non-white, I began to ask different kinds of questions: for example, what was whiteness to him, what was desirable about the attributes he associated with it, and how had these attributes fallen into the category of not-me? More importantly, I asked Michael if he was assuming I was white and what that meant to him. While acknowledging the privilege I have from the fact that I am associated with whiteness, I yet tried to transmute the categories of "white" and "Asian" into what they stood for in a racialized culture and in our mutual racialized imaginations. In consequence, at the same time that whiteness as a narcissistic structure was either denigrated or idealized, there arose a third space of whiteness in which Michael was able to use the fantasy that his ex-boyfriend and I "held whiteness" to explore what he had coveted and what he had shut himself off from in life.

## On politeness and self-absorption, emotion and reason

And now I will turn to the content of the stereotypes and how that content played out in treatment. On numerous occasions, Michael's therapy not only confronted me with my own stereotypes, but it also rendered both conscious and problematic some of the assumptions of health that I have held, assumptions that also get enacted unconsciously in treatment and that serve to sustain a particular power status quo.

As I mentioned earlier, Michael's Western/non-Western binary construct at times seemed to take the form of what I was familiar with as a male/female binary. One day, he told me that his ex-boyfriend had pointed out to him that whenever Michael walked down the street and someone came toward him in the opposite direction, it was always Michael who deferred and moved to the side. Michael also sometimes wondered why he did not feel anger in situations in which he knew his Western friends would be angry. He often noted that Westerners seemed angry a lot – for example, they would say they were having a bad day, rather than merely note that some random thing had not worked out. In other words, he felt Westerners had an irrational way of seeing nonpersonal events – like bad weather – as personal.

More than once, I found myself thinking that, if Michael had been a white female and told me some of the things he did, I would have known right away that we were dealing with problems with self-assertion. But what made me less certain, for this case and perhaps for all, was that I happened to read an article by Rothblum et al. (2000) that brought to my attention the possibility that some of the tension in the therapy, Michael's ongoing discomfort with being in therapy, might have something to do with my conscious and unconscious assumptions and how I was enacting them.

Rothblum et al. argue that the basic tenets of attachment theory – for example, that secure attachment promotes freedom to explore – are not universal, but rather are the product of Western psychological assumptions. Contrasting Western with Japanese child-rearing practices, they note that, while Western parents encourage their children to assert themselves, to figure out what they need and ask for it, Japanese parents tend to anticipate the child's needs and fears, to create an environment in which needs are met without the child's having to ask. The Japanese mother, they argue, fosters emotional closeness, while the Western mother fosters exploration and autonomy. Where the Western ideal of competence values getting what one needs for one's self, versus depending on others to meet one's needs, in Japanese child-rearing practices, the focus is on coordinating one's needs with the needs of others. In the West, babies are encouraged to explore and to be oriented to the environment; in Japan, babies explore less and are encouraged to be more oriented to their mothers, more dependent. While in the West, value is placed on linking attachment and exploration, in Japan, the primary link is between attachment and dependence. This serves the Japanese value of accommodation or social fittedness. "These terms," the authors write, "refer to children's empathy with others, their compliance with others' wishes, and their responsiveness to social cues and norms" (Rothblum et al., 2000, p. 1099).

For Michael, many things made therapy difficult, not least of which was the idea that he was supposed to start the sessions. He told me that he felt he was being "pushy" to talk just about himself; it made him feel as though he was intruding on me. I would interpret this as a problem with self-assertion, but perhaps it was not that at all! And yet, as someone caught between two cultures, it was obvious that Michael struggled, just as Eng and Han (2002) suggest, between being like a Westerner and being like his family.

Am I, then, to be the cultural agent that makes Michael more comfortable operating within Western norms, in effect taking a side of the conflict? Or is my job merely to point out the diverse norms, the conflict, and let Michael find his own path? Consciously, I believe my job is the latter, but I fear I fairly frequently perform the former, relying on the ideals of health that my Western training has championed, ideals incorporated not only in technique, but even in the treatment frame. I suppose one could argue that such performances are conscious, for, after all, I can articulate what the ideals are. But it is my view that, even while the ideals may be conscious, the splitting and devaluation they rest on are not. Repeatedly performing the norms of my profession, I maintain the approval/love of my peers while sustaining a certain distribution of power.

Then one day, Michael presents a dilemma he has with his current boyfriend. Michael doesn't really know whether or not he loves him; he knows that he himself is loved, but that's not enough. I ask him what his feelings are. He says that he knows he loves his parents because he wants them to be happy, and wants to do what he can to make them happy. Is that a feeling, he asks? I float the hypothesis that there is something that inhibits him from feeling and knowing what he feels, and I think it has to do with the way feelings have been identified as Western and bad. He repeats his sense that Westerners react out of proportion to the cause when bad things happen, and he is glad that he doesn't do this. But sometimes he would like to get angry – and he's not sure he should. In fact, he does feel angry sometimes; and then he mentions a new game he's playing with himself, where he waits a little longer before moving out of the way when someone walks toward him on the street. He guesses that, because his ex-boyfriend remarked on the fact that he always moves out of the way first, he now thinks there must be something wrong with this behavior. But he does get angry that others don't step out of the way – it's not fair, and it's rude. He's glad he's like he is – but is he getting stepped on?

I struggled in this treatment because my working hypothesis, based on some things Michael said that showed a desire to express more emotion, was that the Western/non-Western categorization process was one way in which he kept himself inhibited, kept himself from integrating emotion and reason. I also felt that his mother's yelling fits, sometimes paired with humiliation-engendering behavior, made emotion frightening for him. And yet, I certainly agreed with him that Western forms of assertion (or, at least, their U.S. East Coast version) often crossed the line into rudeness and incivility.

At one point, I spoke to Michael about some of my confusions. He was talking about the fun he had had during the past weekend with a visiting friend, a man who laughed a lot at Michael's jokes. He remarked that he generally felt responsible for showing his guests a good time, without focusing on whether he himself was having a good time. Because I again read this as self-abnegation, I brought up the confusions I had been feeling about the Western/non-Western dichotomization. I told him I was concerned that, like the ex-boyfriend, I might have been pathologizing something about these values of civility and duty that guided his behavior, and I told him that my therapy culture tends to understand some of these ways of being as self-abnegation.

I mentioned I was pretty sure that, if I were treating a Western female, I would move in the direction of seeing such behavior as self-abnegating. I said, "I suppose what matters is whether or not you find that these ways of being get in your way; do you want things to be different?"

Michael then revisited some of the examples he saw of Western rudeness, and in the new rendition, matters were more complicated, more East-West: he said that, when he pours tea, he is aware that if there isn't much in the pot, he might not get any; this does, in fact, bother him. Indeed, he said that the responsibility to make others happy was also self-focused: if his friend did not like what he thought would constitute a good time, he would feel devalued as well as guilty.

He then noted how frequently his ex-boyfriend used to leave him alone at parties, and how the boyfriend would rationalize his behavior by asserting a value on independence and a disdain for clinginess. But, Michael said, "I told him more than once that I was uncomfortable in those situations, and he shouldn't have left me alone." "Indeed," I replied, and realized at the same time that this was not about which value system was right; it was about being in tune with your partner, conscious of his vulnerabilities.

At this point, I decided to ask Michael if he might be having any feelings about my upcoming vacation, since he had mentioned being left alone. The rest of the session focused on his question of whether or not he really needed therapy: he associated to the first therapist he saw, the one who had referred him to me over a year earlier, and expressed a feeling that her office was much more conveniently located than mine, and that he would be glad to be able to sleep in while I was gone, and to think, in my absence, about whether he should stop therapy.

He then associated to his friend's girlfriend as not being very good-looking, even though the friend himself was quite attractive. And when I asked what this might have to do with what had come before, he concluded the sequence by saying that his new boyfriend didn't think he really needed therapy. "I think the issues I have, a lot of people have – and I don't think others are in therapy with such issues." I thought to myself that this expression of his discomfort with therapy related to all of what had come before, about what was Western, what was not. I said to Michael, both defensively and nondefensively, that many are in therapy for just the issues he has brought. And then he told me that he would not pay my fee if his insurance were not paying, and he felt guilty about that; he had just learned that his insurance coverage would end in two months' time.

This material is so full of suggestive moments that I hesitate to offer an interpretation, and I imagine that others might have more interesting things to say about it than I do. But my best guess is that Michael may have felt wounded when I suggested a connection between his psychology and that of Western femininity. Had I inadvertently feminized this Asian man who was already sensitive to the feminizing stereotype – both as a gay man and as an Asian man? Perhaps my way of framing things made Michael want to point out to me that he really is much more assertive and self-focused, more masculine, than I think. Perhaps the next association, about abandonment, did not have as much to do with my impending vacation as with the way I had wounded him. Like his ex-boyfriend, I perhaps should have known that what I said would make him uncomfortable. I venture this guess because the material that came after, about whether or not he should quit therapy and whether or not it was worth paying for, had a somewhat hostile edge. It was also not lost on me that the therapist whom he had first seen was not only closer to his home, but was also quite young and beautiful – was he perhaps trying to wound me by questioning *my* femininity?

I would be remiss not to add, however, that Michael's conflict about therapy had other roots as well. A major issue with his current boyfriend was that the boyfriend did not seem to value processing, and Michael was coming more and more to see how much he himself did value it. I believe he found his desire for insight somewhat taboo, and perhaps even associated it with both the degraded feminine *and* the degraded Western.

### What is love?

Another theme that Michael struggled with during the therapy was the question, what is love? Not only was this a presenting problem, but I also invoke it here to demonstrate how the constructs we tend to see as most universal and psychological, least culturally inflected, are in many ways simultaneously psychically and socially constructed.

Earlier, I noted that Michael did not feel sure he was in love with his current partner, and I also noted that he felt he was not very desirable – a feeling the ex-boyfriend heightened, but that the current boyfriend completely contradicted. The current boyfriend had only had two other partners in his life, and both were Asian. My patient wondered about white men who only desire Asians – he averred that, generally, only fat and old white men were into Asians. And Michael wondered why he was never attracted to Asian men either.

Countless works of fiction convince me that love is a social construct as well as a feeling, and that racism can destroy or severely interfere with the capacity for love. No work, perhaps, gets at the socially constructed nature of love better than does *M. Butterfly* (Hwang, 1989). In this play, a white French diplomat, Gallimard, falls passionately in love with a person who he thinks is a diminutive, female, Asian opera singer whom he has heard sing the title role in *Madame Butterfly*. She tells him the tragic story of the American sailor who seduced and then abandoned the Japanese Butterfly, who, in her desperation, committed suicide. And then she taunts Gallimard for finding the story beautiful. In a powerful speech, she deconstructs the white Western male fantasy of the submissive Oriental woman who falls in love with the cruel white Westerner. Underscoring the way power relations infuse love, she asks Gallimard to consider an alternative tale, one in which a blonde Western beauty falls madly in love with a short Asian businessman who treats her badly and then abandons her. In his absence, she remains fixated on him, even turning down a proposal from a young, handsome, affluent white celebrity. When she finds out her Asian lover has married someone else, she commits suicide (see Hwang, 1989, p. 17).

The singer is certain that this reverse tale is one that Gallimard will find laughable, unbelievable, and far from beautiful. And yet, this reversal is precisely what the play enacts: the revenge of the short, thin, Asian male against the white Westerner. Having fallen madly in love with his Butterfly, Gallimard learns that the object of his love is actually a transvestite Asian male. Desperate to preserve his fantasy of true heterosexual love, where white men are dominant and women submissive, Gallimard transforms himself into the female Asian Butterfly – and kills him-/herself for love.

Perhaps no writer better shows the damaging toll that racism takes on love than Toni Morrison. In one of her short stories, "Recitatif" (1983), two girls, one black and one white, are left at an orphanage because their mothers cannot care for them. One mother is physically ill; the other is mentally ill. We do not know which girl is black and which white, and Morrison, mixing up signifiers of class and race, makes her readers face our own racial stereotypes as we frantically try to figure out who is black and who is white. But the story moves us through the girls' lives and shows us how, at every historical point, racism frustrates their possibility of refinding the mutual care and protectiveness that they had once shared, when, on first meeting, each recognized in the other the vulnerability caused by maternal abandonment.

Such literary works suggest why Michael could love only white men, especially those who could not or would not be sexual with him. The BIG History (Davoine and Gaudillière, 2004) of intergenerationally transmitted racism, in which identities are constructed in relation to other identities and marked by differential power relations, also constructs possibilities for love and thus the very nature of love relationships. As the therapy went on, his membership in a gay, Asian activist organization seemed to decrease his homophobia, and he began to be attracted to men from certain Asian subcultures other than his own. It seemed to me that here was an example of the way that essentialist categories and identity politics can, in fact, facilitate growth and defeat internalized racist and sexist prejudice.

But there is more to the story of love and ethnicity in this case. For Michael, love was less a feeling than a sense of duty. He came to understand that the passion he experienced for his ex-boyfriend had to do with the other man's remaining inaccessible and rejecting. Michael's only experiences of passion were on that model of unrequited love. (My interpretation was that his desire was fueled by his wish to have what the fantasied ex-boyfriend seemed to have.) Otherwise, of love, he knew only that he loved his parents, because he wanted them to be happy and because they had sacrificed themselves for him. He wanted to sacrifice for them in return, and he called that love. At the beginning of his therapy, he reported that he only cried in movies during scenes of parent-child love, never adult-adult love. In his view, adult-adult love was never pure: in merely desiring the other, "you are asking for something back for your love." During the treatment, I was never sure whether Michael simply did not love his current boyfriend, and was at best enjoying how much this man loved him, or if we were dealing with an inability to love that had to do with several other factors: the inhibition on feeling and behaving "irrationally"; the self-denigration and internalized homophobia ("I don't want to be a member of any club that wants me as a member"); and the confusion that seemed always to ensue when the other knew what s/he wanted of him. Indeed, it seemed to me that the legacy of Michael's mother's insistent presence – which he experienced as love, but also as control – was to make him unsure of what he felt whenever the other *was* sure. I thought that the constraints on his freedom that he had so disliked growing up had become rationalized as a "true" kind of love, a selfless love.

And then I came across a paper on filial piety in Chinese culture (Gu, 2006). The author of this paper argued that the Oedipus in this culture is different from the Western Oedipus. Specifically, it is marked by a loyalty between parent and child that transcends the loyalty between spouses. Once again, I was decentered by the recognition that my patient's desire was not simply defensive, and perhaps only defensive when seen from within my particular frame. Am I so jaded that selfless love seems absurd to me? I certainly did not hear his rendition of his mother's love as selfless; to me, it seemed that her sacrifices were as much aimed at having her son achieve what she and her husband could not, as they were about her son being happy. But I suppose I should ask: what's happiness got to do with it? Is the idea that we are meant to be happy yet another Western value?

I leave the reader with my confusion rather than with any attempts at answers.

## Conclusion

This summary of my work with Michael gives some sense of the way that racist hierarchies create racial identities that are marked by oscillating idealizing and devaluing dynamics characteristic of narcissism. Norms of race, class, gender, and sexuality, norms transmitted within familial and cultural enclaves of love and hate (P. Williams, 1997), are unconsciously enacted and further legitimized in the very way we assert ourselves in the world and in the very way we connect with others. As Altman (2000) has argued, white clinicians have to assume that their racism pervades the clinical encounter in some way; I hope to have shown here some of the ways that patient and therapist enact the norms that split and racialize emotion and reason, dependence and independence, love and hate. And I hope to leave you with a sense of how every psychological category we contemplate is rife with hauntings from the past – and how our engagements across difference actualize those hauntings.

## Notes

* Used with permission. Adapted from Layton, L. (2006) Racial identities, racial enactments, and normative unconscious processes. *Psychoanalytic Quarterly* 75: 237–269, and Layton, L. (2017) Racialized enactments and normative unconscious processes: Where haunted identities meet. In Salberg, J. and Grand, S. (eds.) *Transgenerational Trauma and the Other*. New York, NY: Routledge, pp. 144–164.

1 For an excellent summary of psychoanalytic theories of race, see Dalal, 2002, Chapter 2. See Stoute (2017) for another historical summary.

2 George (2001, 2016) argues that African Americans may cling defensively to racial identity in order to avoid dealing with the unsymbolized trauma of slavery. According to George's Lacanian schema, racial identities function all too frequently to suture the gap in subjectivity caused by the trauma of slavery. The unsymbolized trauma in the Real gives rise to repetition. While racial identity can be used to further a progressive politics when acknowledged as socially constructed and provisional, racial identity too frequently is used defensively to foreclose the mourning necessary to work through trauma.

3 Dalal (2002) writes that "the terms race, ethnicity and culture are all *names* for differences" (p. 23, italics in original). In his view, the very function of differentiation, usually hidden, is to naturalize power relations. He urges us to look not at difference but at the function of difference, and why any given difference gets "heated up" at particular times.

4 Note that I refer to "rationality," not reason. I do so because I want to emphasize that split polarities tend to be monstrous versions of what they claim to be. As Freud (1915a) once said of repression, the content of what is repressed does not remain what it was when originally repressed. Rather, it "proliferates in the dark . . . and takes on extreme forms of expression" (p. 149). This is true of what is split and dissociated as well, so that when I say emotion and reason are split, I want to make it clear that the result of the split will always be pathological versions of what I take to be the non-defensive capacities for emotion and reason.

5 I am well aware that Japanese Americans, for example, do not have the same background as Chinese or Indian Americans, although, to preserve confidentiality, I obscure those differences at certain points in the paper.

# Section III

# Neoliberal subjectivities and contemporary U.S. life

## Introduction to Section III: neoliberal subjectivities and contemporary U.S. life

The chapters in this section are arranged to reflect my gradually dawning awareness of neoliberalism: what it is; what it entails in the realm of politics, economics, and ideology; and what I slowly and only in pieces came to understand as its psychological effects on the subject formation of both individuals and groups inhabiting different socio-economic sectors of the U.S. population. As I learned more about neoliberalism and the vast income inequalities that it has brought about, I became more convinced that what Bourdieu described as "distinction" (see Chapter 9) quite aptly describes the psychology of U.S. neoliberal raced and gendered class relations: for Bourdieu, distinction describes the motivation in the middle classes to define themselves by distancing by any means possible from the closeness to necessity that marks the lower classes. They do so via such everyday life bodily practices as food and clothing preferences. The chasm neoliberalism has created between the very rich and everyone else has only seemed to heighten anxiety, competition, and a drive to garner marks of distinction.

The chapters each describe some aspect of what neoliberalism is, but because I am interested in the effects of neoliberalism on subject formation – that is, how our ways of being in the world are constructed by the social world and vice versa – I introduce this section by revisiting past moments in my life when something seemed really off, things, however, that in today's reality have come to feel "normal," as simply "how things are." In retrospect, I have come to understand these moments as early harbingers of neoliberal ideological and psychosocial formations.

My first job was in 1980, just a few years after most people date the beginnings of the neoliberal rise to dominance. I was hired as a lecturer in English at Northeastern University, a school known for its co-op model of education. In this model, students take courses for a semester and then work in internships the next semester. I had nothing against this model, and still don't. But what was disturbing, especially after having struggled for eight years to get a Ph.D. in literature, was the lack of interest the school seemed to have in humanities, or, for that matter, any form of education for education's sake, for the formation of a citizenry aware of its history and culture. All the brochures and other public statements focused on how the school was going to prepare the students for jobs. Many students at the school were the first in their families to go to college, and I remember feeling then that because they were not wealthy, they were getting an education that focused not on critical thinking, which had been the undergraduate focus in the public university I had attended in the late 1960s, but on getting a job. It seemed to me that the students were being shortchanged.

If we look at this history in the context of our current climate of precariousness in the job market and difficulty getting a job after college, it looks like Northeastern was presciently focused on concern for the underprivileged. Progressives today are pushing for vocational education for those who may struggle to find jobs in a market that rewards only highly skilled labor. But to see it that way is to ignore the effects of globalization on the working class and to ignore what has happened in higher education over the past 35 years (see Brown, 2015). In the 1980s Northeastern was, in retrospect, a precursor of the neoliberalization of U.S. education: children of the wealthy get a liberal arts education at a cost of $60,000 a year while the lower middle-class and working-class populations struggle for several years to get through community college or four-year college programs that often do not lead to good jobs. And then they are burdened for years with difficult if not impossible to pay off student loans. A recent conversation I had with a liberal consultant to a struggling liberal arts college suggests how deeply neoliberalism has penetrated how we think about even these privileged spaces. The consultant felt strongly, and with no reservation, that the school could survive financially only if it were to eliminate all its liberal arts programs and focus resources instead on the professional preparatory programs that were making money. Neoliberal ideology is the current form of "common sense."

In 1981, I got a job at Boston University in its College of General Studies, which, at the time, was a two-year college that offered a very challenging curriculum to mostly very wealthy students who had not been able to get into the BU program of their choice. During my two years there, John Silber, BU's president, defeated the faculty union by drawing on a precedent court finding that stated that faculty were managers and not workers. Silber also instituted the kind of meritocracy that would come to characterize neoliberalism and its favoring of the 1 percent, a meritocracy in which one or, at most, a couple of people got a lot of fellowship money to go to graduate school and the rest of the class got nothing unless they worked for it. My college also had what felt like a sick obsession with the yearly course evaluation. Many faculty meetings were devoted to discussion of "the instrument." Student ratings determined whether or not a faculty member would get a merit increase. The school provided my first experience of expertise bowing to the sovereign power of the wealthy consumer. I remember being called into the dean's office because a student had called his father to tell him how stupid the college was, using as his example the fact that his humanities professor, me, had not read a play that he had read in high school. Instead of the dean telling the father that his faculty had gone through a rigorous selection process, he called me down to his office to ask if I'd read the play. In retrospect, these experiences speak loudly of the union-busting activity characteristic of neoliberalism; the use of "meritocracy" as a way to undermine worker/student solidarity and create an elite 1 percent; the mania for measurement and imposition of marketing metrics that belong to the domain of consumer preferences and not the domain of education; and the servile relation to the wealthy that began to dominate every institution, including mental healthcare.

By the late 1980s, I was finishing up graduate school in psychology, having decided that I couldn't bear the precariousness of the academic job market and did not want to have to move far away and leave all my friends to get a decent job. That was 30 years ago, and now it is well known that over 60 percent of college faculty are low-paid non tenure-track adjuncts with few or no benefits, a work force change that is totally typical of neoliberalism and its so-called flexibilization of the labor market (see Boltanski and Chiapello, 2005). Not long after I graduated as a clinician, managed care was introduced and, once again, all my colleagues began to feel anxious about being able to make a living, which fostered a more competitive atmosphere among us. My grad school program had been completely psychodynamic, but by the 1990s David Barlow was brought in as chair of the Boston University psychology department, and the program became cognitive behavioral and focused on neuroscience. Managed care had an immediate effect on the psychiatry department in which I worked. Some psychoanalysts who had remained on the hospital staff seemed overnight to have become contemptuous of long-term psychodynamic treatment at the clinic, even labeling it a narcissistic indulgence. It was clear that insurance concerns had begun to drive patient care. I was part of a group that formed in Boston to try to counter managed care by offering a carve-out insurance policy that would not limit the number of sessions, but it never gained enough traction to be taken seriously by employers. All aspects of life were successfully being subordinated to market concerns.

Now psychodynamic graduate clinical psychology programs barely exist and those that are predominantly psychodynamic struggle to get or maintain accreditation from the APA. Undergraduate psychology rarely touches on anything psychodynamic at all. Indeed, when I taught psychoanalysis in the social studies and women's studies programs at Harvard in the 1990s and early 2000s, an undergrad psychology major in one of my classes told me that she had taken my course because she wanted to have at least one course about people before she graduated. Sometime later, positive psychology, which, as Binkley (2011b) and Yakushko (2019) write, promotes happiness and positivity by discouraging reflection on the past, on social embeddedness, on traumatic experience, became one of the most popular courses at Harvard.

A few more autobiographical examples will bring us to the chapters in this section. You may recall from Chapter 8 my experience with the female Harvard undergrads who could not relate to papers about the development of a female relational psychic structure but rather found psychologically familiar only the assigned papers on the development in men of defensive autonomy. Around the same time as I taught this class, I had noticed that several TV shows were featuring white middle-class female professional protagonists who shunned intimacy and were totally focused on their 24/7 careers. I wrote about this turn toward valuing defensive autonomy in women at the time (Layton, 2004b), but it was only later that I came to understand this as an effect of neoliberalism on subject formation. In this case, neoliberal capitalism had appropriated one version of 1960s feminism, the one demanding workplace equality. Nothing, however, had changed in the structure of the workplace, so if women were to enter it, they, like men, would have had to develop a psychic structure based in defensive autonomy. What I mean is that neoliberal economics, politics, and ideology had begun to shape not only middle-class white men but middle-class white women as well. Both were now to be entrepreneurs of the self for whom relational capacities are secondary to the drive to become a self-sufficient member of the 1 percent. As the chapters in this section describe, that ideology is dominant in shaping subjectivity in all cultural subgroups, even as it becomes clearer and clearer that this version of success is barely possible to achieve for any but a small fraction of the upper middle class.

In Chapter 14, I speak about a white middle-class patient of mine who came of age in the 1980s and once told me that she had anxiously translated the pressure her parents put on her to achieve this kind of success as "Yale or Jail." But I did not realize the full meaning of what she said at that time. In fact, when she said it, I was fairly ignorant of the mass incarceration of African Americans that had been occurring since the late 1970s. Then, about 10 years ago, I gave a talk on neoliberalism at a conference. A few hours later, an African American man, not realizing he was talking about me, said that he had heard a talk that morning on neoliberalism and couldn't believe that the speaker had not even mentioned race. How on earth could you talk about neoliberalism, he said, without mentioning race? "Yale or jail," as it turns out, is one of the best ways I have ever heard of grasping the raced socio-economic and political reality of neoliberalism in the U.S.

To make sense of what is going on psychologically in all of these autobiographical examples, I will argue throughout this section that we need to understand the BIG History of neoliberalism in which all players are caught. Chapters 12 through 16 elaborate on the normative unconscious processes that mark neoliberal subjectivities. In Chapter 12, "Who's responsible: Our mutual implication in each other's suffering," published in *Psychoanalytic Dialogues* in 2009, and Chapter 13, "Irrational exuberance," published in *Subjectivity* in 2010, I began to report on some clinical engagements with entrepreneurial, neoliberalized selves. Chapter 12's focus is on the decline of empathic capacities in neoliberal culture and an ensuing decline in the capacity to experience ourselves as responsible and accountable for the suffering of others. Looking at the way conflicts in the area of accountability and responsibility are lived both within some middle-class white patients and within the interaction between patient and analyst, I argue that contemporary definitions of empathy normalize the neoliberal repudiation and devaluation of vulnerability. These ways of constructing empathic capacity foster an experience of empathy in which one can sustain a safe distance from the suffering other and not hold oneself accountable. I propose that achieving a two-way version of empathy, one that would counter neoliberal trends, requires that we examine the ways we unconsciously seek refuge in identifications that distance us from vulnerability – and it requires us to recognize the harm we inflict when we do so.

Chapter 13 describes the perverse fetish structure of neoliberal narcissism as it appears in the white middle class. Three clinical vignettes suggest that understanding the damaging psychosocial effects of neoliberalism – on all of us – can help clinicians make technical choices that counter the tendency in the clinic to reproduce neoliberal versions of subjectivity. Chapter 14, "Yale, fail, jail: Sadomasochistic individual, large-group, and institutional effects of neoliberalism," is a compilation of a few different papers of mine that elaborate both on what neoliberalism is as well as its effects on individuals and on particular classed, gendered, and raced group formations (Layton, 2014b, 2015, 2016). Chapter 14's focus is on the sadistic conscious and unconscious enactments fostered by neoliberal policies and practices. In Chapter 15, "Something to do with a girl named Marla Singer: Capitalism, narcissism and therapeutic discourse in David Fincher's *Fight Club*," first published in *Free Associations* in 2011, I offer an intersectional analysis of the film, *Fight Club*, a film with a sexist and authoritarian "unconscious" that exists in uneasy tension with a critique of neoliberal capitalism. The film, which came out in 1999, grows increasingly resonant and relevant as toxic, racist authoritarian right-wing leaders and subcultures become dominant responses to the real distress fostered by neoliberalism.

## Truth-telling

Finally, in Chapter 16, "Transgenerational hauntings: Toward a social psychoanalysis and an ethic of dis-illusionment," published in 2019 in *Psychoanalytic Dialogues*, I put neoliberalism into historical perspective and delve more deeply into what some have referred to as racial capitalism (Robinson, 2000; Kelley, 2017; Wang, 2018). More specifically, I confront the whiteness of the practice of psychoanalysis. I once again take up the dream reported in Chapter 12, the Hurricane Katrina dream, but here my focus is on the racist history of the U.S. and the historical illusions about ourselves that white U.S. citizens consciously and unconsciously hold. Drawing on earlier psychoanalytic theorists (Freud, Fromm, Erikson), I elaborate what I call an ethic of dis-illusionment that stands in stark contrast to an ethic of adaptation. Clinical vignettes focus on white therapists working with white patients in a neoliberal capitalist era; the vignettes illustrate the tension between an ethic of adaptation and an ethic of dis-illusionment, as well as the seductive temptation to resolve the tension in favor of an ethic of adaptation. An increased awareness of contemporary structural and lived intersecting oppressions – and my own complicity in them – has expanded my thinking about what a social psychoanalysis must encompass. Every day, something I read, or a conversation with a colleague or friend, makes me aware of how normative unconscious processes and resistance to them operate, and I believe that an ethical stance demands a social psychoanalysis that aims at nothing less than transformation of our theories, our clinical practices, and our institutions.

# Chapter 12

# Who's responsible? Our mutual implication in each other's suffering[*]

In a scene in Sarah Schulman's *Empathy* (2006), a novel originally published in 1992, Anna O., the protagonist, comes to Doc, a *very* lay street psychoanalyst, for treatment. She tells him that she is aware that the country is falling apart and that people seem to be acting as though they have nothing to do with the unfolding catastrophe. They do not seem to feel that they are responsible, she tells him. She goes on to say that she herself is content with *her* individual life, but that when she stops to think about things she finds that she gets ideas about what she calls "structure." Doc asks if she means politics. Anna is not sure what he means, but replies that she is aware that there is more to what is going on outside than her own individual happiness. Doc finds this strange. He makes a note. His diagnosis: Anna likely has some past experience that she has not yet faced; he tells her she is suffering from *empathy* (see pp. 51–52).

Schulman's Anna, although suffering from empathy, is nevertheless able psychologically to make a fairly clear separation between her happy personal life and a country that is falling apart – perhaps not as great a separation as the one made by her countrymen, who, it is suggested, do not suffer from empathy. But the capacity to make that separation is part of what I want to look at here. For I've been troubled recently by what I experience as a failure of accountability, a failure not only to take responsibility for the things we sign on for personally, but also for things that my country, the U.S., has signed on for. And I believe this has to do with a failure of empathy, which, I will argue, entails a failure to recognize the ways in which our identity investments and disidentifications implicate us in the suffering of others. I want, then, to consider some possible connections between empathy, responsibility, and accountability in contemporary

U.S. culture. I begin with an analysis of the current U.S. socio-political climate. I then examine the kind of psychic dilemmas about responsibility and accountability that this climate creates for U.S. patients and clinicians alike. To explore this further, I offer some thoughts on the intrapsychic and interpersonal damage that ensues when a culture accepts as normal huge discrepancies between rich and poor, and when it, further, normalizes discourses that make vulnerability and need shameful states. When public institutions abandon their responsibilities toward their citizenry, I will argue, there is a pressure to create ever more individualistic identities that repudiate the vulnerable and needy parts of the self. This, in turn, blocks awareness of the ways in which we are mutually interdependent. Gender, class, racial, sexual, and national collective identities are mobilized to mask vulnerability and to perform the psychological and cultural work of distinguishing ourselves in whatever ways possible from those more vulnerable than ourselves.

## The fate of accountability and empathy in a free market culture

Attempting to account for the increasing income inequality in the U.S., the ever-widening divide between rich and poor, Paul Krugman (2002) has written persuasively that the period of greater equality that occurred between the New Deal and the 1960s was an anomaly in U.S. history – a short span sandwiched between the gilded age of the late nineteenth to early twentieth centuries and our contemporary gilded age. In *A Brief History of Neoliberalism*, David Harvey (2005) suggests that the inflation, surging unemployment, and crisis in capital accumulation that occurred in the U.S. by the late 1960s led the upper classes to panic about their loosening hold on power and wealth. That panic eventuated in the repudiation of Keynesian principles of government intervention in the economy, and led to the embrace of a neoliberal, free market ideology that ended the post-war compromise between labor and capital, broke the back of unions, deregulated public services, and generally made "big government" into a villainous term (even as budget deficits in the U.S. currently soar).

In *The Culture of the New Capitalism*, Richard Sennett (2006) writes about changes that these events have wrought on political and social institutions. Sennett argues that political institutions have modeled themselves on "cutting edge" corporate cultures that have increasingly centralized power, leaving less possibility for subordinates to interpret directives and exercise even a modicum of autonomy. Simultaneously, corporate and political cultures have become less and less accountable for the negative effects their policies have on workers/citizens. Since the 1970s, when changes in monetary policy freed capital to be invested globally and gave more power to shareholders who wanted immediate profit, corporate bureaucracies have come to valorize "flexibility" and innovation over stability and craftsmanship. The consultant, Sennett argues, is the new ideal worker. The consultant model discourages long-term attachments, rewards risk-taking and shaking things up, has little regard for the historical knowledge older workers might have, and valorizes knowing things superficially rather than in depth. In this system, the idealized self, Sennett writes, "publicly eschews long-term dependency on others" (p. 177). Workers in the "cutting-edge" business move around from project to project, which also discourages attachments, and they tend to perform tasks in nonlinear sequences. Indeed, Sennett found that workers who were demoted or reprimanded generally were those who spent too much time tending to relational issues in the workplace, for example, providing too much customer service.

Sennett further points out that in our increasingly individualist meritocracy, a few people are recognized as truly talented and the rest are relegated to the non-special status of a disposable mass. The untalented masses come to feel that they have only themselves to blame for being not special. Along with the self-esteem and harsh super-ego issues that this obviously would produce – it is no surprise perhaps that self psychology, with its focus on self-esteem regulation, develops during this period – Sennett finds that an important consequence for individual psychology is that people feel anxious not so much about failure as about being found useless or redundant. New institutions, he writes, "breed low levels of informal trust and high levels of anxiety about uselessness" (p 181).

Howard Stein (2000) has also written compellingly about what he calls our new feelings of "disposability." His work on the traumatizing ways that workers are fired when deemed redundant or when their jobs are outsourced illustrates how vulnerable white collar workers and professionals have become. And his organizational data well support Sennett's contention that new bureaucracies are marked by a decline of accountability. In Sennett's words, "The new institutional order eschews responsibility, labeling its own indifference as freedom for individuals or groups on the periphery; the vice of the politics derived from the new capitalism is indifference" (p. 164). And Harvey (2005) relates the decline of accountability to conflicts in responsibility as follows:

> As the state withdraws from welfare provision and diminishes its role in arenas such as health care, public education, and social services, which were once so fundamental to embedded liberalism, it leaves larger and larger segments of the population exposed to impoverishment. The social safety net is reduced to a bare minimum in favour of a system that emphasizes personal responsibility. Personal failure is generally attributed to personal failings, and the victim is all too often blamed.
>
> (p. 76)

Indeed, in the past eight years alone [2000–2008], tax cuts for the wealthy, corporate welfare, and the costs of a terribly unpopular war have decimated public services, leaving most of us on our own to fend against very real anxieties that we will end up without healthcare, without pensions, without social security.

Those who strive to make it in this system become in certain ways overly responsible and self-reliant, defending against shameful need with the manic activity necessary to deny how very close we *all* are in the U.S. to falling through what is left of the safety net. Yet, it seems to me that, in other ways, as citizens, people have become less responsible. The individualist individual fostered by neoliberalism is ever more split from the citizen or social individual, which causes a crisis in empathy, responsibility, and accountability. Indeed, government and corporate abdication of responsibility for their citizens and workforce, and the privileged classes' colluding but understandable response – to disavow vulnerability and escape into manic activity – have together brought about a marked decline in social solidarity, the concern and empathy for the vulnerable and for the stranger that characterized the welfare state. On the level of government bureaucracy, a pragmatic and calculating approach to dealing with the vulnerable in society has replaced empathy for fellow citizens. Solidarity toward the stranger, the foundation of the welfare state, has devolved into what sociologist John Rodger (2003) calls an "amoral familism," a term borrowed from Banfield (1958), who, according to Rodger, described it as "behavior which followed the dictum that the individual should maximise the material and short-run advantage of their nuclear family and assume that everyone else in the community would behave similarly" (Rodger, pp. 415–416). The ethic of social solidarity that characterized the U.K. welfare state, Rodger argues, has been replaced by a tendency to limit concern only to the self and to those in one's intimate circle. Perhaps the most dramatic current instance of amoral familism is my – and many people's – sense that were there a universal draft in the U.S., were the middle- and upper middle-classes' children vulnerable to being sent to war, there would be no, and likely never would have been an Iraq War. The volunteer army allows most of us to deny our own vulnerability and our complicity with a government that sends some of its most vulnerable off to die. In our current climate empathy appears as a state in which we are at best concerned by the suffering of certain others, but not implicated in it.

In the U.S., empathic capacities have no doubt been affected as well by the backlash against the social movements of the 1960s to 1970s. Indeed, this backlash began as soon as blacks, women, and gays made social gains. But I think that the backlash *also* has something to do with the rise of neoliberalism. By the mid-1970s, both elected Democrats and Republicans had begun to share the same neoliberal economic worldview, and by the end of the 1970s, debate over redistribution of wealth had virtually disappeared from public discourse. Cultural issues, the so-called "culture wars," became the only issues open to public debate. Dina Georgis (2007) describes the way attachment to collective identities can operate to make loss tolerable, and it just may be that the economic losses and dislocations we have experienced – and neither rebelled against nor mourned – have led many of us, in Georgis's words, to "find consolation in separation from others" (p. 254). The "culture wars" clearly reveal how, once difference becomes distinction and common vulnerabilities are denied, empathy narrows not only to a state in which we cannot imagine ourselves to be implicated in the fate of others but to a feeling which can be given or withheld according to political agendas.

To illustrate, I briefly mention work in progress by Cynthia Burack (2006), who studies homophobia in Christian fundamentalist groups that have developed what she calls compassionate pedagogies. Burack notes that when gay rights activists accuse these groups of being hate-filled, they get nowhere politically, because the groups do not see themselves as hating. Indeed, they see themselves as full of empathy and love. But what Burack points out is that they have carved up the world into who is deserving of empathy and who is not. In this case, those who wish to be rid of their same-sex desire deserve empathy for their struggle, and those who act on such desires do not. Compassionate pedagogy criticizes Christian failures to care adequately for ex-gays, but "*does not* implicate its subjects in destructiveness toward others. It does not acknowledge, for example, histories of targeted violence, police harassment, family rejection, and harmful therapeutic interventions. Instead, it carefully positions Christian conservatives as purveyors of God's law on sexuality and exonerates them for harm-doing against lesbians and gay men" (pp. 19–20).

As the previous paragraph suggests, empathy, like all affects, is a social as well as an individual state, subject to political struggles over how it is to be defined and experienced. In the current era, empathy seems to have been dominantly redefined as something we accord only to people who are most like us, most near and dear – or to very distant suffering strangers, such as tsunami victims in foreign lands. Carolyn Dean (2004) has documented the many social critics who decry an "exhaustion of empathy" in a world in which we are daily bombarded with images of suffering. But perhaps this "exhaustion of empathy" has something to do with neoliberalism and the way that empathy is defined in several dominant discourses. As Paul Hoggett (2006) has pointed out, liberal moral philosophy defines empathy as a one-way state in which the empathizer is figured as separate from the person who suffers, safely distant from the sufferer's pain. To illustrate, he points to Martha Nussbaum's argument that you cannot experience the other as other if you REALLY feel the other's pain.

This argument has a counterpart in mainstream U.S. clinical discourse as well. Indeed, the history of the term empathy, both inside and outside of clinical discourse, reveals that one axis along which its definition has always shifted has to do with its adherents' level of comfort with or anxiety about degrees of fusion and/or separateness from the suffering other. The question of how implicated we are in a patient's suffering has *always* been a point of contention in the definition of empathy. Many psychoanalytic schools' versions of empathy give the impression that the better we are at not getting stirred up by the patient's behavior, the more successful we are at sustaining an empathic stance – as though being stirred up indicates a failure of empathic capacity. There are, of course, counter-discourses, both inside and outside the clinic, that contest one-way definitions of empathy (see, for example, Bolognini, 2004; and Orange, 2007). But in social conditions such as those I described earlier, where fear is constantly stoked, yet vulnerability is deemed shameful, it is unlikely that empathy *would* be experienced as a two-way state, that is, a state in which the one who does not seem to suffer would feel called upon to acknowledge some complicity in or commonality with the suffering of the other.

I'd like now to turn to some ways in which these issues show up in the clinic. What are some of the conscious and unconscious conflicts around responsibility, accountability, and empathy for the other that emerge for the divided individual/citizen that neoliberalism fosters? The following vignettes are from my work with patients who are in their early 30s, and who thus grew up in the period in which the shift to neoliberalism occurred. The first, a female executive in a heavily male-dominated, high-paying field, has mentioned several times that she does not read the news because it makes her feel as though she'd have to do something. A good representative of how the painful issues that emerge from the individualist/citizen split are lived, this patient already feels overwhelmed by responsibilities, many of which were imposed on her by parents who, we have discovered in treatment, repeatedly put their children in difficult or even dangerous situations. This very highly paid patient feels that if she were more aware of the injustices in the world, she actually might be able to do something about them. Her choice until recently has been not to know. "I'm so tired," she often says. One day she came in feeling devastated about a very low offer someone had made to buy a property she had developed. She had become solely responsible for handling this property for her firm. There were numerous legal and other issues that had made this a very onerous project, one that had given my patient many sleepless nights. She had worked tirelessly putting out fires in the previous year. The deal that the prospective buyer offered bore no relation to what he had previously said the property was worth. The patient said to me, "I'd be happy to be a partner in their investment firm, but I'll never do this deal." When I asked what she meant, she said that of course you try to get things for as little as you can pay, but knowing the sweat and tears she had put in over the past year, she felt humiliated and devalued by the offer. She knew, as she put it, that to make money you look for people in desperate straits and try to take advantage of them, but she felt lousy being on the exploited side of the table. A similar issue had come up earlier: although she had entered analysis with some awareness that her manic activity was depleting her and might be contributing to what seemed an inexplicable sadness, and although she eventually decided to stop working 24/7 so that she could have time for herself and for her relationships, at some point she realized that the only way she could ALSO continue to make a lot of money was to require the people she managed to work 24/7. She would get quite angry when her underlings would show the kind of vulnerability that she tends to interpret as an inability or unwillingness to "power through." She misses a bit the adrenaline highs of her days of powering through, but basically she has come to enjoy a life that has space for relationships and reflection. After at one point referring to herself as hypocritical, I offered that, judgment aside, it seems that part of her felt badly about putting people in situations she could no longer tolerate herself.

One thread of our work has involved taking note of the contradictions that keep emerging between her allegiance to accumulating wealth and her allegiance to treating people the way she would like to be treated. We look at why she is so very tired, the toll it has taken on her to bear so much responsibility, the conflict between feeling accountable and needing to distance herself from feeling accountable in order to make money. I am aware that the treatment could, in the end, enable her to feel more at ease being less accountable; for example, at times she says that what she needs is to feel more comfortable with the position of boss, more comfortable recognizing that the rules for bosses and employees simply don't have to be the same. The identification as boss then would successfully block identifications with and thus empathy for her employees. But I wonder what will happen as she increasingly recognizes that what she calls "optimizing" time and money is at odds with what she deems best for her soul and for her relationships with others.

Another female patient with similar issues and of a similar age reveals how these dilemmas regarding responsibility might connect with gender issues, particularly with ways of experiencing dependence and independence. This patient, also in a high-paying and very male-dominated field, also used to working at a manic pace, recently attended a party and was talking with a male colleague about their newborn babies. While talking, the man's boss came near, and he then said loudly enough for his boss to hear: "If you want to talk about this girly stuff, you should give my wife a call." My patient told me that she "whipped out her penis" and made a cutting retort. As we analyzed her feelings further, she realized that he had made her feel "girly," and that she, like he, equates "girly" with something weak and loathsome. So she responded by colluding with his devaluation of women.

Indeed, this patient isn't so sure she likes what for her, since pregnancy, are new feelings of dependence on her husband. For she, like many other professional middle-class women in their 20s and 30s with whom I've worked, has fashioned and has long lived an identity that largely repudiates dependency (see Chapter 8). The repudiation is rooted in her disidentification with a mother who, in her view, incarnates helpless dependency on a charismatic, dependency-denying, and extremely controlling husband. But the disidentification is nurtured by the psychic demands of the space in which contemporary patriarchy and capitalism meet. Traditionally the two have come together to split and gender relationship as female and autonomy male; now, a new form of splitting enables privileged women to inhabit the psychic structure of traditional masculinity. Meanwhile, professional middle-class women such as my patients inherit all the problems that go along with living a version of autonomy that denies its embeddedness in relationships and manically repudiates dependency and vulnerability. In the traditional male version, male dependency was hidden in the caretaking functions of the wife; one way women such as my patients distance from having to be aware of dependency feelings is by purchasing relational services – personal assistants, nannies, housekeepers, and cooks take on the relational work for which the professional classes have less and less time. As I mentioned in Chapter 8, numerous television shows that appeared in the late 1990s and early 2000s legitimized this "I don't need anyone" version of white middle-class femininity; the female protagonists in these shows repudiate or have no time for the intimate and caretaking functions that marked the relational female idealized in the previous era. Neoliberal subjectivity is now available both to males and females of a certain class, but it is a form of subjectivity that promotes manic activity, devalues caretaking, and denies both dependence and interdependence.

Another patient, a white man who was very poor as a child but is now quite comfortable financially, was despondent after seeing the film, *The Pursuit of Happyness* (Muccino, 2006). He felt that he was living his life all wrong, buying all the latest gadgets and defending against old feelings of inadequacy by always having to buy the best. His girlfriend tried to console him by saying, "You shouldn't feel guilty; you worked hard for what you have." He experienced her statement as profoundly unempathic with what he was feeling, for, at that moment, he strongly felt that nobody deserves what he has when people are standing in lines every night waiting for shelter. One of my many reactions was to be surprised that the girlfriend, who herself is quite strapped for money, was not more empathic with my patient's feeling. But he explained to me that when you're poor you tend not to be empathic with poverty; rather, he recalls that his family's attitude toward people in similar struggling circumstances was: "stop complaining and get on with it." Was this view idiosyncratic to his family of poor laborers? A universal sentiment among the working poor? Or did this reflect the beginnings of the decline in social solidarity wrought by neoliberal union busting, a fraying social safety net, the encouragement for poor whites to identify as white and not as poor, and the reprise of a pull yourself up by your bootstraps mentality in the 1980s?

For the patient, the feeling of living his life all wrong surfaces only intermittently; much more salient is his anxiety that he could easily fall from being a winner to being a loser (see Ehrenreich, 1989; Stein, 2000). Perhaps the guilt he expressed after seeing the movie was less about having too much than about not wanting to give up what he has (Altman, 2006a) – in his case, giving it up threatens to thrust him back to where he came from, the shameful place of being a kid on welfare in the 1980s. Perhaps the issue will recur; but if part of my job is to attend to his development as a citizen who recognizes his implication in the suffering of others, and I think it is, then I need to listen carefully for moments where the conflict emerges and might be further explored.

In fact, such moments occur quite often, but not in the sphere of citizenship. This patient has tremendous insight into his thoughts and feelings, but he has had some difficulties acknowledging his implication in the suffering of his intimates. In interpersonal difficulties, he generally prefers to inhabit the position of unfairly treated victim, and yet, even when he moves into that somewhat vulnerable position, he rarely expresses his sense of victimization in terms of his own vulnerability; rather, he tends to express it by taking the moral high ground and accusing the other of bad behavior. Like my female patients discussed earlier, he has nothing but disdain for dependency, and this disdain sometimes limits his capacity for empathy and accountability.

These clinical vignettes suggest that one consequence of the denial of vulnerability that marks neoliberalism is the seeking of refuge in distinction, the defensive use of identity categories to keep oneself safe from criticism and pain. The vignettes reveal that a version of autonomy that repudiates its embeddedness in connection is a version that condemns its perhaps very productive avatar to a life of loneliness and aridity. Although such disconnected achievers suffer, they nonetheless defend tenaciously against exposing relational longings, clinging to the pleasures afforded by what Bourdieu (1984) refers to as "distinction," the cultural cachet that marks them as superior to others and as removed as possible from need and vulnerability. Recall the way my female patient's colleague tried to ally with his fantasy of what his boss would deem properly masculine by distancing himself from things considered feminine. I think it is worth considering whether the wide currency that Bourdieu's concept "distinction" has garnered in recent years might, again, have something to do with the rise of neoliberalism. For "distinction" happens to describe very well the particular ways neoliberalism's effects have mobilized attachments to collective identities that are marked by a denial or disavowal of vulnerability.

## Empathy reconceived: the therapist's implication in the patient's suffering

In Chapter 11, I described some racial/racist enactments that occurred in my work with Michael, a gay first-generation Asian American man. I want to take that material up again here, this time drawing on it to move the conversation on empathy into the relational field of patient and therapist. I do so in order to complicate the definition of empathy, counter its neoliberal version, and describe normative unconscious processes that involve relational repetition compulsions in which patient AND therapist take refuge in distinction. In these next two vignettes, drawn from the case presented in Chapter 11, we can see how shameful vulnerabilities that emerge as the price of inhabiting certain identity positions are split off and return in enactments that sustain inequality and obfuscate awareness of the ways we are implicated in each other's suffering. The vignettes make it clear that when the therapist defends against exposed vulnerability every bit as tenaciously as the patient, empathy devolves from a state of mutual implication to a state in which the empathizer keeps a safe distance from the sufferer.

## Vignettes

Recall that in the case reported in Chapter 11, my gay male Asian American patient, Michael, had ascribed whiteness and all the desirable attributes that go with whiteness to me. When something I had read about minority attempts to inhabit a fictive whiteness (Eng and Han, 2002) made me finally realize that I had assumed that position in the treatment, I began to explore what whiteness meant to him. What whiteness seemed to signify for Michael was a position of invulnerability, which, had he possessed it, would have guaranteed that he never would have to feel the pain of humiliation again – humiliation associated with his race, his masculinity, his homosexuality. In assuming the position of whiteness, I had put myself in an invulnerable position, and, as I said in Chapter 11, I imagine I must have been acting somewhat superior, which probably enabled me to tolerate his envy and idealization, and to empathize with his feelings of inferiority. But I did not realize until later that, by sustaining a superior stance, I was in some ways re-enacting the very scene of humiliation. To the best of my awareness, I feel that I reproduced this racist scene because I unconsciously needed to defend against the emergence of my own ethnic vulnerabilities. I believe that the distancing defense I put up was meant to keep from awareness the price my family and I had paid for the privilege of becoming white (see Cushman, 2019, Chapter 4, on the connection between white Jewish guilt and the loss of Jewish tradition). With this defense against my own losses, I was inviting my patient to collude with me in disidentifying with the attributes associated with non-whiteness.

At another moment in this treatment, I thought that I was being empathic with my patient's difficulty in knowing whether or not he was too deferential to others or, alternately, whether he was adhering to an ethic of politeness that was a norm of his culture. As he saw it, being polite was superior to the norms of a more selfish Western culture. Yet, the situations he described often reminded me of Benjamin's (1988) analysis of domination and submission in gender relations, and one day I told him that if he were a female describing the situations he described to me, I'd have thought that he was indeed assuming a submissive position. I did add that the difference in our cultural norms made me more perplexed about whether this was really submission or something else. What I was not conscious of until I tried to understand why he responded with a hostile zinger aimed at my femininity, however, was that the very mention of a female submissive position was to this gay Asian male a wounding white cultural stereotype. Why had I framed it in those terms? Was I perhaps unconsciously enacting my own dissociated racism and homophobia? Was I imposing my own struggle with sexism, a vulnerable area for me, on his painful struggle with Orientalism and homophobia? What did it stir up for me to sit with a man who didn't assert himself in ways I associate with masculinity? As in the racial enactment, we see the way my own conscious and unconscious identity investments were in part formed in repudiating relation to those of non-whiteness, masculinity, homosexuality. In the first vignette, my patient and I colluded in disidentifying with the attributes associated with non-whiteness. In both vignettes, my investments were deployed to sustain my distinction, which made empathy for the patient something I could only arrive at after inadvertently wounding him, being wounded back, and then thinking about how my own defenses against vulnerability discouraged the identifications that would have made empathy possible.

My work with Michael illustrates why I think that empathy has to be understood as a two-way event – not in the sense that the patient has to empathize with the analyst, though that will also be a likely outcome of treatment, but in the sense that the analyst is so implicated in the pain of the other that the recognition of the multiple ways this is so must lead to a hard-won, slow accretion of empathy that transforms not only the patient but the analyst as well (see Bolognini, 2004, Orange, 2007). Although in this particular situation, I was working with someone who had different cultural, racial, sexual, gender, and ethnic investments from mine, my broader point here is that our histories of racism, sexism, and classism make it so that, in every treatment, *my* psychic investments are likely to come into conflict with those of my patients. Hoggett (2006) has argued that empathy involves identifying "with the point of suffering in the other *and* with the frightened and destructive forces that this suffering unleashes" (p. 156). My vignettes suggest that sometimes, perhaps often, it is we who unleash these forces, particularly when we cannot give up fantasies that we are invulnerable, that we speak from a place of certainty, and that we are separate from the other's pain.

These reflections on the therapist's responsibility and accountability put me in mind of something Cornel West said (as spoken by Anna Deavere Smith in her play *Twilight: Los Angeles* (Levin, 2000)). Speaking about racism in America, West says that white people would be overwhelmed and unable to continue to live their lives of denial were they fully to experience black sadness. He goes on to say that while whites minimize black sadness, they have their own kind of sadness, one connected to the American Dream. The white form of sadness, West maintains, is very different from the black kind. When I heard West's words in the context of Smith's play, I thought that he was certainly right about whites living in denial, but perhaps not quite right to insist on such a radical distinction between the two kinds of sadness. For I believe that the white form of sadness, the one linked to the American Dream and to the dominance of middle-class norms of behavior, has a lot to do with both black upper *and* lower-class sadness. The American Dream was and is built on white privilege and the exclusion of blacks. Thus, what the privileged split off to sustain white privilege in no small measure produces both white sadness and black sadness. And black sadness is sustained not only by continuing inequalities but also by living out the result of what black people had to split off to become "proper" black subjects in a white world that casts them as the inferior "Other." The fact that all of these connections are hidden beneath layers upon historical layers of denial, beneath new forms of the repudiation of vulnerability, and new forms of withdrawal from and retaliation against the vulnerable "Other," make the version of empathy I am calling for very difficult to achieve.

My last vignette gathers together the themes I've explored here: neoliberal subjectivity, responsibility, accountability, empathy, identity investments, and the way these are all shaped by social norms that radically separate the psychic from the social. It centers around a dream that one of my white, middle-class female patients had a week or so after Hurricane Katrina. The dream reveals, I think, the unconscious ways we are implicated in each other's suffering – and the ways we currently deny it. Like many of my patients, this patient had not mentioned Hurricane Katrina at all in sessions immediately following the event. Here is the dream:

> I'm watching this dream unfold: there's a black woman who feels ill. She seems to get progressively worse. Her friends dig up a pit in the dirt and with water make it into a mud bath. They have her in it, rolling her around, back and forth, making more mud all the while. I'm worrying that they might be intending to put her under water. I don't want to be watching and not doing anything; I have to hope they have her best interests at heart and that they know what they're doing. The woman is in a delirium. When just her head is visible, her daughter, who has been watching, cries out, "That's my mama," and rushes closer to her to hug her. I don't remember seeing her submerged or getting better.

In the next scene, there's a whole crew of people escorting her to a tv show where she was supposed to be going on, but they were filling in for her because of her illness. Not only had she recovered, she looked absolutely stunning, glamorous: reminiscent of Oprah. Her friends were rushing ahead and there was commotion as they were letting the tv people know that she was coming and to plan for her to come on.

When I asked for her associations, she first said that it seemed to her the dream was about the personal transformation that she was undergoing, one that held great excitement and promise but also great risks and anxiety. And then she said, "I don't know why the people were black." I asked what came to mind. She said it made her think of Hurricane Katrina and all the poor, black people. She said she was very upset about what was going on and then went on to speak disparagingly about "them," those horrible people in the Bush administration and in New Orleans who didn't think about how poor people without cars were going to get out. I was struck by the part of the dream where she says "I don't want to be watching and not doing anything," and where she *hopes* the people in charge know what they are doing but fears they don't. So I asked her if she perhaps felt complicit in some way. She said she did not; she'd never let such a thing happen.

Shame had set in, and I realized only later that addressing the complicity rather than the helplessness had likely suggested my own refusal of complicity, as though I somehow was able to stand outside as the curious, but NOT HELPLESS onlooker. And I think this prevented me from finding a way to explore with her the richness of this dream, a richness that goes beyond its obvious transferential aspects. I might have drawn on a pact this patient had made with her parents, who were quite critical and quite sure their way was the right way. The silent pact she had made was to do what they told her to do but to take no responsibility for any outcome, positive or negative. We might have talked about her hope that people in charge on all levels, including me, know what they're doing, and the fear they don't – and what do you do when you're pretty sure they don't? We might have talked about her associations to the daughter who cries out, "That's my mama." Perhaps then we would have been able to connect emotionally to the way that the dream and associations suggest a relational unconscious in which we are all interimplicated and interdependent – "that's my mama," while they simultaneously point to a contemporary social reality whose discourses deny interdependence and therefore deny complicity. As I have been arguing, social discourses and norms pull for us to experience the psychic and the social as separate, and for the individual to see him/ herself as responsible only for the self and not for others. Thus Schulman's Anna, like so many of us, can live a happy life while feeling somewhat uneasy about the fact that things are rapidly falling apart in our country. At the same time, you can see how the patient's dream about Katrina captures an underlying feeling many people currently have that they are on their own and responsible for either sinking or swimming.

The dream struck me as perhaps revealing something important about the effects of current social circumstances on the unconscious, for it ends just as every U.S. disaster movie and Oprah show end. Her unconscious turned a tragedy in which we were all complicit, a tragedy of class, race, and the indifference to human vulnerability manifest in neoconservative foreign policies and neoliberal monetary and domestic policies, into a spectacle, a story of personal triumph over adversity. Indeed, the magical reincarnation of the Oprah show is the very thing that cultural authorities offer in lieu of taking responsibility for the welfare of their citizens. My sense is that this abandonment is breeding a resentment and helplessness that shape some of the kinds of conflicts we see in the clinic. Just as the patient's pact with her parents made her simultaneously too responsible and not responsible, so the government's and corporate culture's pact with its citizens makes us too responsible and not responsible enough for either ourselves or others.

## Conclusion

In speaking about failures of empathy and responsibility toward others in neoliberalism, Hoggett (2006) writes that in the place of a politics con- cerned with common welfare, "we find a 'market for care' emerging which colludes with . . . omniscient feelings of invulnerability – the culture of a phantasied 'security' which I can buy for me and my family" (p. 153). The "market for care" is where empathy and vulnerability are still allowed to exist in neoliberal culture, and I think that analysts and therapists, part of that feminized market, hold the culture's split off capacities for empa- thy (Botticelli, 2006). We are perhaps the empathy managers in a culture marked by an "exhaustion of empathy." But, as I have suggested, the *way* that therapists and activists alike hold the culture's split off capacities for empathy is of utmost importance. For one thing, a one-way version of empathy cannot address neoliberal distress. As the vignettes on gender and class suggest, a feature of neoliberal subjectivity lies in the way that identifications are deployed to distance from vulnerability and need. Difference devolves into distinction, which fortifies the polarities of winners and losers, us and them, that neoliberalism encourages. Further, when therapists exclude from clinical consideration the relation between the individual psyche and the kind of cultural material that I have been discussing, we collude with individualism and amoral familism. We make a devil's bargain, in which the culture outsources empathy to us professionals, and we agree not to raise questions in our offices about the harm done by culture.

There is a strong pull to collude – it has become part of what is considered good practice to separate the psychic from the social; those who broach these topics are often criticized for importing politics into the sacred realm of the clinic. But every clinical choice is in fact political, from the frame to the interpretation to, as I have shown, the way affects such as empathy are lived and expressed. As Andrew Samuels (2006, p. 207) has said, yesterday's bad practice has historically often become today's "good or good-enough" practice. In his view (1993), and I agree, the development of the citizen/subject is as integral to mental health as working well and loving well (see also Gutwill and Hollander, 2006); neoliberal subjectivity, along with new backlash versions of sexism, racism, and classism, is bad for your health. In an earlier paper (Layton, 2006b; see Chapter 3), I described our way of separating the psychic and the social as an instance of attacks on linking. Perhaps rather than simply treating neoliberalism's effects, we need to reestablish the links that neoliberal discourse so successfully suppresses. An old joke has it that the difference between an M.D. and a Ph.D. is that the job of the former is to make you well and the job of the latter is to make you sick. It may in fact be that when we restore the suppressed links, we will find that it won't be so easy for those of us who identify with Schulman's Anna to be happy and empathic at the same time, to separate personal happiness from a country and world that are falling apart.

There do exist some counters to the neoliberal trends I have been discussing, a few cultural pockets where we find challenges to prevailing views of empathy, responsibility, and accountability. There are, for example, global political movements in which activists construct new collective identities that yoke together antiracism, anti-capitalism, anti-sexism, and environmental concerns. In clinical psychoanalysis, Benjamin's (2004, 2009, 2017) work urges therapists to acknowledge the harm they inevitably inflict as they get caught up in their own and their patients' repetition compulsions. Other relational analytic clinicians (see, for example, Davies, 2004; Stern, 2004) are exploring the clinical impasses that occur when both therapist and patient defend against exposing their vulnerabilities by attacking, withdrawing, or, as I have suggested here, seeking refuge in distinction. In academic conversations, too, we find a recent tendency to highlight vulnerability and claim it as the source of our common humanity. Butler's (2004) recent work, for example, indebted to Levinas, develops a relational view of subjectivity that re-values vulnerability, dependency, and suffering, and makes them the ground of a politics that would differ significantly from a politics based in rights and an autonomous self. Finally, the artists: Sarah Schulman, for example, or Anna Deavere Smith, whose plays on racial conflicts complicate empathy and accountability, and demonstrate the ways we are implicated in each other's suffering. As clinicians, academics, artists, activists, and citizens, it is important that we recognize where, how, and why we collude with the damaging dictates of neoliberal subjectivity. And it is important for us to think about how we might render conscious the pain we inflict and the losses we incur when we take refuge from the gross inequalities of contemporary life in vulnerability-denying distinction.

## Note

* Used with permission. Adapted from Layton, L. (2009) Who's responsible? Our mutual implication in each other's suffering. *Psychoanalytic Dialogues* 19: 105–120.

# Chapter 13

# Irrational exuberance

## Neoliberal subjectivity and the perversion of truth[*]

In a 2009 *Nation* article titled "Obama and the Return of the Real," Jonathan Schell sets the scene for what I shall discuss in this chapter: disavowal and the perverse modes of subjectivity cultivated by neoliberalism. Schell notes four crises besides the economic meltdown that have suddenly occasioned shock and awe throughout the U.S. public: the shortage of natural resources, the spread of nuclear arms and other weapons of mass destruction, the ecological crisis, and, finally, "the failure of the American bid for global empire and the consequent decline of American influence abroad" (p. 21).[1] These crises, Schell asserts, have "striking features in common, suggesting shared roots" (p. 20). Each is "self-created," and each arises "from pathologies of our own activity, or perhaps hyperactivity . . . the oil is running short because we are driving too many cars to too many shopping malls" (p. 20). Each is "the result of excess, not scarcity," each involves "theft by the living from their posterity," and each is characterized by double standards that block the way to solutions, by which he means that "one group of nations, led by the United States, lays claim to the lion's share of the world's wealth, to an exclusive right to possess nuclear weapons, to a disproportionate right to pollute the environment . . . while everyone else is expected to accept second-class status" (p. 20). Finally, each of the crises has "been based on the wholesale manufacture of delusions" (p. 20).

It is on the subject of the "wholesale manufacture of delusions," what Schell calls "bubble thinking," that a social psychoanalysis has something to teach us. I want to look here at how psychoanalysis can help us understand a culture-wide promotion and acceptance of a lying relation to reality, what I shall call a social perversion. Schell attributes this perversion of truth to the greed of business, government, media, and military organizations "who began to tell lies to themselves and others in pursuit of or subservience to wealth and power" (p. 21), and he goes on to implicate all of us in this madness.[2] I agree that we are all implicated. But rather than attribute the mass madness simply to greed, I want to look at it as possibly being a response to trauma. The trauma I have in mind is not of the shock and awe variety, but of the whittling away over time of a sense of safety, security, and trust in those who are supposed to be watching out for the public's welfare. I want to propose that the excessive greed and political apathy of the past 30 years might be thought of as defensive and perverse responses to social trauma.

## Relational failure and the fetish structure of perversion

Nick Totton (2006) has suggested that rather than look at civilization as neurotic, we think of it as perverse, "structured as a response to massive collective trauma" (p. 144). Freud's (1927a, 1937) elaboration of the relation between disavowal and perversity will be our starting place. At the end of his career, Freud was still struggling to understand the roots of resistance to analysis. In "Analysis Terminable and Interminable" (1937), he wrote that the defenses, originally acquired to ward off threats posed to the ego by a dangerous and unpleasurable outer and inner reality, can themselves become a threat to the self: "if the perception of reality involves unpleasure," he writes, "that perception – i.e., the truth – must be sacrificed" (p. 390). Bion (1962a, 1962b) elaborated on Freud's insight, asserting that the capacity to bear frustration leads to the capacity to think: when the raw emotion evoked by frustration is not adequately contained, lying, rather than thinking, may become a customary way of defending against what he calls catastrophic change.[3]

As some have argued, Freud's late papers suggest he may have been on the verge of replacing repression as the central defense mechanism with disavowal. Disavowal is a simultaneous knowing and not knowing, "a self-deception in the face of accurate perception" (Basch, 1983, p. 133). In his 1927 paper, "Fetishism," Freud argued that disavowal is the defense at the heart of perversion, and his specimen case was the boy's disavowal of the reality of castration. As several analysts have pointed out (see, for example Steiner, 1993, pp. 92–93; Basch, 1983, p. 130; Grossman, 1993, p. 426), among Freud's examples of disavowal in the fetishism paper are two that are not about castration at all but rather about a child's repudiation of the reality of a father's death. This suggests that our understanding of fetishism and, therefore, perversion need not be restricted to the sexual realm. Indeed, as Bass (2000) has convincingly argued, Freud's analysis of fetishism as a solution to castration anxiety does not exemplify what Freud claims it does: the oscillation between a fantasy, that women have a penis, and a repudiated reality. For the repudiated reality is no reality at all, but rather a male fantasy: that girls are castrated boys. The fetish is thus marked by an oscillation between two fantasies: that girls have a penis and that they are castrated boys. There *is* a repudiated reality, but the reality is that girls are different from boys (see, among others, Chasseguet-Smirgel, 1986; Irigaray, 1985). Because of this "phallus-y," we need to re-think the nature of the fetish structure that operates in disavowal, and thus, in perversion.

The dictionary defines perversion as a turning away from the truth. In fact, the first occurrence of disavowal in our lives, according to Freud (1900), appears as a resistance to acknowledging the reality of dependence on others. The hungry baby, who has no control over the appearance or disappearance of the mother, hallucinates the breast, thus finding an omnipotent solution to a painful reality: I don't need you; I'm self-sufficient. Bass (2000) argues that the tension arising from hunger and the need for the breast is a confrontation with the demand to differentiate, which he calls the trauma of Eros. While I do believe that an obstruction to processes of differentiation is at the heart of what I am calling perversion, I do not agree with Bass that the trauma that gives rise to disavowal is the demand to differentiate. Rather, like Bach (1994), Coen (1998), Goldberg (1995), and others, I understand the trauma to derive from consistently unmet dependency needs and profound relational failure. In cases in which the caretaking surround is unable to contain anxiety and meet the dependency and assertion needs of the vulnerable child/citizenry, we will find disturbances in agency and dependency that do have as a consequence an inability to tolerate difference. It is in such conditions that difference becomes traumatic and is experienced in hierarchical pairs of inferior/superior, rather than as mere difference.

The capacity to hallucinate a way out of painful tension and inevitable environmental disappointments (the breast cannot always be there) can be a source of creativity, to be sure. But when that capacity becomes a regularly practiced disavowal of the truth of dependence, interdependence, and vulnerability, we have the makings of a perverse situation. And this is precisely the situation created by the triumph of neoliberalism, and, more recently, in the U.S., the triumph of neoconservatism. In what follows, I will argue that a perverse relation to reality is a solution to the social traumas of profound failures in caretaking and containment that have accompanied increasing economic inequalities and an increasingly dangerous world. The solution is marked by fetish structures that oscillate between two destructive fantasies that we might think of as disorders of disavowed dependency: a fantasy of self-sufficient omnipotence and a fantasy that we will be totally taken care of without any effort on our part.

## Neoliberalism, backlash, and perverse modes of subjectivity

As de Tocqueville (2000) noted in the mid-nineteenth century, individualism has been a dominant feature of U.S. life from the country's earliest days. But to attribute the form of individualism that has been dominant in the past 40 years to an unchanging U.S. character is to collude with the dehistoricizations and decontextualizations that are in fact the very mark of bourgeois ideology. In the U.S. neoliberal social reality of the past 30 years, the free individual of bourgeois ideology has been shaped like perhaps never before by what even some mainstream economists refer to as free market fundamentalism (e.g., Shiller, 2005). I want to look at some of the mediations that operate between culture and psyche and investigate further the traumatic structuring of what I think of as neoliberal versions of subjectivity.

As argued previously, babies and children need containment, holding, and, more generally, the presence of a caretaking attitude toward our vulnerabilities if we are not to be overcome by anxiety. As citizens, we need the same from our social environment. Thus, the welfare state itself becomes an agent that fosters social solidarity and a sense of agency. But over the past 40 years we have been essentially abandoned by our collective containers, and this has bred an anxiety that has, in many ways, been socially channeled toward finding individualistic rather than collective solutions to economic distress and collective social problems. Many theorists (see, for example, Krugman, 2002; Lasch, 1991; Sennett, 2006; Stein, 2000) have ascribed the social trauma that we in the U.S. have experienced to the imposition of free market capitalism, which, they argue, was a response to the economic crises of the 1970s and to the anxiety provoked by demands for economic equality made by various left-wing social movements of the 1960s. In *A Brief History of Neoliberalism*, Harvey (2005) suggests that the inflation, surging unemployment, and crisis in capital accumulation that occurred in the U.S. by the late 1960s led the upper classes to panic about their loosening hold on power and wealth. But panic was hardly restricted to the upper classes. Even before the economic collapse of 2008, many of us were already living in conditions of precarity caused by shifts in labor markets that offer little to no security to the workforce (for example, the loss of secure manufacturing jobs to low-wage service jobs with no benefits; the end of defined pension benefits; the hiring of temporary workers on short-term contracts; the shifting of jobs overseas; the decline of union power to negotiate collective contracts). After the economic collapse, the sense of vulnerability has been all the more widely shared.

In *What's the Matter with Kansas?*, Frank (2004) pondered why the people from his home state would vote consistently against their economic interests and waste their energy fighting against abortion and homosexuality rather than fight for economic equality (see Alford, 2014; Glynos, 2014b). By the 1990s, Kansas had become a bastion of the anti-abortion movement, and Frank details the simultaneous devastation of the state's economy and the rise of backlash movements. Frank's analysis implied that the people of Kansas were conned by the kind of manipulations that did indeed occur in the run-up to the election of Ronald Reagan, our first free market fundamentalist president. Reagan's campaign was rife with messages that encouraged the white working class and white poor, especially in the South, to ally with the white rich rather than with poor people of color. But Frank omitted from his account what his former teacher, Christopher Lasch (1991), had well documented: that the right-wing backlash took off in the very year, 1974, that Democratic neoliberals such as Paul Tsongas and Gary Hart were elected to the Senate. In the wake of the oil crisis and economic recession of the early 1970s, the neoliberal economic agenda that began to be shared by both Democrats and Republicans alike paved the way for social issues to be the *only* topics open to left-right debate. Perhaps the people of Kansas were not stupidly voting against their interests but rather were registering the reality that *no one* was representing their economic interest.

Drawing on Bion, Abel-Hirsch (2006) has noted that one way to think about perversion is as the "choice" to feel pain rather than suffer the painful truth (see Bion, 1962a, 1970). I am suggesting that the trauma of governmental and corporate indifference to increasing economic inequality has indeed been registered but has been disavowed. Rather than experience the extreme vulnerability resulting from the loss of care and containment, one finds in the backlash movements both a hatred of the vulnerable "other" – women of all colors, gays, the poor, Muslims, nonwhites (who, as Zizek, 1991, argues, are paradoxically envied, experienced by the haters as stealing their enjoyment) – and, in the case of the anti-abortion movement, an unconscious identification with the most dependent and vulnerable of all – the helpless fetus. Backlash, I am suggesting, is a perverse solution to the anxiety produced by failures in caretaking, a solution marked by a fantasy of invulnerability and a retaliatory response to injury.[4]

One could argue (see, for example, Lewis, 1996) that the welfare states in their U.K. and less social democratic U.S. incarnations already had implicit within them one kind of benefit that is universal and equal (e.g., early education, social security, and, in the U.K., healthcare) and another kind that marks out difference (such as entitlements for the poor and mandatory desegregation of schools). From the very beginnings of the Johnson era welfare reforms in the U.S., there were struggles over the latter kind of entitlement. But the rise of the neoliberal state has fostered an even greater tendency to collapse difference into distinctions between superior and inferior groups, and refuge has been increasingly sought in the grandiose fantasy of superiority. When a social reality is too traumatic to take in, libidinal attachments to ethnic, racial, and class identities offer many psychological comforts (Georgis, 2007), among which is "safety in an insecure world" (Bauman, 2001). But they simultaneously can operate as defenses against suffering the trauma of a lost sense of interdependence and a failure of care.

## The Bush years: institutional indifference, conflicted vulnerability, and the oscillation between omnipotence and helplessness

In the past 30 years in the U.S., political and institutional orders have primarily served the interests of economic growth and fostered the fantasy that such growth is the only way to address scarcity and vulnerability. One result has been an increasing institutional indifference to the fate not only of the poor but of the citizenry and work force at large. As Obama himself often said (but failed radically to alter), there is a lot of suffering and there has been little accountability or responsibility for what has caused the suffering (see Chapter 12). We are always at the mercy of the indifference of nature to human suffering, but it is quite another thing to be subject to the indifference of our political leaders and our employers. As noted in the last chapter, Sennett (2006) and Stein (2000) have written compellingly about workplace abandonments and the feelings of disposability that they engender. The threats of becoming redundant, of having your job be downsized or outsourced only heightens the sense of precarity for the rest of the population.

During the Bush years, tax cuts for the wealthy, corporate welfare, and the costs of a terribly unpopular war decimated public services, which left the middle classes on their own to fend against very real anxieties that they will end up without healthcare, without pensions, without social security. Vulnerable and dependent feelings, increasingly shameful states since the Reagan revolution, have only become more shameful since the events of 9/11 and the U.S. response to those events: during the Bush years, vulnerability and fear were simultaneously stoked, by both media and government, and treated as shameful. The culture-wide repudiation of vulnerability, which indeed it is less and less safe to feel, makes it hard to tolerate states of dependence and makes it hard to acknowledge how we are all connected to one another.

Bionian Pistiner de Cortiñas (2009) offers some thoughts about the relation between a sense of helplessness and cultures that are committed to lying:

> In thoughts and in the developing of thinking, a tolerance of the emotions that stimulate feelings of helplessness has been achieved, these being uncertainty, ignorance, and the finite-infinite relationship. In lies, when it comes to facing feelings of helplessness, there is an increment in the doses of omnipotence and the need for obtaining collusions that disavow helplessness.
>
> (p. 121)

Key to the capacity for truth-telling is the capacity to tolerate uncertainty, helplessness, and vulnerability rather than disavow the reality that evokes those states. So what happens to possibilities for truth-telling in a culture that makes uncertainty and shame about the vulnerability it evokes a way of life?

## Neoliberal subjectivity and "amoral familism"

Rachael Peltz (2005) has most helpfully traced some of the psychic effects of public indifference on the professional middle-class patients she treats. Like the social theorists cited previously, she, too, argues that when the government abdicates responsibility for containing anxiety and for "holding" the vulnerable and the needy, dependency becomes more and more shameful. She suggests that those who have been lucky enough not to fall through the now huge holes in the social safety net have taken refuge in a manic defense against need. Left on our own by the commitment of government and corporate cultures to greed and power, unable or unwilling to make the links necessary to understand our predicament and rebel against it, many of those fortunate enough to be able to do so have defended against feelings of abandonment, helplessness, and vulnerability with the "lie" of self-sufficiency. As Peltz elaborates, those of us in the professional middle class have accepted as normal a state in which we daily run ourselves ragged: we feel virtuous when we can fit 100 activities into the shortest amount of time and we feel like lazy slobs when we cannot.

Like the patients Peltz describes, most of us in the U.S. professional white middle class have dutifully shaped our subjectivities in accord with dominant individualistic norms that, even more so than in past eras, unlink the social from the individual. And so we consistently rail against ourselves when, for example, our small businesses fail or when we are unable to balance career and child care. We imagine that there are stronger, special others who can do it all and that if only we weren't weak, inferior beings, we, too, would succeed. Adapting to the lack of accountability, the "politics of disengagement" (Bauman, 2001) that have marked our all too recent past, we have successfully made ourselves solely responsible for our so-called failures. In so doing, many of us have anxiously retreated to the private or professional sphere, disavowing our connections to the goings on in the wider world. As mentioned in the previous chapter, sociologist John Rodger (2003) calls the disengaged response to the disengagement of the post-welfare state "amoral familism," another popular response to the culturally fostered denial of mutual interdependence. Amoral familism is a reaction that the clinic, in its general exclusion of any social realm beyond the family, tends to encourage.

We can see, then, that the disavowal of vulnerability and need takes two prominent forms: the retaliation that characterizes backlash and the withdrawal that characterizes amoral familism. And these two classic reactions to trauma can be understood as responses to profound failures in the caretaking environment. Retaliation and withdrawal are at the heart of the sadomasochistic object relations that characterize social perversion (see Chapter 14).

## Containment and care: neoliberal subjectivity in the clinic

It is in this context that I want to explore in more depth some clinical mani-festations of neoliberal subjectivities, which rest on the perverse disavowal of vulnerability, dependency, and interdependence. These disavowals issue in an intensified individualism and thus an intensified version of narcis-sism. By the late 1970s, psychoanalysts, such as Kohut (1971, 1977), and cultural analysts, such as Lasch (1979) and Kovel (1980), were already describing an increased prevalence of the character structure of narcis-sism, the empty selves that need more things, bigger things, better things in order to feel even momentarily adequate (see also Cushman, 1995). Relevant perhaps to the present discussion is the way that Kovel linked narcissistic character to a middle-class family structure in which children came to feel that parental love was contingent on their economic and pro-fessional success (see Chapter 14). A narcissistic individualism has been exacerbated by the vicious circle of heightened vulnerability and increased lack of containment characteristic of neoliberalism. The defenses that sus-tain this version of narcissism are perverse, marked by a fetish structure that oscillates between fantasies of omnipotent self-sufficiency and fanta-sies that one need do nothing to be taken care of. The following vignettes suggest that politics enter the clinic not only in the direct discussion of political events, but in the very conscious and unconscious expression of our subjectivity (Samuels, 2007).

## Vignette #1

Sally, a woman now in her 40s [in 2010], made the decision in her 30s to stop working full-time in her very demanding profession and stay home to take care of her children. She continued to work part-time, but the decision made it difficult to practice her profession and she often feels marginal and frustrated. Sally's husband was a salaried white collar worker when they married, but feeling the pressure of looming college costs and his wife's desire for a bigger house, he has recently tried to parlay his expertise into something more lucrative. His work is now more stressful; he gets manically busy and is away from home a lot more. Sally sometimes feels he is married to his job and, disavowing the way she participates in his drive to get more money, she experiences only abandonment. The business dealings leave the family subject to moments of high promise and big letdown. Whenever her husband's characteristic cockeyed optimism hits a road-block, Sally spirals downward into a familiar despair about the possibility of ever getting what she wants. Of course the wish for a bigger house has multiple meanings, but for a moment let us not reduce it to a wish for a penis – or even a wish for more psychic space, which it certainly is. Let us think of it rather as a fetish object, a stand-in for a traumatic failure of social and individual caretaking.

As in D.H. Lawrence's (2007) short story, "The Rocking-Horse Winner" (see Chapter 9) I imagine that Sally's current house reverberates with the desperate sound of "There must be more money." Sally moved into that house around the time she gave up full-time work. The house is in a very expensive suburb in which housing prices skyrocketed in the late 1990s, which made it impossible for her to move to a bigger house. She keeps trying to fix her current house, but it will never be what she wants. Sally's parents were locked in a miserable marriage and everyone in the family was emotionally abused by the alcoholic patriarch. Her mother was loving but failed Sally by not leaving her husband and so not truly protecting her children and herself from abuse. Her mother, a pre-women's lib subject, felt unable to leave because she had no profession and thus no way to take care of herself and her several children. Sally's psyche is marked by the feeling that nothing will ever change for the better. Attracted at first by her husband's optimism, she has come to see that his optimism is often based in wishful thinking or a need to please, and this has made her sink even further into despair. She has come face to face with the failure of a fantasy that she would get what she wanted without having to do anything to get it.

Sitting with Sally's despair is quite difficult. Like so many of my patients, she can be brutal toward herself with scathing self-recriminations. And like my patients with failing small businesses, I am often amazed by Sally's inability to see her life in any but an omnipotent individualistic or victimized context – she never seems able to remember, for example, that she chose to stay home with her kids, even though, when pressed, she will reiterate that she'd make the same choice today. Instead, she measures herself against those of her friends who have the big house and wonders what the hell is wrong with her, why is she so weak and stupid. A good subject of bourgeois ideology in its neoliberal incarnation, no context, no history enters into Sally's thinking. Indeed, when she is in despair and railing against herself, there is little evidence of a capacity to think.

I have made many interpretations of what it means to Sally to have a better and bigger house, but Sally sticks to her wish with a concreteness and pain that finally made me try a different tack. And that tack was to supply the missing context, which, unanalytic as it may seem at first glance, I have come to regard as an important part of holding, containment, and metabolization. The context here is manifold: Sally's inability to balance a full-time career and childcare is not a sign of character weakness. As I argued in Chapter 8, the result of second wave feminism was a compromise with neoliberalism and patriarchy: rather than alter the structure of domestic and work relations, as socialist feminists had advocated, the version of feminism that succeeded in the of so-called "Third World" women U.S. merely placed middle-class women into the same psychic condition that had prevailed for men, one which demands a repudiation of capacities for nurture, emotionality, and dependence and fosters an omnipotent kind of autonomy: the dominant version of neoliberal subjectivity (see Ehrenreich and Hochschild's 2002 analysis of what they call the "care drain," that is, the importation of so-called "Third World" women to supply the care functions that First World middle-class families no longer have time to perform). When Sally can think, she is aware that her friends who got the big house missed the opportunity to spend as much time as she did with her children, an experience she wouldn't trade for anything, even a bigger house. When Sally can think, she can remember that she made a decision, that she isn't a helpless victim. But that decision was made within social constraints that did indeed rob her of the chance to experience the sense of work fulfillment for which liberal second wave feminists fought.

Sally oscillates between feeling like a helpless victim and a failed omnipotent agent. Her fantasies of self-sufficient omnipotence cause her to berate herself for not having known that housing prices in the suburb in which she wanted to live would, so to speak, go through the roof. And everything in neoliberal culture encourages her to think it *is* her fault – just consider all the books with titles such as *The Courage to be Rich: Creating a Life of Material and Spiritual Abundance* (Orman, 1999), or *The Road to Financial Freedom: A Millionaire in Seven Years* (Schaefer, 1999).

In the wake of the economic collapse of 2007, it may come as a surprise that even some mainstream economists have been warning us for several years that neoliberalism fosters a lying relation to reality that the general population bought into way too eagerly. Robert Shiller (2005), author of *Irrational Exuberance* (a phrase, by the way, coined by Alan Greenspan in a moment of honesty that preceded his own world-altering disavowal), provides context for understanding more about Sally's psychic dilemma. Shiller, a behavioral economist, chronicles the cultural context of what he calls the feedback loops of speculative bubbles and irrational exuberance. And one thing he points to is the shift in cultural values that accompanied the take-over by free market fundamentalism. Shiller well understands that as people became more worried about their well-being, they became more vulnerable to "the kind of feedback that generates bubbles" (p. 27), and his own research documents the fact that materialism became a more and more dominant cultural value in the U.S. beginning in the 1980s. For example, and with regard to the housing market specifically, he writes that

> Before 1960, general public attention to the housing market often tended to take the form of outrage at the exorbitant rents that landlords were able to extract from their tenants, rather than concern about the course of prices of single-family homes. People were . . . not primed to believe that their well-being depended in large measure on their property.
>
> (p. 26)

Until the last decades of the twentieth century, concerns about housing focused on rent control and on a housing cooperative movement. People *expected* government intervention "to prevent home prices from getting out of control" (pp. 26–27) and to keep things fair. Shiller concludes that "Our increasing public commitment to market solutions to economic problems is the ultimate cause of the public's worry about instabilities in home prices." This leaves us "more prone to the kind of feedback that generates bubbles" (pp. 26–27).

Shiller lists some of the sources of such feedback: an internet culture that promotes a false sense of omnipotent control, books on amassing wealth that boldly state as golden rules "the dictum that any stock market decline must soon be reversed" (Shiller, p. 62), and a 24-hour business media whose analysts profit from generating unwarranted optimism. Sally lives in a culture whose character is not unlike that of her husband: a culture of unwarranted optimism that generates fantasies of having it all. For me, this context gives Sally's unbearable despair new meaning, psychosocial meaning.

Psychoanalytic theory tells us that until Sally mourns the psychic wounds of not having been properly cared for, she will be unable to face limits and withstand the burdens of maturity. But nothing in the middle-class culture of the past 30 years has facilitated either mourning or recognition of limits. I have found that, for Sally, caretaking has prominently involved providing context that suggests that there are different narratives within which to frame her life, narratives in which she is not stupid and weak and in which she did exercise agency, but within particular constraints. This has seemed to enable her to begin to internalize my voice as a soothing presence in a way she had not been able to do before. When she begins to get anxious, she says, she hears me talk about the choices she's made, choices in conditions that were not of her own making but choices nonetheless. For Sally, a bit of concerned realism has been one aspect of a containment and transformation that has helped contest the fetish structure and thus helped her mourn her disappointments without descending into helpless, victimized despair. Ironically, the economic collapse has also calmed her; along with my voice, her friends' economic problems and a feeling of being in the same boat seem to have given her permission to cease the self-beratement that was driving her crazy.[5]

## Vignette #2

A colleague presented a very familiar-sounding case in which a middle-class college student performed to perfection in one semester only to collapse into so much binging, purging, and alcohol abuse in the second semester that she could not complete any work and would find herself on the verge of expulsion. The student attempted to comply with parental and cultural demands to be an enterprising self but continued to fall sick from the attempt, rebelling in self-annihilating but powerfully signifying refusals. The therapist felt pulled to help the student complete her work, a very understandable reaction given the student's apparent panic about not getting her work done. But such a pull, I contend, entails an unconscious collusion with one pole of the patient's fetish structure, the one that supports the perverse social norm of non-caretaking and self-sufficient omnipotence to which so many of us, patients and therapists alike, have submitted ourselves in this neoliberal age. Indeed, in attempting to diminish the harshness of my patients' punitive superegos, I often find myself making interventions designed to help them feel less guilty and less bad about enjoying their privilege, but, in so doing, I fear that I consciously and unconsciously collude with neoliberal norms that encourage the privileged not to look at the connection between their fortunate status and the unfortunate status of less privileged others (see Chapter 5).

Lies demand collusion, and, as Gerson (1996) has suggested, resistances in analysis are mutually constructed. In the previous example, the resistances are mutually constructed by normative unconscious processes that sustain the very norms that have made us sick (Layton, 2002). Such collusions create what Ruth Stein (2005) has called a perverse pact: "a relationship between two accomplices, a mutual agreement . . . that serves to cover over or turn the common and mutual gaze of the accomplices from the catastrophic biographical events that had befallen each of them . . ." (p. 787). I am suggesting we add catastrophic social events to our understanding of perversion and to our understanding of that from which our patients suffer. When we leave out the social context of our patients' psychic struggles, we, too, collude with the individualist lie that the psychic and the social are separate, and so we do not analyze a most important determinant of what has made the patient sick in the first place. In this case of the college student, the clinician might have countered neoliberal trends by helping the patient look not only at the destructive symptoms but also at her feelings about the demand to be an enterprising self. Failing that, we unconsciously contribute to sustaining the idea that such pressures for performance are normal.

### Vignette #3

I conclude with one last clinical example, one where I made a direct political intervention into a conversation about politics. After Obama's acceptance of the Democratic Party nomination in 2007 – an event that took place with great drama before a backdrop of the columns of the Lincoln Memorial, or was it an Athenian temple? – a white middle-class patient of mine mocked her 60-something-year-old mother for crying at what, to her, was clearly an event staged to call forth tears. I had also cried, so, feeling a tad annoyed, I asked the patient if she knew why her mother was crying. No, she didn't. But it led to her talking about feeling helpless to do anything political, a comment I have heard many times from patients. When she repeated this a few weeks later, I told her there were things she could do, such as volunteering for Obama. I uncharacteristically mentioned that I'd been going to New Hampshire to volunteer. The next week she seemed angry about everything and complained about how much therapy cost and a variety of other things. I thought the anger might have come from what I'd said. But the following week she opened the session with a hearty "thank you." An African American friend of hers had persuaded her to campaign in a swing state for Obama over the weekend, and although she was loath to give up a WHOLE weekend of academic work, she found the experience exhilarating and an antidote to her feelings of helplessness. Afterwards, she asked her mother why she had cried at the Obama nomination, and her mother said that it was because she had never thought that she would see an African American nominated for president in her lifetime. Her mother has been politically active most of her life, but her daughter, my patient, came of age in the 1980s, the time of withdrawal from politics, of career uncertainty, and the perverse disavowal of need and interdependence. I noted that the week before she had seemed very angry and I asked her if she had been bothered by my having mentioned my own volunteer activities. She said no, that she was grateful, that I don't ever give advice but that it felt like I knew her well enough to know that this would be helpful to her. She began to cry and said it had felt like a caretaking response to her feelings of helplessness.

My interventions in these examples are not classically analytic, that is, the provision of context and suggestion of activity are quite different from our usual notions of interpretation of unconscious conflict – but they do confront what I am calling perverse defenses of omnipotent self-sufficiency and the cynical or apathetic sense of helplessness. Given the cultural trajectory that I have been tracing, it is interesting to note that in the U.S. of the 1990s, a new psychoanalytic school, relational analysis, rose to prominence. The dominant influences on that school are psychoanalytic theories that value holding, containment, and the real relationship as highly as interpretation, as well as theories that locate the core of trauma in relational failures of caretaking and in traumatizing responses to dependency needs (see Chapter 5). The more hatred toward dependency there is in the culture, the more disorders of dependency and attachment come to the center of analytic attention – and the more our capacity to care (Hollway, 2006) is called upon.

The definition of social perversion that I have offered centers on the self-estrangement we practice in order to live in a precarious state that systematically makes dependency shameful and frightening, that unlinks the individual and the social in a way that makes it possible to deny the ways in which we are all interconnected, and that therefore encourages the collapse of difference into hierarchies of superior/inferior. Neoliberal subjectivity of course takes on different forms depending on one's place in the social structure, but it is to be hoped that the wake-up call that led to the election of Obama will help us to reckon with the many painful truths that neoliberalism has encouraged us to disavow.[6] Whether or not this will be the case remains to be seen. A January 2010 U.S. poll shows (see Allstate/National Journal Heartland Monitor Poll Topline, January 3–7, 2010), as Atlantic Media Director Ron Brownstein reports (January 15, 2010a), "a populist uprising against all institutions" (with 40% of the poll subjects saying that banks benefited most from the government's response to the financial crisis, 20% choosing major corporations, 16% wealthy individuals, 9% middle-class individuals, and 8% low-income individuals). Brownstein (January 16, 2010b) adds: "respondents expressed little trust in any institution beyond their own family to help them navigate the financial rapids – giving government, major corporations, and financial institutions all dismal grades." The question, as Brownstein and other pundits are putting it, is what will be the target of the populist anger? Conservatives are waging a thus far successful campaign to make government the principal target; the pundits are predicting a Democratic defeat in 2010 that would repeat the 1994 "Gingrich revolution" that brought conservative Republicans to power. Obama, who thus far has governed like his neoliberal Democratic predecessor, bailing out banks and cutting deals with big business, needs to take up the cause of the vulnerable and re-build a sense of social solidarity. And whether or not he does so may largely depend on what use the U.S. population makes of their growing anger against institutional indifference.

## Notes

* Used with permission. Layton, L. (2010) Irrational exuberance: Neoliberal subjectivity and the perversion of truth. *Subjectivity* 3(3): 303–322.

1 Note that Schell wrote this piece seven years before Trump became president (and before the Tea Party came to power), proving, should proof be necessary, that Trump's election was no accident but rather an extreme of a trend fully present during the Obama administration.

2 Schell does not mention the terrorist attacks of September 11, 2001, and I think that such omissions of traumatic events make it difficult to account fully for the psychological complexities of popular and even political response.

3 When, following Freud and Bion, I use the terms "truth" and "lying," I do not mean to imply that the turn away from painful experience is conscious; nor does my use of "truth" imply transparency. Indeed, I am not speaking here of facts that can be labeled true or false. As I shall elaborate, I am speaking about relational interactions and interactions with the environment that are painful and defensively managed or avoided rather than, to use Bion's term, "suffered" (see Abel-Hirsch, 2006, for a connection between perversion and Bion's distinction between feeling pain and suffering pain). Hoggett (2000) has usefully distinguished between delusional dogmas and creative illusions. Drawing on Winnicott's (1971) use of transitional phenomena, Hoggett understands illusion to be a subject's way of negotiating the inevitable tension between what is internal and what is external. This is a felicitous way to handle the postmodern problem of speaking naively about truths. And yet, in the clinic, one is constantly faced with the patient's and therapist's habitual modes of self-deception, the resistance to acknowledging what, at some level, one knows to be true or will discover to be true. The power of resistance is in no small measure due to the fact that often what we take to be the most central aspects of the identity we have constructed, our very way of being in the world, relies on sustaining such deceptions.

4 Distinguishing between an ethic of justice and an ethic of care, Hoggett (2000, pp. 159–160) has pointed out that the British welfare state never adequately concerned itself with care, that is, with attention to the emotional needs and vulnerabilities of the population (as opposed to a focus on material needs). Thus, he finds it not surprising that the Thatcher/Reagan backlash against the welfare state centered on an attack against the so-called culture of dependency (pp. 164–165, p. 179). The attack was further executed by Blair and Clinton, who promulgated what became the widely shared fantasy that economic growth is the only way to address scarcity and vulnerability.

5 Of course, it is quite possible that the symptomatic part of this picture will re-emerge elsewhere in Sally's life. But I have been struck by how, at times, a

change in circumstances can make something that has looked unconscious and deep-seated (see, for example, Volkan, 1988) seem rather easily changeable when the environment changes. For example, research by social psychologists Gaertner and Dovidio (2005) has shown that a change in environmental conditions makes a kind of unconscious racism seen in liberal subjects who consciously understand themselves to be non-racist (what Gaertner and Dovidio call aversive racism) seem to disappear.

6  I chose to leave this conclusion from 2010 as it was, sadly, predictive of things to come.

Chapter 14

# Yale, fail, jail

## Sadomasochistic individual, large-group, and institutional effects of neoliberalism[*]

Long before the Occupy movements began, I asked a friend why he was so concerned that his children go to law school, and he replied: "The U.S. is well on its way to being like a third world country, where there is a tiny minority of rich people and the rest of the population in poverty, and I want my children to be among the rich." One could interpret his response as an expression of greed, and, indeed, it shows little concern for the poor. But I understand it also as an expression of anxiety, an anxiety that is daily being passed down to middle-class children – along with indifference, if not contempt, for the poor: "Yale or jail" is how one of my white middle-class patients interpreted the parental message.

Our current social conditions of increasing income inequality, downsizing, outsourcing, high unemployment – extremely high in some groups – and generally precarious feelings about the economic situation have created much anxiety about class status and well-being in all classes. This has led, on the one hand, to split states of immense vulnerability and insecurity, and on the other, to public hatred of any signs of vulnerability and dependency. Dependency has come to signify "poor" and "failure." From a psychological perspective, however, we know that denying dependency leads to a kind of grandiose sense of omnipotence in which one feels that one needs nobody and nothing. As a result, it becomes hard to see how rich and poor, powerful and vulnerable, are connected to each other, how we are all part of the same social system and thus mutually interdependent.

Grandiose states tend to be unstable and crash, precisely because we do need others. Fluctuations between grandiose omnipotent self-states and states of low self-worth are, in fact, symptomatic of the difficulties regulating self-esteem that clinicians refer to as narcissism, a dialectical disorder marked by oscillations between self-deprecation and grandiosity, devaluation and idealization of others, and longings to merge versus needs radically to withdraw from others (Layton, 1988; Shaw, 2013). The form these oscillations take will differ depending on how the class inequalities that cause splitting intersect with the wounds of racism, sexism, and other social inequalities. I look here at some individual and large-group psychological effects of neoliberal social and economic policy and explore the relational dynamics of what I think of as social narcissism. I argue that in all social groups, on both individual and large-group levels, the stark inequalities ushered in by neoliberal governance lead to sadomasochistic and instrumentalized relational scenarios marked by domination and submission – and by the eroticization of positions of power and weakness.

## Neoliberalism

In the U.S., "neoliberalism" is not a term commonly heard outside of academic circles. And yet, the effects of neoliberalism have become increasingly pervasive in public and private life over the past 40 years, promoting and/or exacerbating particular forms of narcissistic and perverse states. What is meant by neoliberalism and what have been its effects on psychic life?

In his lectures of 1978–79, Foucault (2008) suggested that the origins of various forms of neoliberalism appeared in the 1940s, noting that whereas neoliberal ideologies in Germany arose in reaction against the all-powerful Nazi state, in the U.S. they developed in reaction against the New Deal, Keynesian economic policies, and, only later, against LBJ's Great Society programs, e.g., the War on Poverty, all of which came to be summarized and demeaned under the heading "big government." In the 1940s in the U.S., neoliberal economic and political policies were based on the assumption that government ought to function largely as the facilitator of and handmaiden to free markets. Neoliberal backlash legislation was passed in several states in the 1940s, policies that included right-to-work legislation that sought to undermine the power of unions (which were considered communist).

Nonetheless, as Paul Krugman (2002) and others have written, in the post-World War II period, 1945 to the early 1970s, there remained a general consensus in favor of the welfare state. The dominant assumption, post-depression, was that the free market creates inequalities and crises that most affect the vulnerable, and that government needs to step in to protect the whole polity from capitalism's excesses. Government, for example, should be active in redistributing wealth through progressive taxation, make sure labor has a voice in negotiating with capital for such things as length of the work week and benefits, and ensure as close to full employment as possible. This was probably the most egalitarian period in U.S. history, especially for white people. It was a time during which the white working and middle classes enjoyed a rising standard of living, new government benefits, and a contract of sorts between labor and capital. To the dismay of those who benefitted, this period turned out to be a short blip between two Gilded Ages dominated by the wealthiest members of society and hostile to middle and working classes, and, most especially, to the poor of all races.

Naomi Klein (2007) coined the phrase "disaster capitalism" to refer to moments of crisis that allowed neoliberals to begin to institutionalize the policies they had begun to formulate in the 1940s, first in Latin America and then in the U.S. Most of those who write about neoliberalism date the beginnings of neoliberal dominance to the late 1970s. They argue that the first phase of neoliberalism in the U.S. was ushered in during the mid-1970s crisis years of high unemployment, high inflation, and high oil prices (Harvey, 2005; Peck and Tickell, 2002). In this period, a decline in capital accumulation caused rising anxiety among the capitalist elite. Besides high inflation and high unemployment, U.S. national identity in this era was battered and fragmented by the terrible human losses of Vietnam, the humiliating defeat and ultimately unanswered question of what we were doing there in the first place, the unsettling of the social status quo brought about by black protest movements, student movements, and several other social justice movements confronting racial, class, gender, and sexual discrimination. A crisis of authority emerged as a crooked president chose to resign rather than face impeachment.

Although Ronald Reagan and Margaret Thatcher have become the poster children of neoliberalism through their loudly proclaimed disdain for big government, the story of U.S. neoliberalism's rise as a subject-forming socio-political-economic ideology really starts earlier, during the Carter administration. The Nixon administration had in fact passed quite a bit of progressive legislation, including signing into law Supplemental Security Income, establishing the Environmental Protection Agency (EPA), and the Occupational Safety and Health Administration (OSHA). In the early

1970s, heads of major corporations and right-wing ideologues began to go on the offensive against labor, progressive movements, and against government regulation. They created foundations, business organizations, and think tanks that eventually began to formulate and promote legislation favorable to the wealthy, for example, legislation that would drastically cut taxes on the wealthy, deregulate everything from banking to environmental policy, disempower unions, and take the teeth out of any consumer protections. The elections of 1974 brought to the Senate Democrats such as Gary Hart and Paul Tsongas, who, like many Republicans of the time, embraced neoliberal principles of free market capitalism. Although Carter himself was eager to promote progressive legislation, and Democrats controlled all branches of government when he took office, he was unable to do so. The first attacks were on the EPA, consumer affairs, and labor legislation. A bill to create an Office of Consumer Representation, legislation that had at first seemed as though it would be easy to pass, was defeated in 1978 with 3/5 of the new class of Democrats voting against it. The capital gains tax – which taxes investment income – was reduced from 48 percent to 28 percent.

In the U.S., beginning in the 1970s, business interests became more and more organized and entrenched, exerting influence on the government via a massive rise in lobbying activity (Hacker and Pierson, 2010). The neoliberal partnership between business and government began to dominate U.S. life, and by the 1990s neoliberalism had become the new normal, abetted by the rise to power of the Democratic Leadership Council (DLC). One of the DLC's leaders, Bill Clinton, faced with an increasingly radical right wing Republican Congress, continued to dismantle pieces of the welfare state while simultaneously promoting globalization, free trade agreements, and banking deregulation. These policies resulted in the outsourcing of manufacture and the decimation of the industrial working class. As Krugman (2019) has said of the effect of neoliberal economic policies on the working class, the decline we have seen in workers' wages has little to do with advances in technology but rather with "a political environment deeply hostile to labor organizations and friendly toward union-busting employers." Eventually, all of these neoliberal policies culminated in the crash of 2007.

Because of the high cost of winning a seat in the U.S. government, most legislators, including those liberal on social issues, end up beholden to corporate interests. The huge income inequality we experience today has been achieved, in government, both through active legislation, like continuous tax cuts for the rich, as well as through passive ways of making sure progressive legislation, like attempts to impose regulations on Wall Street, goes nowhere. All of this has abetted the vast expansion of the wealth and power of multinational corporations and the finance sector. With the Occupy movements these machinations were finally publicly named as the cause of the largest income gap in the U.S. between the very rich and everyone else since the Gilded Age of capitalism (Krugman, 2002). The betrayals by both government and corporations have created crisis conditions for the poor as well as for both the white and nonwhite working and lower middle classes (Lamont, 2000; Silva, 2013), what Hollander and Gutwill (2006) have referred to as a traumatogenic environment.

## Neoliberalism and social policy

In classical liberalism, the market was conceptualized as a sphere separate from government. Neoliberalism, as noted previously, is marked by a partnership between government and market, one in which government extends market values such as cost-benefit analysis and privatization into areas formerly understood to be part of the common good – e.g., health, education, and social security. Whereas the welfare state shifted responsibility for market risks from the individual worker to collectivist solutions such as disability and unemployment insurance, neoliberal policies shift risk back onto the individual. As it retreats from providing a social safety net, neoliberalism promotes a particular vision of human nature: the individual is conceived of as an entrepreneur whose "nature" is competitive and based in self-care and self-interest (for descriptions of "homo entrepreneur" see Rose, 1999; du Gay, 2004; Read, 2009). The function of the state becomes one of "facilitation": individuals and organizations are "set free to find their own destiny;" the state "is relieved of its powers and obligations to know, plan, calculate and steer from the centre" (Rose, 1999, p. 476).

Citizenship itself is reduced to an individualist and consumption-driven form of self-care rather than being defined by an interest in the public good (Brown, 2006, p. 695). Social problems are reconceptualized as individual problems that market forces such as privatization and consumer products can solve. Brown writes (2006):

Examples in the United States are legion: bottled water as a response to contamination of the water table; private schools, charter schools, and voucher systems as a response to the collapse of quality public education; anti-theft devices, private security guards, and gated communities (and nations) as a response to the production of a throwaway class and intensifying economic inequality; boutique medicine as a response to crumbling health care provision; "V-chips" as a response to the explosion of violent and pornographic material on every type of household screen; ergonomic tools and technologies as a response to the work conditions of information capitalism; and, of course, finely differentiated and titrated pharmaceutical antidepressants as a response to lives of meaninglessness or despair amidst wealth and freedom.

(p. 704)

The neoliberal reconceptualization of the individual rationalizes the radical split between those who have a chance of making it in the system and those who do not and cannot: social divisions, produced by neoliberal policies themselves, become understood not as system failures but as "failures of *individual* choice and responsibility" (Hamann, 2009, p. 50). These so-called individual failures are what therapists are called upon to treat. As Hamann puts it (p. 43), "Exploitation, domination, and every other form of social inequality is rendered invisible *as social* phenomena to the extent that each individual's social condition is judged as nothing other than the effect of his or her own choices and investments." In the middle and upper middle classes, paradoxical psychological states of too much responsibility (for the self) and too little (for the common good) ensue (see Chapters 12 and 13).

In the U.S., then, neoliberalism is thus quite a bit more than merely an economic system or an ideology; rather, neoliberalism encompasses a whole way of living, what Brown (2006) calls a political rationality and Foucaultians call a governmentality, that is, "a particular mentality, a particular manner of governing, that is actualized in habits, perceptions, and subjectivity" (Read, p. 34). The extension of market rationality into social life entails "marketing" the subjective practices that will turn subjects into entrepreneurs who rationally choose to maximize opportunity when possible and, at the same time, will agree to shoulder much of the responsibility formerly taken on by public agencies (du Gay, 2004). Read (2009) draws some of the consequences: "The model neoliberal citizen is one who strategizes for her or himself among various social, political and economic options, not one who strives with others to alter or organize these options" (p. 35). The politics of neoliberalism, Read (2009) writes, entails "a generalization of the idea of the 'entrepreneur,' 'investment' and 'risk' beyond the realm of finance capital to every quotidian relation . . ." (p. 32): "the discourse of the economy becomes an entire way of life, a common sense in which every action – crime, marriage, higher education and so on – can be charted according to a calculus of maximum output for minimum expenditure; it can be seen as an investment" (p. 31).

As noted in Chapter 6, sociologist Sam Binkley has studied self-help books, the field of coaching, and positive psychology and has identified some of the practices that experts encourage people to adopt to be success-ful, "enterprising" selves. Subjects, he found, are dissuaded from intro-specting, dwelling on problems, putting their experience in a relational context, or looking into the past to understand the present; rather, they are exhorted to be forward-looking, optimistic, and to set goals to maximize what is in their self-interest. Yet, such responsibilized individuals always feel expendable in a world in which the only value driving decisions in any domain is whether or not the action fosters economic growth.

## Psychic effects of neoliberalism: Yale

By the 1990s, the psychic effects of neoliberalism on middle and upper middle-class whites began to appear everywhere in the culture. Some-time in the 1990s, when I as yet had no understanding of neoliberalism, I remember coming across a magazine cover that only later struck me as a horrifying example of the new normal: a full-page picture of a baby was accompanied by a caption that read "Is Having Children Cost-Effective?" I began to hear many of my middle- and upper middle-class patients talk about maximizing effectiveness and optimizing just about everything (see Peltz, 2005; Chapter 12). Most of them seemed to feel a sense of virtue when they ran themselves ragged, and a sense of shame and anxiety about just sitting around and experiencing what we used to call "downtime." In her study of the dignity of working men, Lamont (2000) had found that the white working-class men she interviewed in the 1990s dealt with the heightened feelings of vulnerability created by neoliberalism by drawing moral boundaries between the deserving and the undeserving poor (the latter of whom they generally associated with blackness (see also Wac-quant, 2001b)). On the contrary, the upper middle-class professionals and managers she interviewed were psychically caught up in competitively comparing themselves to others of their class: their psychosocial energy focused on how much money they were earning, their job status, and which schools their children were getting into. Their capacity to separate their fate from the fate of those all around them is one hallmark of what I refer to as social narcissism.

As my friend's words in the chapter's opening vignette suggest, the white middle and even upper middle classes began in the 1990s to experience what Barbara Ehrenreich (1989) called the fear of falling. Anxieties about falling, failing, being disposable began to be intergenerationally transmitted in prescriptions of what it means to be a proper human being. A growing literature focuses on the vast amount of work that middle-class parents, particularly mothers, currently put into assuring that their children get ahead and stay ahead in the world (what Lareau, 2003, has called 'concerted cultivation'; Vincent and Ball, 2007; Reay et al., 2011; Walkerdine et al., 2001). Examples include paying for costly after school activities and college prep services, as well as writing/editing their children's essays. In March 2019, news broke of a college admissions scandal in which rich parents bought their children's way into college by faking test scores and by bribing coaches to turn a blind eye to faked athletic achievements. As many pointed out, this was merely the illegal version of the legal and culturally condoned means that rich people have used for years to get their children into top-tier colleges (e.g., by giving huge sums of money to their alma maters). As Carey (2019) writes: "[The college admissions scandal] is in some ways a case of one-percenters lusting after the privileges of one-tenth-of-one-percenters."

What are some of the ways these cultural phenomena are lived psychically? One stark example of how practices of concerted cultivation transmit to individuals an ideology of what it means to be a proper and successful neoliberal human being was captured in an episode titled "Grover" (Krisel, 2012) of the sketch comedy, *Portlandia*. In this vignette, a pre-school boy, Grover, sits at a kitchen counter as his parents try to engage him in understanding how important it is that he do well at his upcoming private pre-school interview. Holding up a chart that graphs the trajectory that will follow if he successfully gets into the Shining Star Pre-school – and noting that they have trademarked his name – the parents point to the first symbol that will mark his upward mobility: an ivy-league college. Then, asking him if he can spell Ferrari, they point to a picture of the car he will drive if he gets into the pre-school. As a cautionary tale, they then hold up a chart that graphs failure. If he does not get into the pre-school, they tell him, he will have to go to a public school, pictured on the graph as a prison. They spew denigrating comments about the lower-class children he will be subjected to in public school, the dumb and low-class kids he will encounter in community college, and the guns and drugs that will inevitably lead to jail or to a life of shooting birds and squirrels for dinner. The crowning touch of the satire is when the father, following one of his contemptuous comments about the lower classes, tells his child, "Never judge."

Grover knows that he is supposed to like the first graph a lot better than the second one, and yet, with each new close-up of his face, we find him looking increasingly bewildered and depressed. Still, when his parents ask him to say which graph he prefers, he readily endorses the success graph. The episode well illustrates Lawler's (2005b) assertion that middle-class disgust for the working class is at the heart of distinction – and thus at the heart of the creation of a middle-class identity built on NOT being disgusting and repellent.

The demand to be an entrepreneurial self is conveyed not only by parents but by other agents of the middle class as well. A former student, born around 1980, told me that in her upper middle-class elementary school lessons were taught that were designed to humiliate the children into striving for upward mobility (reported in Layton, 2014a, p. 470): in 5th grade, one of her teachers asked his students where their parents had gone to college. As each child responded, it became clear that the predominant answers were Ivy League and elite schools. "Well," he concluded, "none of you is going to any of these schools because you don't work hard enough. You won't get your first choice." My student remembers that from that time forth she anxiously repeated to herself the mantra, "I must have my first choice, I must have my first choice." She and her peers were exhorted to incarnate "the exhausting self-inventions" of what Hey (2005, p. 864) calls "reflexivity winners"; they were "forced" to choose, while less privileged others lack the resources to choose. You can almost taste the invitation here to oscillating and split states of grandiosity and low self-worth, to a punishing superego that marks a sadomasochistic relation to self; indeed, this student suffered from depressions that had at their core a questioning of what she was doing – and for whom.

Reay (2005) suggests that different kinds of anxieties animate, motivate, and, in some cases, cripple working-class versus middle-class subjects. Her sense is that while the working-class students she studied were plagued with anxieties, the middle-class students had less at risk, their cultural and emotional capital endowing them with more confidence (pp. 921–922). This may be true, because the effects of class inequality fall differently on different social classes. But the effect of class demands for distinction may be as psychologically damaging to middle-class achievers as to those who internalize a sense of themselves as unable to achieve. And, as described in the case vignettes in Chapter 10, the demand to rise in class, to be an economic winner in a world in which all others are considered losers, causes its own version of intense psychosocial distress. A central question is: do the different forms of damage perpetuate distinctions of superior/inferior, and, if so, how do they do it – and how do they perpetuate cycles of sadomasochistic relating? The Grover example suggests that processes of acquiring distinction require a distancing indifference toward and contempt for those who fail or cannot compete – and require as well a hatred of a self never quite successful enough to feel safely distinguished.

## Psychic effects of neoliberalism II: fail

How does neoliberalism affect the psychosocial positioning of those people toward whom the middle classes are encouraged to effect a distancing sense of disgust and distinction? In Jennifer Silva's (2013) interview study of cross-racial working-class young adults, *Coming Up Short*, she finds that the traditional markers that once defined adulthood in the working class – dignity in work, marriage, family, class solidarity – no longer seemed relevant to her interviewees, largely because they were not felt to be realizable. Subject to all the precariousness of so-called flexible labor markets and the shift from a manufacturing to a low-paid service economy, her interviewees had few chances of paying back massive school loans or finding stable employment. Paradoxically, however, their experience led many of them to support the neoliberal agenda of devaluing dependency and explicitly repudiating interdependence and any kind of group solidarity. Because they generally felt they had been betrayed by everyone and could rely on no one and no institution – not family, not education, not government – they took pride in their always precarious capacities for self-reliance. Silva writes, "Over and over again, the men and women I interviewed told me that growing up means learning not to expect anything from anyone . . ." (p. 83). They also drew sharp boundaries between themselves and those who needed government handouts, and this boundary-drawing usually had a racist dimension: the white subjects seemed to feel that if they had to make it on their own, everyone should (it is worth noting that, as economist Suzanne Mettler (2011) writes, most people, including those most vocally against big government, are unaware of the fact that, on average, nearly everyone in the U.S. enjoys at least four kinds of government benefit). Silva's subjects felt that to struggle on your own is morally right, and even the African American members of her sample, who knew the system was unfair, subscribed to belief in meritocracy. As Silva writes, they "make a virtue out of not asking for help, out of rejecting dependence and surviving completely on their own . . ." (p. 97).

Again, we find that sadomasochistic features mark Silva's interviewees: she reports that they tended to cut ties, turn inward, and numb themselves emotionally. They learned that choice is simply an illusion. Perhaps most alarming is that Silva's subjects tended to define markers of maturity and adulthood in purely therapeutic terms: their stories of what had made them most proud revolved not around connections with others or finding work that was meaningful but rather around emotional self-management, that is, how they had struggled to overcome their demons, like drug addiction or familial abuse (childhood betrayals and early experiences of profound uncertainty were quite common in the sample). In compliance with neoliberal dictates, they largely separated their psychological selves from any connection with social conditions. These findings, I think, ought to send shivers down the spines of therapists; they remind us, as I have been claiming throughout this book, that therapists are called upon to treat social problems as if they are individual problems.

Even the so-called "pure relationship" that Giddens (1991) saw as anchoring "modern" subjectivity (see Chapter 5) was not an option for these working-class young adults. Many of Silva's heterosexual female subjects rejected relationships with men, blaming the men they knew for not being good enough breadwinners. In their study of a South Wales working-class community, Walkerdine and Jimenez (2012) found similar gender dynamics. A casualty of globalization and neoliberal deindustrialization, the steel works had been shut down in 2000. This caused all kinds of new psychological difficulties for a community that had been built for 200 years around iron and steel work as the central male occupation. Young adult males were no longer able to live up to the traditional image of working-class solidarity and proud, hard masculinity. The only jobs available to those who stayed were in pizza delivery or janitorial services. The neoliberal tendency to see problems as psychological rather than systemic also permeated this community. Many of the young men's fathers were ashamed of their sons' new status, and their mothers, and even their peers colluded in the shaming. These findings suggest that those who try but fail to make it in a neoliberal order have good reason not to trust anything or anybody, and the psychosocial effects in this group, too, generally tend toward enactments in which rage is either turned inward or turned onto those even less socially powerful.

## Psychic effects of neoliberalism III: jail

All of us, no matter what our social class, have to contend with the current mainstream ideal that the most successful human is a rich human and not a dependent human. All of us have been enjoined to become entrepreneurial selves even if we belong to ethnic, racial, or class groups that practice norms that challenge those of neoliberal individualism, for example, identities rooted in community and caregiving. For some social groups, neoliberal policies have severely damaged formerly tight communal bonds, and such policies have increasingly marginalized and denigrated many groups, especially poor people of color. Neoliberalism has indeed spawned its own unique iteration of U.S. structural racism. In fact, many commentators – including right-wing white conservatives – have noted that neoliberal calls for small government and for drastic cuts to social programs were and still are primarily motivated by white anxiety about losing political, cultural, and economic power to people of color (Bouie, 2019).

In *The New Jim Crow*, Michelle Alexander (2010) describes how the decline in urban manufacturing in the 1980s and 1990s created massive unemployment among unskilled and semi-skilled male urban African American workers, up to 50 percent in some cities. Racist government policies, particularly the invention and execution of the war on drugs, combined with neoliberal economic policies to turn poor but formerly socially cohesive ghettos into wastelands. In her book, *Carceral Capitalism*, Wang (2018) brings together a wealth of material to show how cities and municipalities have become starved for cash not because of "big government" programs but because of massive tax incentives for corporations. In the age of neoliberalism, local governments have not only shifted their wealth from public services to corporations and financial institutions, but have then financed what is left of their public services, e.g., police and other departments, by levying fees and fines on poor people of color (pp. 179–187). The U.S. 2018 midterm elections revealed a panoply of Republican short- and long-term strategies designed to keep people of color from voting.

The mass incarceration of African American men, normalized by ubiquitous media images of black men as criminals, led sociologist Loïc Wacquant (2001a) to examine the systemic ties between what he calls neoliberal hyperghettos and neoliberal prisons. This complex, he argues, is the most recent incarnation of four U.S. "peculiar institutions" forged from racism (slavery, Jim Crow, and the urban ghetto were the three preceding incarnations). Describing the prison-like conditions of public housing and inner city schools (what Wang, 2018, p. 189, calls "carceral spaces," where people are afraid to go out of the house), Wacquant quotes an elderly resident of a DC housing project who said: "It's as though the children in here are being prepared for incarceration, so when they put them in a real lockdown situation, they'll be used to being hemmed in" (p. 108). The New Jim Crow, a series of late twentieth century and early twenty-first-century laws that obstruct or prevent those who have ever been in the penal system from voting, living in public housing, receiving public assistance, operates alongside neoliberal economic changes that make it very difficult to get a well-paying job or have the means to get to a job.

As I have been arguing, it is a hallmark of U.S. neoliberal political life that the more people are rendered vulnerable and disposable, the more the state of vulnerability seems to become figured as shameful. As many have noted (see, for example, Centeno and Cohen, 2012), increased income inequality has led the privileged to rationalize their privilege, which in turn has led to decreasing empathy for the poor. Homelessness, for example, is criminalized, and the incarcerated poor are deemed to have deserved their fate. By the 1990s in the U.S., the white imaginary offered two predominant socially reviled subject positions to poor African Americans: the omnipotent male criminal, who terrorizes vulnerable whites with his criminal entrepreneurial skills, and his split off other side, the female welfare dependent, who, since Reagan, has held all of the country's disavowed need and has been used as a signifier of the failures of big government. In this form of splitting, typical of and endemic to neoliberal practices and ideologies, omnipotent narcissistic versions of autonomy are pitted against degraded narcissistic versions of dependence. This incarnation a racist white imaginary well exemplifies how a radical split between autonomy and dependence can be projected seamlessly onto a racialized and gendered divide. The options of "Yale or jail" between which my white middle-class patient felt she had to choose reveal a tragic truth about the deep social divides that mark everyday life in the U.S. As Wang (2018) compellingly argues, the safety and freedom of dominant, largely white, groups cannot be thought separably from the creation of disposable groups, most of whom are black and brown people.

## Social narcissism and neoliberalism: sadistic institutional-level enactments

Skeggs (2005) has suggested that in order to find the truth in what has been projected onto marginalized and disempowered groups we need to look not at those on whom the projections fall, but rather at those who do the projecting. When we do so, we easily find traces of the dependency needs that have been split off to attain the neoliberal fantasy of invulnerability. Anti-abortion movements, for example, seem intensely to identify with a dependent, helpless, and vulnerable fetus (Burack, 2014; Gentile, 2016). In work on trauma, Alford (2013) describes what he calls "group-reinforced denial," which "too often depends on placing large numbers of people beyond its aegis, their existence representing an unbearable reality" (p. 268). Group-reinforced denial of vulnerability, he continues, "generally requires as its correlate the existence of others who are naked and vulnerable. My group is powerful because yours is weak, my group is invulnerable because yours is vulnerable" (p. 268). Such denial can easily become destructive, "creating a community of the fit inflicting the feared trauma on outgroups and others" (p. 268).

Highlighting the distinction between projection and projective identification, Alford complicates Skeggs's point: "Unlike simple projection, projective identification not only attributes one's psychic state to others, but acts in such a way as to bring about the attributed state in the other ..." (p. 268). The evacuation of unbearable emotions and states into others "works its way behind the other's ego defenses, creating the psychological state it would evoke ..." (p. 268). Projective identification can only "work," however, when the disowned and projected vulnerability becomes concretized in the kind of policies, practices, and distinctions described by Wang and Wacquant, i.e., the ones that exacerbate the vulnerability of those already most vulnerable. The exacerbation, too, is disavowed, as "omnipotent and invulnerable" selves cast all blame for worsening life chances on the already vulnerable. But as clinicians well know, the very fragility and instability of narcissistic states require a constant search for ways to reinforce the fantasy of omnipotence. The normative unconscious processes nurtured by neoliberalism set the stage, on both the individual and large group level, for relational repetition compulsions that are marked by sadomasochism.

I have elsewhere elaborated two particular large-group reactions to the anxiety-producing changes wrought by neoliberalism, globalization, and the attacks of 9/11 (Layton, 2006c; Chapter 13): retaliation and withdrawal, two typical reactions to trauma that merely reproduce trauma. In response to U.S. civil rights legislation of the 1960s and 1970s that was designed to protect vulnerable populations and extend citizenship rights to formerly socially excluded and devalued groups – gays, minorities, the poor, women – social conservatives, themselves beginning to experience the dislocating effects of neoliberal economic policies, immediately launched retaliatory movements that have, over decades, increased in vehemence and meanness. Since the election of Donald Trump as President, these movements have reached a fever pitch, manifesting in white nationalist racist violence and vicious attacks on women's reproductive rights. Miyazaki (2010), citing Hage (2003), describes a kind of attachment to the state that may well shed some light on what motivates such retaliations. Hage argues that those who have given up hope that their nation will provide, yet who cannot truly face the reality that the state is no longer providing, continue affectively to attach to the state, but in a perverse and paranoid fashion subtended by "no hope." The attachment of the "no hopers" becomes "a paranoid form of nationalism . . ." (Hage, cited by Miyazaki, p. 238). This paranoid attachment seems to manifest as a sense that the poor and extremely vulnerable are responsible for the fact that the state has abandoned those only moderately less vulnerable.

Among privileged liberals, a more prevalent response over time has been withdrawal from a commitment to sustaining public life (for examples, see contributions to the special section on the psychic effects of neoliberalism in the journal *Psychoanalysis, Culture & Society* 19(1), 2014: Adams, 2014; Archangelo, 2014; Glynos, 2014a; Samuels, 2014; Lesser, 2014; Roseneil, 2014). The withdrawal has many determinants, including (1) disappointment, as purportedly progressive leaders seem, post-election, to turn center if not center-right; (2) a growing sense, as traditional sources of solidarity erode and as risk shifts from the public to the private sphere, that every man is for himself; and (3) the fact that those at or near the top have done extraordinarily well economically. As noted in previous chapters, Rodger (2003) has referred to this withdrawal as amoral familism, a retreat into an individualistic private sphere and a tendency to extend care only to those in one's family and immediate intimate circle. Describing what he calls the obsessional narcissism of the privileged, Samuels (2009, 2014) goes further, arguing that the withdrawal response also signifies the mainstream population's desire not to have its fantasy of American exceptionalism or U.S. domination of world resources disturbed by awareness of their consequences.

These large-group reactions have been facilitated by the government's abandonment of its caretaking functions at the very moment when the citizenry feels most vulnerable. As the safety net erodes, political leaders encourage vulnerable populations to "stay strong" or go shopping, which only makes those affected more ashamed of ongoing vulnerability, feelings of helplessness, and depression. Further, neoliberalism, as Fisher (Fisher and Gilbert, 2013) pointed out, is marked by new forms of bureaucracy that create new kinds of vulnerability as well as heightened anxiety about maintaining privilege. In such conditions, new social defenses emerge to deal with these anxieties (Menzies, 1960): those who can will seek refuge from an increasing sense of precariousness and vulnerability in identifications that psychically distance them from more vulnerable populations. Empathy becomes defined in such a way as to allow the privileged to feel distant and other from less privileged and suffering groups. This distancing is active as well as passive; it contributes to the many practices and policies that obstruct recognition of the interdependence of privileged and vulnerable/dependent populations and masks the complicity of the privileged in the suffering of those less privileged (see Chapter 12). The large-group responses of withdrawal and retaliation are at the heart of social narcissism.

The "group-enforced" denial of dependence and interdependence central to social narcissism (Alford, 2013) not only issues in individualistic feelings of "every man for himself" but also produces vicious circles marked by sadistic and sadomasochistic forms of relating. Scanlon and Adlam (2013), who consult to caregivers of vulnerable populations in the U.K., well describe one such typical vicious circle, in which more privileged groups inadvertently inflict what they call "reflexive violence" on those less privileged. As they describe it, the circle begins with neoliberal policies that create categories of people, like the homeless, victims of rising income inequality, who are first socially excluded, then pathologized and not deemed proper citizens. Disavowing the effect of these prior processes of social exclusion, caregivers fail to recognize or acknowledge the way neoliberal conceptions of subjectivity are embedded in their very caregiving practices and attitudes (e.g., the demand to "just do it," as if improvement in the condition of these populations is a matter of free choice, of making good versus bad choices). Scanlon and Adlam observe that when caring efforts are met with hostility or indifference, caregivers tend to become enraged or disengaged, completing a vicious circle of sadomasochistic relating.

Friends who are educators and familiar with failing inner city schools in the U.S. describe another such vicious circle. This one begins in a neoliberal refusal to take responsibility for poverty levels not seen since before the 1960s U.S. War on Poverty. Instead of addressing poverty, recent education policies hold teachers in inner city schools accountable for the poor performance of their students on high stakes tests. In many poor inner city neighborhoods, very high percentages of students have witnessed or experienced violence. Poverty and violence can severely damage the capacity to learn (Archangelo, 2010, 2014). What all children need, my friends asserted, is a safe environment that fosters creativity and a capacity to think. What these children get instead is a punishing regimen of teaching to the test from teachers who themselves face punishment for not improving scores. I sometimes teach teachers in suburban wealthy districts. They believe that their duty is to foster creativity and a capacity for critical thinking; where possible, they refuse to teach to the test. Teaching to the test damages all children, but it plays a particular role in reproducing inequality and will continue to do so as long as the willful disavowal of poverty and racism remains normative (see also, Adams, 2014, who describes the vicious circle of relations between poor, young black men, and various disciplinary systems).

In 1960, Menzies described the "social defenses" that marked the nursing system that she was called on to consult to in the U.K. Menzies found that the anxieties stirred up in student nurses by their work task, e.g., treating the ill and dying, were actually exacerbated by the structures put in place by their superiors, structures that were ostensibly meant to reduce work task anxiety. For example, nurses were given rigid task lists that actually interfered with their ability to create a relationship with any of their patients. As it turned out, only those nurses whose defenses aligned with the social defenses set up by the larger system were able to succeed in that system; Menzies found that the most capable and competent of the nursing students dropped out. More recently, in a chapter of a book that updates the social defenses group analytic tradition (Armstrong and Rustin, 2015), Cooper and Lees (2015) challenged the Menzies study for not having taken into account the broader social currents affecting social defense systems. In their study of youth protective service workers, they found that workers experienced and described two different kinds of anxieties. The first kind, anxieties connected to the workers' actual work task of protecting children from harm, were depressive in nature (see Klein, 1946). The second set of anxieties, which came not from the work task but from the neoliberal austerity, surveillance and audit culture within which they operated, were persecutory (paranoid-schizoid). Workers reported that despite the difficulties entailed in protecting the children, the work was gratifying. What made their jobs most stressful, they reported, were neoliberal surveillance and audit policies.

In the sphere of neoliberal mental health services, Rizq (2014) well describes how such persecutory social defense systems operate and how they issue in a series of sadomasochistic institutional enactments. A patient complained that an intake worker at a National Health Service clinic (the U.K. single-payer health plan) had made her feel treated as a number. This complaint issued in new surveillance and audit procedures. At first, affected clinicians used their process group to express their anxieties about providing care given their work overload. But soon they began to blame the complaining patient, insisting that the therapist had been correctly following the rules. Rizq was supervising a group leader, who himself was now required to take attendance, and he reported that because the groups were now largely focused on sharing information about the techniques they were using to help them be more efficient with paperwork, he wasn't sure what his purpose was. Rizq herself was becoming ever sleepier in sessions. When the supervisee missed a session, he anxiously hoped Rizq wouldn't record the miss. Rizq agreed, but soon realized that the letter of complaint had set off a chain of events that had led to massive disavowal of how uncared for the new procedures had made people feel. Instead, the clinicians had embraced the procedures as legitimate and used them to reassure themselves that following the policies was tantamount to demonstrating care.

Rizq's case example well illustrates how the new accounting regulations created a perverse and sadomasochistic situation, an untenable conflict between the therapists' ethic of care and a neoliberal ethic of surveillance based in demands for economic austerity. The bureaucratic rituals of verification began to seem like the only logical way of proceeding: government cutbacks made it impossible for the therapists to care well for everyone. The needs were overwhelming. So they struck a deal in which complying with the ethic of surveillance would come to feel like an adequate substitute for care: where doing the paperwork became experienced as care itself.

Describing the anxiety fostered by neoliberalism's creation of new forms of competition in spheres such as education and healthcare (with the focus on the ubiquity and constancy of rating and self-rating instruments, merit ratings that pit worker against worker, and the creation of what he calls "spurious quantificatory data" (p. 92)), Fisher suggested that workers like those Rizq describes become isolated, subdued, and passive, their confidence eroded, their capacity for acting collectively undermined (p. 93). Thus, Gilbert (2013) finds that, even for the more privileged, collective action and political resistance, let alone participation in the public sphere, become severely hampered by a constant anxiety about just getting by day to day.

The perverse nature of such interactions seems to me to be endemic to neoliberalism (see Hoggett, 2013), which suggests, again, that we look at the disavowal defense that is at the heart of perversion (Freud, 1927a). Our public officials' disdain for facts (so well captured in Franken's 2003 book title, *Lies: and the Lying Liars Who Tell Them*) points to the connection between perversion and lying that I described in Chapter 13. Another way of thinking about the retaliation and withdrawal responses to neoliberal dislocations, then, is as social defenses erected upon a disavowal of what we know to be true but cannot bear to know.

As described earlier, Binkley (2009, 2011a, 2011b, 2014) and other non-psychoanalytic thinkers focus on neoliberal subjective practices that demand a shift from comfort with dependence to repudiation of dependence. In a psychoanalytic frame, however, which recognizes no possibility or desirability of overcoming dependence, the task is to comprehend the psychic effects of a cultural lack of attunement to dependency needs and a cultural encouragement to split off and project dependency needs and vulnerability. Such effects, as we have seen, include intense shame about dependence (see Jimenez and Walkerdine, 2012), omnipotent versions of autonomy, and narcissistic processes that include oscillations between grandiosity and self-deprecation with regard to the self, and idealization and devaluation with regard to the relation with others. These narcissistic states and oscillations, fostered by a perverse society that disavows a reality marked by gross failures of accountability and proper caretaking by those in authority, underlie sadomasochistic enactments at the individual, interpersonal, and institutional levels.

## Conclusion

In all of this, where might we find hope for social change? Progressive social movements clearly offer the most promise (see also Hall, Massey, and Rustin's Kilburn Manifesto: www.lwbooks.co.uk/soundings/kilburn-manifesto). But professional counter-discourses to neoliberalism also exist. Binkley's work (2014) reveals the complicity of psychological discourses with neoliberalism (see also Rose, 1989; Cushman, 2019). He describes psychological theories and practices based in the rational actor theory that guides neoliberal policy: that repudiate the idea that it is important to look within or to the past to understand present causes of suffering, that do not think about an individual's problems in the context of relationships, that have no notion of unconscious process that divides the self against the self. All of the psychoanalytic theories of which I am aware certainly counter what Binkley describes as the versions of subjectivity promoted in neoliberal discourses. In "normalizing" vulnerability, dependency and interdependence as part of what it means to be human, in insisting on the importance of attending to thwarted needs for caretaking that result in obstructed capacities for basic trust, and in critiquing versions of autonomy that deny an embeddedness in relation, most schools of contemporary psychoanalytic theory offer something of a counter-discourse to hegemonic neoliberal discourses. But psychoanalysis colludes with neoliberal narcissism in generally refusing to understand what people suffer from as having to do with societal conditions (see Layton et al., 2006; Cushman, 1995, 2019). We see effects of this refusal when clinicians unconsciously reproduce neoliberal versions of subjectivity (see Chapters 5 and 13), or when clinicians learn to turn a blind eye to the disparity between those treatments available to the rich and those available to the poor (see Debieux Rosa and Mountian, 2013; Goodman, 2015). Due in part to the psychoanalytic establishment's disavowal of the effects of the social on the psyche, the profession – in the U.S. at least – has had little impact on public policy. The marginalization of psychoanalysis is of course also in no small measure due to the dominance of neoliberal discourses that promote short-term cognitive behavioral treatments. But psychoanalysts could certainly play more of a public role in countering neoliberal values and practices, and the creation of the Psychotherapy Action Network (https://psian.org/) is one encouraging development designed to challenge the dominance of neoliberal mental health practices in the U.S. and promote the principles of a progressive psychodynamic therapy. I believe, as well, that further examination of the connections between neoliberalism, social narcissism, and perverse sadomasochistic dynamics and social defenses can and should stimulate creative thinking about strategies to bring about progressive social change.

## Note

* Used with permission. Adapted from Layton, L. (2014a) Grandiosity, neoliberalism, and neoconservatism. *Psychoanalytic Inquiry* 34(5): 463–474; Layton, L. (2014b) Some psychic effects of neoliberalism: Narcissism, disavowal, perversion. *Psychoanalysis, Culture & Society* 19(2): 161–178; Layton, L. (2015) *Neoliberalism and Its Psychic Effects*. Keynote presentation at Reflective Spaces/Material Places conference, San Francisco, September 12; and Layton, L. (2016) Yale or jail: Class struggles in neoliberal times. In Goodman, D.M. and Severson, E.R. (eds.) *The Ethical Turn*. New York, NY: Routledge, pp. 75–93.

# Chapter 15

# Something to do with a girl named Marla Singer

## Capitalism, narcissism, and therapeutic discourse in David Fincher's *Fight Club**

Arguing that the "dilemmas of the traumatized male subject are a recurring theme of contemporary cinema" (p. 304), Bainbridge and Yates (2005) capture in their film analyses a sense of masculinity in crisis. Set within a contemporary social context, the analyses reveal twin tendencies toward the emotionalization and 'feminization' of Western culture, tendencies that seem to produce a "hysterical defense against the perceived trauma of loss and difference" (p. 304). Drawing on media theories that suggest that dominant discourses are always contested by subordinate discourses that circulate in culture, Bainbridge and Yates theorize that although there has been a general shift toward filmic representations of men who express their emotions, representations of masculinity exist on a continuum. At one pole of this continuum lie what they call fetishistic or rigid masculine representations, and at the other pole lie transitional spaces that allow for various renegotiations of masculinity. The authors suggest that films of the 1990s perhaps offered male spectators more possibility for such renegotiations than do recent films; discussing *Fight Club* (Fincher, 1999), for example, they write that because the two male protagonists turn out to be two sides of the same person, the spectator is alerted to "the schizoid status of masculinity," which forces the spectator "to imagine the originary moment of trauma and then to contemplate more radical alternatives" (p. 307).

In what follows, I look more closely at the nature of the trauma represented in *Fight Club*, a trauma I shall root in cultural conditions that offer increasing opportunities for individualization (in fact, they demand it; see Beck and Beck-Gernsheim on the "multi-option" society, 2002) while simultaneously encouraging a narcissistic individualism. After a discussion of the relation between narcissism and capitalism, I suggest that *Fight*

*Club* offers a particularly compelling example of filmic attempts to solve problems posed by the cultural contradictions of neoliberalism and late modernity (Giddens, 1991). *Fight Club* is noteworthy not only because it addresses the crisis of masculinity/autonomy in a free market consumer culture, but also because it invokes therapeutic discourses as possible solutions to cultural crisis.

## Capitalism and narcissism

From the late 1970s to the mid-1980s, several left wing historians, sociologists, and psychoanalysts took as their object of study the relation between capitalism and narcissistic personality disorder. Christopher Lasch's (1979) *The Culture of Narcissism*, which drew on contemporary writings on clinical narcissism by Kernberg (1975) and Kohut (1971, 1977), influenced authors such as Kovel (1980), Livesay (1985), Holland (1986), and myself to explore a 'social character' that seemed peculiar to our times.[1] The sociological aspect of my own writings on capitalism and narcissism, beginning in 1986, are influenced by Frankfurt School critiques of capitalism, particularly their focus on the pervasive dominance of instrumental reason, but my psychoanalytic understanding of narcissism is based on Kohut's (1971, 1977) and Fairbairn's (1954) definition (with some additional ideas drawn from Kernberg, 1975). Thus, as described in the previous chapter, I see as central to the syndrome a fragility of self structure that results in an oscillation between grandiosity and self-deprecation, and between devaluation and idealization of the other, and, finally, between longings to merge and isolating defenses against merger. The state shift from grandiosity to self-deprecation, from idealization to devaluation, from merger to isolation, from elation to depression depends in part on differences in power relations and relational context – a bully in one relational matrix can be submissive in another (a classic example is the man who is submissive with his boss but domineering with his wife and children). Emotionally, the shift is notably set off by an empathic break, a slight to the fragile self whose needs for recognition, connection and care have consistently not been met.

Slights evoke what Kohut called narcissistic rage, a punitive, annihilating anger that issues from an archaic harsh and punishing superego. Kernberg's (1975) Kleinian perspective on narcissism, in which rage and hostility are central to the syndrome, adds to this picture an emphasis on the primary defense mechanisms of narcissism: splitting and projective identification. In his explanation of etiology, Kernberg highlights a failure to integrate good and bad representations, self-states, and affects, a failure caused either by traumatic treatment by the environment or by an excessive amount of constitutional aggression. Because of this difficulty integrating good and bad, that is, the difficulty achieving, in Klein's (1946) terms, a somewhat stable depressive position, narcissistic disorder is marked by an inability to tolerate ambivalence and ambiguity. The use of defenses such as splitting and projective identification produces the oscillation between polarized states that is endemic to the disorder.

People suffering from narcissistic personality disorder do not experience themselves as what Kohut described as "separate centers of initiative" and what Frankfurt School heirs call autonomous selves. This is due to their difficulty differentiating themselves from others. There are at least two relational sequelae of this failure: in one, merger with an other stabilizes the fragile self; in the second, a repudiation of the need for the other issues in a pseudo-separation. In either case, those who suffer from a narcissistic psychic structure have difficulty setting their own agenda, as their sense of self-worth is overly dependent on how they are thought of by others. Indeed, they use others, ideas and ideologies, and things – for example, food or consumer goods – as necessary props to shore up what Kohut called "empty" selves (because so many of his patients spoke of feeling empty, of having an empty depression).[2]

Psychoanalytic theorists of narcissism tend not to connect narcissistic personality disorder with capitalism (although Kohut does link "Guilty Man's" eclipse by "Tragic Man" to certain socio-historical conditions). The Frankfurt School and their heirs have done most of the work that links the two. Like his Frankfurt School influences, Lasch (1977, 1979) located the origins of narcissistic personality disorder in the decline of the patriarchal family and the supposedly firm ego and superego that developed from its Oedipal dynamics. He argued that this decline emerged from the entrenchment of bureaucracy, the eclipse of entrepreneurial by monopoly and consumer capitalism, and the rise of a reliance on experts. It is especially the latter, according to Lasch, that increasingly weakens the autonomy of the individual. As many feminists were to point out, the villains of Lasch's piece were not just capitalism and bureaucracy, but female dominated families and a "feminized" culture (see, for example,

Engel, 1980). Refuting Lasch and the Frankfurt School on this point, feminist theorists such as Benjamin (1977, 1988) charged that the very Oedipal dynamics they idealize in fact create the version of autonomy that defensively devalues emotionality, vulnerability, and dependency, a kind of autonomy marked by pseudo-differentiation and pseudo-rationality. Autonomy, in Western culture, has been understood to rest not on mutual interdependence but on radical alone-ness. And it is this narcissistic autonomy that has been associated with traditional ideal versions of white heterosexual masculinity.

Kovel (1980, 1988) and Livesay (1985) focused their understanding of narcissism not only on the decline of autonomous selves but on the decline of any sense of collectivity or social selfhood. Agreeing with Lasch that what produces narcissism are the core features of late capitalism – a massive state apparatus, experts that delegitimize parents, especially when both parents have to work, mass media, and consumerism – Kovel (1988) argued that the late capitalist bourgeois family, cut off from any direct influence on politics or production, is an increasingly isolated unit whose functions have been reduced over time to the raising of children and to consuming goods. A "de-sociated" entity of intense and contradictory kinds of relating, the white middle-class family's children are simultaneously made to feel special and omnipotent, and they are infused with the anxieties of the parents' unfulfilled dreams. Narcissistic rage, Kovel argues, arises from the awareness of being loved not just for who they are but for the return they can bring on their parents' investment in them. These children of contemporary middle-class families might not suffer gross trauma, but nonetheless they become hostilely dependent on and enraged at their parents because, at some level, they are aware that their parents' relation to them has "the quality of capital invested for a future yield" (1988, p. 197). Narcissism, then, is a disorder of differentiation and dependency, which best explains a paradox frequently noted by commentators on U.S. social character: the odd co-existence of defiant self-reliance with an anxious dependence on what experts tell you to do and what the Joneses tell you to buy.[3]

Both Livesay and Sloan (1996) draw attention to the fact that in late capitalist society, bureaucracy, markets, the media, and other cultural apparatuses undermine at every juncture the necessary preconditions for autonomy and intersubjectivity: the capacity to differentiate from the other without repudiating the other, the capacity to tolerate ambivalence, the capacity for mature dependence (Fairbairn, 1954), and the recognition of mutual interdependence. As Frankfurt School theorists have always warned (e.g., Horkheimer and Adorno, 1944), the fantasmatic drive to predict, calculate, and standardize contingency out of existence leads also to the standardization of internal life, which quashes spontaneity and so issues in automatic responses and defenses that impede the capacity to reflect on the self – another pre-requisite of autonomy.

## Masculinity, femininity, and narcissism

While writing about narcissism was popular in the late 1970s to the mid to late 1980s, the whole notion of social character was somewhat eclipsed by the academic focus on aspects of identity such as gender, sexuality, and race. In part, the eclipse had to do with the fact that class dropped out of these analyses as well as to the tendency, from the 1970s to late 1980s, to study one identity element at a time rather than their intersection – and to claim that the one element under examination, for example, gender oppression, could explain all other types of oppression. Feminist psycho-analytic film studies of the 1970s and 1980s did indeed, however, describe a narcissistic male psychic structure, even if the term narcissism was not used. Mulvey's (1975) version of the Lacanian imaginary, for example, overlaps in significant ways with the Kohutian definition of narcissism (although not at all with its etiology).

Extending Chodorow's (1978) object-relational gender theory and Ben-jamin's (1988) work on gendered versions of domination and submission, I argued in *Who's That Girl?* (Layton, 1998) that capitalist and patriarchal formations have together promoted dominant "ideal" versions of mas-culinity and femininity that split and render mutually exclusive human longings for both agency and connection. In traditional dominant forms of masculinity, so-called masculine attributes crystallize around a kind of autonomy that arises when one receives recognition and esteem from the repudiation of connections and the dependency needs that go along with them; this version of subjectivity remains a cultural ideal in the U.S. and is increasingly inhabited as well by middle-class women (see Chapter 8). Traditionally feminine attributes crystallize around a kind of connection or relatedness that arises when one is consistently not recognized and/ or humiliated for asserting one's own agenda. These split masculine and feminine subject positions incarnate two different versions of narcissism. Although all who suffer from narcissistic disorder show both sides of these splits, generally people lead with one set of defenses and hide the other side. Thus, one dominant masculine version of narcissism articulates grandiosity with devaluation of the other and with isolating defenses against merger, while a traditionally dominant female version articulates self-deprecation, idealization of the other, and a defensive longing to merge and lose oneself in the other (Layton, 1988). Because it is a dialectical disorder, the two types tend to seek out one another to couple, generally causing lifelong misery as each tries to heal the split in ways that simply fortify it. To fully understand the narcissistic injury brought about by the demand to split off longings such as dependency or agency is to recognize that such longings do not disappear from the psyche. Indeed, those who repudiate dependency keep their distance from connection precisely because they are extremely vulnerable to any kind of rejection. Ashamed of and full of self-loathing for continuing to have dependency longings, any stirring of them produces defensive enactments and narcissistic rage.

What definitively got lost in filmic gender studies of the 1970s and 1980s was the connection between gender theory and capitalism or class (one notable exception is Walkerdine, 1986). Now that social class is back on the academic radar screen and there is agreement on the necessity of analyzing the way identity elements intersect, it seems a good time to return to the relation between gender, race, class, narcissism, and capitalism, this time with the advantage of the more sophisticated analyses of the way ideology works that we find in the theories of Hall (1982), Laclau and Mouffe (1985), Stavrakakis (2007), Glynos (2008), and Žižek (1989). What those who write about capitalism and narcissism tell us is that key to the production of narcissism is the radical separation of the individual from the social that marks U.S. culture, and the fact that capitalism's instrumental forms of domination find their way into the very heart of the family. And what feminist theory suggests is that the repudiation of dependency, demanded by both that radical separation and by disavowal, finds its way also into split, narcissistic gender/race/class/sexual identities. Those theorists, like myself, who feel that psychoanalysis can most fruitfully be used to understand social character, generally believe that a given era engenders particular collective psychological responses to its social contradictions, particular kinds of transferences and particular repetition compulsions.

## Popular culture and therapeutic culture

Fantasy productions symbolize and seek solutions to the psychic problems that a culture of narcissism creates. So-called "chick flicks," for example, wrestle with the seeming impossibility to integrate relatedness and agency. And the "crisis of masculinity" films analyzed by Bainbridge and Yates reflect, among other things, the longing to find a way out of the paradoxical command to be both self-reliant and emotionally sensitive and connected. But what we often find in "crisis of masculinity" texts is that the threats to male autonomy are located not in the contradictions of capitalism and class domination from which they originate, but rather in women, blacks, the poor, and other subjects onto whom the despised dependency and need have been ragefully projected. Narrative incoherencies that signal the unconscious of these works often simultaneously reveal and conceal the dread of dependency and vulnerability that ever more starkly marks the U.S. culture in which they were produced (especially after 9/11 and the economic crisis of 2008).

In following the Frankfurt School and its heirs, my cultural analysis thus far has not been as dialectical as it needs to be to understand the complexity of contemporary subjectivity. Like Beck and Beck-Gernsheim (2002) as well as Giddens (1991), I do believe that the disembedding from all traditional anchors of selfhood that has rapidly increased since the end of WWII has both progressive and anti-progressive moments. Individualization, the opportunity and the demand to create a life of one's own exists in tension with narcissistic individualism (or what I and others refer to as neoliberal versions of subjectivity). As Giddens (1991) and Beck and Beck-Gernsheim (2002, p. 7) write, the do-it-yourself biography teeters on the edge of an ever-present possibility that it will become a breakdown biography. There is no question that, as Bainbridge and Yates (2005) suggest, contemporary popular representations of masculinity "open up spaces in which alternative modes of masculinity can be imagined through the affectively-nuanced process of spectatorship that they demand" (pp. 306–307). And their notion of a continuum well captures the reality that a "masculinity in crisis" narrative sometimes resolves in a rigid narcissism and sometimes in the opening of transitional space.

Affects such as anger can, in fact, put one more deeply in touch with the self and others – or they can defensively function to tear down self and others. To account for what they understand to be a fairly recent shift in Western culture toward valuing emotional expression, Richards and Brown (2002) have argued that we live in a "therapeutic culture," the key features of which are expressivity (id), knowledge (ego), and compassion (superego). To be authentically therapeutic, however, they argue that such a cultural constellation must also include a reparative impulse (p. 101). Without such an impulse, an "id-type emotionality" substitutes for what they call "thoughtful feeling." Like Bainbridge and Yates, Richards and Brown are mindful of the tension between the progressive possibilities of therapeutic culture, in which emotionality is linked with thought, and its regressive possibilities, in which emotionality is linked with sentimentality, false selves, and artifice.

Popular media can, as the authors suggest, clearly promote thoughtful feeling-type expressions of therapeutic culture. In clinical work, I have often found that patients use popular media representations as one means of forging identifications that counter the restrictive and damaging identifications on offer in their families: for example, one patient used Patrick Stewart's version of masculinity in *Star Trek* to contest his conviction that only macho versions of masculinity counted as masculine (see Layton, 1998, Ch. 7). Another used the same figure to enable her to reflect on alternative modes of leadership besides the sadomasochistic ones to which she continued to find herself prey.

Media texts, however, are complex phenomena. As Jameson (1979) pointed out many years ago, popular texts' popularity is in no small measure due to their tendency to combine both progressive and anti-progressive elements, and they do so in various ways, for example, by creating contradictory identificatory and transferential possibilities, or by throwing up contradictions between form and content (where, for example, anti-progressive form might undercut progressive content). Promoting both id-type and thoughtful feeling versions of emotional expression, popular texts provide audiences with both non-normative and normative transferential possibilities. They may provoke in the spectator normative unconscious processes or enactments that invite unconscious collusions with such oppressive norms as sexism or racism. At the same time, since meaning can never be fixed and identities are fluid, the very same popular texts may well invite unpredictable decodings that challenge oppressive norms and normative transferences (Hall, 1980). And media texts contain unconscious subtexts that defy the intentionality of their authors and that disrupt any possibility of narrative coherence.

David Fincher's 1999 film, *Fight Club*, provides a compelling example of these popular culture theses as it wrangles with the fine lines existing between a culture of individualization and a culture of narcissistic individualism. After numerous viewings and numerous teaching experiences (in which I have found that students see the film very differently from how I see it – an argument for the necessity of audience studies), I continue to find the film puzzling in its strange mixture of anti-capitalist critique and simultaneous proffering of id-type and thoughtful feeling-type solutions. Indeed, in the film, therapeutic discourse is evoked as a solution to the protagonist's cultural malaise, only to be abruptly discarded and replaced by a sadistic and violent discourse (that itself, at times, draws on psychological narratives). Narrative discontinuities seem to signal the film's confusion in this regard. In what follows, I offer my own reading of the film and end with some alternative readings. I hope along the way to elucidate some of the normative and non-normative transference possibilities that arise from the film's particular way of linking masculinity, narcissism, and capitalism.

### Fight Club

*Fight Club* came out in 1999, at the end of two decades of filmic testaments to white male anger. So many of these films – an uncommonly large number of which starred Michael Douglas – pinned blame for threats to male autonomy squarely on women. A prime example is Barry Levinson's (1994) *Disclosure*, in which Michael Douglas is passed over for an expected promotion that goes instead to Demi Moore, an ex-girlfriend. Moore engineers a scene that makes it look as though Douglas sexually harassed her, and most of the film focuses on Douglas's attempts to clear his name, which he does at the end. At one or two moments, the film's class unconscious erupts and it becomes clear that the real causes of Douglas's and other unemployed men's problems are the machinations of upper class male bosses focused solely on the bottom line. But this truth is very much background to the foreground fear of female emasculators.

*Fight Club* is far more explicitly critical of capitalism than most films in the white male anger genre. Its protagonists are also younger than those the genre usually depicts. And yet, rage about the way capitalism and hegemonic masculinity thwart longings both for agency and connection are deflected onto women in this film as well. Like Lasch's analysis of narcissism, the film simply cannot seem to decide whether or not its male protagonists' problems are caused by instrumentalized, meaningless, and morally bankrupt work; emotional isolation; parental abandonment, particularly abandonment by fathers; and consumer capitalism – or if their problems are caused by feminization, mothers, and females in general. Consumerism, as is often the case, is figured as feminine, and in several pivotal scenes blame slips incoherently from fathers and capitalism to mothers and to the film's sole female character, Marla Singer.

In brief, *Fight Club* is the story of a 30-something man (Ed Norton) who is mildly critical of the consumer culture and meaningless job that define his life. He can't sleep, and, in the first part of the film, he seeks relief from his insomnia by frequenting many self-help groups. Marla Singer's (Helena Bonham Carter) presence at the same groups ruins this solution for him, and after his apartment mysteriously blows up, destroying all his possessions, he goes to live with Tyler Durden (Brad Pitt), a soap manufacturer and explosives specialist he had sat next to on a plane during a business trip. He and Tyler start fight club, a weekly meeting where men gather to beat each other up. Men are drawn to fight club like moths to a flame, and fight clubs begin to proliferate all over the country. Tyler develops various homework assignments designed to turn the members of fight club into an anti-conformist corps of revolutionaries dedicated to the destruction of consumer capitalism and the remasculinization of men. Simultaneously, Tyler begins to have sex with Marla Singer, which makes the narrator feel marginalized and rejected. As Project Mayhem, Tyler's plan to blow up consumer debt institutions, proceeds, the narrator becomes more and more uncomfortable with Tyler's authoritarian and dehumanizing leadership style; what began as a philosophy of radical anti-conformity seems to have devolved into sadomasochistic ways of obliterating individuality and demanding complete obedience to the charismatic leader. As the narrator intervenes to stop Project Mayhem from going forward, he – and, simultaneously, the audience – discovers that he and Tyler are, in fact, the same person. Realizing that Marla is in danger of being killed by his own troops, he rescues her and kills off his Tyler self. The film ends as he and Marla, holding hands, watch the buildings blow up.

In the first frames of *Fight Club*, Tyler forces a gun down the narrator's throat on the top floor of a skyscraper, and the narrator's voiceover suggests that something terrible is about to happen, buildings are about to blow up, and that he knows this because Tyler knows it. At this point, the audience presumes that Tyler is someone separate from the narrator. In a terrifying foreshadowing of 9/11, only with young white male protagonists who are closer kin to 1999's homegrown Columbine terrorists than to the 9/11 terrorists, Tyler announces they are standing at Ground Zero. The narrator, a former yuppie turned revolutionary, is filmed in anxious close-up, face sweating. While the narrator worries about whether or not the gun in his mouth is clean, Tyler, filmed at butt and penis level, is cocksure and proud of the destruction they are about to wreak, the reduction to "smoldering rubble" of a few square blocks of buildings in which the business of consumer capitalism is transacted. The narrator and Tyler incarnate the two oscillating states of one narcissistic personality: one conformist, dependent, and self-deprecating, the other rebellious, antisocial, and grandiose. As two, we can mistake one for feminine and the other for masculine, which is one of the film's misogynist strategies. The secret to understanding the disorder, however, is to recognize them as one, the product of splitting two sets of human capacities, connection and agency – for only when the split off side is owned can these two distortions become something other than monstrous.

The feminization of the narrator also makes him the locus of the film's avowed and disavowed homoerotic desire. The very next thing the narrator tells us is that he and Tyler have been living out the cliché that you always hurt the one you love. Throughout the film, such homoerotic confessions are immediately taken back as the narrator locates the blame for all of what has happened not on Tyler, but on a woman: all the mayhem, all the bombs and guns, he suddenly realizes, has something to do with a girl called Marla Singer.[4] The film then cuts to the self-help group for testicular cancer, Remaining Men Together, and we see the narrator's dazed and sleep-deprived face smooshed between Bob's steroid-enhanced breasts. Bob intones that they are still men. The narrator responds in monotone that, yes, they are still men. And then he tells the sad tale of Bob, a former body-builder whose attempt to be hypermasculine through use of steroids and too much testosterone left him without balls, and now with breasts. The theme has something to do with failed masculinity and the blame seems to lie with men who bought into a cultural fantasy about perfect bodies. But also, the film makes visible a wish that the narrator's symptom, terrible insomnia, might be cured by a world without women, here by a man with breasts, later by the male only fight club. Just as Bob gives the narrator permission to cry, the narrator stops the narration again. He tells the audience, in direct address, that he needs to go back further in time so that all this information about castrated men and buildings that are about to blow up will make sense to them.

In this second attempt to find the right place to begin the story, the narrator tells us more about himself. He works for a major car manufacturer, and his job is to investigate car accidents and calculate mathematically whether or not it is in his company's interest to initiate a recall or, rather, quietly to settle an insurance claim and be done with it, even if the car is, to quote Ralph Nader, unsafe at any speed. He's single, isolated, travels a lot for work, knows exactly how immoral his job is, and he creates what meaning there is in his life, creates a personality, via consumerism. Indeed, he describes his entire generation as slaves to consumer capitalism.

The narrator, who fittingly remains nameless, has not been able to sleep for six months. Subjection to a meaningless bureaucracy, to a kind of rationality that puts the cash bottom-line before any other set of values, to the pressure to fill an empty self with consumer goods recommended by experts and endorsed by peers, to disrupted possibilities for social connection – these are the quickly sketched-in origins of the character's malaise. So how does a girl named Marla come to take the blame?

Seeking respite from his social symptom, severe insomnia, the narrator goes to a doctor who refuses to give him sleeping pills. His rage at the doctor is visibly marked by a quick flash in which Tyler appears, a clue (admittedly difficult to decipher) that the way the narrator will psychically resolve his problem will be to split his self into two and project onto Tyler his own rage at those who have failed to recognize his vulnerability and his needs, those who deny him care. In the film, those who do so are just about always men. The doctor suggests that if he wants to see real pain, he should attend a self-help group for men with testicular cancer. And so he comes to Remaining Men Together and the scene with Bob. Now we learn that what cured the narrator's symptom was the moment at the end of the self-help group when the leader has people pair off and open themselves up to the other. Bob gives him permission to cry; eventually the narrator's cynical distance gives way and he sobs into Bob's breasts to the sound of medieval religious music. And then he tells us how well he slept that night.

After a year of treating his symptoms in this way, going each night to a different group of sick and dying people, Marla Singer shows up, ghostly and Goth and smoking her way through the same self-help cancer meetings that the narrator attends, including Remaining Men Together. The narrator finds that, because Marla's lie makes him too conscious of his own lie, he can no longer cry. Because he can no longer cry, he can no longer sleep.

The narrator tries to get Marla to stop attending meetings, and Marla asks him why these groups matter so much to him. He begins to tell her that it is only when people think you are dying that they really listen. Marla interrupts to finish his sentence: in ordinary conversation, she says, people are not listening but rather are waiting until it is their turn to speak. The narrator agrees. This interchange indicts a narcissistic world in which the chances for subject to subject relating in everyday life are almost nil. In moments such as this the film crucially links capitalism with the destruction of capacities for intimacy. But the narrator cannot sustain awareness of this connection. Instead, Marla is blamed for ruining this one chance the narrator has found to feel alive and recognized. They agree to split up the different groups between them, and Marla disappears from the narrative for a while.

The film now takes a very different turn, one that I have always found narratively incoherent, and, for this reason, symptomatic. The narrator, again afflicted with insomnia and praying that the plane he's on will crash or have a mid-air collision, is seated next to Tyler, who is dressed in 1970s Superfly attire. The narrator again suggests that his ills derive from capitalism's destruction of capacities for meaningful relating, telling us that the single people who happen to sit next to him on a plane pretty much exhaust his social life. When the narrator arrives home from this particular trip, he discovers that his apartment and all his belongings have blown up. In the rubble, he finds Marla's number and he calls her, but when she picks up, he hangs up. He calls Tyler instead, and so he chooses to address his pain by conjuring a macho alter whose compelling critique of consumer capitalism is only part of his attraction: the other part is his conscienceless fucking, fighting, and authoritarian exploitation of others. While the call to Tyler reflects the narrator's choice at that moment for a certain kind of re-masculinization, a violent, exploitive, and misogynist kind, the call to Marla reflects the unconscious of the film, the narrator's wish for a different solution to the meaninglessness of his life than the one fight club represents. The different solution is at least partly captured in the self-help groups, which the narrative discards the same way Tyler discards Marla after fucking her. Perhaps what the final conflagration has to do with a girl named Marla Singer is that the narrator was more afraid to call her than he was to call Tyler.

The unconscious symptom of the film is reflected in the narrator's difficulty establishing a narrative. A narrative incoherence separates part one, in which the cure to the character's ills lies in mourning losses in a context of what he considers to be meaningful relating, and part two, in which the cure lies in the kind of sadomasochistic male bonding that denigrates women as it claims for itself a revolutionary subject position that in fact looks more like a militarized hate group than like the antiglobalization movements that currently fight global capitalism.

The oscillation between capitalism critique and misogyny is repeated in the next scene. After the narrator calls Tyler, they meet at a bar, and he tells Tyler that all his things are gone. In what seems like a non-sequitur, Tyler replies that this is not the worst thing that could happen: it would be worse if he were asleep in a moving car and a woman had cut off his penis and thrown it out the window. Then Tyler asks him if he knows what a "duvet" is, and of course the narrator does. Tyler then launches into a critique of consumer capitalism, encouraging the narrator to agree that they are a generation indifferent to world problems like poverty and instead obsessed with celebrities, branding, and products like Viagra that promise to enhance their masculinity. Tyler names a series of such products, and, again, in a seeming non-sequitur the narrator interrupts by calling out the name of Martha Stewart. Tyler shouts agreement, damning Martha Stewart. And then he says it's all going down (Martha Stewart was, indeed, about to "go down" for the kind of unethical business practices that would soon after be understood to be endemic to neoliberal capitalism.). Tyler finishes his tirade by asserting that the things we own end up owning us.

Tyler's analysis recalls that of Lasch, blaming it all on women, feminizing consumer capitalism as if capitalism has anything to do with femininity. He does so not just by summing it all up in the figure of Martha Stewart, which is precisely what the media did in 2004. The blame is also evident in Tyler's first comment about the worse fate being castration by a woman. And while this comment goes by as quickly as the subliminal cuts of Tyler do before his character is introduced, we should note the fear that is expressed here: the subtext of the film figures women not just as agents of castration, but also as agents of rejection who could toss your penis out the window.

It is in the next scene that fight club is initiated, and here again we can glimpse a fear of rejection behind a surface bravado. The narrator and Tyler leave the restaurant and the narrator says goodnight. Tyler is astounded by the fact that even after three pitchers of beer, the narrator can't ask him if he can stay with him. He encourages the narrator to stop with the "foreplay" and ask for what he really wants. The narrator asks, Tyler accepts, and then Tyler asks for his favor: that the narrator hit him as hard as possible. As Steve Neale (1983) has written, the very intimation of male homoeroticism on screen usually gives way to sadomasochistic fireworks, and this film, a male buddy movie of sorts and, as I said earlier, certainly part of the 1980s and 1990s "oppressed white male" film genre, canonizes male-on-male aggression as a solution to emasculation. So the aggression defends against the desire. But I think one could argue that the erotic desire itself defends against the longing for intimacy, and it is this longing against which the film consistently defends, perhaps right through to the end. Male dependency and vulnerability is the last taboo (bedrock, Freud (1937) would have called it), not male homoeroticism.

And why is the narrator so terribly vulnerable, so defended against narcissistic wounding? The film tells us that the narrator and Tyler both hate their parents. Shortly after they begin to expand fight club and remasculinize men, there is a scene in which Tyler is in the bathtub and the narrator is sitting on the floor of the bathroom, treating his wounds. Tyler asks who the narrator would most want to fight. The narrator replies that he would fight his boss. Tyler is surprised – he would fight his father. The rest of the conversation turns on the revelation that both men had fathers who abandoned them, who every few years remarried and started new families, like they were setting up franchises. In their yearly calls with their fathers, they got generic advice like "go to college" (which their fathers had not done) or "get a job." When they turned 25, their fathers advised them to get married. The narrator, now 30, protests that marriage is not possible because he is still a boy. At that point, the critique of long-distance abandoning dads breaks off and once again yields to female-bashing. Tyler asserts that it is absurd to think that women could possibly heal a generation of men that were raised by women.

Several other scenes also locate the source of the narrator's problems in rejection and abandonment. In one scene, Tyler, slapping the narrator around after pouring lye on his hand, yells that if their fathers were their models for God and their fathers abandoned them, it is likely that God hates them and never wanted them in the first place. He concludes that they need neither God nor redemption. After this scene, the narrator begins to act like Tyler.

For all its critique of capitalism, what the film flirts with but fails to articulate are capitalism's connections to a dominant version of masculinity that has traditionally been tied to an "autonomy" based in a denial of dependence and interdependence. This version of autonomy psychologically carries capitalism's assault against possibilities of achieving the kind of intimacy and connection for which the narrator yearns. In neoliberal times, this version of autonomy's formerly exclusive tie to white masculinity has been loosened, but, in the U.S., it has become the dominant version of autonomy on offer to white middle-class subjects. *Homo entrepreneur* (du Gay, 2004; Foucault, 2008; Read, 2009), the "proper" subject of neoliberalism, can be gendered male or female – but this version of subjectivity, as Kovel presciently foresaw, is marked by a reality in which all relations are infected by the market logic of investment for a future yield, of what is cost-effective and what maximizes opportunity. Films such as *Fight Club* can be understood as part of a backlash that blames women for the loss of real autonomy that men and women alike have sustained in the wake of neoliberalism: where social risk has been shifted from collectives to individuals, where social problems are responded to with market-based solutions, where the social contract that offered at least a modicum of good social objects on which one could conceivably depend is repeatedly violated, and, thus, where individuals focus their concern on self-care rather than social citizenship. When you look closely at what happens both in the film and the novel on which it is based (Palahniuk, 1996), it becomes clear that the narrator splits himself into two not because he needs to be remasculinized by Tyler, but as a defense against the wounds caused by repeated humiliations and abandonments that come from both individual and institutional sources. Humiliating slights from his father, the medical system, his boss, the way he is instrumentally used by others, even Tyler – all these are visible in the film but are avenged by blaming Marla and seeking solace in an all-male, authoritarian, violent organization. The narrative is incoherent because the narrator's chosen solutions enact his split off rage and defend against experiencing the narcissistic wounds that caused the rage in the first place.

## Alternate interpretations

In this chapter, I have played with a few different popular culture theories to account for filmic representations of a crisis of white middle-class heterosexual masculinity: Richards and Brown on id-type versus thoughtful feeling-type emotionality (and the implications for therapeutic culture); Bainbridge and Yates on the continuum from rigidified representations of masculinity to representations that open transitional space for possible renegotiations of masculinity; Jameson's reflections on the reified and utopian possibilities on offer in most media representations that become very popular; and theories about the unconscious subtexts that disrupt narrative coherence. What theory needs to account for is the contradictory qualities of any popular text and how those contradictions contend with what I have taken here to be a central contemporary problematic for all cultural subjects: the tension between a narcissistic individualism and opportunities for individualization (the latter of which, in *Fight Club*, are simultaneously allowed to the leaders and refused to the nameless followers).

Jameson's (1979) thesis on contradiction, Hall's (1980) thesis that culture enacts the hegemonic struggle between dominant and subordinate discourses taken up differently by different audiences, and the idea that texts have unconscious subtexts all suggest we look for other possible interpretations of the film besides my own, and, as I mentioned earlier, my students through the years have helped me see these other possibilities. In one alternate interpretation, the film can be seen to narrate the way a macho and narcissistic version of masculinity utterly fails to cure the ills of anomic modern existence. Evidence for this reading lies in the fact that when the narrator realizes that Project Mayhem has spun completely out of control, he destroys Tyler, his split off macho alter. It is Tyler, though, who in fact has all the left-wing charm and who voices the critique of consumer capitalism. Nonetheless, perhaps the film recognizes that his version of masculinity, based as it is in a hatred of women and what they culturally stand for, leads to an impersonal destruction of self, others, and any sense of connection. Indeed, the film's turning point is the death of Bob, a victim of Project Mayhem's violence. Bob was the narrator's old self-help partner in the testicular cancer survivors' group, Remaining Men Together. Rebelling against Tyler and against the "rules" of Project Mayhem, the narrator insists that Bob's human dignity and specificity be recognized, even in death.

As I mentioned earlier, there is also evidence in the film that the narrator is unclear from the outset whether it is Marla or Tyler who provides the key to solving his troubles. In this reading, the narrator becomes a real revolutionary only when he rejects Tyler's version of masculinity, the violent and authoritarian organization this version spawns, and his hostility toward Marla and women in general. Realizing that Project Mayhem is killing the very humanity it was created to save, the narrator saves Marla from the destruction his own rageful fantasy is about to enact. In the final scene, he and Marla hold hands and watch the symbols of consumer capitalism blow up, which perhaps suggests that Tyler has found a way to value love and connection while holding on to his desire to destroy capitalism.[5] But even if this ending suggests that one can remain human and still wish to destroy capitalism, it can nonetheless only be read as an individual and not a collective solution – perhaps too much to ask of a Hollywood film. For the film definitely does not imagine a functioning revolutionary collective but rather an authoritarian hierarchy in which the minions are encouraged to conform to the leader's rules and not to think or ask questions.

Indeed, a third psychoanalytic reading, one that takes account of the individualist strain of the film, might argue that, as in a dream, Marla, Tyler, and the narrator are all parts of one person and that Tyler can only disappear when the narrator connects with the part of himself represented by Marla. Evidence for this interpretation includes the fact that Marla takes the place of the narrator's power animal in his meditation and that Marla is a ghostlike figure who walks out into traffic and doesn't die. The narrative perhaps makes most sense, best coheres, with this interpretation. But it took several viewings and a few student comments for me to find this way of establishing some narrative coherence, and that is because the film's excitement derives neither from Marla's filmic presence, which is rare, nor from the narrator's struggle to acknowledge those parts of himself that humanize him. Not only are such moments of struggle few, but they are mostly repudiated explicitly in the narrative. The weight of the narrative is on narcissistic masculinity as a solution to both the problems of consumer capitalism and emasculation; most of the film's pleasure comes from fight club, not from its dissolution in the final frames or from the hero's early flirtation with self-help groups.

## Conclusion

Regardless of the interpretation that most speaks to us, it is clear that both fight club and the narrator's insomnia emerge from a social structure that splits autonomous from relational capacities and does so in support of a neoliberal, global order of consumer and finance capitalism. The result of this split is narcissistic self structure and narcissistic relations: urges either to conform or to rebel in a violent form stem from experiences of never feeling good enough, never feeling listened to, never feeling connected to others in any but exploitive ways. The film and its narrative structure reveal the intimate connection between capitalism and the kind of injury in the private sphere that produces a narcissistic defensive autonomy. This version of autonomy wreaks violence on the self and the environment; it disparages relations with others as it struggles against a dreaded dependency and vulnerability. Because the narration chooses as its dominant solution the very narcissistic masculinity that is a source of the problem, it well illustrates the way normative unconscious processes work. Hurt by dominant forms of masculinity and femininity, the male characters, who know consciously who and what the real enemies are, nonetheless are pulled unconsciously to repeat the very dynamics that caused their problem in the first place.

A psychoanalytic reading of the film could easily focus only on the critique of capitalism, the denial of loss, and the film's critique of the fantasy that all loss can be made good by the right consumer products. But any psychoanalytic reading that omits the many things the narrator has to say about his failed relationships will miss that important link between social character and capitalism for which I am trying to make the case. It is through looking at the historical specificity of the characters' relationships that we can move from the particular to any kind of meaningful analysis of the collective. And, as I have suggested, the film downplays the only thing that can possibly give it narrative sense – the narrator's experience of repeated rejections and abandonments by friends, lovers, parents, and society (see my discussion of Silva, 2013, in the previous chapter). The film reveals as well that what makes women easy to villainize is not that they represent castration or lack, but rather that they are made, unfairly, to represent the agents of rejection and abandonment.[6] In the novel, in fact, the real target of the explosives is not capitalism but the national museum, the dead white abandoning fathers. A reading of the film's unconscious suggests that we have to look for the roots of omnipotent grandiose destructiveness in the way capitalism and traditional forms of dominant masculinity instrumentalize both public and private relationships, creating narcissistic wounds that are not in fact healed but rather are fortified by consumerism, misogyny, and homophobia.

# Notes

* Used with permission. Layton, L. (2011) Something to do with a girl named Marla Singer: Capitalism, narcissism, and therapeutic discourse in David Fincher's *Fight Club*. *Free Associations* 62: 112–134. Reprinted and updated in Sheils, B. and Walsh, J. (2017) *Narcissism, Melancholia and the Subject of Community*. Cham, Switzerland: Palgrave Macmillan, pp. 91–118.

1 The notion of 'social character' itself derives from the work of early left-wing analysts such as Otto Fenichel (1953), Wilhelm Reich (1933/1972), and Erich Fromm (1941). This work was further elaborated by Frankfurt School theorists: Fromm's (1941) "modern man," escaping from freedom via conformity, and Adorno et al.'s (1950) authoritarian personality both bear more than a passing resemblance to the narcissistic personality Kohut and Kernberg were to elaborate in the 70s and 80s.

2 I still find Kohut's definition of narcissism compelling, although I have come to believe that narcissistic selves are not marked by a deficit of structure and lack of conflict, as Kohut argued, but rather by what Kernberg (1975) and Fairbairn (1954) identified as pathological, conflict-ridden psychic structures.

3 This is, of course, a very different interpretation of the role of experts in late modernity from that offered by, for example, Beck (1999), Beck and Beck-Gernsheim (2002) and Giddens (1991). But perhaps what gets lost in their analyses is the "dark side" of expertise so well chronicled by, for example, Rose (1990). See Chapter 6 of this volume.

4 It is worth noting that the first chapter of the novel (Palahniuk, 1996), unlike the film's first scene, does NOT end with the statement about Marla's guilt. Rather, it ends with the Norton character trying to find a way out of being murdered by his alter ego. In the book version, the statement about hurting the one you love is taken back in a different way. After confessing that he wants Tyler, Tyler wants Marla, and Marla wants him, the book's narrator starts to talk about Tyler's wish to be a legend. Gun in mouth, he likens himself to the gospel writers who told Jesus's story: since he was there from the beginning, he will tell Tyler's story and make him a legend (pp. 14–15).

I underline this difference in the novel because of its resonance with Columbine and other school shootings, that is, for what it tells us about the wishes of alienated young men for some kind of celebrity to give meaning to their lives, even if that celebrity has to occur at the moment of self-inflicted death. This particularly male version of the celebrity fantasy, tied as it is with death, takes to absurd extremes the simultaneous longing for specialness and awareness of the impossibility of achieving it (in life) that marks a narcissistic culture intolerant of the ordinary (Stein, 2000). And with regard to that impossibility, the novel makes far clearer than the film the narcissistic oscillation between grandiosity and self-deprecation – for example, Marla and the narrator constantly refer to themselves as human butt-wipe and both long for death as release from the meaninglessness of life. Nonetheless, in film and novel a longing for something that would make life meaningful is present throughout. The solutions are disastrous; the expression of the longing is what is radical about both novel and film.

5 Interestingly, the novel ends differently and does not suggest such an integration. The novel ends when the narrator repudiates Tyler and acknowledges he likes Marla, at which point Marla and the people from the support groups come after the narrator to rescue him. In the novel, the buildings don't blow up – because the narrator (as Tyler) used paraffin, knowing full well that paraffin impedes the explosion. Furthermore, the buildings that are being blown up are not the centers of finance but national museums that symbolize the dead white fathers.

6 When Marla re-enters the narrative as Tyler's fuck buddy, the narrator is enraged that she has come between him and Tyler. In the novel, the narrator goes on to blame women more generally for his loss of male intimates. Since college, he complains, all his male friendships ended after his friends got married (p. 62).

# Chapter 16

# Transgenerational hauntings

## Toward a social psychoanalysis and an ethic of dis-illusionment[*]

On September 6, 2005, the Tuesday after the week when Hurricane Katrina devastated New Orleans, a 55-year-old white middle-class female told me the following dream (first reported in Layton, 2009; see Ch. 12):

> I'm watching this dream unfold: there's a black woman who feels ill. She seems to get progressively worse. Her friends dig up a pit in the dirt and with water make it into a mud bath. They have her in it, rolling her around, back and forth, making more mud all the while. I'm worrying that they might be intending to put her under water. I don't want to be watching and not doing anything; I have to hope they have her best interests at heart and that they know what they're doing. The woman is in a delirium. When just her head is visible, her daughter, who has been watching, cries out, "That's my mama," and rushes closer to hug her. I don't remember seeing her submerged or getting better.
>
> In the next scene, there's a whole crew of people escorting her to a tv show where she was supposed to be going on, but they were filling in for her because of her illness. Not only had she recovered, she looked absolutely stunning, glamorous: reminiscent of Oprah. Her friends were rushing ahead and there was commotion as they were letting the tv people know that she was coming and to plan for her to come on.

I asked the patient for her associations, and she first said that it seemed to her the dream was about the personal transformation she was undergoing, one that held great excitement and promise but also great risks and anxiety. And then she said, "I don't know why the people were black." I asked what came to mind. She said it made her think of Hurricane Katrina and all the poor, black people. She said she was very upset about what was going on and then went on to speak disparagingly about "them," those horrible people in the Bush administration and in New Orleans who didn't think about how poor people without cars were going to get out. I was struck by the part of the dream where she says, "I don't want to be watching and not doing anything," and where she *hopes* the people in charge know what they are doing but fears they don't. So at some point I clumsily asked her if she perhaps felt complicit in some way. She said she did not; she'd never let such a thing happen.

Shame had set in for her, and I realized only later that in addressing the complicity, rather than her helplessness and her wish to do something, I had likely suggested that I was NOT complicit, as though I somehow was able to stand outside as the curious, but NOT HELPLESS onlooker.

The dream has many meanings at many levels, as all dreams do. We explored together, for example, the transferential question she raised about whether I, the person in charge of her analysis, knew what I was doing. But the dream's meaning field extends out into historical transgenerational directions as well, and its social meanings are no less personal and deep than are the individual and family-centered meanings on which we usually base our interpretations. Indeed, the ghosts of past and present U.S. history are all over this dream, and I think you can see here both the opportunity I had to bring that history into the treatment as well as the way I unconsciously resisted doing so. Had I not bypassed what I suspect was my own shame, we might together have been able to connect emotionally to the dream's complex duality. On the one hand, the dream and associations point to a relational unconscious, formed in history, in which we are all interimplicated and interdependent. The dreamer feels concern and even love for the distressed black woman – "That's my mama." But whites, as perpetrators and bystanders, are called out as complicit in the ongoing destruction of poor black people.

At the same time, the dream and associations point to a contemporary social reality whose dominant discourses deny interdependence and therefore disavow complicity. The disavowal is seen in the dream's Hollywood ending, in which a tale of hardship ends in the success of special individuals. Here, the poor black woman becomes a rich black woman. Race and class get split, and poverty is disavowed, although it reappears in the dream associations – in all those poor people who couldn't get out. By the end of the dream, my patient's unconscious seems to have turned a tragedy in which we were all implicated into a spectacle. The tragedy of classism, racism, and the indifference to human vulnerability, manifest in all our contemporary domestic and foreign policies, becomes a colorblind story of rags to riches, of personal triumph over adversity. But the ghostly shadow of white classed indifference haunts the attempt to take refuge in this version of the American Dream.

I can think of no better way to think about psychoanalysis, transgenerational haunting, illusion and dis-illusionment than to begin with this dream. In what follows, I explore the way in which the dream and my responses to it reflect the ghostly intersectional workings of racialized as well as classed psychosocial unconscious processes. I seek some of the ways in which, for white people, these processes simultaneously unsettle white privilege and then work very hard to re-center it. Although I imagine myself white (Coates, 2015) and am very economically privileged, I am aware that white advantage is lived in different ways depending, in part, on class, and, in part, on one's identifications. Some whites, like those my patient referred to as "in charge," wield official power. Some whites have little class power but yet benefit from being white. Among the latter, some think that people of color are all that stand in their way of achieving the Dream. Others, like my patient and myself, know we benefit from being white and feel a lot of guilt and shame about it: these states arise largely from being consciously committed to progressive antiracist politics while knowing that we have made few to no changes in our everyday lives that would actually address systemic racism (for example, we continue to live in all white neighborhoods and have all white friends and lovers). With that in mind, I hope to contribute here to the pedagogical project George Yancy (2012) proposes in his book, *Look, A White!*: to help white people acquire our own version of double consciousness, to try to see ourselves through the eyes of people of color so that the ghostly and destructive presence of white and class advantage become as visible to white people as they are to most people of color.

## The duality of unconscious processes

The ghosts that haunt past and present U.S. history make themselves known in unconscious processes that are fully psychosocial. Earl Hopper (2003) defines a social unconscious as:

> the existence and constraints of social, cultural and communicational arrangements of which people are unaware: unaware, in so far as these arrangements are not perceived (not 'known'), and if perceived not acknowledged ('denied'), and if acknowledged, not taken as problematic ('given'), and if taken as problematic, not considered with an optimal degree of detachment and objectivity.

> (p. 127)

While I like Hopper's definition, I don't think it quite captures the way that, as my patient's dream suggests, psychosocial unconscious processes point simultaneously away from and toward truth. I used to teach popular culture, and one of my favorite articles was Jameson's (1979) "Reification and Utopia in Mass Culture," which argues that the most popular mass cultural products generally become popular because they contain both progressive and reactionary ideological trends. Other pop culture critics have shown how the endings of mostly progressive works, like the end of my patient's dream, generally tie things up in a reactionary direction. Works of popular culture, like everything else, are shaped by unconscious process, and so, like dreams, they reveal the dual way that psychosocial unconscious processes work: resisting and conserving.

In the week I began this chapter, I saw a documentary called *Whose Streets?* (Folayan, 2017), about the black protest movement that emerged against police violence in Ferguson. The person introducing the film warned black audience members that the film would be hard to watch, and he encouraged them to get up and leave the room if they needed to. White people, he said, need to sit still and watch every frame. I felt unsettled. That night I dreamed there was a flood in one room of my house. The rug in that room, interestingly one that we refer to as "Oriental," was ruined, but all the other rooms remained unaffected. In the dream, my unsettled state gets connected to a flood – at the very moment that I had begun writing about white complicity in the tragedy of Hurricane Katrina. My unsettled state calls to mind DiAngelo's (2018) concept, white fragility, which describes how the evocation of white racism often evokes defensiveness in whites. In the dream, I seem to be wrestling with the ghosts of racism and with how much privilege I'm willing to give up – an "Oriental" rug, ruined. Race and class privilege live, too, in my very ability to imagine that the other rooms CAN remain unaffected. No such compartments, no safe spaces existed for many poor African Americans caught in the traumatic reality of Katrina New Orleans. As in my patient's Katrina dream, here, too, what I have called normative unconscious processes push forcefully to restore the psychic equilibrium conferred by having, or even aspiring to have, white upper class advantage.

Slowly, I am coming to understand such dreams as offering a chance to experience a ghost of U.S. history that, in this case, is manifest in the ways in which whiteness, white fragility, and class privilege intersect. As I look back over my career, my writings, my life, what strikes me is how I alternate between two different states of consciousness: in one, I am, as Ta-Nehisi Coates (2015) would say, a Dreamer, imagining myself as white, blindly enacting in so many ways, in the clinic and out, my class and race privilege. And then, at moments, something happens, maybe an interpersonal encounter, maybe something I read that puts me in touch, viscerally, with the ghosts of U.S. history. Suddenly, concepts like white privilege and intersectionality come alive and I become a little bit more "woke." I am part of a cross-racial and cross-class group of therapists on a steering committee of a Boston chapter of Reflective Spaces/Material Places. More than once, the people of color in the group have found themselves pitted against each other while the white folks sit silently and seemingly innocently by, enacting what Solnit (2017) has referred to as "the willed obliviousness of privilege." We clash over whether class trumps race or race trumps class. When these interpersonal conflicts arise, it FEELS like we are unconsciously acting out trans-individual and trans-historical forces of structural racism and class struggle that we carry unconsciously, like ghosts, in our bodies and minds.

## Psychosocial ghosts

In her book, *Ghostly Matters*, sociologist Avery Gordon (1997) puts forward the idea, now widely recognized by those in our field who write about transgenerational transmission of trauma, that "impossible memories and unwritten histories continue living and often come to us as ghosts

. . ." (Ferreday and Kuntsman, 2011, p. 1). Examining works of literature and photography, Gordon notes that ghosts often lie just outside a work's frame, and yet something inside the frame itself points toward the ghosts. Many contemporary psychoanalytic theorists have offered ways to understand and access these ghosts: Apprey's (2014) pluperfect errand; Faimberg's (2005) telescoping of generations; Abraham's (1994) encrypted phantom; Salberg's (2015) attention to transmitted attachment patterns; Grand (2000, 2009) on malignant dissociation. Gordon widens the frame, in a crucial way, of what most of our theorists of transgenerational transmission of trauma understand as ghostly. "The ghost," she writes, "is not simply a dead or a missing person, but a social figure, and investigating it can lead to that dense site where history and subjectivity make social life" (1997, p. 8). Haunting is "an animated state in which a repressed or unresolved social violence is making itself known" (Gordon, 2011, p. 2), a "socio-political-psychological state when something else, or something different from before, feels like it must be done, and prompts a something-to-be-done" (p. 3). Ghosts come "demanding attention, looking for justice, challenging the way we know, act, and feel" (Ferreday and Kuntsman, 2011, p. 1). In the Katrina dream, my patient wishes she could DO something to make things different. What haunts, Gordon (2011) writes, are "the 'historic alternatives' that could have been" (p. 7, citing Marcuse). Her vision of the ghost conjures Davoine and Gaudillière's (2004) plea that clinicians seek out the multiple ways that we and our patients are caught up, together, in what they call the BIG History: "That's my mama."

To even begin to understand what Gordon means by the historic alternatives that could have been, we have to look honestly at U.S. history, a history rife with ghosts that call out the savagery haunting our illusory fantasy of being civilized. The exceedingly dangerous illusion of American exceptionalism, is, as Coates rightly recognizes, the ideological centerpiece of our disavowed history of genocide and slavery, a disavowal that infantilizes the population. In 1955, James Baldwin (1955/1998) warned of the damaging psychic effects of living in illusion about ourselves. Baldwin wrote:

I do not think . . . that it is too much to suggest that the American vision of the world, which allows so little reality . . . for any of the darker forces in human life . . . tends until today to paint moral issues in glaring black and white – [and] owes a great deal to the battle waged by

Americans to maintain between themselves and black men a human separation which could not be bridged. It is only now beginning to be borne in on us . . . that this vision of the world is dangerously inaccurate. For it protects our moral high-mindedness at the terrible expense of weakening our grasp of reality. People who shut their eyes to reality simply invite their own destruction, and anyone who insists on remaining in a state of innocence long after that innocence is dead turns himself into a monster.

(pp. 128–129)

Gump (2000, 2010), Leary (2000), White (2002), Holmes (2006, 2016), Fletchman-Smith (2011), Apprey (2014), Jones and Obourn (2014), Vaughans (2016), Altman (2000, 2003, 2006b), Wachtel (2003), Suchet (2004, 2007, 2017), Harris (2012), Gentile (2014), Grand (2014, 2018), Hassinger (2014), Hellman (2017), Parker (2019) and others have spoken of the many ways that the disavowed legacies of slavery live on in the psychologies of and interactions among whites, blacks, and other people of color. An all too often missing part of this story, however, is the link between slavery, genocide, and the history of U.S. capitalism, the disavowed ghostly presence that haunts all our institutions (including psychoanalysis). U.S. history offers many instances of the disavowed intersection of race and class, a disavowal that always serves the interest of capitalism. One sees it strikingly, for example, in government documents' perverse inversion of the terms savage and civilized: civilization is repeatedly equated with ownership of private property; Native Americans' communal relation to the land is deemed savage. The distinction is then used as an excuse to take the land (see Dunbar-Ortiz, 2014). Such perversions repeatedly enshrine white class privilege while offering a sense of superiority, of psychic and physical comfort, to all classes of whites.

In *Between the World and Me*, Coates (2015) makes visible the ghost as social figure by deconstructing the illusion of whiteness. He accomplishes this by repeatedly referring to white people as Dreamers who call  themselves white. Dreamers' projections outward of their vulnerability and destructiveness are manifest in racist institutions and policies that trap people of color and enable Dreamers to go on dreaming. Coates is writing a good 40 years into a period of neoliberal dominance, when class and race have been dissociated in different ways. Not long after Martin Luther King, Jr. planned a poor peoples' campaign to make manifest the united interests of poor whites and poor people of color, King was murdered and the Republicans' right-wing Southern Strategy offered, for the nth historical time, an invitation to poor whites to identify with whiteness and dis-identify with people of color. By the late 1970s, Democrats, every bit as invested in finance capital and the globalization of capitalism as Republicans, began to practice their own form of dissociation of race and class, advocating a multicultural identity politics that disavows class difference (see Fraser, 2017). Both strategies have initiated new ruptures in the link between people and their social world, new betrayals of trust in what Benjamin calls a moral third (2004, 2017). Both strategies underwrite white race and class privilege. Among whites, they largely benefit the upper class, but all Dreamers live in the illusion that whiteness is a guarantee of superiority and of relative invulnerability. This illusion, as Baldwin said and current U.S. events tragically demonstrate, makes whites dangerous to themselves and to others.

For me, looking at this history has brought on a horrific sense of dis-illusionment, a loss of comforting illusions. Dis-illusionment, the undoing of disavowal, is a painful process. It first entails a willingness to become conscious of historical trauma (Salberg and Grand, 2016), a process that renders visible the ways this trauma, alive in intersectional ghosts, haunts all of our institutions in the U.S., including the theories and practices of psychoanalysis. Facing these ghosts evokes shame at harm done, at benefitting from harm done, what Watkins (2018) refers to as deserved shame. When we bypass deserved shame, we are likely to repeat the conditions that keep oppression in place. Unconscious deals get struck between conflicting demands to turn toward the truth and to turn away from it. It was my bypassed shame that shut my patient down as she began to question why black people appeared in her dream. It was my bypassed shame that made me miss the chance to explore her love for the woman in the mud, her wish not just to stand by but rather to heed the ghost's call for something-to-be-done.

Like Watkins, Jacobs (2014), too, calls on us not to bypass deserved shame but rather to move closer into it, a second moment of the work of dis-illusionment. As Cushman (2000) and Straker (2004) have suggested, white deserved shame arises from experiencing a conflict between ideals of equality and awareness of benefitting from racial and class inequities. Moving closer into shame can lead to feeling a real concern for the other, to remorse, and, most importantly, to ethical action (Gobodo-Madikizela, 2016).

It seems to me that it is only through the painful process of undoing the disavowals that underlie psychosocial illusions that we might become able to imagine historical alternatives, to conceptualize and address the ghosts' demand for justice, for a something-to-be-done. A particularly dangerous psychosocial illusion is that dominant culture is healthy. Psychoanalysis can and has addressed this illusion. In what follows, I briefly sketch a history of what we might call a psychoanalytic ethic of dis-illusionment. Such an ethic, I suggest, might attune us to and call on us to disrupt the constant reiterations of laws and norms that sustain systemic racism and class inequality, attune us to individual and group unconscious processes that we ignore at our peril.

## An ethic of dis-illusionment

As a feminist psychoanalyst who spent my early career writing and teaching about gender, I did not expect to find my starting point for elaborating an ethic of dis-illusionment in Freud, but indeed I did, and I found it in his work on disavowal (1927a, 1937). Alan Bass (2000) has persuasively argued that, late in life, Freud began to sense that disavowal, and not repression, was the primary defense mechanism at the heart of all repetition compulsions and resistances (Freud, 1937, pp. 235–238). Freud (1937) wrote:  "If the perception of reality involves unpleasure, that perception – i.e., the truth – must be sacrificed" (p. 236). Freud's insight about turning away from painful truths became central to Bion and to many of his followers. Bion (1962a, 1962b, 1970) asserted that when the raw emotion evoked by frustration is not adequately contained, lying, rather than thinking, may become a customary way of defending against what he called catastrophic change. According to Bion, lies may well be painful to live with, but they are less painful than the truth, which can threaten to annihilate the self and its bonds. Only if the truth can be tolerated is it possible to learn from experience. For both Bion and Freud, then, disavowal, turning a blind eye to painful truths, is at the heart of perversion, repetition, and the inability to learn from experience.

The Freud that is usually taught in institutes is generally not the Freud who wrote social treatises like *Totem and Taboo* (1913), *The Future of an Illusion* (1927b), *Civilization and its Discontents* (1930). I have had the good fortune to teach Freud in extra-analytic spaces, and the Freud I teach argued, early on, that neuroses are collective responses to oppressive social conditions (Freud, 1908). This Freud critiqued the oppressive side of the bourgeois norms of his era and the symptoms that spoke loudly of that oppression. His early example, of course, was hysteria, a disease largely seen in extremely intelligent white middle-class female patients whose developmental paths were blocked by sexist patriarchal norms. Think Anna O., Bertha Pappenheim, feminist social work pioneer who coined the term "talking cure." But, unfortunately, we must also think Dora (Freud, 1905), with whom Freud re-enacted those sexist norms. In these early Freudian works, we find the duality of unconscious process I spoke of earlier, a tension between radical and conservative forces. When the tension is broken by disavowing truths that contest dominant social norms, here heterosexism, the psychic equilibrium of those who benefit from conforming to those norms is restored. Meanwhile, for those oppressed by these norms, enactments like the one with Dora become fresh instances of betrayal. At our field's very origin, we find a split between a radical Freud offering a psychoanalytic ethic of dis-illusionment and a conservative Freud enacting a psychoanalytic ethic of adaptation. The tension between these two ethics haunts our field (see Zaretsky, 2015); too often, disavowal wins the day and we lapse into an ethic of adaptation.

For the radical Freud, psychoanalysis was an heir to the Enlightenment project of questioning authority and resisting conformity. Freud's contribution to the Copernican Revolution was his discovery of the unconscious, that which decenters our illusions about ourselves, specifically, our fantasy that we are master in our own house. "A great part of my life's work," Freud said, "has been spent to destroy my own illusions and those of humankind" (cited in Barglow, 2018, unreferenced epigram). During WWI, Freud (1915b) wrote that to understand the horrors that his country and countrymen were perpetrating in the name of civilization, which, here and elsewhere, he named as white (p. 276), we would have to reckon with the fact that we humans are neither as evil nor as good as we think we are. Freud called out the hypocrisy of the state, which, at that very moment, was enacting unimaginable barbarities that its own laws prohibited its citizens from enacting. Evil, he argued, cannot be eradicated, and conscience, "is not the inflexible judge that ethical teachers declare it, but in its origin is 'social anxiety' and nothing else" (p. 280). Freud was quite aware that an ethic of dis-illusionment is far from pleasurable, but as a lover of truth he hoped it might deter us from committing the kinds of savagery perpetrated in the war, savagery, again, that hides behind claims to being "civilized."

## From a radical ethic of dis-illusionment to a psychology of adaptation

Erich Fromm, one of radical Freud's most radical heirs, took another step in developing an ethic of dis-illusionment. Like Jacobson, Fenichel, Reich, and others of his left-wing contemporaries (see Jacoby, 1983), he saw capitalism as a perpetrator of evils. Fromm (1941, 1962) developed the concepts of the social unconscious, what a given social order requires its subjects to repress, and social character, including what he called, as early as 1947, consumer capitalism's marketing orientation. In his prescient 1970 book, *The Crisis of Psychoanalysis*, Fromm warned against the devastating effects of harboring illusion: "The grave danger to the future of man," he wrote, "is largely due to his incapacity to recognize the fictitious character of his 'common sense'" (p. 26). Fromm argued that the crisis within psychoanalysis had ensued in part from a betrayal of the radical Freud, a betrayal most manifest in ego psychology. The conformist Freud of ego psychology, he felt, fit with the common sense of an historical era in which a radical bourgeois liberalism had itself become coopted by a consumerist, individualist ethic. Like many others, Fromm accused ego psychology of fostering a psychology of adaptation. Indeed, Leah Gordon's (2015) compelling and dis-illusioning study of twentieth-century historical shifts in academic work on racism reveals the prominent role played by psychology in fostering adaptation: in the interwar years, Gordon reports, racism was treated as systemic; in the post-WWII period, psychology entered and became dominant in interdisciplinary work groups, at which time racism began largely to be conceptualized and studied as an artifact of individual attitudes and prejudices.

Fromm claimed that treating patients with an eye toward deconstructing the phenomenon of common sense would require analysts to engage in "a radical critique of their society, its overt and especially its hidden norms and principles" (1970, p. 3). He called for a psychoanalysis that examines the "pathology of normalcy," "the psychological phenomena which constitute the pathology of contemporary society" (1970, p. 29). Too often, Fromm said, his contemporaries colluded with patients to make analyses not too disturbing.

## Erik Erikson: ethics versus moralism

Fromm praised a few contemporaries who he felt had resisted betraying the radical ethic of psychoanalysis, and one of those was Erik Erikson.

Like Freud, Erikson (1976) made a very important distinction between moralism and ethics, one that directly challenges an ethic of adaptation. Moralism, he wrote, derives from an early superego structured by the rules of conduct of one's culture, while ethics develop later and center on what he calls "the more affirmative sense of what man owes to man, in terms of the developmental realization of the best in each human being" (p. 414). Erikson felt that, throughout life, we struggle with conflicts engendered by contradictions between our formation within conventional norms and our wish to be better and fuller human beings. These conflicts reveal themselves in what Erikson calls "deals" (pp. 413–414) between "our ethical and our most moralistic sides . . ." (p. 414). Such deals, he says, "eventually permit us to commit or to agree to the commission of enslavement, exploitation and annihilation in the name of the highest values" (p. 414). In my patient's Katrina dream, and in my response to it, for example, we can see the deal we struck between our awareness of white complicity in the tragedy of structural racism and our wish to take refuge in goodness and innocence.

Freud would not have disagreed with Erikson. Already in 1915, he argued that the internal factor that disposes us to be able to attain ethical capacity, to transform egoistic into social instincts, to curb our tendencies toward savagery, is our need for love, "an advantage for which we are willing to sacrifice other advantages" (1915b, p. 282). But needs for love and belonging can just as well dispose us to conformity, Fromm's concern, as to the call of truth. Unlike moralism, ethics requires the capacity to reflect on what has been merely taken in as convention. Translated to the clinic, I imagine that an ethical stance, in Erikson's view, would primarily entail helping patients become conscious of the deals they have struck between adhering to convention and heeding the less safe call of truth. Again, our attention is called to the psychic struggle between illusion and dis-illusionment.

## Normative unconscious processes

I consider my own work on normative unconscious processes to be in the tradition of dis-illusionment laid out by radical Freud, by Fromm, and by Erikson. Most of what I've written about centers on conflict between normative unconscious processes, which work toward reproducing cultural inequalities of all kinds, and what I've called counterhegemonic processes that work to reintegrate those crucial parts of us that we have split off from ourselves under the pressure of social norms and the need for love and recognition. This was my way of capturing the duality of psychosocial unconscious process. I like Erikson's way of describing what I'm after as "deals" we make to negotiate our conflicts between what has brought us love, social approval, and security, financial and otherwise, and what, to my mind, has simultaneously made us sick and destructive to ourselves and others.

Psychic deals – resistance to and compliance with the historically specific norms that have built and that sustain dominant culture – begin very early in the process of identity formation, and they make their presence known in a ghostly fashion. "What Makes Me White," a short video by Aimee Sands (2010), powerfully describes the psychic deal that emerges in the process of becoming white and middle-class in the 1950s. In the video, two little girls living in white Westchester County, New York, are picked up by their grandfather in his large 1950s car and taken for a visit to their grandparents' New York City home. As the car enters a poor black neighborhood, the grandfather clicks down the door locks and rolls up the windows. One girl gazes out the window with a perplexed look. Her awareness of what it means to be white, the video suggests, comes into being as a fear of blacks and black neighborhoods. Blacks are cast outside; whites are shut inside. The poverty of the black neighborhood is the ghost that haunts the scene of the grandfather's fear and the granddaughters' introduction to racial difference. The disavowed history, if confronted honestly, would reveal that the grandfather's fear is firmly built on what Yancy (2012) calls missilic projections, on disavowals of complicity, on white rage (Anderson, 2016) enacted first in genocide and slavery, and later in convict leasing, Jim Crow, redlining, school segregation, and mass incarceration.

The psychosocial material these girls will draw upon to shape their identities and desires is intergenerationally transmitted by grandparents, parents, teachers, and the white geographies that segregate them from intimate contact with people of color and their living conditions. These girls will likely be taught NOT to know what historical forces produced these conditions. Any sense of complicity, as in the Katrina dream, will most likely register as not-me experience. As Patricia Williams (1997) writes, hatred and fear learned in the context of love, in a private sphere dissociated from the public sphere, upholds and reproduces the norms of dominant culture – and damages both self and other.

## White class advantage and the psychoanalytic frame

White upper class advantage, the contemporary neoliberal version of whiteness, is built both into our institutions and into the work we do; psychoanalytic space is haunted by deals that normalize structural inequalities. In what follows, I ask: What are the psychic costs of clinging to the illusion that dominant culture is healthy? How might we identify the ghostly presence of resistance as well as the ways that whites counter that resistance by seeking psychic equilibrium?

Let us first look at a key psychoanalytic structure, the frame. On the institutional level, an important frame is the psychoanalytic conference, attended largely by white people and whoever else can afford the high costs of attending. At the 2017 Division 39 Spring meeting, several people of color experienced microaggressions involving white administrators, enactments that, whatever was consciously intended, served to keep the space safe for white people. For example, people of color spoke about having been directed to the registration table of an adjoining conference of African American activists, a conscious and unconscious enactment that suggests to people of color that they cannot possibly be psychology professionals like "us." I am not talking here about bad racist individuals; this is a structural problem, a normative unconscious process that caters to white fragility and thus works to keep white people comfortable. Yancy (2012) writes about his discomfort in the all-white spaces of philosophy conferences. "One ought to wonder," he says, "about the specific white normative frame that structures such spaces . . . its disciplining effects on bodies of color" (loc 1992). For Yancy, the frame is race. But, as I have been arguing, the frame is both raced and classed. Indeed, I am pretty sure that not all conference attendees who call ourselves white DO feel at home at professional conferences. I think, however, that whites unconsciously imbibe in these white upper-class spaces what we need to be and do to become the kind of person that WILL feel comfortable. How to speak, how to use our bodies, etc. This psychic work lies very much at the intersection of race and class. Gender, too.

Bleger (1967) called the frame a 'ghost world' that is never noticed unless it changes or goes missing. Focusing on the psychoanalytic situation as an institution, Bleger wrote: "we must accept that institutions and the frame *always* make up a 'ghost world,' that of the most primitive and undifferentiated organization" (p. 512). Bleger argued that the frame sustains the patient's fantasy of omnipotence and safety; if uninterpreted, it becomes the site of a perfect repetition compulsion that leaves the patient at risk of ending treatment with an adaptive ego. In Bleger's definition, an adaptive ego takes comfort in belonging but is not self-directed.

We can render Bleger's work psychosocial by placing the frame in a historicized relational context. In a recent two-part series in *Psychoanalytic Dialogues* (Seligman et al., 2017a, 2017b), in which therapists reflected on their clinical experience post-election, we see the tension that arises when therapists confront the politics of the frame. Several therapists spoke of having had to break their own frame rules as the political reality crashed into the room. Spielberg (2017) says, for example, "that my rules about the boundary between the political and the clinical no longer made sense" (p. 367). Many spoke of patient frame breaks, like lateness, but also how they themselves began enacting frame breaks, like letting sessions go over time. What was striking to me was how few writers questioned the politics of the frame from which they had shifted. To me, the lesson here was that keeping politics out of the therapy frame IS in fact the enactment of a politics. A politics that fosters adaptation.

Our field's strong tendency to dissociate the psychic from the social is a premier instance of an institutional level enactment of normative unconscious process (Cushman, 2019; Layton, 2006b). Normative unconscious processes reproduce inequality precisely where the link between the psychic and the social has been disavowed; in limiting our concept of social context to a socially decontextualized family, a radical ethic of disillusionment gives way to an ethic of adaptation. Frie (2017) has recently suggested that so long as we police our psychoanalytic frame in such a way that family memory remains distinct from collective memory, from the BIG History, we will not be able adequately to deal with the soul wounds of class inequities and classed racism. I believe we need to consider the possibility that what we call depth merely touches the surface, a surface on which the disavowals of history, our illusions, are allowed continuously to repeat themselves.

To make more visible the politics of the clinical frame, we might look at Hollander's (2017) "Who is the Sufferer and What is Being Suffered?". I highlight this vignette in part because it is a rare instance in which the race-class intersection is explored – and it is explored where it is perhaps most difficult for white people to see the ghosts of white class privilege: in a white-white patient-therapist dyad (see Cushman, 2000, note on p. 616; Bodnar, 2004; Hellman, 2017). Hollander writes about her work with L., a white upper middle-class female corporate lawyer "whose frenetic life leaves little opportunity for her to be with her infant daughter" (p. 644). L. had come to resent and envy her child's Latina nanny, which played out in the treatment as a demand for special attention from Hollander and fears that Hollander would retaliate and reject her. Hollander describes how the working through of the maternal transference based on familial etiology led to the patient being able more easily to assert herself with the nanny "and to claim her place as her baby's mother" (p. 644). However, as Hollander goes on to note, there was something "uncannily absent in the frame" (p. 645), what I'm here calling a ghost. The ghost as social figure, in this case the figure that marks what the destructive white neoliberal subject destroys in both self and other, became visible to Hollander when the patient said something that reminded her that her patient was paying the nanny less than minimum wage and was requiring of the nanny "excessively long work days and nights" (p. 645). At that moment, Hollander realized that she and her patient, both white, had unconsciously occluded the way that the nanny had been treated as an "other" in their work, how both had unconsciously projected "dissociated and denigrated emotional states of insecurity and vulnerability" (p. 646) onto the nanny. Hollander then "struggled" to find a way to raise this in the treatment. She simply noted that they had "not talked much about the nanny's personal life and experience and [wondered] what that might mean" (p. 645). L. was surprised to recognize that this was true. Eventually, she began to talk about how paying the nanny low wages had violated her own social values while simultaneously giving her an enigmatic gratification. And this made her realize that she had been denying how much of her anxiety had been generated by her firm's downsizing policies. L's "privileged class/racial position" allowed her "to experience her agency through her role as a boss with absolute control over her worker" (p. 646). The perverse repetition of our race/class history lies in what L. resorted to in order to be able to tolerate the dehumanizing conditions of her neoliberal workplace: she created intolerable conditions for the nanny, thereby becoming a little less human herself.

We can see how Hollander, her patient, and the normative parameters of treatment itself are all caught up in the BIG History, a neoliberal and globalized history that includes the demand to be a defensively autonomous entrepreneurial self in a precarious employment world. It includes as well what Ehrenreich and Hochschild (2002) called the "care drain," the immigration of mostly female caregivers from the so-called Third World to the First World. Leaving the nanny's story out of the frame perhaps LOOKS like what Bleger refers to as the creation of a self-directed self, mark of a successful analysis. But, as Hollander asserts, what it really does is reproduce a neoliberal entrepreneurial subject that, in projecting vulnerability outward, draws its ego boundaries around exclusion and devaluation of the nonwhite, lower-class other.

To me, this vignette very well exemplifies what Erikson called a "deal." And it is a deal on three levels: intrapsychic, interpersonal, and institutional/systemic (i.e., between the self and a psychoanalytic and social status quo). Normative unconscious processes of both therapist and patient, one might say, at first collude to reproduce egos safe in their feeling of belonging to the institutions of dominant culture, here, respectively, psychoanalysis and the corporate world. An ethic of adaptation. Hollander concludes that had she not seen what I am calling the cast-off and disavowed ghost of white neoliberalism, she would have left "intact the neoliberal split between the private individual and the social individual or citizen, a split that hinders the development of empathy and accountability" (p. 645; see also Layton, 2009 and Chapter 12, this volume). But she didn't leave the split intact – demonstrating that we have the power either to preserve white upper-class psychic equilibrium or to resist and enact an ethic of dis-illusionment. Indeed, this vignette clearly reveals that technical choices that focus on the individual as psychosocial, as embedded in history, are quite different from those that focus on the individual as separate from the social.

## Conclusion

Fromm (1970) argued that patients seek therapy because they have a vision of a better life, one of being rather than of having and using. The ethic of having and using, of course, has long been dominant in the U.S. It has historically been ideologically centered in The American Dream. In a *New York Times* op-ed, David Brooks (2017) cited de Tocqueville's 1830s commentary on white Americans as follows:

> They owe nothing to any man, they expect nothing from any man; they acquire the habit of always considering themselves as standing alone, and they are apt to imagine that their whole destiny is in their

own hands. Thus not only does democracy make every man forget his ancestors, but it hides his descendants and separates his contemporaries from him; it throws him back forever upon himself alone and threatens in the end to confine him entirely within the solitude of his own heart.

(cited on p. A23)

Belief in the American Dream is a classic example of an Eriksonian deal; the Dream has always thrived by disavowing the racism and classism on which it was built, on disavowed slavery and genocide. De Tocqueville's words reflect on the psychic toll paid by white patriarchal Americans who buy into the Dream. Confined in the solitude of his own heart. As Baldwin (1972/1998) put it more than 200 years later: ". . . I have always been struck, in America, by an emotional poverty so bottomless, and a terror of human life, of human touch, so deep, that virtually no American appears able to achieve any viable, organic connection between his public stance and his private life" (p. 385). Both men evoke the effect on whites of segregating themselves from situations that might evoke deserved shame.

The ghost of being demands that we look honestly at our history. It haunts the ethic of having and doing, a raced and classed ethic. In its current neoliberal version, the American Dream radically measures the worth of human beings in terms of productivity and economic success, a success its version of capitalism simultaneously keeps most people from being able to attain. Altman (2005) and Peltz (2005) coined the term, "the manic society," to describe the contemporary psychic effects of an ethic of having, using, doing, optimizing, of disavowing dependence, vulnerability, and need. The children of the white middle class exhaust themselves trying to attain the dream of having and using, and they appear in our offices with familiar symptoms. A white middle-class patient of mine once said that the message she got from her educated parents was "Yale or Jail," a BIG History message that well captures the connection between the white dream and its disavowed nightmare of mass incarceration, ghettos, and other forms of structural classed racism (Layton, 2016, and Chapter 14, this volume; Kita, 2019). Recall my patient's association to her Katrina dream: "I don't know why the people were black."

To heed the ghost's call for something-to-be-done, we need to demand change in our psychoanalytic institutions. We need to know the history of our profession and to recover from it the precious insights about group unconscious process that analysts like Bion and his followers have given us. We should demand courses that are psychosocial, not the ones that celebrate diversity, but the ones that look squarely at the psychic effects of the history of class, gender, sexuality, and race inequalities. Demand that white institutions reflect on their whiteness, that they invite and make financially possible the inclusion of people of color. And then listen to what people of color have to say. Demand technique courses that point up the differences between conceptualizing ourselves as sovereign individuals rather than as psychosocial historical beings, courses that reflect on the ways in which we often are called upon to treat social problems as if they are individual problems. I invite you to begin to imagine the techniques we would need truly to reach historical psychic depth (Layton, 2018, and Chapter 5, this volume). Heed Kim Leary's (2014) call for psychoanalytic training to include a community component and for us all to work at higher structural levels than the individual private practice level. White people need to get up close, get proximate (Stevenson, 2015), to be able truly to see the ongoing destructive psychosocial effects of white supremacy – and to begin to make reparation.

This historical moment offers a good chance for us and our profession to wake up. We've had such opportunities before, and we didn't go there. Indeed, if anyone in dominant psychoanalytic institutions had listened to Fromm and Fanon (1963) in the 1950s and 1960s, I'd probably not have to argue, these many years later, that psychic process is permeated by history and social circumstance. It is late, but hopefully not too late to see the ghost, not too late to reflect on the tension between unconscious processes that resist conformity, confront truth, lovingly seek repair, and unconscious processes that work to restore the destructive psychic equilibrium of the dominant. Not too late to turn away from the temptations of a psychoanalytic ethic of adaptation. Not too late to commit to a psychoanalytic ethic of dis-illusionment.

## Note

* Used with permission. Layton, L. (2019) Transgenerational hauntings: Toward a social psychoanalysis and an ethic of dis-illusionment. *Psychoanalytic Dialogues* 29(2): 105–121.

# References

Aarseth, H., Layton, L. and Nielsen, H.B. (2016) Conflicts in the habitus. The emotional work of becoming modern. *Sociological Review* 64(1): 148–165.

Abel-Hirsch, N. (2006) The perversion of pain, pleasure and thought: On the difference between "suffering" an experience and the construction of a thing to be used. In D. Nobus and L. Downing (eds.) *Perversion: Psychoanalytic Perspectives/Perspectives on Psychoanalysis*. London: Karnac, pp. 99–107.

Abraham, N. (1994) Notes on the phantom. In N. Abraham and M. Torok (eds.) *The Shell and the Kernel*, Chapter 9. Chicago, IL: University of Chicago Press, pp. 171–196.

Adams, C.J. (2014) The impact of neoliberalism on the psychological development of low-income black youth. *Psychoanalysis, Culture and Society* 19(1): 39–46.

Adorno, T. (1967) Sociology and psychology. *New Left Review* 46: 67–80.

Adorno, T. (1968) Sociology and psychology. *New Left Review* 47: 79–91.

Adorno, T., Frenkel-Brunswik, E., Levinson, D. and Sanford, R.N. (1950) *The Authoritarian Personality*. New York, NY: Harper.

Alexander, M. (2010) *The New Jim Crow: Mass Incarceration in the Age of Colorblindness*. New York, NY: The New Press.

Alford, C.F. (2013) Winnicott and trauma. *Psychoanalysis, Culture and Society* 18(3): 259–276.

Alford, C.F. (2014) Voting against one's interests: The hatred of big government. *Psychoanalysis, Culture and Society* 19(2): 203–208.

Allstate/National Journal Heartland Monitor Poll Topline. (2010, January 3–7). Retrieved from www.nationaljournal.com/img/topline100114.pdf, p. 8. Accessed January 16, 2010.

Althusser, L. (1971) Ideology and ideological state apparatuses (Notes towards an investigation). In L. Althusser (ed.) *Lenin and Philosophy and Other Essays*. Trans. B. Brewster. New York, NY and London: Monthly Review Press, pp. 127–186.

Altman, N. (1995) *The Analyst in the Inner City*. Hillsdale, NJ: The Analytic Press.

Altman, N. (2000) Black and white thinking: A psychoanalyst reconsiders race. *Psychoanalytic Dialogues* 10: 589–605.

Altman, N. (2003) How white people suffer from white racism. *Psychotherapy and Politics International* 1(2): 93–106.

Altman, N. (2005) Manic society: Toward the depressive position. *Psychoanalytic Dialogues* 15(3): 321–346.

Altman, N. (2006a) Is politics the last taboo in psychoanalysis? A roundtable discussion with Neil Altman, Jessica Benjamin, Theodore Jacobs, and Paul Wachtel. Amanda Geffner, moderator. In L. Layton, N.C. Hollander, and S. Gutwill (eds.) *Psychoanalysis, Class and Politics. Encounters in the Clinical Setting.* New York, NY: Routledge, pp. 166–224.

Altman, N. (2006b) Whiteness. *Psychoanalytic Quarterly* 75(1): 45–72.

Anderson, C. (2016) *White Rage. The Unspoken Truth of our Racial Divide.* New York, NY: Bloomsbury Publishing.

Anzaldúa, G. (1990) La conciencia de la mestiza: Towards a new consciousness. In G. Anzaldúa (ed.) *Making Face, Making Soul. Haciendo Caras.* San Francisco: Aunt Lute Books, pp. 377–389.

Apprey, M. (1993) The African-American experience: Transgenerational trauma and forced immigration. *Mind & Human Interaction* 4: 70–75.

Apprey, M. (2014) A pluperfect errand: A turbulent return to beginnings in the transgenerational transmission of destructive aggression. *Free Associations*, July, 66. Retrieved from http://freeassociations.org.uk. Accessed October 5, 2017.

Archangelo, A. (2010) Social exclusion, difficulties with learning and symbol formation: A Bionian approach. *Psychoanalysis, Culture and Society* 15: 315–327.

Archangelo, A. (2014) A psychosocial approach to neoliberalism, social exclusion and education. *Psychoanalysis, Culture and Society* 19(1): 29–38.

Armstrong, D. and Rustin, M. (eds.) (2015) *Social Defences Against Anxiety: Explorations in a Paradigm.* London: Karnac.

Aron, L. (1995) The internalized primal scene. *Psychoanalytic Dialogues* 5: 195–237.

Aron, L. (1996) *A Meeting of Minds. Mutuality in Psychoanalysis.* Hillsdale, NJ: The Analytic Press.

Aron, L. and Starr, K. (2013) *A Psychotherapy for the People.* New York, NY: Routledge.

Aron, L., Grand, S. and Slochower, J. (eds.) (2018) *De-Idealizing Relational Theory. A Critique From Within.* New York, NY: Routledge.

Aviram, R. (2009) *The Relational Origins of Prejudice.* New York, NY: Jason Aronson.

Bach, S. (1994) *The Language of Perversion and the Language of Love.* Northvale, NJ: Jason Aronson.

Bainbridge, C. and Yates, C. (2005) Cinematic symptoms of masculinity in transition: Memory, history and mythology in contemporary film. *Psychoanalysis, Culture & Society* 10(3): 299–318.

Balbus, I. (2004) The psychodynamics of racial reparations. *Psychoanalysis, Culture & Society* 9(2): 159–185.

Baldwin, J. (1955/1998) Stranger in the village (Notes of a native son). In T. Morrison (ed.) *Collected Essays*. New York, NY: Library of America, pp. 117–129.

Baldwin, J. (1972/1998) No name in the street. In T. Morrison (ed.) *Collected Essays*. New York, NY: Library of America, pp. 353–475.

Balint, M. (1968) *The Basic Fault*. Evanston, IL: Northwestern University Press.

Ball, S.J., Vincent, C., Kemp, S. and Pietikainen, S. (2004) Middle-class fractions, childcare and the 'relational' and 'normative' aspects of class practices. *Sociological Review* 52(4): 478–502.

Banfield, E. (1958) *The Moral Basis of a Backward Society*. New York, NY: Free Press.

Barglow, R. (2018) Why Freud matters. *Skeptic* 23(1): 53–59. Retrieved from https://pocketmags.com/skeptic-magazine/231/articles/327032/why-freud-matters. Accessed October 12, 2018.

Barthes, R. (1957/1972) *Mythologies*. Trans. A. Lavers. New York, NY: Hill & Wang.

Basch, M.F. (1983) The perception of reality and the disavowal of meaning. *Annual of Psychoanalysis* 11: 125–153.

Bass, A. (2000) *Difference and Disavowal: The Trauma of Eros*. Stanford, CA: Stanford University Press.

Bassin, D. (1996) Beyond the he and the she: Toward the reconciliation of masculinity and femininity in the postoedipal female mind. *Journal of the American Psychoanalytic Association* 44(Suppl.): 157–190.

Baudrillard, J. (1983) *Simulations*. Trans. P. Foss, P. Patton, and P. Beitchman. New York, NY: Semiotext(e).

Bauman, Z. (2001) *Community. Seeking Safety in an Insecure World*. Cambridge, UK: Blackwell.

Beck, U. (1999) *World Risk Society*. Cambridge, UK: Polity Press.

Beck, U. and Beck-Gernsheim, E. (2002) *Individualization. Institutionalized Individualism and its Social and Political Consequences*. London: Sage.

Beebe, B. (1985) Mother-infant mutual influence and precursors of self and object representations. In J. Masling (ed.) *Empirical Studies of Psychoanalytic Theories*, Vol. 2. Hillsdale, NJ: Lawrence Erlbaum.

Benjamin, J. (1977) The end of internalization: Adorno's social psychology. *Telos* 32: 42–64.

Benjamin, J. (1988) *The Bonds of Love*. New York, NY: Pantheon.

Benjamin, J. (1990) An outline of intersubjectivity: The development of recognition. *Psychoanalytic Psychology* 7(Suppl.): 33–46.

Benjamin, J. (1991) Father and daughter: Identification with difference – A contribution to gender heterodoxy. *Psychoanalytic Dialogues* 3(1): 277–299.

Benjamin, J. (1996) In defense of gender ambiguity. *Gender & Psychoanalysis* I: 27–43.

Benjamin, J. (1998) *Shadow of the Other: Intersubjectivity and Gender in Psycho-Analysis*. New York, NY: Routledge.

Benjamin, J. (2004) Beyond doer and done-to: An intersubjective view of thirdness. *Psychoanalytic Quarterly* LXIII(1): 5–46.

Benjamin, J. (2009) A relational psychoanalysis perspective on the necessity of acknowledging failure in order to restore the facilitating and containing features of the intersubjective relationship (the shared third). *International Journal of Psychoanalysis* 90: 441–450.

Benjamin, J. (2017) *Beyond Doer and Done-to: Recognition Theory, Intersubjectivity, and the Third*. New York, NY: Routledge.

Bennett, T., Savage, M., Silva, E., Warde, A., Gayo-Cal, M. and Wright, D. (2009) *Culture, Class, Distinction*. London: Routledge.

Bhabha, H.K. (1994) *The Location of Culture*. London: Routledge.

Binkley, S. (2009) The work of neoliberal governmentality: Temporality and ethical substance in the tale of two dads. *Foucault Studies* 6: 60–78.

Binkley, S. (2011a) Psychological life as enterprise: Social practice and the government of neo-liberal interiority. *History of the Human Sciences* 24(3): 83–102.

Binkley, S. (2011b) Happiness, positive psychology and the program of neoliberal governmentality. *Subjectivity* 4(4): 371–394.

Binkley, S. (2014) *Happiness as Enterprise: An Essay on Neoliberal Life*. Albany, NY: SUNY Press.

Bion, W.R. (1962a) *Learning from Experience*. Northvale, NJ: Jason Aronson.

Bion, W.R. (1962b) The psycho-analytic study of thinking. *The International Journal of Psychoanalysis* 43: 306–310.

Bion, W.R. (1970) *Attention and Interpretation*. London: Karnac.

Bion, W.R. (1984) Attacks on linking. In W.R. Bion (ed.) *Second Thoughts*. New York, NY: Jason Aronson, pp. 93–109.

Bleger, J. (1967) Psycho-analysis of the psycho-analytic frame. *International Journal of Psychoanalysis* 48: 511–519.

Bodnar, S. (2004) Remember where you come from: Dissociative process in multicultural individuals. *Psychoanalytic Dialogues* 14: 581–603.

Bolognini, S. (2004) *Psychoanalytic Empathy*. Trans. M. Garfield. London: Free Association Books.

Boltanski, L. and Chiapello, E. (2005) *The New Spirit of Capitalism*. London: Verso.

Bonovitz, C. (2005) Locating culture in the psychic field: Transference and countertransference as cultural products. *Contemporary Psychoanalysis* 41: 55–76.

Botticelli, S. (2006) Globalization, psychoanalysis, and the provision of care. *Studies in Gender and Sexuality* 7(1): 71–80.

Botticelli, S. (2007) Return of the repressed: Class in psychoanalytic process. In M. Suchet, A. Harris, and L. Aron (eds.) *Relational Psychoanalysis, Volume 3: New Voices*. New York, NY: Routledge, pp. 121–134.

Botticelli, S. (2012) Weak ties, slight claims: The psychotherapy relationship in an era of reduced expectations. *Contemporary Psychoanalysis* 48: 394–407.

Bouie, J. (2019) Undemocratic democracy. *New York Times Magazine*, August 18, pp. 50–57.

Boulanger, G. (2007) *Wounded by Reality: Understanding and Treating Adult Onset Trauma.* New York, NY: Routledge.

Bourdieu, P. (1984) *Distinction: A Social Critique of the Judgement of Taste.* Trans. R. Nice. Cambridge, MA: Harvard University Press.

Bourdieu, P. (1999) The contradictions of inheritance. In P. Bourdieu et al. (eds.) *The Weight of the World: Social Suffering in Contemporary Society.* Cambridge, UK: Polity Press, pp. 507–513.

Bromberg, P. (2001) *Standing in the Spaces.* New York, NY: Routledge.

Brooks, D. (2017) The GOP rejects conservatism. *New York Times*, June 27, p. A23.

Brown, W. (2004) Paper presented at Radcliffe Institute for Advanced Study conference on Cultural Citizenship. Varieties of Belonging, Cambridge, MA, February 20.

Brown, W. (2006) American nightmare: Neoliberalism, neoconservatism, and de-democratization. *Political Theory* 34: 690–714.

Brown, W. (2015) *Undoing the Demos: Neoliberalism's Stealth Revolution.* Cambridge, MA: Zone Books.

Brownstein, R. (2010a) Report on *Morning Joe. MSNBC*, January 15.

Brownstein, R. (2010b) *A Season of Discontent.* Retrieved from www.national journal/njmagazine/nj_20100106_9394.php. Accessed January 16, 2010.

Burack, C. (2006) *The Psychology of Political Strategy.* Paper presented at conference of the Association for the Psychoanalysis of Culture & Society, Rutgers University.

Burack, C. (2014) Keeping government out of my medicare and in her uterus: The paradox of small government conservatism. *Psychoanalysis, Culture & Society* 19(2): 190–195.

Butler, J. (1990) *Gender Trouble.* New York, NY: Routledge.

Butler, J. (1995) Melancholy gender – Refused identification. *Psychoanalytic Dialogues* 5: 165–180.

Butler, J. (2004) *Precarious Life: The Powers of Mourning and Violence.* London: Verso.

Carey, K. (2019) What's a degree like that worth, anyway? For the underprivileged, a lot. *New York Times*, March 16, p. A16.

Centeno, M.A. and Cohen, J.N. (2012) The arc of neoliberalism. *Annual Review of Sociology* 38: 317–340.

Chase, E. and Walker, R. (2012) The co-construction of shame in the context of poverty: Beyond a threat to the social bond. *Sociology* 47(4): 739–754.

Chasseguet-Smirgel, J. (1986) *Sexuality and Mind: The Role of the Father and the Mother in the Psyche.* New York, NY: New York University Press.

Chodorow, N.J. (1978) *The Reproduction of Mothering.* Berkeley, CA: University of California Press.

Clarke, S. (2003) *Social Theory, Psychoanalysis and Racism*. London: Palgrave Macmillan.

Coates, T. (2015) *Between the World and Me*. New York, NY: Spiegel and Grau.

Coen, S. (1998) Perverse defenses in neurotic patients. *Journal of the American Psychoanalytic Association* 46: 1169–1194.

Combahee River Collective (1977) *The Combahee River Collective Statement*. Retrieved from http://circuitous.org/scraps/combahee.html. Accessed January 9, 2018.

Cooper, A. and Lees, A. (2015) Spotlit: Defences against anxiety in contemporary human services organizations. In D. Armstrong and M. Rustin (eds.) *Social Defenses Against Anxiety*. London, UK: Karnac, pp. 239–255.

Cooper, S. (2000) *Objects of Hope*. New York, NY: Routledge.

Corbett, K. (2001a) Faggott = loser. *Studies in Gender and Sexuality* 2(1): 3–28.

Corbett, K. (2001b) Nontraditional family romance. *Psychoanalytic Quarterly* 70(3): 599–624.

Corpt, E.A. (2013) Peasant in the analyst's chair: Reflections, personal and otherwise, on class and the forming of an analytic identity. *International Journal of Psychoanalytic Self Psychology* 8: 52–69.

Crenshaw, K. (1989) Demarginalizing the intersection of race and sex: A black feminist critique of antidiscrimination doctrine, feminist theory and antiracist politics. *Chicago Legal Forum* 1, Article 8. Retrieved from https://chicagounbound.uchicago.edu/cgi/viewcontent.cgi?article=1052&context=uclf. Accessed July 7, 2019.

Cushman, P. (1990) Why the self is empty: Toward a historically situated psychology. *American Psychologist* 45: 599–611.

Cushman, P. (1991) Ideology obscured: Political uses of the self in Daniel Stern's infant. *American Psychologist* 46: 206–219.

Cushman, P. (1995) *Constructing the Self, Constructing America*. Reading, MA: Addison Wesley.

Cushman, P. (2000) White guilt, political activity, and the analyst: Commentary on paper by Neil Altman. *Psychoanalytic Dialogues* 10(4): 607–618.

Cushman, P. (2019) *Travels with the Self: Interpreting Psychology as Cultural History*. New York, NY: Routledge.

Dalal, F. (2001) Insides and outsides: A review of psychoanalytic renderings of difference, racism and prejudice. *Psychoanalytic Studies* 3(1): 43–66.

Dalal, F. (2002) *Race, Colour and the Process of Racialization: New Perspectives from Group Analysis, Psychoanalysis and Sociology*. Hove, England: Brunner-Routledge.

Danto, E. (2005) *Freud's Free Clinics – Psychoanalysis and Social Justice, 1918–1938*. New York, NY: Columbia University Press.

davenport, d. (1983) The pathology of racism: A conversation with third world wimmin. In C. Moraga and G. Anzaldua (eds.) *This Bridge Called My Back: Writings by Radical Women of Color*. New York, NY: Kitchen Table Press, pp. 85–90.

Davies, J.M. (2004) Whose bad objects are we anyway? Repetition and our elusive love affair with evil. *Psychoanalytic Dialogues* 14(6): 711–732.

Davies, J.M. and Frawley, M.G. (1994) *Treating the Adult Survivor of Childhood Sexual Abuse*. New York, NY: Basic Books.

Davoine, F. and Gaudillière, J-M. (2004) *History Beyond Trauma*. Trans. S. Fairfield. New York, NY: Other Press.

Dean, C. (2004) *The Fragility of Empathy After the Holocaust*. Ithaca, NY: Cornell University Press.

Debieux Rosa, M. and Mountian, I. (2013) Psychoanalytic listening to socially excluded young people. *Psychoanalysis, Culture & Society* 18(1): 1–16.

Demos, J. (1981) Oedipus and America: Historical perspectives on the reception of psychoanalysis in the United States. In R.J. Brugger (ed.) *Our Selves/Our Past: Psychological Approaches to American History*. Baltimore, MD: Johns Hopkins, pp. 292–306.

Derrida, J. (1976) *Of Grammatology*. Trans. G. Spivak. Baltimore, MD: Johns Hopkins University Press.

Derrida, J. (1978) *Writing and Difference*. Trans. A. Bass. Chicago, IL: University of Chicago Press.

de Tocqueville, A. (2000/1835) *Democracy in America*. Ed. J.P. Mayer and trans. G. Lawrence. New York, NY: Perennial Classics.

DiAngelo, R. (2018) *White Fragility*. Boston, MA: Beacon Press.

Dimen, M. (1991) Deconstructing difference: Gender, splitting, and transitional space. *Psychoanalytic Dialogues* 1: 335–352.

Dimen, M. (1994) Money, love, and hate: Contradiction and paradox in psychoanalysis. *Psychoanalytic Dialogues* 4(1): 69–100.

Dimen, M. (2003) *Sexuality, Intimacy, Power*. Hillsdale, NJ: The Analytic Press.

Dimen, M. (ed.) (2011) *With Culture in Mind*. New York, NY: Routledge.

Dinnerstein, D. (1976) *The Mermaid and the Minotaur*. New York, NY: Harper & Row.

Domenici, T. and Lesser, R.C. (eds.) (1995) *Disorienting Sexuality*. New York, NY: Routledge.

du Gay, P. (2004) Against 'Enterprise' (but not against 'enterprise', for that would make no sense). *Organization* 11: 37–57.

du Plessis, M. (1996) Blatantly bisexual; or, unthinking queer theory. In D.E. Hall and M. Pramaggiore (eds.) *RePresenting Bisexualities*. New York, NY: New York University Press, pp. 19–54.

Dunbar-Ortiz, R. (2014) *An Indigenous Peoples' History of the United States*. Boston, MA: Beacon Press.

Eadie, J. (1996) Being who we are (and anyone else we want to be). In S. Rose, C. Stevens et al. (eds.) *Bisexual Horizons*. London: Lawrence & Wishart, pp. 16–20.

Eadie, J. (1997) Living in the past: Savage nights, bisexual times. *Journal of Gay, Lesbian, and Bisexual Identity* 2: 7–26.

Ehrenreich, B. (1989) *Fear of Falling: The Inner Life of the Middle Class*. New York, NY: Pantheon.

Ehrenreich, B. (2001) *Nickel and Dimed.* New York, NY: Henry Holt.

Ehrenreich, B. and Hochschild, A.R. (eds.) (2002) *Global Woman.* New York, NY: Metropolitan Books.

Elias, N. (1991) *The Symbol Theory.* London: Sage.

Elise, D. (1997) Primary femininity, bisexuality, and the female ego ideal: A reexamination of female developmental theory. *Psychoanalytic Quarterly* LXVI: 489–517.

Elise, D. (1998) Gender repertoire: Body, mind, and bisexuality. *Psychoanalytic Dialogues* 8: 353–371.

Elise, D. (2000) Woman and desire: Why women may not want to want. *Studies in Gender and Sexuality* 1(2): 125–145.

Eng, D.L. and Han, S. (2002) A dialogue on racial melancholia. In S. Fairfield, L. Layton, and C. Stack (eds.) *Bringing the Plague. Toward a Postmodern Psychoanalysis.* New York, NY: Other Press, pp. 233–267.

Engel, S. (1980) Femininity as tragedy: Re-examining the new narcissism. *Socialist Review* 53: 77–104.

Erikson, E.H. (1950) *Childhood and Society.* New York, NY: W.W. Norton.

Erikson, E.H. (1959/1980) *Identity and the Life Cycle.* New York, NY: W.W. Norton.

Erikson, E.H. (1976) Psychoanalysis and ethics – Avowed and unavowed. *International Review of Psycho-Analysis* 3: 409–414.

Faimberg, H. (2005) *The Telescoping of Generations.* New York, NY: Routledge.

Fairbairn, W.R.D. (1954) *An Object-Relations Theory of the Personality.* New York, NY: Basic Books.

Fairfield, S., Layton, L. and Stack, C. (eds.) (2002) *Bringing the Plague: Toward a Postmodern Psychoanalysis.* New York, NY: Other Press.

Fanon, F. (1963) *The Wretched of the Earth.* New York, NY: Grove Press.

Fanon, F. (1967) *Black Skin, White Masks.* New York, NY: Grove Press.

Fast, I. (1984) *Gender Identity: A Differentiation Model.* Hillsdale, NJ: Analytic Press.

Fast, I. (1993) Aspects of early gender development: A psychodynamic perspective. In A.E. Beall and R.J. Sternberg (eds.) *The Psychology of Gender.* New York, NY: Guilford Press, pp. 173–193.

Fenichel, O. (1953) The drive to amass wealth. In *The Collected Papers of Otto Fenichel. Second Series.* New York, NY: W.W. Norton, pp. 89–108.

Ferenczi, S. (1949) Confusion of the tongues between the adult and the child – (The language of tenderness and of passion). *International Journal of Psycho-Analysis* 30: 225–230.

Ferreday, D. and Kuntsman, A. (2011) Haunted futurities. *Borderlands* 10(2). Retrieved from www.borderlands.net.au.

Fincher, D. (dir.) (1999) *Fight Club*, VHS. Retrieved from www.script-o-rama.com/movie_scripts/f/fight-club-script-transcript-fincher.html. Accessed July 4, 2010.

Fisher, M. and Gilbert, J. (2013) Capitalist realism and neoliberal hegemony: A dialogue. *New Formations* 80/81: 89–101.

Fletchman Smith, B. (2011) *Transcending the Legacies of Slavery: A Psychoanalytic View*. London: Karnac.

Folayan, S. (dir.) (2017) *Whose Streets?* [Film] USA: Magnolia Pictures.

Fors, M. (2018) *A Grammar of Power in Psychotherapy*. Washington, DC: APA Books.

Foucault, M. (1978) *Discipline and Punish*. Trans. A. Sheridan. New York, NY: Pantheon.

Foucault, M. (1980) *The History of Sexuality*, Vol. 1. Trans. R. Hurley. New York, NY: Vintage.

Foucault, M. (2008) *The Birth of Biopolitics. Lectures at the Collège de France 1978–1979*. Senellart, M. (ed.), Burchell, G. (trans.). New York, NY: Palgrave Macmillan.

Frank, T. (2004) *What's the Matter with Kansas? How Conservatives Won the Heart of America*. New York, NY: Metropolitan Books.

Franken, A. (2003) *Lies: And the Lying Liars Who Tell Them*. New York, NY: Dutton.

Fraser, N. (2017) From progressive neoliberalism to Trump--and beyond. *American Affairs* 1(4). Retrieved from https://americanaffairsjournal.org/2017/11/progressive-neoliberalism trump-beyond/#.WiksQ67LIyM.email.

Freud, S. (1900) The interpretation of dreams. *SE* 5. London: Hogarth Press.

Freud, S. (1905) Fragment of an analysis of a case of hysteria. *SE* 7: 1–122.

Freud, S. (1908/1959) 'Civilized' sexual morality and modern nervous illness. In E. Jones (ed.) *Sigmund Freud. Collected Papers*, Vol. 2. New York, NY: Basic Books, pp. 76–99.

Freud, S. (1913/1955) *Totem and Taboo*. In J. Strachey (ed.) *SE* 13. London: Hogarth Press, pp. 1–161.

Freud, S. (1914/1959) Recollection, repetition, and working through. In E. Jones (ed.) *Sigmund Freud. Collected Papers*, Vol. 2. New York, NY: Basic Books, pp. 366–376.

Freud, S. (1915b) Thoughts for the times on war and death. *SE* 14: 273–300.

Freud, S. (1915a/1964) Repression. In J. Strachey (ed.) *SE* 14. London: Hogarth Press, pp. 143–158.

Freud, S. (1922) *Group Psychology and the Analysis of the Ego*. Strachey, J. (ed.). *SE* 18: 65–141. London, UK: Hogarth Press.

Freud, S. (1927a) Fetishism. *SE* 21: 147–158.

Freud, S. (1927b) The future of an illusion. *SE* 21: 1–56.

Freud, S. (1930) Civilization and its discontents. *SE* 21: 57–146.

Freud, S. (1933) Femininity. *SE* 22: 112–135.

Freud, S. (1937) Analysis terminable and interminable. *SE* 23: 209–253.

Freud, S. (1939) *Moses and Monotheism*. New York, NY: Vintage Books.

Frie, R. (2017) History flows through us: Psychoanalysis and historical understanding. *Psychoanalysis, Self, and Context* 12(3): 221–229.

Friedman, S.S. (1995) Beyond white and other: Relationality and narratives of race in feminist discourse. *Signs* 21: 1–49.

Fromm, E. (1941) *Escape from Freedom*. New York, NY: Holt, Rinehart and Winston.

Fromm, E. (1947) *Man for Himself: Towards a Psychology of Ethics*. New York, NY: Rinehart.

Fromm, E. (1962) *Beyond the Chains of Illusion*. New York, NY: Simon & Schuster.

Fromm, E. (1970) *The Crisis of Psychoanalysis*. New York, NY: Holt, Rinehart, Winston.

Fromm, E. (1984) *The Working Class in Weimar Germany: A Psychological and Sociological Study*. Oxford, UK: Berg Publishers.

Gaertner, S.L. and Dovidio, J.F. (2005) Understanding and addressing contemporary racism: From aversive racism to the common ingroup identity model. *Journal of Social Issues* 61(3): 615–639.

Garber, M. (1995) *Vice Versa: Bisexuality and the Eroticism of Everyday Life*. New York, NY: Simon and Schuster.

Gaudillière, J.-M. (2012) Madness as a form of research targeting the historical scotomas in the life and mind of the analyst. *Psychoanalysis, Culture & Society* 17(4): 348–355.

Gentile, K. (2013) Bearing the cultural in order to engage in a process of witnessing. *Psychoanalytic Psychology* 30(3): 456–470.

Gentile, K. (2017) Collectively creating conditions for emergence. In S. Grand and J. Salberg (eds.) *Wounds of History: Repair and Resilience in the Transgenerational Transmission of Trauma*. New York, NY: Routledge, pp. 169–188.

Gentile, K. (ed.) (2016) *The Business of Being Made*. New York, NY: Routledge.

George, S. (1993) *Women and Bisexuality*. London: Scarlet Press.

George, S. (2001) Trauma and the conservation of African-American racial identity. *Journal for the Psychoanalysis of Culture & Society* 6(1): 58–72.

George, S. (2016) *Trauma and Race: A Lacanian Study of African American Racial Identity*. Waco, TX: Baylor University Press.

Georgis, D. (2007) The perils of belonging and cosmopolitan optimism: An affective reading of the Israeli/Palestinian conflict. *Psychoanalysis, Culture & Society* 12(3): 242–259.

Gerson, S. (1996) Neutrality, resistance, and self-disclosure in an intersubjective psychoanalysis. *Psychoanalytic Dialogues* 6: 623–645.

Gerson, S. (2004) The relational unconscious: A core element of intersubjectivity, thirdness, and clinical process. *Psychoanalytic Quarterly* 73: 63–98.

Giddens, A. (1991) *Modernity and Self-Identity: Self and Society in the Late Modern Age*. Stanford, CA: Stanford University Press.

Gilbert, J. (2013) What kind of thing is 'neoliberalism?' *New Formations* 80/81: 7–22.

Gilroy, P. (1993) *The Black Atlantic*. Cambridge, MA: Harvard University Press.

Glynos, J. (2008) Ideological fantasy at work. *Journal of Political Ideologies* 13(3): 275–296.

Glynos, J. (2014a) Neoliberalism, markets, fantasy: The case of health and social care. *Psychoanalysis, Culture & Society* 19(1): 5–12.

Glynos, J. (2014b) Hating government and voting against one's interests: Self-transgression, enjoyment, critique. *Psychoanalysis, Culture & Society* 19(1): 5–12.

Gobodo-Madikizela, P. (2016) Psychological repair: The intersubjective dialogue of remorse and forgiveness in the aftermath of gross human rights violations. *Journal of the American Psychological Association* 63(6): 1085–1123.

Goldberg, A. (1995) *The Problem of Perversion.* New Haven, CT: Yale University Press.

Goldner, V. (1991) Toward a critical relational theory of gender. *Psychoanalytic Dialogues* 1(3): 249–272.

Gooding-Williams, R. (ed.) (1993) *Reading Rodney King/Reading Urban Uprising.* New York, NY: Routledge.

Goodman, D. (2015) The McDonaldization of psychotherapy: Processed foods, processed therapies, and economic class. *Theory and Psychology* 26(1): 77–95.

Gordon, A.F. (1997) *Ghostly Matters: Haunting and the Sociological Imagination.* Minneapolis, MN: University of Minnesota Press.

Gordon, A.F. (2011) Some thoughts on haunting and futurity. *Borderlands* 10(2). Retrieved from www.borderlands.net.au. Accessed August 1, 2017.

Gordon, L.N. (2015) *From Power to Prejudice: The Rise of Racial Individualism in Mid-Century America.* Chicago, IL: University of Chicago Press.

Gramsci, A. (1971) *Selections from the Prison Notebooks.* Q. Hoare and G.N. Smith (eds.). New York, NY: International Publishers.

Grand, S. (2000) *The Reproduction of Evil.* Hillsdale, NJ: The Analytic Press.

Grand, S. (2007) Maternal surveillance: Disrupting the rhetoric of war. *Psychoanalysis, Culture & Society* 12(4): 305–322.

Grand, S. (2009) *The Hero in the Mirror: From Fear to Fortitude.* New York, NY: Routledge.

Grand, S. (2013) God at an impasse: Devotion, social justice, and the psychoanalytic subject. *Psychoanalytic Dialogues* 23: 449–463.

Grand, S. (2014) Skin memories: On race, love and loss. *Psychoanalysis, Culture & Society* 19(3): 232–249. Reprinted in Grand, S. and Salberg, J. (eds.) (2017) *Trans-generational Trauma and the Other.* New York, NY: Routledge, pp. 38–58.

Grand, S. (2018) White shame & the native American genocide. *Contemporary Psychoanalysis* 54(1): 84–102.

Grand, S. and Salberg, J. (eds.) (2017) *Trans-generational Trauma and the Other: Dialogues Across History and Difference.* New York, NY: Routledge.

Grossman, L. (1993) The perverse attitude toward reality. *Psychoanalytic Quarterly* 62: 422–436.

Gu, M.D. (2006) The filial piety complex: Variations on the Oedipus theme in Chinese literature and culture. *Psychoanalytic Quarterly* 75(1): 163–195.

Gump, J. (2000) A white therapist, an African American patient – Shame in the therapeutic dyad: Commentary on paper by Neil Altman. *Psychoanalytic Dialogues* 10(4): 619–632.

Gump, J. (2010) Reality matters: The shadow of trauma on African American subjectivity. *Psychoanalytic Psychology* 27: 42–54.

Guralnik, O. and Simeon, D. (2010) Depersonalization: Standing in the spaces between recognition and interpellation. *Psychoanalytic Dialogues* 20: 400–416.

Gutwill, S. and Hollander, N.C. (2006) Class and splitting in the clinical setting: The ideological dance in the transference and countertransference. In L. Layton, N.C. Hollander, and S. Gutwill (eds.) *Psychoanalysis, Class and Politics*. New York, NY: Routledge, pp. 92–106.

Haaken, J. (1998) *Pillar of Salt: Gender, Memory, and the Perils of Looking Back*. New Brunswick, NJ: Rutgers.

Habermas, J. (1971) *Knowledge and Human Interests*. Boston, MA: Beacon Press.

Hacker, J.S. and Pierson, P. (2010) *Winner-Take-All Politics*. New York, NY: Simon and Schuster.

Hall, D.E. and Pramaggiore, M. (eds.) (1996) *RePresenting Bisexualities: Subjects and Cultures of Fluid Desire*. New York, NY and London: New York University Press.

Hall, S. (1980) Encoding/decoding. In S. Hall, D. Hobson, A. Lowe, and P. Willis (eds.) *Culture, Media, Language*: Working Papers in Cultural Studies, 1972–79. London: Hutchinson, pp. 128–138.

Hall, S. (1982) The rediscovery of "ideology": Return of the repressed in media studies. In M. Gurevitch, T. Bennett, J. Curran, and J. Woollacott (eds.) *Culture, Society and the Media*. London: Methuen, pp. 56–90.

Hall, S., Massey, D. and Rustin, M. (eds.) *After Neoliberalism? The Kilburn Manifesto*. Retrieved from www.lwbooks.co.uk/journals/soundings/manifesto.html. Accessed January 1, 2014.

Hamann, T. (2009) Neoliberalism, governmentality, and ethics. *Foucault Studies* 6: 37–59.

Harris, A. (1991) Gender as contradiction. *Psychoanalytic Dialogues* 1: 197–220.

Harris, A. (2005) *Gender as Soft Assembly*. Hillsdale, NJ: The Analytic Press.

Harris, A. (2011) The relational tradition: Landscape and canon. *JAPA* 59: 701–735.

Harris, A. (2012) The house of difference, or white silence. *Studies in Gender & Sexuality* 13: 197–216.

Hartman, S. (2005) Class unconscious: From dialectical materialism to relational material. *Psychoanalysis, Culture & Society* 10(2): 121–137.

Harvey, D. (2005) *A Brief History of Neoliberalism*. Oxford: Oxford University Press.

Hassinger, J. (2014) Twenty-first century living color: Racialized enactment in psychoanalysis. *Psychoanalysis, Culture & Society* 19(4): 337–359.

Hellman, T. (2017) *Race-Talk: White Identified Dyads in Dialogue*. Paper presented at Division 39, APA, Spring Meeting, New York City, April 27.

Herman, J.L. (1992) *Trauma and Recovery*. New York, NY: Basic Books.

Hey, V. (2005) The contrasting social logics of sociality and survival: Cultures of classed be/longing in late modernity. *Sociology* 39(5): 855–872.

Hirsch, I. (1998) Further thoughts about interpersonal and relational perspectives. Reply to Jay Frankel. *Contemporary Psychoanalysis* 34(4): 501–538.

Hirsch, I. (2008) *Coasting in the Countertransference*. New York, NY: Routledge.

Hochschild, A.R. and Machung, A. (1989) *The Second Shift: Working Parents and the Revolution at Home*. New York, NY: Penguin.

Hoffman, E. (1989) *Lost in Translation: A Life in a New Language*. New York, NY: Penguin.

Hoffman, I.Z. (1998) *Ritual and Spontaneity in the Psychoanalytic Process*. Hillsdale, NJ: The Analytic Press.

Hoffman, I.Z. (2005) Standard dominance versus creation of interludes of power in the psychoanalytic situation. Discussion of case presentation by Joseph Newirth. *Psychoanalytic Inquiry* 25: 328–341.

Hoffman, I.Z. (2009) Therapeutic passion in the countertransference. *Psychoanalytic Dialogues* 19: 617–637.

Hoggett, P. (2000) *Emotional Life and the Politics of Welfare*. London: Palgrave Macmillan.

Hoggett, P. (2006) Pity, compassion, solidarity. In S. Clarke, P. Hoggett, and S. Thompson (eds.) *Emotion, Politics and Society*. Houndmills, Basingstoke: Palgrave Macmillan, pp. 145–161.

Hoggett, P. (2013) Governance and social anxieties. *Organisational & Social Dynamics* 13(1): 69–78.

Holland, E. (1986) On narcissism from Baudelaire to Sartre: Ego-psychology and literary history. In L. Layton and B. Schapiro (eds.) *Narcissism and the Text: Studies in Literature and the Psychology of Self*. New York, NY: New York University Press, pp. 149–169.

Hollander, N.C. (2017) Who is the sufferer and what is being suffered? Subjectivity in times of social malaise. *Psychoanalytic Dialogues* 27(6): 635–650.

Hollander, N.C. and Gutwill, S. (2006) Despair and hope in a culture of denial. In L. Layton, N.C. Hollander, and S. Gutwill (eds.) *Psychoanalysis, Class and Politics: Encounters in the Clinical Setting*. New York, NY: Routledge, pp. 81–91.

Hollway, W. (2006) *The Capacity to Care*. New York, NY: Routledge.

Hollway, W., Venn, C., Walkerdine, V., Henriques, J. and Urwin, C. (1984) *Changing the Subject: Psychology, Social Regulation, and Subjectivity*. London: Routledge.

Holmes, D.E. (2006) The wrecking effects of race and social class on self and success. *Psychoanalytic Quarterly* 75(1): 215–236.

Holmes, D.E. (2016) Culturally imposed trauma: The sleeping dog has awakened: Will psychoanalysis take heed? *Psychoanalytic Dialogues* 26(6): 641–654.

Hopper, E. (2003) *The Social Unconscious*. London: Jessica Kingsley.

Horkheimer, M. and Adorno, T.W. (1944/1972) *Dialectic of Enlightenment*. New York, NY: Herder and Herder.

Hwang, D.H. (1989) *M. Butterfly*. New York, NY: Plume.

Illouz, E. (2012) *Why Love Hurts*. Malden, MA: Polity Press.

Irigaray, L. (1985) The blind spot of an old dream of symmetry. In L. Irigaray (ed.) and G. Gill (trans.) *Speculum of the Other Woman*. Ithaca, NY: Cornell University Press, pp. 13–129.

Jacobs, L.M. (2014) Learning to love white shame and guilt: Skills for working as a white therapist in a racially divided country. *International Journal of Psychoanalytic Self Psychology* 9(4): 297–312.

Jacoby, R. (1983) *The Repression of Psychoanalysis*. New York, NY: Basic Books.

Jameson, F. (1979) Reification and utopia in mass culture. *Social Text* 1: 130–148.

Jimenez, L. and Walkerdine, V. (2012) Shameful work – A psychosocial study of father-son relations, young male unemployment, and femininity in an ex-steel community. *Psychoanalysis, Culture & Society* 17: 278–295.

Jones, A. and Obourn, M. (2014) Object fear: The national dissociation of race and racism in the era of Obama. *Psychoanalysis, Culture & Society* 19(4): 392–412.

Kaftal, E. (1991) On intimacy between men. *Psychoanalytic Dialogues* 1: 305–328.

Kelley, R.D.G. (2017) What did Cedric Robinson mean by racial capitalism? *Boston Review*, January 12. Retrieved from https://bostonreview.net/race/robin-d-g-kelley-what-did-cedric-robinson-mean-racial-capitalism.

Kernberg, O. (1975) *Borderline Conditions and Pathological Narcissism*. New York, NY: Jason Aronson.

Kirsner, D. (2000) *Unfree Associations*. London: Process Press.

Kita, E. (2019) "They hate me now, but where was everyone when I needed them?": Mass incarceration, projective identification, and social work praxis. *Psychoanalytic Social Work* 26(1): 25–49.

Klein, F. (1993) *The Bisexual Option*, 2nd Edition. London: Routledge.

Klein, M. (1946) Notes on some schizoid mechanisms. *International Journal of Psycho-Analysis* 27: 99–110.

Klein, N. (2007) *The Shock Doctrine: The Rise of Disaster Capitalism*. New York, NY: Metropolitan Books.

Kohut, H. (1971) *The Analysis of the Self: A Systematic Approach to the Psychoanalytic Treatment of Narcissistic Personality Disorder*. New York, NY: International Universities Press.

Kohut, H. (1977) *The Restoration of the Self*. New York, NY: International Universities Press.

Kovel, J. (1970) *White Racism – A Psychohistory*. London: Free Association Books.

Kovel, J. (1980) Narcissism and the family. *Telos* 44: 88–100.

Kovel, J. (1988) *The Radical Spirit: Essays on Psychoanalysis and Society*. London: Free Association.

Krisel, J. (2012) Grover. *Portlandia, Season 2, Episode 4*. Aired January 27. Retrieved from www.youtube.com/watch?v=qjn7c7Szc-8. Accessed December 20, 2013.

Krugman, P. (2002) For richer. *New York Times Magazine*, October 20. Retrieved from www.lexisnexis.com. Accessed September 8, 2007.

Krugman, P. (2019) Don't blame robots for low wages. *New York Times*, March 15, p. A31.

Kubie, L.S. (2011; orig. 1974) The drive to become both sexes. *Psychoanalytic Quarterly* 80(2): 369–440.

Lacan, J. (1977) *Ecrits: A Selection*. Trans. A. Sheridan. London: Tavistock.

Lacan, J. (1998) *The Four Fundamental Concepts of Psychoanalysis*. New York, NY: W.W. Norton.

Laclau, E. and Mouffe, C. (1985) *Hegemony and Socialist Strategy: Towards a Radical Democratic Politics*. London: Verso.

Lamont, M. (2000) *The Dignity of Working Men*. Cambridge, MA: Harvard University Press.

Lareau, A. (2003) *Unequal Childhoods: Class, Race, and Family Life*. Berkeley, CA: University of California Press.

Lasch, C. (1977) *Haven in a Heartless World: The Family Besieged*. New York, NY: Basic Books.

Lasch, C. (1979) *The Culture of Narcissism*. New York, NY: W.W. Norton.

Lasch, C. (1991) *The True and Only Heaven: Progress and Its Critics*. New York, NY: W.W. Norton.

Lawler, S. (2005a) Introduction: Class, culture and identity. *Sociology* 39(5): 797–806.

Lawler, S. (2005b) Disgusted subjects: The making of middle-class identities. *Sociological Review* 3(3): 429–446.

Lawrence, D.H. (2007; orig. 1926) The Rocking-Horse Winner. In *The Complete Short Stories*. Pickering, UK: Blackthorn Press, pp. 530–540.

Layton, L. (1986) Narcissism and history: Flaubert's *Sentimental Education*. In L. Layton and B. Schapiro (eds.) *Narcissism and the Text: Studies in Literature and the Psychology of Self*. New York, NY: New York University Press, pp. 170–191.

Layton, L. (1988) *An Empirical Analysis of the Self and Object Love: A Test of Kohut's Conception of the Self*. Ph.D. Thesis, UMI Dissertation Information Service, Ann Arbor, MI.

Layton, L. (1990) A deconstruction of Kohut's concept of the self. *Contemporary Psychoanalysis* 26(3): 420–429.

Layton, L. (1998/2004) *Who's That Girl? Who's That Boy? Clinical Practice Meets Postmodern Gender Theory*. New York, NY: Routledge.

Layton, L. (2000) *Maternally Speaking: Mothers, Daughters, and the Talking Cure*. Paper presented at Division 39 meeting, San Francisco, April 7. Revised version published in Bueskens, P. (ed.) (2014) *Mothering & Psychoanalysis*. Bradford, ON: Demeter Press, pp. 161–176.

Layton, L. (2002) Cultural hierarchies, splitting, and the heterosexist unconscious. In S. Fairfield, L. Layton, and C. Stack (eds.) *Bringing the Plague: Toward a Postmodern Psychoanalysis*. New York, NY: Other Press, pp. 195–223.

Layton, L. (2004a) Relational no more: Defensive autonomy in middle-class women. In J.A. Winer, J.W. Anderson, and C.C. Kieffer (eds.) *The Annual of Psychoanalysis 32, Psychoanalysis and Women*. Hillsdale, NJ: The Analytic Press, pp. 29–42.

Layton, L. (2004b) Working nine to nine: The new women of prime time. *Studies in Gender and Sexuality* 5: 351–369.

Layton, L. (2004c/2006) That place gives me the heebie jeebies. *International Journal of Critical Psychology* 10: 36–50. Reprinted in Layton, L., Hollander, N.C. and Gutwill, S. (eds.) *Psychoanalysis, Class and Politics: Encounters in the Clinical Setting*. New York, NY: Routledge, pp. 51–64.

Layton, L. (2004d) A fork in the royal road: On defining the unconscious and its stakes for social theory. *Psychoanalysis, Culture & Society* 9(1): 33–51.

Layton, L. (2005) Notes toward a non-conformist clinical practice: Response to Philip Cushman's "Between arrogance and a dead-end". *Contemporary Psychoanalysis* 41(3): 419–429.

Layton, L. (2006a) Racial identities, racial enactments, and normative unconscious processes. *Psychoanalytic Quarterly* 75: 237–269.

Layton, L. (2006b) Attacks on linking: The unconscious pull to dissociate individuals from their social context. In L. Layton, N.C. Hollander, and S. Gutwill (eds.) *Psychoanalysis, Class and Politics: Encounters in the Clinical Setting*. New York, NY: Routledge, pp. 107–117.

Layton, L. (2006c) Retaliatory discourse: The politics of attack and withdrawal. *International Journal of Applied Psychoanalytic Studies* 3(2): 143–155.

Layton, L. (2008) Relational thinking: From culture to couch and couch to culture. In S. Clarke, H. Hahn, and P. Hoggett (eds.) *Object Relations and Social Relations*. London: Karnac, pp. 1–24.

Layton, L. (2009) Who's responsible? Our mutual implication in each other's suffering. *Psychoanalytic Dialogues* 19(2): 105–120.

Layton, L. (2010) Irrational exuberance: Neoliberalism and the perversion of truth. *Subjectivity* 3(3): 303–322.

Layton, L. (2011a) On the irreconcilable in psychic life: The role of culture in the drive to become both sexes. *Psychoanalytic Quarterly* LXXX(2): 461–474.

Layton, L. (2011b) Something to do with a girl named Marla Singer: Capitalism, narcissism, and therapeutic discourse in David Fincher's *Fight Club*. *Free Associations* 62: 112–134. Reprinted and updated in Sheils, B. and Walsh, J. (2017) *Narcissism, Melancholia and the Subject of Community*. Cham, Switzerland: Palgrave Macmillan, pp. 91–118.

Layton, L. (2013a) Normative unconscious processes. In T. Teo (ed.) *Encyclopedia of Critical Psychology*. Retrieved from www.springerreference.com/docs/html/chapterdbid/307088.html.

Layton, L. (2013b) Dialectical constructivism in historical context: Expertise and the subject of late modernity. *Psychoanalytic Dialogues* 23(3): 271–286.

Layton, L. (2013c) Psychoanalysis and politics: Historicising subjectivity. *Mens Sana Monographs* 11(1): 68–81.

Layton, L. (2014a) Grandiosity, neoliberalism, and neoconservatism. *Psychoanalytic Inquiry* 34(5): 463–474.

Layton, L. (2014b) Some psychic effects of neoliberalism: Narcissism, disavowal, perversion. *Psychoanalysis, Culture & Society* 19(2): 161–178.

Layton, L. (2015) *Neoliberalism and Its Psychic Effects*. Keynote presentation at Reflective Spaces/Material Places conference, San Francisco, September 12.

Layton, L. (2016) Yale or jail: Class struggles in neoliberal times. In D.M. Goodman and E.R. Severson (eds.) *The Ethical Turn*. New York, NY: Routledge, pp. 75–93.

Layton, L. (2017) Racialized enactments and normative unconscious processes: Where haunted identities meet. In J. Salberg and S. Grand (eds.) *Transgenerational Trauma and the Other*. New York, NY: Routledge, pp. 144–164.

Layton, L. (2018) Relational theory in socio-historical context: Implications for technique. In L. Aron, S. Grand, and J. Slochower (eds.) *De-Idealizing Relational Theory*. New York, NY: Routledge, pp. 209–234.

Layton, L. and Bertone, K.L. (1998) What's disclosed in self-disclosures? Gender, sexuality, and the analyst's subjectivity: Commentary on paper by Samuel Gerson. *Psychoanalytic Dialogues* 8(5): 731–739.

Layton, L., Hollander, N.C. and Gutwill, S. (eds.) (2006) *Psychoanalysis, Class and Politics. Encounters in the Clinical Setting*. New York, NY: Routledge.

Layton, L. and Schapiro, B. (eds.) (1986) *Narcissism and the Text: Studies in Literature and the Psychology of Self*. New York, NY: New York University Press.

Leary, K. (1995) "Interpreting in the dark": Race and ethnicity in psychoanalytic psychotherapy. *Psychoanalytic Psychology* 12(1): 127–140.

Leary, K. (1997a) Race, self-disclosure, and "forbidden talk": Race and ethnicity in contemporary clinical practice. *Psychoanalytic Quarterly* 66: 163–189.

Leary, K. (1997b) Race in psychoanalytic space. *Gender & Psychoanalysis* 2: 157–172.

Leary, K. (2000) Racial enactments in dynamic treatment. *Psychoanalytic Dialogues* 10: 639–653.

Leary, K. (2003) *How Race Is Lived in the Consulting Room*. Paper presented to Massachusetts Association for Psychoanalytic Psychology, Boston, MA, October 29.

Leary, K. (2012) Race as an adaptive challenge: Working with diversity in the clinical consulting room. *Psychoanalytic Psychology* 29: 279–291.

Leary, K. (2014, April 25) *On the Arts of Conflict and Confligere (Striking together)*. Keynote address at the Spring Meeting of Division 39, New York, NY.

Lesser, R.C. (2002) Discussion of "A Dialogue on Racial Melancholia". In S. Fairfield, L. Layton, and C. Stack (eds.) *Bringing the Plague: Toward a Postmodern Psychoanalysis*. New York, NY: Other Press, pp. 269–278.

Lesser, R.C. (2014) Notes on neoliberalisms and psychoanalysis. *Psychoanalysis, Culture & Society* 19(1): 13–18.

Levenson, E. (1972/2005) *The Fallacy of Understanding*. Hillsdale, NJ: The Analytic Press.

Levenson, E. (1983/2005) *The Ambiguity of Change*. Hillsdale, NJ: The Analytic Press.

Levin, M. (dir.) (2000) *Twilight: Los Angeles*. Screenplay by Anna Deavere Smith. PBS Pictures.

Levine-Rasky, C. (2011) Intersectionality theory applied to whiteness and middle-classness. *Social Identities* 17(2): 239–253.

Levinson, B. (dir.) (1994) *Disclosure*, VHS. Warner Brothers.

Lewis, G. (1996) Welfare settlements and racialising practices. *Soundings* 4: 109–119.

Lipsitz, G. (1990) The meaning of memory: Family, class, and ethnicity in early network television. In *Time Passages: Collective Memory and American Popular Culture*. Minneapolis, MN: University of Minnesota Press, pp. 39–75.

Lipsitz, G. (1998) *The Possessive Investment in Whiteness. How White People Profit from Identity Politics*. Philadelphia, PA: Temple University Press.

Livesay, J. (1985) Habermas, narcissism, and status. *Telos* 64: 75–90.

Lyons-Ruth, K. (1991) Rapprochement or approchement: Mahler's theory reconsidered from the vantage point of recent research on early attachment and relationships. *Psychoanalytic Psychology* 8: 1–23.

Magee, M. and Miller, D.C. (1996) What sex is an amaryllis? What gender is lesbian? Looking for something to hold it all. *Gender & Psychoanalysis* 1: 139–170.

Mahler, M., Pine, F. and Bergman, A. (1975) *The Psychological Birth of the Human Infant*. New York, NY: Basic Books.

Marcuse, H. (1955) *Eros and Civilization: A Philosophical Inquiry Into Freud*. Boston, MA: Beacon Press.

Marcuse, H. (1964) *One-Dimensional Man: Studies in the Ideology of Advanced Industrial Society*. Boston, MA: Beacon Press.

Maroda, K. (1999) *Seduction, Surrender and Transformation*. New York, NY: Routledge.

Martin, B. (1996) Extraordinary homosexuals and the fear of being ordinary. In *Femininity Played Straight: The Significance of Being Lesbian*. New York, NY and London: Routledge, pp. 45–70.

McNall, S.G., Levine, R.F. and Fantasia, R. (eds.) (1991) *Bringing class back. In Contemporary and Historical Perspectives*. Boulder, CO: Westview Press.

Menzies, I.E.P. (1960) A case-study in the functioning of social systems as a defense against anxiety: A report on a study of the nursing service in a general hospital. *Human Relations* 13: 95–121.

Mettler, S. (2011) *The Submerged State: How Invisible Government Policies Undermine American Democracy*. Chicago, IL: University of Chicago Press.

Michel, F. (1996) Do bats eat cats? Reading what bisexuality does. In D.E. Hall and M. Pramaggiore (eds.) *RePresenting Bisexualities*. New York, NY: New York University Press, pp. 55–69.

Mitchell, S.A. (1988) *Relational Concepts in Psychoanalysis*. Cambridge, MA: Harvard University Press.

Mitchell, S.A. (1993) *Hope and Dread in Psychoanalysis*. New York, NY: Basic Books.

Mitchell, S.A. (1997) *Influence and Autonomy in Psychoanalysis*. Hillsdale, NJ: Analytic Press.

Miyazaki, H. (2010) The temporality of no hope. In C.J. Greenhouse (ed.) *Ethnographies of Neoliberalism*. Philadelphia, PA: University of Pennsylvania Press, pp. 238–250.

Moraga, C. and Anzaldúa, G. (eds.) (1983) *This Bridge Called My Back: Writings by Radical Women of Color*. New York, NY: Kitchen Table Press.

Morgan, H. (2002) Exploring racism. *Journal of Analytic Psychology* 47: 567–581.

Morrison, T. (1983) Recitatif. In A. Baraka and A. Baraka (eds.) *Confirmations*. New York, NY: Morrow Press, pp. 243–261.

Moss, D. (ed.) (2003) *Hating in the First Person Plural*. New York, NY: Other Press.

Muccino, G. (dir.) (2006) *The Pursuit of Happyness*. Columbia Pictures Corporation.

Mulvey, L. (1975) Visual pleasure and narrative cinema. *Screen* 16: 6–18.

Neale, S. (1983) Masculinity as spectacle. *Screen* 24: 2–16.

Orange, D. (2007) *Kohut Memorial Lecture: Attitudes, Values, and Intersubjective Vulnerability*. 30th Annual Conference on the Psychology of the Self: Self and Systems. Los Angeles.

Orman, S. (1999) *The Courage to be Rich: Creating a Life of Material and Spiritual Abundance*. New York, NY: Riverhead Books.

Palahniuk, C. (1996) *Fight Club*. New York, NY: Henry Holt and Company.

Parker, R. (2019) Slavery in the white psyche. *Psychoanalytic Social Work* 26: 84–103.

Parsons, T. (1949) The social structure of the family. In R. Anshen (ed.) *The Family: Its Functions and Destiny*. New York, NY: Harper & Row, pp. 241–273.

Peck, J. and Tickell, A. (2002) Neoliberalizing space. *Antipode* 34(3): 380–404.

Peltz, R. (2005) The manic society. *Psychoanalytic Dialogues* 15(3): 347–366. Reprinted in Layton, L., Hollander, N.C. and Gutwill, S. (eds.) *Psychoanalysis, Class and Politics. Encounters in the Clinical Setting*. New York, NY: Routledge, pp. 65–80.

Philipson, I.J. (1993) *On the Shoulders of Women: The Feminization of Psychotherapy*. New York, NY: Guilford.

Pistiner de Cortiñas, L. (2009) *The Aesthetic Dimension of the Mind. Variations on a Theme of Bion*. London: Karnac.

Pollack, W.S. (1995) Deconstructing dis-identification: Rethinking psychoanalytic concepts of male development. *Psychoanalysis and Psychotherapy* 12(1): 30–45.

Rabine, L.W. (1988) A feminist politics of non-identity. *Feminist Studies* 14: 11–31.

Rapoport, E. (2019) *Desiring in the Real: From Psychoanalytic Bisexuality to Bisexual Psychoanalysis.* New York, NY: Routledge.

Read, J. (2009) A genealogy of homo-economicus: Neoliberalism and the production of subjectivity. *Foucault Studies* 6: 25–36.

Reay, D. (2005) Beyond consciousness: The psychic landscape of social class. *Sociology* 39(5): 911–928.

Reay, D. (2015) Habitus and the psychosocial: Bourdieu with feelings. *Cambridge Journal of Education* 45(1): 9–23.

Reay, D., Crozier, G. and James, D. (2011) *White Middle-Class Identities and Urban Schooling.* Basingstoke: Palgrave Macmillan.

Reich, W. (1933/1972) *Character Analysis*, 3rd Edition. Trans. V.R. Carfagno. New York, NY: Farrar, Straus and Giroux.

Reich, W. (1966) Sex-Pol: Essays 1929–1934. In L. Baxandall (ed.) *Dialectical Materialism and Psychoanalysis, 1929, 1934.* New York, NY: Random House, pp. 1–74.

Richards, B. and Brown, J. (2002) The therapeutic culture hypothesis: A critical discussion. In T. Johansson and O. Sernhede (eds.) *Lifestyle, Desire and Politics: Contemporary Identities.* Goteborg, Sweden: Daidalos, pp. 97–114.

Riesman, D. (With Glazer, N. and Denney, R). (1950/2001) *The Lonely Crowd.* New Haven, CT: Yale University Press.

Rizq, R. (2014) Perversion, neoliberalism and therapy: The audit culture in mental health services. *Psychoanalysis, Culture & Society* 19(2): 209–218.

Robinson, C.J. (2000; orig. 1983) *Black Marxism.* Chapel Hill, NC: University of North Carolina Press.

Rodger, J. (2003) Social solidarity, welfare and post-emotionalism. *Journal of Social Policy* 32(3): 403–421.

Rose, J. (1986) *Sexuality in the Field of Vision.* London: Verso.

Rose, N. (1989) *Governing the Soul: The Shaping of the Private Self.* London: Free Association Books.

Rose, N. (1999) Inventiveness in politics. *Economy and Society* 28(3): 467–493.

Rose, S., Stevens, C. et al. (eds.) (1996) *Bisexual Horizons. Politics, Histories, Lives.* London: Lawrence & Wishart.

Roseneil, S. (2014) On meeting Linda: An intimate encounter with (not-)belonging in the current conjuncture. *Psychoanalysis, Culture & Society* 19(1): 19–28.

Rothblum, F., Weisz, J., Pott, M., Miyake, K. and Morelli, G. (2000) Attachment and culture: Security in the United States and Japan. *American Psychologist* 55(10): 1093–1104.

Rozmarin, E. (2009) I am yourself: Subjectivity and the collective. *Psychoanalytic Dialogues* 19(5): 604–616.

Rozmarin, E. (2014) Talking about Gaza in psychoanalysis. *Public Seminar* 1(2). Retrieved from www.publicseminar.org/2014/08/talking-about-gaza-in-psychoanalysis/#.U-nyIaOodEN. Accessed August 15, 2014.

Rust, P.C. (1995) *Bisexuality and the Challenge to Lesbian Politics: Sex, Loyalty, and Revolution*. New York, NY: New York University Press.

Rustin, M. (1991) *The Good Society and the Inner World*. New York, NY: Verso.

Rustin, M. (2014) Belonging to oneself alone: The spirit of neoliberalism. *Psychoanalysis, Culture & Society* 19(2): 145–160.

Ryan, J. (2006) 'Class is in you': An exploration of some social class issues in psychotherapeutic work. *British Journal of Psychotherapy* 23(1): 49–62; Reprinted in Lowe, F. (ed.) (2014) *Thinking Space*. London: Karnac, pp. 127–146.

Ryan, J. (2009) Elision and disavowal: The extrusion of class from psychoanalytic theory and practice. *Sitegeist* 3: 27–40.

Ryan, J. (2017) *Psychoanalysis and Class: Landscapes of Inequality*. London: Routledge.

Salberg, J. (2015) The texture of traumatic attachment: Presence and ghostly absence in transgenerational transmission. *Psychoanalytic Quarterly* 84(1): 21–46.

Salberg, J. and Grand, S. (2016) *Wounds of History: Repair and Resilience in the Trans-generational Transmission of Trauma*. New York, NY: Routledge.

Samuels, A. (1993) *The Political Psyche*. London: Routledge.

Samuels, A. (2001) *Politics on the Couch: Citizenship and the Internal Life*. London: Routledge.

Samuels, A. (2006) Response to roundtable: Politics and/or/in/for psychoanalysis. In L. Layton, N.C. Hollander, and S. Gutwill (eds.) *Psychoanalysis, Class and Politics: Encounters in the Clinical Setting*. New York, NY and London: Routledge, pp. 202–209. Originally printed in *Psychoanalytic Perspectives* 2(1): 39–47.

Samuels, R. (2009) *New Media, Cultural Studies, and Critical Theory after Postmodernity*. New York, NY: Palgrave Macmillan.

Samuels, R. (2014) Neoliberalism and higher ed. *Psychoanalysis, Culture & Society* 19(1): 47–51.

Sander, L. (1983) Polarity, paradox, and the organizing process in development. In J.D. Call, E. Galenson, and R.L. Tyson (eds.) *Frontiers of Infant Psychiatry, No 1*. New York, NY: Basic Books.

Sands, A. (2010) *What Makes Me White*. Retrieved from www.youtube.com/watch?v=dOFsNRhRvJs.

Sayer, A. (2005) *The Moral Significance of Class*. Cambridge, UK: Cambridge University Press.

Scanlon, C. and Adlam, J. (2008) Refusal, social exclusion and the cycle of rejection: A cynical analysis? *Critical Social Policy* 28: 529–549.

Scanlon, C. and Adlam, J. (2013) Reflexive violence. *Psychoanalysis, Culture & Society* 18(3): 223–241.

Schaefer, B. (1999) *Der Weg zur Finanziellen Freiheit: In Sieben Jahren die Erste Million (The Road to Financial Freedom: Your First Million in Seven Years)*. Frankfurt: Campus Verlag.

Schell, J. (2009) Obama and the return of the real. *The Nation*, February 9, pp. 18–22.

Schulman, S. (2006; orig. 1992) *Empathy*. Vancouver: Arsenal Pulp Press.

Schwartz, D. (1995) Current psychoanalytic discourses on sexuality: Tripping over the body. In T. Domenici and R.C. Lesser (eds.) *Disorienting Sexuality*. New York, NY: Routledge, pp. 115–126.

Seligman, S. (1999) Integrating Kleinian theory and intersubjective infant research: Observing projective identification. *Psychoanalytic Dialogues* 9(2): 129–159.

Seligman, S., Ipp, H. and Bass, A. (eds.) (2017a) Working in the shadow of the election: The day after, at work in the aftermath of the Trump victory. *Psychoanalytic Dialogues* 27(2): 111–129.

Seligman, S., Ipp, H. and Bass, A. (2017b) Working in the shadow of the election: The day after, Part II at work in the aftermath of the Trump victory. *Psychoanalytic Dialogues* 27(3): 354–387.

Sennett, R. (2006) *The Culture of the New Capitalism*. New Haven, CT: Yale University Press.

Shaw, D. (2013) *Traumatic Narcissism*. New York, NY: Routledge.

Shiller, R.J. (2005) *Irrational Exuberance*, 2nd Edition. New York, NY: Doubleday.

Silva, J.M. (2013) *Coming Up Short: Working-Class Adulthood in an Age of Uncertainty*. New York, NY: Oxford University Press.

Simon, W. (1996) *Postmodern Sexualities*. London: Routledge.

Skeggs, B. (1997) *Formations of Class and Gender: Becoming Respectable*. Thousand Oaks, CA: Sage.

Skeggs, B. (2005) The making of class and gender through visualizing moral subject formation. *Sociology* 39(5): 965–982.

Sloan, T. (1996) *Damaged Life: The Crisis of the Modern Psyche*. New York, NY: Routledge.

Slochower, J (2003) The analyst's secret delinquencies. *Psychoanalytic Dialogues* 13: 451–469.

Solnit, R. (2017, May 30) *The Loneliness of Donald Trump*. Retrieved from http://lithub.com/rebecca-solnit-the-loneliness-of-donald-trump.

Spielberg, W. (2017) A tale of two firefighters and Trump. *Psychoanalytic Dialogues* 27(3): 366–368.

Stavrakakis, Y. (2007) *The Lacanian Left*. Edinburgh: Edinburgh University Press.

Stein, H. (2000) Disposable youth: The 1999 Columbine high school massacre as American metaphor. *Journal for the Psychoanalysis of Culture & Society* 5(2): 217–236.

Stein, R. (2005) Why perversion? "False love" and the perverse pact. *International Journal of Psychoanalysis* 86(3): 775–799.

Steiner, J. (1993) *Psychic Retreats*. London: Routledge.

Stern, D.B. (1997) *Unformulated Experience. From Dissociation to Imagination in Psychoanalysis*. Hillsdale, NJ: The Analytic Press.

Stern, D.B. (2004) The eye sees itself: Dissociation, enactment, and the achievement of conflict. *Contemporary Psychoanalysis* 40(2): 197–237.

Stern, D.B. (2010) *Partners in Thought*. New York, NY: Routledge.

Stern, D.B. (2013) Responses to commentaries by Ferro and Civitarese, Carnochan, Peltz and Goldberg, and Levine. *Psychoanalytic Dialogues* 23(6): 674–682.

Stern, D.N. (1985) *The Interpersonal World of the Infant*. New York, NY: Basic Books.

Stevenson, B. (2015) *Just Mercy: A Story of Justice and Redemption*. New York, NY: Scribe Publications.

Stimmel, B. (1996) From "nothing" to "something" to "everything": Bisexuality and metaphors of the mind. *Journal of the American Psychoanalytic Association* 44(Suppl): 191–214.

Stoute, B.J. (2017) Race and racism in psychoanalytic thought: The ghosts in our nursery. *The American Psychoanalyst* 51(1): 10–29.

Straker, G. (2004) Race for cover: Castrated whiteness, perverse consequences. *Psychoanalytic Dialogues* 14(4): 405–422.

Straker, G. (2006) The anti-analytic third. *Psychoanalytic Review* 93(5): 729–753.

Suchet, M. (2004) A relational encounter with race. *Psychoanalytic Dialogues* 14: 423–438.

Suchet, M. (2007) Unraveling whiteness. *Psychoanalytic Dialogues* 17(6): 867–886.

Suchet, M. (2010) Face to face. *Psychoanalytic Dialogues* 20: 158–171.

Suchet, M. (2017, April 27) *The Narcissism of Whiteness*. Paper presented at Division 39, APA, Spring Meeting, New York City.

Sullivan, H.S. (1953) *The Interpersonal Theory of Psychiatry*. New York, NY: W.W. Norton.

Tartakoff, H. (1966) The normal personality in our culture and the Nobel Prize complex. In R.M. Loewenstein, L.M. Newman, M. Schur, and A.J. Solnit (eds.) *Psychoanalysis – A General Psychology. Essays in Honor of Heinz Hartmann*. New York, NY: International Universities Press, pp. 222–252.

Totton, N. (2006) Birth, death, orgasm, and perversion: A Reichian view. In D. Nobus and L. Downing (eds.) *Perversion: Psychoanalytic Perspectives/Perspectives on Psychoanalysis*. London: Karnac, pp. 127–146.

Touraine, A. (2009) *Thinking Differently*. Trans. D. Macey. Cambridge, UK: Polity Press.

Tucker, N. (ed.) (1995) *Bisexual Politics: Theories, Queries, & Visions*. New York, NY: The Haworth Press.

Vaughans, K.C. (2016) To unchain haunting blood memories: Intergenerational trauma among African-Americans. In J. Salberg and S. Grand (eds.) *Wounds of History: Repair and Resilience in the Trans-generational Transmission of Trauma*. New York, NY: Routledge, pp. 226–241.

Vincent, C. and Ball, S.J. (2007) 'Making up' the middle-class child: Families, activities and class dispositions. *Sociology* 41(6): 1061–1077.

Volkan, V. (1988) *The Need to Have Enemies and Allies*. Northvale, NJ: Jason Aronson.

Volkan, V. (2004) *Blind Trust*. Charlottesville, VA: Pitchstone Publishing.

Wachtel, P.L. (2003) The roots of racism: A psychoanalytic perspective. *Black Renaissance* 5(1): 45–50.

Wacquant, L. (2001a) Deadly symbiosis: When ghetto and prison meet and mesh. *Punishment and Society* 3(1): 95–134.

Wacquant, L. (2001b) The penalization of poverty and the rise of neo-liberalism. *European Journal on Criminal Policy and Research* 9: 401–412.

Walkerdine, V. (1986) Video replay: Families, films and fantasy. In V. Burgin, V. Donald, and C. Kaplan (eds.) *Formations of Fantasy*. London: Methuen, pp. 167–199.

Walkerdine, V. (1992) *Didn't She Do Well?* London: Metro Pictures.

Walkerdine, V. (1997) *Daddy's Girl: Young Girls and Popular Culture*. Cambridge, MA: Harvard University Press.

Walkerdine, V. (2003) Reclassifying upward mobility: Femininity and the neo-liberal subject. *Gender and Education* 15(3): 237–248.

Walkerdine, V. and Jimenez, L. (2012) *Gender, Work and Community after De-industrialisation: A Psychosocial Approach to Affect*. Basingstoke: Palgrave Macmillan.

Walkerdine, V. and Lucey, H. (1989) *Democracy in the Kitchen: Regulating Mothers and Socializing Daughters*. London: Virago.

Walkerdine, V., Lucey, H. and Melody, J. (2001) *Growing Up Girl*. London: Palgrave Macmillan.

Walls, G. (2006) Racism, classism, psychosis and self-image in the analysis of a woman. In L. Layton, N.C. Hollander, and S. Gutwill (eds.) *Psychoanalysis, Class and Politics: Encounters in the Clinical Setting*. London: Routledge, pp. 129–140.

Wang, J. (2018) *Carceral Capitalism*. Semiotext(e) Intervention Series 21. South Pasadena, CA: Semiotexte.

Wark, M. (1996) Double agency. In S. Rose, C. Stevens et al. (eds.) *Bisexual Horizons*. London: Lawrence & Wishart.

Watkins, M. (2018) The social and political life of shame: The US 2016 presidential election. *Psychoanalytic Perspectives* 15(1): 25–37.

Weinberg, M.S., Williams, C.J. and Pryor, D.W. (1994) *Dual Attraction: Understanding Bisexuality*. Oxford: Oxford University Press.

Weise, E.R. (ed.) (1992) *Closer to Home: Bisexuality and Feminism*. Seattle: Seal Press.

White, K.P. (2002) Surviving hating and being hated. *Contemporary Psychoanalysis* 38(3): 401–422.

Whitson, G. (1996) Working class issues. In R. Perez-Foster, M. Moskowitz, and R.A. Javier (eds.) *Reaching Across Boundaries of Culture and Class*. Northvale, NJ: Jason Aronson, pp. 143–158.

Williams, P. (1997) The ethnic scarring of American whiteness. In W. Lubiano (ed.) *The House that Race Built*. New York, NY: Pantheon, pp. 253–263.

Williams, R.M. (1997) Living at the crossroads. In W. Lubiano (ed.) *The House That Race Built*. New York, NY: Pantheon, pp. 136–156.

Winnicott, D.W. (1965) *The Maturational Processes and the Facilitating Environment*. Madison, CT: International Universities Press.

Winnicott, D.W. (1971) The use of an object and relating through identifications. In *Playing and Reality*. London: Tavistock Publications, pp. 86–94.

Winograd, B. (dir.) (2014) *Black Psychoanalysts Speak*. PEP Video Grants 1(1): 1. Retrieved from www.pep-web.org/document.php?id=pepgrantvs.001.0001a.

Yakushko, O. (2019) *Scientific Pollyannaism: From Inquisition to Positive Psychology*. New York, NY: Springer.

Yancy, G. (2012) *Look, A White! Philosophical Essays on Whiteness*. Philadelphia, PA: Temple University Press.

Young-Bruehl, E. (1996) *The Anatomy of Prejudices*. Cambridge, MA: Harvard University Press.

Young-Bruehl, E. (2011) Psychoanalysis and social democracy: A tale of two developments. *Contemporary Psychoanalysis* 47(2): 179–201.

Young-Bruehl, E. (2012) *Childism*. New Haven, CT: Yale University Press.

Zaretsky, E. (2015) *The Political Freud*. New York, NY: Columbia University Press.

Žižek, S. (1989) *The Sublime Object of Ideology*. London: Verso.

Žižek, S. (1991) *Looking Awry: An Introduction to Jacques Lacan through Popular Culture*. Cambridge, MA: MIT Press.

Žižek, S. (1994) How did Marx invent the symptom? In: Žižek, S. (ed.) *Mapping Ideology*. London: Verso, pp. 296–331.

# Index